# Contents

# Preface

I am greatly honoured by the request of Mr Billy Kay, the radio producer and editor of the series which forms the origin of this book, that I should write the prefatory note to this volume. I do so as an historian of migration and I begin by emphatically seconding Mr Kay's remarks respecting the significance of oral history. History as we first came to know it was oral history: Herodotus depended heavily upon it, and, as has been established by the work of Professor Momigliano and others, his presentation of his findings remains in many ways a model for modern historians. Herodotus was careful to record stories which he himself sometimes did not believe to be true, but which he preserved for us with a clarity and fidelity alongside his own disclaimers, and on which in some cases modern knowledge has shown his informants to be justified. The point remains true today. There remains in oral source-material much that the historian does not know, and much that he might scout, which if it be recorded, some future generation might yet find verifiable.

But the fundamental point lies in a different sphere from simple questions of verifiable fact. It is from oral history that we get blood, otherwise all that remains to us are the dry bones. It is not simply a question of reality, but of multi-dimensional reality being provided by the evidence of those who heard, saw and felt the historical experience with which we are concerned. Historians become readily hypnotised by written evidence, whether from individual persons or from corporate bodies. They ask themselves far too seldom how selective such evidence may be, whether by reason of 'salting' of critical evidence by interested custodians, or by the sheer accident of the survival of material. In the last analysis, those with money can afford to preserve documentary evidence. The poor in history are often illiterate and, even when writing is theirs, they have had little ability to hoard their letters or, until recently, to persuade archivists to accept them.

Mr Kay's programmes did outstanding work in tapping a vein of historical source-material of which far too little has hitherto been made, and on which historians have frequently been self-deafened. He and his associates have created an outstanding work in obtaining the oral evidence of the survivors of the migration experience. It is fair to say that if they only had a sufficiency of predecessors in the past two centuries in every country in the world, the history of migration as we know it would be very different. Inevitably, recollection has its lapses and additions, its subtractions and multiplications, whether of joy or sorrow, loss or pain. But the cumulative material gives a sense of reality which can nowhere else be paralleled.

This is a book that can be interpreted as a unity in very different ways. It is chapters of Scottish social history. It is the background to folk art and song. It is human drama, and the wellsprings of literature. It is in the last analysis, all of us.

OWEN DUDLEY EDWARDS

# Introduction

At one time, all history was oral. *The Odyssey* is a collection of stories told around hearths for hundreds of years, before finding a permanent and fixed form in the works of Homer. In ancient Greece there was no distinction made between folk stories and 'factual accounts' of events in the past, history was simply the *mutho logos*, the expression of the people's knowledge about themselves. As recently as the eighteenth century, many historians still relied on oral history, proud to cite their personal involvement in the period covered in their writing, and seeking credence by dint of the fact that they or their informants had experienced the events themselves. Voltaire consulted oral and documentary sources, considering both equally valid for his purposes. In the introduction to his *History of Charles XII* (1731), his claim for the work's authenticity rests on the fact that he had 'not ventured to advance a single fact, without consulting eye-witnesses of undoubted veracity'. Since the early nineteenth century, however, history has been the realm of an élite of professional historians for whom the written document is sacred, and who regard oral evidence as unsound and irrelevant. In their eyes written evidence is the only true source of history, oral evidence is simply 'hearsay' . . . *until it is written down*. Sadly, this established view of history is the only one available to students at university, who in turn become teachers and pass on to their pupils a modern history as remote and dry as the paper it is printed on, ignoring the old folk of the same area, class and dialect as the children who could bring events such as the Great War dynamically alive for them through their own life stories. The historian's skill has been developed in the library, where he is master. In collecting oral material, however, the interviewee is all important and through a mixture of inhibition and reluctance to accept the value and relevance of an ordinary person's recollections, very few historians leave their niche and make the effort to communicate. Consult the people? A preposterous idea put down by A. J. P. Taylor himself, "In this matter, I am an almost total sceptic . . . old men drooling about their youth — No."

The Odyssey series refutes that statement with a resounding Yes! The people here present their own version of their past; stories of work, unemployment, hardship and leisure which illustrate vigorously the changing lifestyle of the masses and contrast strongly with the 'Chronicle of Kings and Great Men' version of the past found in the history books.

The radical difference between written and oral history can be illustrated from an incident in my own education. I recall reading with astonishment the school history books' unqualified praise for Churchill as Statesman, War Hero and Saviour of Britain. In my home there was unqualified hatred for him as the man who advocated the use of tanks and troops against the workers in Glasgow in 1919 and who sent the Scots regiments in to be slaughtered at the Dardanelles. Both versions have elements of truth, they simply reflect differing standpoints. The former type of history invariably indicts the wisdom of those in authority, the latter shows how the choices of those in power affected and were interpreted by the people. The coherence of the working-class view was revealed to me while making the Odyssey programme 'They Fairly Mak Ye Work' in 1980, when the old jute workers of Dundee, describing their own experiences in the early 'twenties, expressed exactly the same opinion of Churchill as that passed on to me in Ayrshire in the early 1960s. It is in this sense that the presentation of the working-class view through oral material adds not only another dimension to history, but one which is intrinsically radical. It is the potential multiplicity of versions which oral history offers that make it so compelling and indeed necessary, if a more democratic view of the past is to be arrived at.

The subjects covered in Odyssey are as diverse and varied as Scotland itself. For the reader who has relied on 'official' histories or the often verkitsch Scotland represented on the media, the people's stories will appear at times as exotic as any in Homer's masterpiece . . . folk alive today stepping from crag to crag and killing fulmars on St Kilda . . . working at the age of ten in the jute mills of Dundee . . . speaking Irish Gaelic in the Gorbals . . . belonging to secret Horsemen's societies in the East coast . . . escaping the Depression of the 'thirties and climbing icy rock faces in stocking soles . . . describing Lithuanian weddings in Bellshill . . . seeing colours invisible to you or I, which indicate the presence of herring in the waters off Kintyre . . . all of these interconnected layers of culture bubbling vital and alive beneath the stifling surface of clichés which Scotland is in danger of becoming. By unearthing these subjects and revealing some of the diversity which exists, I hope that others will be encouraged to explore the rich seam of their own culture and discover their own 'gold'. In his beautiful poem, *Scotland Small?*, Hugh MacDiarmid shows that it is all there for those who look beneath the surface with commitment and compassion.

### SCOTLAND SMALL?

*Scotland small? Our multiform, our infinite Scotland small?*
*Only as a patch of hillside may be a cliché corner*
*To a fool who cries "Nothing but heather!" where in September another*
*Sitting there and resting and gazing round*
*Sees not only heather but blaeberries*
*With bright green leaves and leaves already turned scarlet,*

*Hiding ripe blue berries; and amongst the sage-green
        leaves
Of the bog-myrtle the golden flowers of the
        tormentil shining;
And on the small bare places, where the little
        Blackface sheep
Found grazing, milkworts blue as summer skies;
And down in neglected peat-hags, not worked
In living memory, sphagnum moss in pastel shades
Of yellow, green, and pink; sundew and butterwort
And nodding harebells vying in their colour
With the blue butterflies that poise themselves
        delicately upon them,
And stunted rowans with harsh dry leaves of glorious
        colour.
"Nothing but heather!" – How marvellously
        descriptive! And incomplete!*

Odyssey attempts to look at Scotland in the same way, drawing from one of the greatly untapped sources of her strength, oral history.

The role of oral tradition in Scotland is made all the more important in the fostering of pride and identity, due to the fact that many of the official institutions of culture are as likely to be as English or Anglo-American as they are Scottish. The strongly rooted Scottish identity which a child derives from the oral tradition is given little support through knowledge of the country's intellectual achievement during his or her school career. Indeed, in many cases the identity is undermined and devalued as official neglect of Scots language and literature implies that it is not worthy of attention, while the concentration on British history implies that Scotland is a historical desert after 1707!

The schizophrenia induced by such attitudes in education can often be balanced by the stories and songs recalling the struggles and achievements of their own folk told in the homes of family and friends. It is in the homes of ordinary working people that the life stories which gave the Odyssey series such virr and smeddum were collected. Radio is a beautifully simple medium, recorder and microphone are soon forgotten if the conversation is compelling, and with people expressing the essential moments of their lives, the desire to communicate overcomes any artificiality in the situation. Speaking broad Scots helped too, as that tongue has an intimacy and identity for those who use it which official disapproval perhaps serves to reinforce. Of course, the rich accents and dialects of Scots are more easily savoured when heard on the air, yet in these accurate transcriptions, the flavour of the different speech forms comes across and although written down, the words literally jump off the page and demand attention.

Basil Bernstein's theory that the working class is imprisoned linguistically by limited speech forms is refuted categorically in the Odyssey tapes. In making these programmes, I have yet to come across an inarticulate man or woman. In James Mooney's story

of the end of an era, when a mechanical digger challenges the supremacy of the Irish navvies in 'From the Gorbals to Gweedore', or in Bobby Peterson's tales of the Antarctic whaling from 'Da Merry Boys', there is an unconscious narrative skill at work, which I heard repeated many times while collecting material for the programmes. In 'Fishermen of Kintyre', the old ring-net men's description of the way they absorbed all the natural signs around them to detect herring is beautifully recalled; colours and textures, the smells and sounds of the sea all woven in words which give the listener or reader an almost uncanny physical sense of being there. The dependence on, and sensitive awareness of the environment which these men possess is matched by their high ideals. I recall being moved by the sadness in Donald MacIntosh's voice when he described the inability of the modern method of fishing to let the young fish go free. Contrast the beauty of the word picture painted by the ring-net men with young Donald Paterson's summing up of modern-day fishing as "Dog eat dog, round in a circle", and you see the evocative power for encapsulating change which oral history possesses.

Through the words of the people who experienced it, history is alive. It is one thing to read an account of clearance and emigration to Canada from the Hebrides, another to hear the people's version of the dispersal of their community and their adaptation to a foreign land. One can read in official histories the various parliamentary debates about poor relief, but one feels the problem when Mrs Craig and Cockburn of Dundee describe the humiliation of an inspector's visit and the conditions they had to raise a family under. In the case of recording work experiences, oral history is the only possible source of knowledge. I daresay manuals have been published describing the weaving process, but only the weaver can describe what it is actually like to stand there for hours and days and eventually years, weaving jute. It is one thing to read 'outsiders' reports about the 'problem' of alien immigrants, another to hear about the experience of ethnic communities told from the inside, information which again is only available from oral sources. During the recent riot in Bristol all the newspapers adopted the usual approach, outsiders analysing expert opinion about the 'immigrant problem'. No one printed the St Paul's people's version of what happened! In Odyssey's 'The Lanarkshire Lithuanians', read Mrs Miller's account of her departure from her rural homeland, her arrival in the mining area of Bellshill and the marriage that was arranged for her there, and you are inside the experience of these people with an immediacy which would be impossible if the stories were written by an outsider. Fortunately oral history is slowly being given the recognition it deserves, and through collection by institutions such as The School of Scottish Studies, interested bodies such as the Oral History Group, and Odyssey, stories like those in this book are preserved to inform future generations.

While making these programmes it has often struck me how close the parallels between the life stories and the literature of the period are, surely a vindication of our writers' success at portraying accurately the culture surrounding them. Read George MacDougall Hay's novel *Gillespie*, or his son George Campbell Hay's fishing poems and you will find the tone, style and 'feel' of the writing paralleled in Odyssey's 'Fishermen of Kintyre'. Similarly in 'From the Gorbals to Gweedore', there is no division between the language of those interviewed and the speech of the characters in Patrick MacGill's novels such as *Children of the Dead End*. The transcript of this programme could also be read as a companion to *No Mean City* or the rest of the more sensational novels about Glasgow, where violence is as common as pease brose, if only to contrast the writers' depiction of the Gorbals with that of the Donegal community — Bridget Connolly: "Well, I never seen anything wrong with the Gorbals. In those days, you could walk in it any hour of the night and see nothing worse than yourself!"

The culture of the rural north-east portrayed so brilliantly in Lewis Grassic Gibbon's *Sunset Song* is described in the words of the ploughmen in 'A Weel Plou'd Rig'. More striking similarities are to be found in a comparison between Odyssey's 'They Fairly Mak Ye Work' and the final part in Gibbon's trilogy 'A Scots Quair' — the novel *Grey Granite* in which he describes the conditions in a fabled city of the north-east during the Depression. Gibbon's re-enactment of the police breaking up the workers' protest march could almost have been based on Sarah Craig's recollections of a similar incident in Dundee in 1930. Were they both witnesses of the same event, one writing it down in 1933, the other recalling the event with equal vigour for my tape recorder in 1980?

Another medium which mells with the oral history is that of traditional music. In Odyssey the oral history was embellished by the songs and tunes which preserved another version of the people's past in such an emotive and evocative form. For the book I have chosen a selection of this type of song, for example, 'The Micky Dam' about the Irish navvies, or Mary Brooksbank's 'Jute Mill Song', give a heightened version of the same story superbly blended with music. In these mediums of music, literature and oral history we have the very essence of the lives lived in this nation in this century, preserved and ennobled.

Most of the folk interviewed for Odyssey belong to a generation of the Scottish working class born in the first decade of this century. John Murray of Galston, an old miner whom I visited until he died, was typical of a type of working man of that era, full of moral integrity and high principles. A catholic provost elected by a mainly protestant town, John was a self-educated Socialist, a personification of the dignity of the working man and a defender of his rights. He died before I began working in radio, so like others with their own unique insight into the past, he went unrecorded. However, I had the honour of meeting and recording for posterity, his type time and time again while making these programmes. Odyssey has attempted to give history back to the people who made it, allowing them to speak without interruption or editing by an 'expert' from outside their culture. It has also given them the central role in broadcasting where they have been ignored for so long. As a generation, these people tholed appalling housing, unemployment, decimation by war and abject poverty to survive with their spirit intact. Through their words, programmes full of honesty, vitality and beauty have emerged, helped by the guiding hand of knowledge and commitment shared by all those who have contributed to this book. I have grown to appreciate even more Scotland's interwoven tapestry of cultures, and have learned from the experience I have had collecting the people's stories. If I have succeeded in reflecting truthfully their enduring human dignity in adversity, then Odyssey has been worthy of them.

BILLY KAY

*Irish shearers in the Lothians, c. 1910.*

## FREE AND EASY

Freely

The first of my ram -bles I- now will sing, L-ike any small bird or thursh o-n wing, When the
sun a-rose f-or to bless th-e morn, I was free and eas -y for to jog a- long.

2   *The first place I rambled was to Derry quay*
*A few miles distant from Ballybofey*
*With a cheerful heart and a happy song*
*I was free and easy for to jog along.*

3   *The next place I landed was in Glasgow Green*
*Where the lads and lassies were to be seen*
*But I being the blithest of the throng*
*I sang free and easy for to jog along.*

4   *I scarcely travelled a very short space*
*When a beautiful damsel smiled in my face*
*She asked of me was I a married man*
*No, I'm free and easy for to jog along.*

5   *I took this wee lassie into an inn*
*Where we drank whisky, strong ale and gin*
*She asked of me to pledge heart and hand*
*And give o'er free and easy for to jog along.*

6   *Says I my wee lassie, this thing can't be*
*For I am bound for Americay*
*When a man gets married, his race is run*
*He's no more free and easy for to jog along.*

7   *Look at yonder stream as it gently glides*
*It can go no further than its allowed*
*It can go no further without command*
*I'll stay free and easy for to jog along.*

# From The Gorbals To Gweedore

When the Galloway coast is not shrouded in mist, the green hills of Antrim can be seen clearly shimmering across the water. Twelve miles of Irish Sea separate us from the turmoil of Ulster, but at different points in history the influence of the Irish on Scotland and the Scots on Ireland has been profound. The Gaelic Scots of Ulster who crossed to Argyll in the fifth and sixth centuries gave Scotland her name, her initial experience of Christianity and her ancient tongue, which survives to this day in the Gaidhealtachd of the North and West. After 1603 the migration was reversed when thousands of Calvinist Lowlanders followed their landlords to the estates granted them by James VI during the plantations of Ulster. The settlers' uncompromising brand of Presbyterianism still dominates the life of the six counties while dialects of their Lallans tongue remain in the speech of County Antrim. But it is a more recent migration which has changed the character of the industrial heartland of Scotland — the movement of thousands of Catholic, mainly Irish-speaking people from the coast of Donegal to the farms and eventually the cities of the Lowlands.

The radical improvement in Scottish agriculture in the latter half of the eighteenth century turned the Eastern Lowlands into a vast granary of corn. Also the Napoleonic Wars at the turn of the nineteenth century increased corn prices and produced an incentive to encourage farmers to increase the cultivation of the crop. With the urban population increasing rapidly due to the impact of industrialisation, the corn was essential in feeding the urban masses. With inclement weather a constant threat to the crop, it was necessary to harvest it quickly and efficiently, and in the days before mechanical reapers and binders, the job was done by strong arm and heuk. Thousands of men were required, and as the 1820s saw the introduction of cheap regular sailings between Ireland and Scotland, it fell to the poor population of Donegal to join and in some areas replace those shearers from the Scottish Highlands and Islands who had come down for the Lowland Hairst since the early days of farming improvement, a century before. Both the Highland and Irish shearers have passed into the folklore of Scotland in songs such as *The Band o' Shearers*, *The Lothian Hairst* and *The Rambling Shearer*:

> *I am a shearer Bred and Born, I oft times crossed the ocean,*
> *And all my life, through hot and cold for honour and promotion.*

These songs always conjured up an image in my mind of a bygone age until I met Mrs Coll, a vivacious old lady from Gweedore, Co. Donegal, who lived in the South Side of Glasgow, before her death in March 1980, aged 93.

"I left Donegal in 1908. They all come to Scotland that time and I came over first in May and then I used to go back and come back to the harvest again. They carried it under their oxter their hooks, for to cut the corn. I mind that as well. I come on the — did ye ever hear o' the Gola boat — a boat that used tae leave from where we stayed just and we got the boat there and she left us in Glasgow. We only paid four shillins."

Patrick Roarty:

"The original shearers had sickle hooks and they carried them with them from Ireland. Later, they had the scythes and — there were three in a squad — one cutting, one lifting and binding and the other stooking."

Donegal did not suffer the mass starvation in the western and southern counties of the non-Ulster provinces of Ireland during the Potato Famine of 1845-50, as many of the people there could turn to the sea as a source of food. But as the population increased and the crofts were sub-divided to be shared equally among sons and daughters, the land could barely feed the existing population. It was expected of the young to leave home for seasonal work in Scotland, where they could earn money to help tide the family over the winter. This seasonal migration continued throughout the nineteenth century until after the Second World

*A sod house, Donegal, c. 1895. Probably a temporary accommodation following an eviction. Many families avoided this fate by sending sons and daughters to earn money in Scotland.*

War. It seems that almost every man or woman I spoke to over the age of 40 in the Rosses and Gweedore, had spent some years of his or her life travelling around the farms of Scotland.

For more than a century the Donegal workers travelled via the cattle boats which plied the route between Derry and Glasgow. According to newspaper accounts of the mid-nineteenth century the journey was far from being a pleasant one.

*Scots Times*, 11th May 1836:
> Every boat that arrives at the Broomielaw from Derry is literally crowded on deck with hundreds of poor creatures, who are huddled together and mixed up with horned cattle, pigs, sheep and lambs.

*Scottish Guardian*, 24th August 1849:
> The *Londonderry* brought over from Ireland the extraordinary number of 1,700 human beings at one trip . . . the poor creatures filled every corner from stem to stern, clustering round the bulwarks as thick as bees.

The parallel with these descriptions and those of the slave ships of the middle passage in the same period is striking. The callousness of the steamship owners is revealed in the fact that the captain of the good ship *Londonderry* in the year before the above description,

found 72 corpses in the steerage section of his ship when he arrived at Derry Quay after a stormy overnight crossing.

The passing of 100 years did not make a great difference to conditions on board the Derry Boat. Mr Kearney of Derry describes a crossing in the 1940s.

Mr Kearney:

"Manys the time I travelled on the boat going back to Glasgow, on a cattle boat, and, they called that part of the boat 'Steerage' . . . I suppose now they'd maybe call it second class. But the boats were always crowded in these days, as the man says, ye jist hid tae kip down where ye could. And there was always that smell of cattle on the boats. They used to clean them out right enough, hose them down inside, but there was always that smell of cattle about, and this would maybe make you sick, more than the sea waves. It got pretty packed at times, pretty rough, the water used to come in through the sides of the boat when they used to open the doors, to put the gangway up. If there was a heavy sea the water used to bash in through the open doors — the place was pretty wet inside, you know. It was pretty rough, the cattle used tae get sick — used to make a lot of noise ye know. But the people used to be kept separate as much as they could, ye know, but you could hear them all night. I used to get sick myself and be walking about for two or three days, thinking I was still on the boat, ye know.

*A steamer for cattle and people at Derry Quay, c. 1910.*

"There was enjoyable times, because the bar used to be opened and older people used to take a drink, or the younger people used to have a sing-song, maybe someone with an accordion or a fiddle or something. Well, when the bar was open, as the man says, the gas was good. They always sang the Hills of Donegal. I thought maybe that when they were goin' to Scotland, they were glad to see the last o' the Hills of Donegal.

"We used to get a lot of people travelling backwards and forwards like, that were lookin' for work, ye know. I suppose in them days, they'd probably be goin' away broken hearted. Although it was only from Ireland to Scotland, to them they were leavin' home and they were sort of like immigrants wondering what they were goin' to find on the other side."

Unlike their predecessors, the immigrants in Mr Kearney's day found employment in digging, trenching, singling turnips and tattie howking, rather than shearing. Once in Scotland, they would disperse in groups organised by gangers contracted by the farmers, to every airt of the Lowlands and Borders. The conditions of employment were very poor.

Mr McGarvey:

"We went away up to the Kelso. And we'd start at the harvest and when the harvest was finished we went away over to Dunbar, we started potatoes, gathering potatoes in a farm. And then that was finished I came in to Mossend again and then my brother brought me down into the pits. I was working there for a couple of years and then I thought I would take a trip o'er here you know. It was a custom, going back and forward you know all the time. And then when you were a while here, maybe in the winter time, then you would go back in the summer time again d'ye see? And that's the way we used to carry on ye see, that way. But eh, they were hard times that time.

"I've seen me lying at the harvest time at a place called Windywalls, and the rats was lying on top of my breast at night when I would waken. That's true enough. And when you put out your hand the rats would walk away. You could see them on the beams. You were lyin' in a stable — that's where you were — a stable barn. Oh and what would you do, you had to do it."

Kitty Mooney:

"They had to sleep rough, boys and girls. I visited one of my friends one time, and she was very sick and a friend I called to see her and we went in to where she was staying. She was lying on the floor, with a few bags or something under her and she was waiting on the doctor to call. And I thought it was an awful way to live or make an earning, you know, working very hard out in the fields and then they hadn't a decent place to sleep."

In some places the tattie howkers were locked into the barns at night, a practice which resulted in the appalling tragedy at Kirkintilloch in 1937. There, ten people were burned to death, unable to escape when their sleeping quarters caught fire.

Although seasonal migration continued throughout the nineteenth and early twentieth centuries, thousands of Donegal folk decided to make Scotland their

*Tattie howkers, Ayrshire, 1940s.*

permanent home. By 1851 there was already a settled Irish community which numbered well over 200,000, and this figure does not include those children born in Scotland who considered themselves Irish. At this time there was a marked Irish presence in the textile industry, where they became skilled spinners, weavers and dyers. For many of the single men the pull of the road was strong, and generations of Donegal men helped to build the railways in the nineteenth century, and roads, dams and tunnels in the twentieth century. The life of the navvies is vividly described in the writings of Patrick Macgill, who undoubtedly modelled characters such as Carrotty Dan on people like the Hashy Dan, described by James Mooney of Gweedore:

James Mooney:

"Early in my life when I was first in Scotland there was a job goin' on along the Galloway coast and myself and a few comrades started off up to the Galloway coast and got work. We started workin' and there was a lot of those old men of the road workin' there, one of them, the best known was the Hashy Dan and a few more along with him. And they were hashy — they would try to beat one another when digging out and good luck to a new starter that wasn't able to handle a shovel — he would get it hard. So we worked out there for a few weeks and the rumour went about that there was a mechanical digger comin' in on the job. Well that was the start of mechanical diggers for nobody ever saw any of them before around there. Anyhow, the Hashy Dan was talkin' to some of his mates and they said that now when this machine would come they would get a showin' up. The Hashy Dan says 'They'll not show me up for there's no mechanical digger that'll dig me out of it'. That was all right till the day the digger came

*Navvies building a road in Glencoe, c. 1900.*

and got rigged up. As soon as the digger started, the Hashy Dan started and it was only as hard as the Hashy could go throwing out. And, of course, the digger was only finding its way till it could get set in proper. And the Hashy was takin' out fairly good but at dinner time he was pretty tired and the digger wasn't making much progress either. After dinner they were at it again. The Hashy started into it again as hard as he could go and the digger started movin' away from him, started leavin' him behind. Every minute he was losin'. He went on for a while, and when he saw that he could do no more he just flung the shovel from him as far as he could send it — walked away to the office and demanded his books.

"There's something about the travelling that gets into you. There's men that go across there that I knew that went into one job and never in another job but the one they were in. Some of them had over 40 years service with the one firm — that's recently too, and they never went anywhere else. But I couldn't stick to one firm. If things were goin' good it was all right for a year or two, but good or bad, whatever it would be, I was away again. The whole lot of them are like that. Now I knew men that did three weeks and that was the height of it and they would be off again."

John Diver:
"I worked in the north of Scotland — making dams. It was some dangerous work in it. I worked at a place in Pitlochry where we had to sink a trench down where there was a river — an underground river. And it was running at 30 feet deep. We had to sink this trench down over 117 feet deep to get a solid foundation for the dam wall.

"There was one time in Pitlochry that I had to put up what they called a coffar dam — that was a temporary dam until they got the right dam built. On one night, there were two rivers, there was the Garry and the Tummel and they both joined upstream together and there was a strong flow in it and this night there was terrible rain and it burst the whole coffar dam away, smashed it away and that was a terrible night that night."

Con Greene:
"The working man's community was poor and the white collar and tie were always on top, and they looked down upon the working man as if he was nothing — not even second class. He was always looked upon as if he was part of a machine and nothing else and they often thought more of an old wheelbarrow than what they did to a working man, for if the man and a wheelbarrow went up a scaffold they'd run to see if the barrow broke for they didn't mind if his neck was broke or not."

James Mooney:
"I couldn't understand how men could be like yon at all. When you at first went into those camps — there was not even beds. You went into a hut, you had a bag of straw, and you lay on it and then you went out into another place to get your food, well, it wasn't fit for pigs. No it was not. You got porridge in the morning and ye got tea and bread and there was no dishes washed, no nothing. But you were just used to the roughness. You just would soon fall into the same way as the whole lot of them. Now on a Saturday night some of them would sing and some of them were good singers.

And then they would fight and they might fight till morning and they would start gambling — that's how the money went — a lot went on the Crown and Anchor. When a man would lose he'd be angry, he'd smash the place up. And his money was gone."

## THE MICKEY DAM

Vigorously

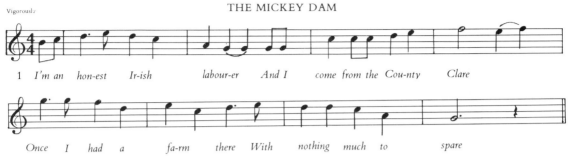

1 I'm an hon-est Ir-ish labour-er And I come from the Cou-nty Clare
Once I had a fa-rm there With nothing much to spare

2 But I had to sell my donkey
And my famous billy goat
And with the money I received
To Glasgow took the boat.

3 In the morning when I landed there
Before me hair got dry
I was started in the Mickey Dam
In a place they called Milngavie.

4 Now the ganger that I started with
They called him John the Mouse
And the very first day that I was there
At me he made to grouse.

CHORUS
Oh, I'm as strong as any lion
I was raised on eggs and ham
I'm a terror to all fighting men
Around the Mickey Dam.

5 But I quickly surprised him
I said, You little rat
I'll tie a string around your neck
And throw you to the cat.

6 Now this rose the Mouse's temper
And at me he made to jump
He swore he'd paralyse me with
The handle of a pump.

7 But I quickly surprised him
I grabbed him by the throat
And I shook that little monkey till
The tail fell off his coat.

8 Now the big hotel we're stopping in
They call them navvies' huts
And the bugs and fleas are in the beds
As big as coconuts.

9 On Saturday nights when I get drunk
I stand behind the door
And as they come out one by one
I bash them to the floor.

*Breakthrough at Butterbridge tunnel on hydro-electric scheme at Loch Sloy, 1949. A group of Irishmen and Poles.*

Eventually the great public works projects of the '20s and '30s were completed and there was no longer the demand for an army of itinerant workers. The Gorbals with its settled Donegal community and its job prospects was a magnet to the men of the road.

Con Greene:
"It was a Donegal community and is still ye know, although they're scattered more out at all the housing schemes. But it, it was a good community. Well, on a Saturday night, you might go down about the Gorbals. Ye might just fall out about somethin' and ye would see a wee fight and that was that. But for the rest of it, they were all good people and they all went to their religious duties even on a workin' day and goin' to their work you would see them goin' early to get to the early mass. They were always good livin' that way."

Father Canning:
"Religion was virtually the only security they had, 'cause they hadn't much of the world's goods and they found comfort and strength in their religion. Also they found security in that they could go for example to the local priest and he was there to assist them in many ways, very often doing things that we now take for granted — like writing letters, getting houses, jobs and so on. Also fighting their battles for social equality. So the priest played a very important role in their life and also the Church afforded them an opportunity for meeting their fellow countrymen, or fellow county men, or even fellow townsmen and this itself was a source of help to them, because they were able to rely on each other."

Mrs McGarvey:
"The old tenements — they didn't look too good on the outside, but when you walked into the houses, they all had lovely houses, and in these days there was no hot and cold water — no baths, but everything was nice, you know, inside."

Patrick Roarty:
"We had so many neighbours and friends who were here, that coming into Glasgow, especially the parishes of St John's and St Francis' in the south side, and St Luke's, was like coming home because there was a strong Gaeltacht in Glasgow in 1950 when I came here. On the south side of the city coming out from 11 o'clock mass or 12 o'clock mass from St John's in Portugal Street, you heard more Irish spoken outside that church than you did actually hear in my own native Annagry. So I think that made it easier for the young person coming across."

Kitty Mooney:
"It was for a holiday I went first, and when I went there I was very young, I was under sixteen years of age and I liked the place so much and I got a nice job and I decided that I would stay there for

a while. . . . So I was lucky enough to get in with this lovely couple, they were very good to me. As a matter of fact she was an Irish woman she was from Dublin and they were Jews and I was a mother's help lookin' after her wee girl.
"Now when I went to Scotland I was naive and I thought everybody had the same religion and with me being a Catholic I decided to teach the wee Jewish girl her prayers, and she picked it up very quick. She used to stand in the cot every morning and she would say her Hail Mary and God bless this and that and I thought I was doin' a wonderful job until I got a fortnight's holidays and the mother took over then. She shared the room with the little girl while I was away, and she couldn't believe it. The first morning, her daughter stood up in the cot and started saying her Hail Mary and all this sort of prayers and she laughed at it all right, and she knew that I hadn't the sense to know the difference between Jews and Catholics. However, when I came back they were very very nice about it, and they came into the kitchen and I remember Mr Fruitin saying, 'Now Kitty,' he said, 'there's a wee bit of difference between our religion and your religion, and you're not to teach Roz these prayers any more,' and I said that was alright. Well the local priest, anyway, heard the story about me teachin' the wee girl her prayers and he said, 'I heard you were teachin' the wee Jewish girl her prayers', and I said I was, and he said, 'Well, keep on with the good work!'."

During the nineteenth century there were several clashes between the Irish and the Orangemen of Glasgow including the great riot in Partick in 1875 when a demonstration in support of Irish Home Rule was attacked by hundreds of Orangemen.
Earlier this century there was discrimination in employment opportunities for the Irish, particularly in some of the older firms engaged in the shipbuilding industry. These days are thankfully gone and the only contemporary source of Protestant-Catholic tension which can still flare into violence is at Rangers v. Celtic football matches. However, the general opinion of the Donegal folk who lived in the Gorbals when it was supposed to have been seething with Billy and Dan gang hatred, was that the violence existed more in newspapers and novels than on the streets of the city.

Mrs Connelly:
"Well, I never seen anything wrong with the Gorbals. In those days you could walk in it any hour of the night and see nothing worse than yourself."

John Diver:
"You would get an odd, what we would call an old blackguard that would be inclined to raise trouble sayin' that the Irish people shouldn't be here. It was only the low class of people who said that, I couldn't say I found any discrimination."

*The Gorbals: a second-hand clothes store, 1948.*

Since Irish Independence has been achieved, and the nationalist aspirations of the Donegal community satisfied, the working class of both Scots and Irish origin share the same political identity.

Patrick Roarty:

"Now in local politics most of them supported Labour. I would say that 90-95 per cent of them supported Labour. I think the reason for that was the treatment they got at home from the Tories, the Liberals that were ruling Ireland at that time, made them naturally turn to Labour. Unfortunately they did not get involved in politics as they should, as the numbers of Irish in Glasgow of Donegal extraction must be huge, I would put it at perhaps two hundred thousand or maybe more, I think that had they been really so interested in politics, they could have had a stronger representation in the Glasgow City Chambers."

Today some branches of the culture of old Donegal still flourish in Glasgow. Very little Irish is now spoken in the city although it is still strong in the parts of Donegal from which the Glasgow Irish stemmed, the Irish Government having conferred official Gaeltacht status on the Rosses and Gweedore. In Glasgow there is a strong Rosses Association, Gaelic sports are played at Eastfield, Irish dancing classes are held throughout the city and perhaps most important of all, there is a thriving branch of Comhaltas Ceoltóirí Eirann, the Irish traditional music association. Today young traditional musicians in Scotland derive many features of their style from recordings by the successful Irish bands like Planxty and the Bothy Band. A generation ago musicians in Donegal were attracted to the tunes of Scott Skinner and recordings by Jimmy Shand brought home by the migrant workers. The great doyen of the Donegal style of fiddling with its speed and excitement, Johnny Docherty, like most of his generation worked and travelled in Scotland, absorbing our musical tradition during his stay. Today a large number of the people playing in the Scottish folk scene are of Irish origin — Dick Gaughan, Tony Cuffe, the Jacksons of Ossian and Kevin Mitchell to name but a few. The Jacksons like thousands of others of Irish origin still have family ties in Donegal and visit the place regularly.

George Jackson:

"There always seems to be this amazing traffic every week going back and forth from Donegal, it just doesn't seem to stop. To me it just seems like goin' to the Western Isles, it just seems like another island off the West Coast. And funnily enough, when we were in Ireland in the summer, at the festival in Balisodare there were some people from Kerry in the very south and they were asking whether I had any Irish connections and I was telling them about Donegal and they said 'Oh they're Scots anyway really', ye know. And they [the Donegal people] were sayin' as well, that they had more in common with the Scots than they had with the people down in Kerry and they even said that Donegal was just like an island off the west coast of Scotland."

Many of the travellers do go back and forward regularly, carried by mini bus and bus from a pick-up point in the old Gorbals.

Feda O'Donnell:

"I would be carryin' somethin' in the region of say 60-70 people per day. There's another five or six operators. They work from the Rosses, Gweedore and Cloneely. They do the same as I do."

If you are 'in the know', you can catch a bus to Donegal almost every day of the year and the same service exists on the other side. Some people travel from Donegal to Glasgow to do their shopping, visit their relatives and go back home a day later.

It is as if the wheel of fortune was turning in both areas, for the once proud industries of the West of Scotland are in decline while the Irish economy is booming. There can be few places in Europe which have undergone such a rapid transformation as Gweedore in the last two decades.

As late as the early '60s it still clung to the old ways. George Jackson's description of his grandmother's house would compare with that of an eighteenth-century traveller in Donegal.

George Jackson:

"My earliest recollections of Donegal are probably of when I was about three years old and that was goin' to my grandmother's home in Gweedore. It was a one-roomed cottage — thatched roof, peat fire, black pot, candlelight, rain coming in the door, smoke coming down the chimney, a sort of constant battle between either being soaked to death on the doorstep or being smoked to death inside. It was going into a different world."

Now new bungalows are standing beside the black houses and the once maligned Gaelic language is aided

*Children of Donegal descent continue the tradition of Irish dancing. The annual Columba Feis at Uddingston. August 1980.*

by grants to Gaelic-speaking families who wish to move back there and build houses. A far cry from our Government's attitude to the culture and economy of the Western Isles where the signs of neglect are everywhere.

Patrick Roarty:

"The younger generation have actually stopped coming from Donegal to Glasgow. In fact there has been an increase of twelve thousand in the population of Donegal at the last census taken and I can see that myself in my own parish of Annagry when I go home on holiday — the number of houses that are being built there and the number of families actually returning there. Especially since that industrial estate was established at Gweedore and the Gaeltarra factory in Annagry which is doing very well at the moment. People find that it's better to go back because there is a high standard of living there at the moment. And leaving the city of course and going and living and bringing up a family in that environment is much better. And even if they had to sacrifice a drop in income if they found work there they would be prepared to go back and live in it. But that isn't the case, they haven't found that there is a drop in their income. The economy there is really booming at the moment, because, for people going back and building their own houses, there are several grants that they can get to help them build their own homes. With the result that you have lots of people going back and nobody coming."

Mary McGarvey, a girl in her early teens, moved back from Glasgow to Donegal a few years ago. She is now absorbed totally in the language and culture of the Rannafast Gaeltacht. I spoke to Mary and her grandfather, Con Greene, on a douce summer evening. Con Greene's house is perched amidst rocky inlets and patchwork fields overlooking the sea. The scene was perfectly still and serenely beautiful . . . a stark contrast to the grey tenements they had left behind.

Mary McGarvey:

"Gaelic's my main language and I speak it nearly all the time. I like the beach and the countryside — I didn't like the city. I was sorry to leave all the same but I'd rather live here now than Glasgow. You get more freedom and, like in Glasgow there's lots of gangs goin' about and ye're afraid to open the door at night time. But here, ye can leave the door lyin' open when ye go to bed and nothin' would happen — as long as ye lock up the chickens in case the foxes come on them, that's all."

Many of those who have stayed on in Scotland feel a sense of mixed identity, a strong pride in where they have come from and in what they have become.

The Scots Irish, unlike smaller ethnic groups in Britain, derive strength from having a strong recognisable culture here in Scotland, while retaining close ties with a homeland which is more prosperous now than it has ever been. There seems to be no conflict in feeling Scots or Irish, no ethnic dichotomy to pull their allegiancies in opposite directions. They retain a strong pride in their Irishness, yet appear totally integrated within the context of Scottish culture. In this they are supported by the huge numbers of people of Irish extraction in West Central Scotland and also by the numbers of Scottish institutions — from the Catholic Church to the Football League — over which the Scots Irish exercise such a profound influence. They appear to enjoy the best of both worlds.

Mrs Coll:

"I like goin' to Gweedore for a run but I don't like stayin' in it now. The people's all changed ye know, no the same as the old people that used to be there. I'm Irish to the backbone, but all my children was born here."

*Granny Coll at home in the South Side of Glasgow, 1979.*

George Jackson:

"When I'm in Ireland, I feel Irish, although not too Irish. I feel more Scottish than I do Irish."

Father Canning:

"They first regard themselves as Scots, there's no doubt about it, after all it's a poor hen that despises her own nest ye see. But by and large I'd say that they are proud of their ancestry and some of them indeed are more Irish than the Irish are themselves. I can think of an old lady for example in the last parish I was in and she was furious when the parish priest had introduced a redecoration scheme and removed St Patrick's statue. She said afterwards that the parish had never had a day's luck from the day he was moved."

BILLY KAY

*Two neighbouring ring-net crews pictured on the Kintyre shore, c. 1895. The crews are composed mainly of members of the Brodie (Brodelty) family of Campbeltown, whose regular fishing station during the camping era was Cour Bay, between Carradale and Skipness. For the eldest men of the group, camping would undoubtedly have been a regular summer experience.*

# Fishermen Of Kintyre

The Scottish ring-net originated from irregular use of traditional drift-nets in the 1830s. The year cannot be established with certainty, but the available evidence indicates either 1833 or 1835.

Ninian Ballantyne, who began fish-curing at Tarbert in 1826, claimed to have purchased the first great catch of herring taken in the new way. He remembered that, in December 1833, two men had stretched drift-nets across the mouth of a Lochfyne bay and enclosed 6,700 barrels of herring. He paid out £400 or £500 for his share of the catch, the rest of which went to farmers and other fish-curers in the neighbourhood.

Within a few years, nets were being designed at Tarbert specifically for ring-netting, but the expansion of the method raised a public outcry. The drift-net fishermen, those of upper Lochfyneside particularly, petitioned the Fishery Board and the Government with complaints of the use of narrow-meshed nets and of resultant destruction of massive quantities of immature herring and spawn.

In 1851, all nets other than the drift-net were declared illegal in the herring fishery. The Fishery Board's policing methods proved futile, however, and the policing force itself was discredited in June 1853. HMS *Porcupine* was merely a month stationed on Lochfyne when, during an evening encounter with patrolling naval crews off Skipness, 28-year-old Colin MacKeich of Tarbert was shot and wounded. A gunner and marine from the ship were later convicted of reckless and culpable discharging of firearms and were sentenced to three months' imprisonment.

By 1858 the law had ceased to be enforced and a repeal was expected. In that year, however, the Tarbert ring-net fishermen ventured for the first time north of Otter Spit and into the narrow upper loch. Fighting broke out in Inveraray between them and the upper loch fishermen. The state of tension continued, and in 1860 an amended Act of Parliament was passed. Having proved useless in the prevention of ring-netting, it was replaced less than a year later by a harsher and more thorough piece of legislation.

The year 1861 was a calamitous one for ring-net fishermen. The Act was calculated to hit them hard, and succeeded. It received a premature baptism in the blood of a teenage Ardrishaig fisherman, Peter MacDougall, shot dead on a hazy June night off the wooded shore of East Otter. An officer and marine of HMS *Jackal* were tried at the High Court, Edinburgh, on charges of culpable homicide, but were acquitted.

The face of opposition was set firmly, as never before. Of the Tarbert fishermen, 26 would spend, in that year, periods of 14 or 20 days in jail at Campbeltown. In 1862 the effects of the repression touched every corner of the Tarbert community. Families starved; payment of rent was neglected; debts accumulated; and the young men began to leave the village.

Evidence of these hardships was heard in Tarbert by a Royal Commission appointed that year to investigate the operation of the laws. In the following year, 1863, that commission's report explicitly condemned the repressive legislation, and two years later a second commission added its criticism.

By 1866 the ring-netters were again out in force. The zone of defiance extended north of Otter Spit and into the very communities which, seven years before, had been prepared to reject ring-netting by uncompromising violence. Naval and fishery officers were beginning to admit that ring-netting could not be halted except by overwhelming force. That force was not granted and in 1867 the law, which had proved both ill-advised and unworkable, was repealed.

*The west end of Tarbert's Back Street, c. 1885. The men were working at a net, hung on the gable of the house.*

Ring-net skiffs of the original class were small and lightly-built. Their lightness was essential because the fishermen preferred, until about 1870, to haul their nets directly on to the shore, and so had to land and beach their craft. These early skiffs ranged in length from 20 to 25 feet and were about six feet of beam. They were open from stem to stern and the fishermen got about principally by rowing, though the boats were generally equipped with a small lugsail. Such a vessel would have cost, in 1852, from £12 to £20.

Some crews, when fishing at a distance from home, were accompanied by a smack which provided shelter after a night's work and which, in the absence of herring-carrying steamers, ran catches to market. Tents and huts raised ashore in the vicinity of the fishing grounds also served as shelters, particularly for those fishermen without a smack at their disposal.

These boats carried to sea with them a small brazier for brewing tea or cooking a meal of herring and potatoes during the night. Usually, however, their food consisted solely of a 'piece' (sandwich) wrapped in a big, fresh handkerchief and tied beneath athwart to keep it dry. Oatcakes and herring milt (the roe of the male fish) were eaten, often raw, at sea by many of the upper Lochfyneside fishermen.

The role of the 'floating market', as the herring-carriers were collectively known to fishermen, was of singular importance in the marketing of herring, from the 1870s until the 1930s, when the traditional skiffs began to be replaced on a general scale by powerful decked motor-boats, themselves capable of running catches to the railheads. These little *herring-screws*, owned by the fish-merchants of Glasgow, accompanied the fishing fleets from one fishing ground to another, their operational principle being simply to quickly secure a load of fish and set off before dawn to catch the early market at Glasgow.

Donald MacIntosh:

"We used tae haiv a couple o' flambeaux [kettle-shaped paraffin torches]; there wir a flambeau in each boat. . . . They used tae light wan on each boat if they wir waantin' tae sell. There might be six or seven o' the steamers cam' tae ye. An' then, when they'd come, the steamers used tae lower thir small boat an' the buyer wid come aboard ye, an' then they wid start biddin' up. . . . If ye got them in the first o' the night, well ye got a better price, because they wir away for the early market. By the mornin' the market might be flooded — there might be that much fish caught — that ye'd always the best chance if ye wid catch them in the evenin'. . . . They always used tae go away, away for Fairlie, for tae catch the early train for the Glasgow market. An' ye could haiv them for yer breakfast in Glasgow in the mornin'.

Angus Martin:

"A seen us wan night, och it was aweh back aboot 1912, we got a good puckle herrin' — seeventy or echty baskets — [and] we went alongside the steamer an' discharged them. We left

*Two Lochfyne skiffs moored off Dalintober beach, while (left) the hulk of a redundant drift-net smack lies rotting.*

the steamer an' we never went a mile tae we cam' into the herrin' agane, an' we got another good shot. We had three times at that steamer the sem night."

In 1882, with the launch of a pair of part-decked skiffs, began the elimination of the custom of camping ashore. These boats, the *Alpha* and the *Beta*, were 25 feet of keel and were built at Girvan to the order of Edward McGeachy of Dalintober (now merged with Campbeltown, but once a distinct community on the northern shore of the loch). Designed by McGeachy's father, a native of Gigha and a retired ocean-going ship's carpenter, these skiffs' forecastles provided accommodation — albeit cramped — and improved cooking facilities for the fishermen, and they were the prototypes of the famous Lochfyne Skiff.

The final development of ring-netting began in 1907 with the installation of a 7-9 h.p. petrol-paraffin engine in the *Brothers* of Campbeltown. There followed a rapid mechanisation of the ring-net fishery, and within 25 years most of the familiar working ways would have vanished. By 1970, the ring-net method itself had declined into insignificance, superseded by the more efficient — and more destructive — mid-water trawl method.

The skills of ring-net fishermen in locating herring constituted, in their particularity and diversity, a remarkable accomplishment, and it is with that branch of the fishermen's expertise — largely eliminated by technology — that this account will now deal.

The transition from drift-netting to ring-netting forced the fishermen to develop a new range of abilities. The traditional method was fundamentally a passive one, the fleet of nets being set out in the form of a drifting wall, into which fish might or might not swim and become enmeshed. The ring-net, on the contrary, was an active method, the net being set around a shoal. Herring, therefore, had ordinarily to be located before the ring-net was shot, whereas at drift netting the nets were set out on chance, more or less, and comparatively little attention was paid to signs of fish. Ring-net fishermen, therefore, became adept at recognising signs of herring, and that net of knowledge was heavy. These signs were called *appearances*, in Gaelic *coltais*.

On a calm, dark night the main-sheet would be tightened on the 'back' — or starboard — side of the skiff, so that, with sail taut, the skiff would be "more driftin' than sailin'. . . . Ye could go along," said Hugh MacFarlane of Tarbert, "an' the boat wid take steerin' wey, an' that wis aa' they waanted." The men would listen, with hands cupped about their ears, for the jump of a herring. One plop was sufficient to justify the shooting of the net, for, as David MacLean of Campbeltown remarked, "That wan herrin' jumpin' gies away the millions below him."

An extensive range of terms existed to express the various degrees of sound, principally among the fishermen of Tarbert, where a vigorous Gaelic vocabulary survived the failure of the spoken language. A *bling* or *bleeng* was the merest disturbance of the

water's surface by tail, fin, or nose, likened by some fishermen to a 'spittle'.

George Newlands:
"We wir in the Kyles wan night, the Kyles o' Bute, an' we wir lyin' on a lovely moonlight night, an' I wis in a boat they callt the *Glad Tidings*, an' we felt just like a spittle in the waater, like a spittle, an' just tae pass the time we thought we'd just have a go at it, get a wee bit o' work, because there wir nothin' doin'. An' we shot, an' we got the fuul o' the net. We'd tae get help, we'd tae get another perr alongside. . . . An' we nearly fillt the four boats — wi' one spittle. It wis that calm; it wis dead calm, not an err [air] o' win'."

The *plout* or *ploop* of a leaping fish could, by a practised listener, be identified as that of a herring, or else dismissed as *peuchtie* or *gleshan* (young saithe of comparable size) or some other fish.

---

*The Lochfyne skiff* Good Hope *of Campbeltown (skipper-owner Hugh MacLean) leaving Campbeltown harbour under unbarked regatta rig, c. 1905.*

George Newlands:
"Oh, ye could hear them playin' in the mornin' or in the evenin', just lik' flutterin' in the water. But ye could always tell a herrin' besides a saithe — gleshans we called them — it made a sort o' smack in the water. When you heard a herrin', it wis a clean jump."

For a small flurry of herring the Tarbert fishermen might use any one of three terms: *bratan* (difficult to define, but probably 'small covering'); *fras* or, in its oblique case, *frois* ('shower'); or *fliuchan*, which was also known to Carradale fishermen, and described by Duncan 'Denis' MacIntosh as "a wee watery spot o' herrin' ". The Scots *plooder* ('to splash') was used by Campbeltown fishermen for herring jumping regularly, as in "They're plooderin' away here."

A turbulent mass of herring or, oftener, mackerel— a noisier fish — could be expressed by any of four Gaelic terms: *raibheic*, *gàir*, *toirm*, and *eas*.

There was a real division of opinion among fishermen on the degree of accuracy attainable when listening for herring, but an unmistakable sound was a

*A 'daylight ring'. Dugald Blair of Campbeltown's* Glad Tidings III. *The net is being winched on board, while a towing strain is maintained by the neighbour-boat, or* conjug, *from the stern of which the photograph was taken.*

big *play* of herring rushing in bulk on the surface and 'renting the hills'. Before daybreak, herring might be heard — often from a distance of several miles away — 'playing off the shore', that is striking out from the shallow water towards the deep. Decided skill was required to successfully surround playing herring then, so quickly would they leave the coast. The mouth of the net would almost invariably be set across the shore to block their passage.

The fishermen preferred to shoot their nets on herring jumping singly, believing that a shoal so signified was 'steady'. A big play, especially far into night, suggested that the shoal was shifting away, or was about to sound to the deeps. "On dark nights when we'd hear a big play we'd say — 'That's them, they're shiftin' away clear o' that, or they're goin' tae lie doon.' They might go an' lie doon for weeks, away doon in the deep, an' they winna rise at all," said Donald MacIntosh of Carradale.

During 'the burning fishing', in the late summer and autumn nights, when phosphorescence lit the sea, herring were located principally by sight. A man or two men would lie watching over the bow of the boat, and one would intermittently strike the gunwale with the anchor-shank. The sound-wave transmitted would cause a shoal of herring to start, producing an incandescent flash. That reaction, which was peculiar to the herring, was termed 'answering the anchor'. The Gaelic-speaking fishermen called phosphorescence *losgadh*, the meaning of which is represented exactly in the English term which has totally replaced it, *burning*.

The organism most likely to produce 'fire in the water' is the dinoflagellate *Noctiluca*, a very abundant member of the *phytoplankton* (minute drifting plants) in western Scottish waters. It emits a glow when disturbed, for an as yet obscure reason.

A 'trained eye' was required to distinguish between a shoal of herring and a shoal of other, unwanted fish; but, more especially, to discern a glow deep down. The response of deep-swimming herring was often noted as a mere 'change in the water'. Tommy Ralston Jr.,

formerly of Campbeltown, recalled that "Jock MacKenzie, one of the most expert deck-hands I ever sailed with, used to shout, 'There's a change in the water' when he saw a lot of herring in the burning." MacKenzie, attempting to explain to his young shipmate the nature of that change which his unwavering vision had perceived, told him that "the water went milky". Jock MacKenzie would *dunner* not with the anchor, but with a personal mallet which he considered so indispensable to his technique that when it finally snapped he was virtually inconsolable until a satisfactory replacement could be found for him.

Robert McGown of Campbeltown remembered: "Wi' the big herrin' ye used tae say there wir a blue flash off them. Ye always thought they wir good herrin', whether it wis the solidness o' them that made them dim." David MacLean remarked: "Sometimes the big herrin' show just lik' a dim wisp o' smoke."

George Newlands:

"You're on the bow, ye see, an' ye're *chappin'* the anchor, ye know strikin' the anchor as ye're goin' along. They wid start, ye see. If they wir in a sheet they wid gie this blue sort o' flash off them. Other times ye'd jeest see hoot [what] we called a *scatter*.

The ability to detect the evanescent glow of an 'answering' shoal deep down was, as Robert McGown remarked, "really expert work". Expertise was, however, the product of many years of observation, both of the night waters and of the skills of an experienced man on the bow, and young boys fresh at fishing were invariably awed by the mysterious abilities of their seniors to locate and catch fish of which they themselves had seen not a sign. Said Robert McGown: "When I went tae the fishin' first, I'd be lyin' for'ard on the bow wi' my father, an' my father wid be shoutin', 'Right round wi' her — here's a fine spot!'. I'd be lookin' an' couldna see a thing. Ye marvelled at them until ye got intae the way o' it yerself." A young Carradale fisherman, born in 1950, had this to say.

Donald 'Dan' Paterson:

"Ye lay up for'ard with them an' ye looked for what they looked [for], and if they said, well, 'Slow her down, there a scatter', ye saw what they slowed down for, but, och, it wid take years really tae learn. . . . It's there for everybody tae see, but, it's . . . lik', machrel show different than herrin' in the water; small herrin'll show different than big herrin'; deep herrin', herring on the surface . . . they're all different. This is how the man on the bow, the experienced man, knows to differentiate between [them], whether it's worth shottin' on a scatter, a length o' a scatter, a deep scatter. It wis all up tae him on the bow. The skipper took his word for it an' that was it. But the burnin' wis all around ye, ye know in the summertim' wi' the phosphorescence in the water, an' all the crew more or less always lay for'ard on the good nights, the summer nights. An' some nights wi' maybe a moon or a northerly breeze, northerly sky, there wasna the same dark, it didna darken the same. There wir less burnin' in the water or it wis harder tae see, an' ye'd only maybe see lik' wee stars, lik' bits o' stardust. Well, the experienced man could tell again whether there wir herrin' wi' this, jeest a wee odd sparkle in the water, which again wis jeest experience an' age."

*The writer's grandfather, Duncan Martin, on Dalintober quay scraping the mast of his skiff, the* Fame, *prior to revarnishing. Boats were annually overhauled in May.*

Although the author was born many years too late to witness the most magnificent spectacles of 'fields' or 'parks' of herring suddenly luminous in a dark reach of sea, he has vivid memories of lying night after summer night and watching, enchanted, the swirls of glittering water at the stem, and the ubiquitous darting mackerel which left like comets a gleaming trail, and the sluggish dog-fish which seemed to curl upon themselves as they broke out of the way of the advancing boat.

That imperial fish-hunter, the gannet (in Tarbert *sollan*, and elsewhere solan goose), unwittingly led generations of fishermen to great catches. His presence was always investigated if his behaviour suggested that he might be working on herring. Indeed, summer daylight fisheries were periodically based on the presence of great concentrations of the birds. Daylight

fishing was uncertain work, however, because the herring were able to see the nets set around them and might evade capture by *dooking* below the nets before their closure. "Ye missed them of'ner than ye got them," John McWhirter of Campbeltown remarked ruefully.

A gannet prowling in the sky with a peculiar persistence was an almost sure indication that a shoal was below it. "When ye see them hingin' thon way, cockin' thir nebs," said Donald MacIntosh, "that's when the herrin' wir right thick." An explanation of the phenomenon of the uncertain bird was offered by Robert McGown: "We always knew when a gannet circles round and round [that] it's on a spot. It must just be waiting to get the edge o' the herrin'."

A high vertical plummet — an almost infallible indication of herring — was termed a *stroke*. The height from which a gannet struck was considered proportionate to the depth of penetration necessary. Gannets were especially valuable to fishermen in late evening, and it was during that gloaming period that the fishermen might 'ring on a gannet'. If a bird was working on *sile* or *haaz* (small herring) or mackerel, his dive would be shallow and angled, though gannets fishing with that technique on evening herring close to the surface were not absolutely unknown.

When fishermen came into an area where gannets were resting full-bellied on the surface after intensive feeding, upon approaching one it would invariably regurgitate the contents of its stomach to lighten itself for take-off. In that way, the fishermen would discover whether or not the unlucky bird had been feeding on herring. Eight or nine herring might be *boaked* up by a bird so disturbed.

'Herring whales' — a collective name, probably applied to common rorquals and lesser rorquals — were once abundant visitors to the Kilbrannan Sound and Lochfyne, but come no more in great numbers — indeed, tragically, and by the agency of man, do not exist in great numbers.

Both the whale (known to the Gaelic fishermen as *muc-mhara*, 'sea-pig') and the porpoise herded the herring and fed on the outer fish. Archibald Stewart of Campbeltown expressed delightfully their strategy: "They jeest swept round and round and nibbled a wee yin now an' agane." The fishermen claimed to know when a whale was working around a shoal of herring by the infrequency of its blowing.

When it did blow, the stench exuded was, by all accounts, unbearable. The author of a newspaper contribution, *A Night with the Herring Fishers*, published in 1901, told of an engineer on the herring-steamer the *Rob Roy* who, after a whale had surfaced to blow, was "made so faint that he was glad to escape to his sweltering engine-room". Hugh MacFarlane remembered, with amusement, that "If they'd come up tae win'ard, they'd damn near take yer breath away. When ye wid get a whiff ye'd be boakin' away. Talk aboot foul air!'

A whale bursting to the surface clear of a dense shoal of herring was naturally a valued sign. Hugh

*A Campbeltown crew discharging a catch of herring on to lorry. Wearing soft hat, on left, is Archiblad 'Baldy' Stewart, a noted 'character' and sound fisherman. Third from right, also wearing soft hat, is David Robertson, for many years fish-salesman at Campbeltown.*

MacFarlane: "The old men used tae say, the whale wis throwin' it off 'er back at such a place. . . . It wis jeest lik' a bing o' silver up in the air, an' then it wis all spread away."

Donald MacIntosh:

"Aye, we liked tae see the whales, aye. Sometimes if there wir a big shoal in't, the whale wid rise in the centre o' them an' ye wid hear them, like ye wid think it wis somebody riddlin' grevel or that. She wid throw them right off 'er back, jeest make a splash. I've seen them lik' that, especially in the wintertime. She wid jeest maybe rise in the shoal that way, an' they would be up on the surface an' she wid knock them right oot the water."

There was, as Donald MacVicar of Kames, Loch Gair, recalled, a whale repellent practice among upper Lochfyne fishermen. Fearing for their safety in the small skiffs, which they believed were readily capsizable by whales, they would scatter astern ashes from the forecastle fire, and these, they maintained, would turn a following whale out of their wake.

In daylight or at evening, strings of bubbles might be seen rising to the surface of the sea. The Tarbert fishermen of the nineteenth century called that appearance *frying*, but the later general term was *putting up*, with *belling* (from Scots *bell*, to bubble) also sometimes used, mainly by Campbeltown fishermen.

The phenomenon has been scientifically investigated, notably by T. H. Huxley in the 1880s. It is

caused by the expulsion of gas from the swim-bladders of the fish as they rise from a depth, and enables them to maintain their natural buoyancy.

Of the lesser appearances little account can be given, by reason of space restriction.

'Smelty water' or 'greasy water' was a calm on the surface of the sea, caused by a patch of fish oil, which might be accompanied by a 'raw smell'.

George Newlands:

"Ye could go intae a bay, an' ye could actually feel them, an' ye could feel them out in the deep jeest the sem. If there wir a waft o' win' an' there wir herrin' about, ye felt this sort o' raw smell."

'Red feeding'—in Tarbert 'croy' (Gaelic, *crò*, 'blood') — described concentrations of copepods, in particular calanus. The red colouration is caused by oil contained in a sac which lies along the gut. When the copepods drifted close to the surface in banks, the herring would rise to feed on them. In breezy weather, the fishermen would search for herring along lee shores, where the patches of feeding would be carried.

'The herring cleaning', when that feeding was all excreted, was an autumn phase which preceded the herrings' departure from Lochfyne and the Kilbrannan Sound to the spawning grounds of the Ballantrae Banks. The 'herring dirt', or *glar*, resembled tiny red worms on the water's surface, and was most noticeable when the tide gathered it.

When the herring did leave Lochfyne, their departure might transiently be marked by the wash they caused. Referred to as a 'herring wave', it was evident on a calm sea, and such would be the speed of the shoal that any attempt to surround it would almost certainly fail.

When dog-fish were rampaging among herring and biting, here and there, chunks from the fish, the oil so released would rise and form patches on the surface, letting off a distinctive and detectable odour.

Fishermen noted that herring were often present in the vicinity of basking-sharks, which likewise feed on copepods. Storm-petrels and seagulls might also put the observant fisherman on to herring.

Donald MacIntosh:

"An' then sometimes ye would see the wee stormy-petrels. They come an' they jeest skim on the water. They're jeest wee burds, lik' swallows. They skimmed up the fish oil. Ye wid see them

there, an' maybe if ye'd look about there, sometimes ye'd come on [herring]."

Once the fisherman's accepted companion by night and day, the seagull is now denied even the right of existence. Innumerable birds are yearly destroyed on certain Campbeltown trawlers, ostensibly to check a so-called nuisance, but actually as a form of amusement which resists reasonable explanation. An indication — one among many — of how far removed are the generality of younger fishermen from that sense of being in the natural world which their forebears enjoyed and would not violate for miserable ends.

*Surprised in the act, a gull coming to grips with a herring fallen from a box.*
*Photograph by W. J. Maclean.*

ANGUS MARTIN

## THE OLD FISHERMAN

Greet the bights that gave me shelter,
they will hide me no more with the horns of their forelands.
I peer in a haze, my back is stooping;
my dancing days for fishing are over.

The shoot that was straight in the wood withers,
the bracken shrinks red in the rain and shrivels,
the eyes that would gaze in the sun waver;
my dancing days for fishing are over.

The old boat must seek the shingle,
her wasting side hollow the gravel,
the hand that shakes must leave the tiller;
my dancing days for fishing are over.

The sea was good night and morning,
the winds were friends, the calm was kindly—
the snow seeks the burn, the brown fronds scatter;
my dancing days for fishing are over.,

GEORGE CAMPBELL HAY

# JŠEIVIU DRAUGAS.

Skiriamas svetimoj šaly gyvenantiems lietuviams.

'Iseiviu Draugas'–The Friend of the Emigrant from rural Lithuania to industrial Lanarkshire and to picnics among the coal bings.

# The Lanarkshire Lithuanians

The origins of the Lithuanian community in Scotland remain something of a mystery. It has been suggested in some accounts that the first Lithuanian immigrants arrived as prisoners of war from the defeated Russian army after the Battle of Sebastopol in 1855. It was not until the 1890s, however, that the Lithuanians began to arrive in considerable numbers. Included among the early immigrants was my grandfather, Antanas Augustaitis, who arrived in Scotland around 1897 and settled first in Stevenston, Ayrshire, before later moving to Coatbridge in Lanarkshire. There, amidst the coal mines and iron and steel works that dominated the area, he joined the largest settlement of Lithuanians in Scotland, estimated to number between 5,000 and 6,000 by 1914. In this less than salubrious quarter the first generation Lithuanians established a community with a strong ethnic identity where their language and culture was preserved almost intact. Some three generations later the Lithuanian community has disappeared almost without trace and only a handful of those original immigrants are still alive. Their story is, as yet, untold and little recognition has been given of their contribution to the history of the area in which they settled.

The Lithuanians were a farming nation and almost all of the immigrants who arrived in Lanarkshire in the 1890s and 1900s came from agricultural backgrounds. Most of them left Lithuania for economic reasons. Agriculture had changed little over the centuries: farming techniques were primitive, land-holdings on average were small, and the vast majority of the peasantry lived at not much more than subsistence level. In the latter half of the nineteenth century a combination of a rapid increase in population, heavier government taxation, and a fall in grain prices after 1885 pushed many Lithuanians to the very margin of existence. Emigration took place on an unprecedented scale and between 1870 and 1914 over 650,000, or one in four of the total population, left their homeland to seek a more secure future elsewhere.

But not all emigrants chose to leave. For in Lithuania, as in other parts of the Russian Empire, there was a groundswell of opposition to Tsarist rule. Abortive insurrections in 1830 and 1863 had resulted in an intensification by the government of the policies of colonisation and russification. These measures only stiffened the resolve of the newly emergent Lithuanian nationalist movement.

Frank Dullick:
"My parents described the difficulties that they had to undergo being under the Tsar and they told us about the smuggling of books over the border from East Prussia. My parents lived near the border. One of the acts passed by the Tsarist government, Lithuanian print was forbidden and all books had to be printed in Cyrillic script even though it was in the Lithuanian language. So, there was a tremendous smuggling went on and most books were printed in a place called Tilse [Tilsit in East Prussia] and because of this the book smugglers became well sought by the Russian police."

If convicted the book-smugglers could expect sentences of up to five years' imprisonment locally or deportation to Siberia for three to five years. To avoid such a fate emigration was often the only solution.

Mrs Mitchell:
"My father had to leave Lithuania because he was a book-smuggler. The village in which he stayed it was policed by Russian soldiers and my father was very friendly with a Colonel, and one night he said to my father, 'Kazis,' which is Charles, 'I would not be at home tonight. I can say no more but I would not be at home tonight.' So my father crossed the river, actually stood in the river with the proverbial reed in his mouth, got across, went to Germany eventually, and my mother and her first born daughter, my sister Mary, had to join him there later."

The ultimate destination of most of the emigrants was the United States and Scotland, at least initially, was probably no more than a stepping-stone on the journey from Lithuania to America. With well-established shipping routes between, for example, Hamburg or Bremen and Leith and Dundee, Scotland was easily accessible from the continent. Travel was also cheap and a ticket from Hamburg to Leith around 1900 cost only £1 5s. 0d.

It seems unlikely, nevertheless, that the first Lithuanians in Lanarkshire arrived there by chance.

Frank Dullick:
"From what our parents told us the ironmasters in Coatbridge went to Lithuania recruiting men to dig coal. When you talk to a farm labourer of digging, what he foresees is using a spade, as if he's delving and digging ground. Now, they didn't realise that digging for coal meant going into the bowels of the earth. I'm not too sure about the name but it was the ironmasters recruited men and paid their fare over to this country only. Such that, when the men came over here, they didn't know the language and they saw the conditions. Well, they had no money to leave, or even to go back to America, or leave here and go back to their own country. In the last decade of the century this was how it began because they were told 'You're coming to Scotland to dig coal'."

If recruitment did take place, whether at home or abroad, it solved three of the most immediate problems facing the pioneer immigrants: accommodation, money and communication. Firstly, employment with the large companies in the area such as Baird, Merry and Cunninghame, Wilson or Dixon, included provision of company-owned housing. Secondly, wages in Scotland were high by Lithuanian standards and could only be substantially improved by a further move to America. And thirdly, the language difficulties were minimised by the unskilled nature of the work being done by the Lithuanians in the blast furnaces and mines.

*Lithuanian workers in the Summerlee iron works, Coatbridge, c. 1917. The author's father is on the extreme left.*

The 'attractions' of Lanarkshire, conveyed by letter to friends and relatives in Lithuania and in other parts of Britain, undoubtedly contributed to the growth of the Lithuanian community. Although numerically insignificant in terms of the total population of the area, the Lithuanians, or 'Poles' as they were called, tended to 'colonise' certain streets and districts.

Jenny Sinclair:

"I found that where we lived, at the 'Pole Barracks' [in Bellshill], I mean, the majority were Lithuanians. There were quite a lot of single men because there wasn't enough women to go round them. But I never knew any that married Scots women. And you found that these single men, they usually lodged with Lithuanians. My mother used to have two lodgers, Lithuanian bachelors."

Matt Mitchell:

"There's part of the old Carfin that we used to call 'The Bell'. And coming from New Stevenson, past Hefferman's house, the row on the right hand side, I can still repeat the Lithuanian names. First house: Yafortskus, Baukauskus, Kvedera, Curzeatis, Lizdus and Koshinsky. That was the first building in Carfin coming from New Stevenson. It was totally Lithuanian and the left was nearly the same."

The relatively sudden appearance of these immigrant 'colonies' throughout Lanarkshire alarmed the local population and, like the Irish before them, the Lithuanians became a convenient 'scapegoat' to explain all the ills of society.

The main allegations came from the mining unions who regarded the Lithuanians as a threat to employment and wage rates and to safety in the mines because of their inexperience and inability to understand the language. They illustrated the latter point by frequently citing the gruesome example of the young Lithuanian who was decapitated when he failed to understand the warning of an engineman to keep his head in as the pit-cage descended the shaft. One unexpected problem that confronted the unions was the difficulty of identifying the number of Lithuanians involved in accidents. For it was common practice when a Lithuanian first arrived on the job for the overseer or manager to change his name to something more easily spelt and pronounced. Thus, names like Bernotaitis, Kanapinskas, and Augustaitis were changed to Smith, Kane and Rodgers. It was the new name that was registered in the company records and, if an accident occurred, in the district Mining Inspectorate's report. The choice of name was completely arbitrary and local newspaper reports have revealed some unusual Scottish surnames such as Frank Gorilla, Joseph Coalbag and Antanas Kipper. One rather inappropriate name was given to a Lithuanian whose frequent court appearances were hardly in keeping with its biblical origins: Mathew Mark.

But the failure of the Lithuanians to understand verbal instructions or warnings was clearly not the only problem of communication that existed down the mines.

Anne Russell:

"A friend o' mine told me that his father worked in the pits and the pony that they used for the hutches, he used to speak Lithuanian to it. So one day he went on holiday and someone, a Scotsman, had to take his place. So the pony didn't understand what he was sayin' to him, to go ahead. So when the fellow came back from his holidays the Scots fellow says: 'How do you speak to that pony, it doesn't move for me'. So he says, 'I just say v—— r—— [Lithuanian expletive] — 'Go on ya B——!'."

On the question of the threat to employment and wages there is little doubt that initial union fears were quite justified. The Lithuanians were often introduced to break strikes or to force down wage rates and the local employers were not slow to exploit the weakness of the immigrants' bargaining position. By 1910, however, it was generally recognised that the Lithuanians had proved themselves to be 'good union men' and capable miners. This was no mean achievement for a group of farmhands, many of whom had never seen a mine in their life before.

Vince Davidson:

"Aye that was one thing about them, they were very adaptable. I don't know if you remember the Bevan Boys. They were taking young boys and putting them into coal mines, they couldn't get miners. Well, this was a queer thing, they were giving them six months' training to be a miner and the Lithuanians they came over and they were miners inside three days. And nobody taught them. They could always improvise and all this."

The ability to improvise manifested itself in many ways and the Lithuanians, the women in particular, quickly gained a reputation for their handiwork.

Mrs Smith:

"The men were normally good joiners or carpenters. In fact my father [Antanas Augustaitis] was a handy man like that. He used to make tables and he made a violin. He built a violin for my brother and a golf club. And they made their own 'rag-rugs' with cloth, strips of cloth, and they designed them and some of the designs were really marvellous. Some were just plain, diamonds and hearts and what not. They were self-sufficient among themselves, they worked hard."

Mrs Millar:

"I'm used to crochetin', I'm used to knittin', I'm used to sewin'. I'm used to do everything. Ma husband he used to go to bed and I'm get a chance to work. And he's used to say: 'Well, it's time goin'

to bed'. Well, I'm sayin': 'I'll need to make a money for my family'. Och, I manage all right. An' I made a jerkin and a pair o' trousers oot o' ma old coat. And it was the teacher said: 'Where d'ye get that suit, son?'. Said: 'My mammy made it'. Said: 'No wonder you're always nice dressed'."

The resourcefulness and thrift of the women was in marked contrast with the profligate spending, particularly on drink, of some of the Lithuanian men. In this respect the men were no different from their native counterparts although their 'alien' status accorded them much greater publicity in the local press when they ended up in court. Christenings and weddings were a great source of enjoyment among the immigrant community and during the first generation of settlement the ceremonies continued to follow traditional lines.

Vince Davidson:

"They worked hard and they lived hard and they always enjoyed themselves you know. They werena' a crowd for savin' at that time, most of it went on booze. Even a christening used to last about three days. They used to buy a barrel of beer and they put it in the corner and if you went to the christening you just helped yourself. . . . As far as weddings were concerned, they carried on their old tradition. A whole week it went on. I played at the weddings in Lithuania, I played the violin. The fiddlers stood at the door and they played something that was really sentimental and

*Lithuanian miners from Bellshill, c. 1910, note the 'Scotch bunnets'.*

everybody, everybody was crying. And then their
cart, it was all decorated with flowers, the wheels
were all covered with flowers, the horses, the lot.
Beautiful it was. The whole mob went out to the
chapel and then when they got married, if you are a
fiddler, you are standing at the door to catch them
coming back. Well every time you were playing
this they were always dropping coins you know in
the slit in the violin. You could hardly carry the
damned thing. Oh, it was beautiful, a beautiful
custom.''

Another traditional practice still in evidence at that
time was the 'arranged' marriage.

Mrs Millar:
    "Well, I'd a boyfriend in Lithuania and he want
to get married, and another boy friend stayed with
ma' sister [in Lanarkshire] and is writin' letters to
come over. And my father said: 'Well,' said 'if you
goin' to Scotland you go an be a lady. If you get
married here, you need to work day and night'.''

But for Mrs Millar the prospects of an easy life were
quickly dashed.

Jennie Sinclair:
    "When my mother came she was supposed to be
gettin' married to this boy, he'd sent the fare for
her tae come over. But when she did come over
eventually he'd got married, ye see. So her sister
says 'how can you stay here, we've got to get you
married, we can't feed you, ye can't get a job'. So,
a marriage was arranged.''

Mrs Millar:
    "Well, [ah'd met him] maybe two or three times.
But once he was up in the house and were drunk,
and his cousin came up to ma' house and she said
'well' she said, 'you should get married to John'.
And I'm thinkin', that man looks kinna' funny for
me, is a drunk, and oh, dear God! But after all, at
that time, women werena' workin'. There's nae
jobs for womens naewhere. So ah just stayed in the
house, look after ma family.''

    The survival of traditional Lithuanian customs under
the murky skies of Lanarkshire illustrates the degree of
independence achieved in this period. For by 1914 the
Lithuanians had their own clergy, shops and stores,
insurance societies, two weekly newspapers — the
Socialist *Rankpelnis* and the Catholic *Iseiviu Draugas* —
and a variety of political, religious and recreational
groups.
    The Lanarkshire community had acquired
considerable status among the exiled Lithuanian
population and attracted some prominent Lithuanian
politicians to its midst. For example, Dr Juozas
Bagdonas, who was one of the leading members of the
nationalist movement, came to Bellshill and edited the
newspaper *Laikas* in 1905 and 1906 and on his return to
Lithuania became Dean of the Faculty of Medicine at
Kaunas University. 1915 saw the arrival of Vincas
Mickevicius-Kapsukas who for fifteen months was
editor of *Rankpelnis* before returning to Lithuania (via
America) in 1917. Kapsukas was the first president of
the short-lived Lithuanian Soviet Republic and now
has a Lithuanian town named after him.

Vince Davidson:
    "The Lithuanians were definitely a funny crowd
because their tradition and their culture was
everything to them although they had nothing.
They believed in it and they, when they did come
over here, they wouldn't associate with the Scots
people. They wouldn't even bother about the
language. My father was in the country for what,
oh about twenty-eight years, and he couldn't speak
the language. Same wi' ma mother.''

The reluctance of some of the older Lithuanians to
learn English had important ramifications. Besides
prolonging the isolation of the Lithuanians from the
local community, it produced a generation of young
Lithuanians who were bi-lingual.

Mrs Smith:
    "The Lithuanian had to be spoken because my
father wrote out a paper and put it on the wall
that: 'In this house Lithuanian was the only
language to be spoken'. We used to sit and talk
English between ourselves and my father would just
yell out: 'None of that English' he says, 'Keep to
your own language!'. He just wanted us to be able
to speak the Lithuanian language and keep to the
Lithuanian. . . . They seemed to want to be on their
own, they didn't want to mix too much with the

*The Lithuanian press.*

*Three Lithuanians who returned to Russia in 1917 and became members of the Siberian police.*

Scots. But that was all in the early days. Later on, when we grew up, he became a wee bit more 'Englified' and started to back horses. In fact, I'd tae read up for him in the newspapers with the result that he started learning English."

The linguistic talents of the children were of great practical benefit when dealing with official documentation and frequent calls were made upon them to appear as interpreters at court cases. It was an important function especially during the First World War when many Lithuanians found themselves in court for violation of the residence clauses of the newly-imposed Aliens Restriction Act of 1914. Infant interpreters were also used during the military exemption tribunals that followed the implementation of the Anglo-Russian military convention of July 1917. The effect of the convention on the community was little short of disastrous.

Vince Davidson:
"Well, the Lithuanians living in this country, they'd a choice, either to go into the British Army or go and fight for Russia. . . . Now, och there were hundreds of Lithuanians did join the British Army, but others said: 'No, I'm a Russian subject, why should I fight for Britain?' And they went over to Russia in 1917. But when they landed there the Tsar had been overthrown and eh, the Commies had taken over so they wanted to put them in the Communist Army. Some of them went in but the

majority says 'no', they says, 'we came over to fight for the Tsar'! So my father, he joined the Commie Army, not because he loved them, he just joined them because he was going to get fed there. Well, he was in the army for about three years and then he got fed up with it. And then he went to the Commissar and he told him he was fed up servin'. It just gives you an idea what sort of a rag-time army it was. The Commissar says, 'well, if you don't want to fight the Capitalists, go wherever the hell you like!'. So my father, he walked and travelled from Russia to Lithuania. Well, in 1920 we got word that he was alive in Lithuania. . . ."

The fate of the 900 Lithuanians from Scotland who embarked for Archangel in October 1917 is uncertain. Some of the Socialists in the Lanarkshire community fought with the Bolsheviks and later joined the First Soviet Chumysh Division, others tried to reach Lithuania, and some joined the interventionist British forces in northern Russia as a way of guaranteeing a passage home. For the anxious dependants, correspondence was sporadic and in most cases censored.

The following letter, written in broken English, was received by a Lithuanian woman in Carfin from her husband in Camp Zarapu in Siberia. It was dated 8 December 1918, and was uncensored:

My Dear and Loving Mary,
I have written to you so many letters in which I was asking you of yours and our dears and amiable childrens helth and life, but I had got no answer yet. Dear Mary and you my lovely daughter Ona, write though one letter to me which I will wait day and night for and I will be very much thankfully to you. If you will be so kind and to inform me of all your lives in Carfin, especially my dear son Jonas, who has remained without father for so long time. . . . I am so sad and unfortunate man here living in Siberia. Here is a very cold weather at present time. Dear Mary, If you could ask some of the good and intelligent man will I could return to Scotland or not? . . . Excuse me my dears for that but I left you alone for such long time. You should understand that it is not my fault. I had made mistake only this, that I had not away to France in the trenches to help the Britishers fight against Germans. I could be more happy in the front than in the Siberia. Goodbye my dears, I remain a very sad and unhappy man,

Petras Geraitis.

The unfortunate Geraitis never returned and his wife, like many of the other Lithuanian women, had to rely upon Parish Relief. The allowances of 12/6 for a wife and 2/6 per child were less in total than half the average miner's wage at that time and some women were forced to take up employment in the local brickworks and as surface-workers in the mines.

*A group of Scottish and Lithuanian workers at the brickworks near Carfin, c. 1923.*

Despite the support of local councillors and MPs and such notable figures as John Maclean and Sylvia Pankhurst, little was done to alleviate the suffering of the Lithuanian dependants. In fact, their position worsened, for in 1920 the Treasury decided to withdraw their meagre allowances and 'offered' repatriation to those who wanted it. This completed the decimation of the community as over 400 women and children returned to Lithuania in March of that year.

Repatriation was a convenient way of removing the financial burden of Parish Relief payments as well as easing the acute housing shortage that existed in the Lanarkshire area and it could be argued that, in this case, there was more than a hint of official discrimination against the Lithuanians. It is quite possible too that this was not an isolated episode.

Mr Smith:

"But the thing that stuck out tae me was quite a few of them [Lithuanians] were deported for just generally the least wee thing, for instance, there were an uncle of mine he was deported. It was a card game that he had got into and they had a bit of a fight or 'Stramash' or whatever it was. However, the outcome of it was he was deported and his wife and two children were left here. So after a few months or so, there were nothing else

for her, she went out to try and see if she could get him but she never saw hilt nor hair of him."

The suspicion of official discrimination is given added weight by the fact that some deportations were ordered for breach of the peace offences, crimes which normally warranted a £2 fine or 30-day prison sentence.

At a local and more personal level, relations with the native population were better, if only because opposition was of a less serious nature.

Mr Smith:

"Well, people used to taunt us that we used to eat waggon grease and so on . . . about the nettle soup that we used to have and about the toadstools — mushrooms. Of course, I'm 77 now and they tell me: 'You're looking awfully well, you don't look your age' and so on. Well I just give them an answer back: 'Well, that was all the good waggon grease that I used to eat, so it must be stickin' to my ribs'."

The Lithuanian children suffered the usual playground taunts and the cry of 'Dirty Poles' appears to have been heard in most Lanarkshire schools at one time or another during this period.

Irene Dickson:

"Well, I don't think there were any problems because I think in a mining village they all had similar problems. Working very hard and not much money. . . . They [Lithuanians] worked hard and played hard and that was about it, but they did keep together, and as far as I understand they all got on very well. . . ."

Compared with the earlier period, the community in the inter-war years was only a shadow of its former self. Apart from the loss in numbers, the education of second and third generation Lithuanians effectively dismantled the barriers that had hitherto kept the community in a state of isolation. Some of the organisations continued, mainly those run by the clergy, and in the 'thirties there were still several Lithuanian choirs performing throughout the country. In the post-war years the decline in interest and involvement became more marked, despite a fresh influx of Lithuanians who came to Lanarkshire in 1947 as DPs (displaced persons) from the refugee camps in Germany. By that time the process of assimilation was well advanced and it has been a constant struggle since then for the Lithuanians to keep their language and culture alive.

Msr. Gutauskas:
"We have in this aspect some failures and in this aspect some victories. First of all, we have our Lithuanian societies . . . we Lithuanians have a Lithuanian chaplain, that is myself. . . . We have here two places with Lithuanian choirs. One choir in Bellshill, another choir in Glasgow. We believe this community will be still alive for many days. I cannot profess but we are not going to die as fast as I expect some of them will."

There is still a strong identification with a Lithuania of a bygone era among the older members of the community even though some of them have lived all their days in this country. It is a romanticised view of the past but it has created in some a feeling of not belonging, or not quite belonging.

Frank Dullick:
"We keep up the traditions of the British people but we also keep up the traditions of our parents . . . our nationality is Lithuanian, our citizenship is British."

Irene Dickson:
"The stories that Mum and Dad used to tell us about Lithuania, I always felt that if I ever got to

'Naiyas Laikas': the New Era. A glossy bi-lingual publication which ran to eight editions in 1930. It was part of a programme to revive interest in Lithuanian culture among second-generation immigrants and to encourage local (i.e. Scottish) participation in Lithuanian organisations.

Lithuania, I'd recognise it and know it. We are very proud of our Scottish nationality but also we are Lithuanian and we cannot forget that. You do feel that little bit different."

Mrs Mitchell:
"I'm going to make a very honest statement, I made this before. I don't feel I really belong anywhere yet, I've leanings this way and leanings that way."

For one grand old lady in her eighties, Mrs Millar, who has gone through the whole immigrant experience, there is no doubt as to where her heart lies.

Mrs Millar:
"I was in Canada, I was in America and I was in Lithuania, and I was all over. You couldna' get a better country than here. It's the best country in the world."

MURDOCH RODGERS

*Village bay, c. 1900, looking towards the Dun. In the foreground are some cleits, the St Kildan drystone storehouses.*

# St. Kilda

The old lady in a black dress and shawl, out walking the country roads near a village on the fringes of industrial Lanarkshire, was being helped by her grandson to collect the fleece caught in the barbed wire by the roadside. At her home in the evenings it would be carded, spun and finally knitted up. My grandmother, Christina McQueen, had been born on St Kilda, and the habit of constant work remained with her all her life.

St Kilda is an island archipelago in the Atlantic, 50 miles west of Uist in the Hebrides. These spectacular islands, for centuries the possession of the McLeods, are the breeding ground of the greatest number of gannets in the world, and visited annually by vast numbers of other sea birds, including puffins and fulmars. Hirta, the main island of the group, for centuries also supported a human population, an ancient and self-supporting community who spoke a peculiar dialect of Gaelic and who wrested a living from the cliffs, the sea and the little available arable land. The foundation of their life on St Kilda was in the annual harvest of the birds. The feathers were sold, the flesh was eaten, the oil was used to lubricate wool for spinning and weaving, and as fuel for their primitive lamps, while the very bones were used as fertiliser. The population had remained constant at around 200 till the mid-nineteenth century when it started to decline. The reduction continued until the Government responded to the islanders' petition and evacuated the remaining 36 inhabitants on the 29th August 1930.

Life on the island was dominated by the necessity to work constantly for survival. Like the other girls on Hirta, my grandmother learned her skills through sharing in the work of the community. Miss Chrissie Cameron, daughter of one of the last missionaries to St Kilda, recalls the work of the women of the island.

Miss Cameron:

"St Kildan mothers were always knitting — knitting, knitting, knitting — and the girls learned to knit at a very early age. They would put many a mainlander to shame — how quickly they could turn out a pair of socks — and how accurately the socks were finished, and it really was amazing to see how they could manipulate the turning of a heel at a very early age, without advice or guidance from their mother.

"The wool eh, they spun it all themselves — they sheared the sheep and spun the wool into yarn and imported nothing really, apart from the cloth for the lady's gowns — they all wore a navy-blue gown. The St Kildan's work was weaving really, their livelihood was weaving, because, eh, well they had crofts, but eh, very little was produced from the crofts but hay, and there was a super-abundance of it. But what they made was sent to an agent, one of their own number, Alexander G. Fergusson, who

was a merchant in Glasgow and he sent them, em, instead of paying them for their work he paid them in kind, some of it was flour, some of it was meal, and there was this cloth which he sent and the men did all the sewing for themselves and for the women. And the ladies all wore the same type of gown. They loved bright colours, an unmarried woman would tie a bright coloured shawl round her head — Spanish fashion — they were really like the

*Christina McQueen (left) and sister knitting gloves just before the Great War.*

Spaniards in that they doted on bright bright colours — and when a girl was married, she was allowed to put a white mutch underneath her coloured shawl. And then as time passed, if she became a widow — the mutch was taken off and she put her plaid over her head, that was her mourning. And even a funeral, everybody went to a funeral and even the married women, everybody put their plaid over their head while they were proceeding to the cemetery, that was how they mourned. The plaid itself was most uninteresting looking, it had a dark ground, I'm not very sure whether it was black or navy-blue, but they must have woven it themselves. It had a most uninteresting check, eh, almost like a chess board a narrow, narrow check maybe, rather more than an inch wide — that was their coat."

This was the society that Christina McQueen left when she was 18 to go to Glasgow. Her move was a reflection of the desire common among the younger St Kildans to make a new life away from their island home. But although many married and had families on the mainland, they would often return 'home' in the summer taking their children to meet the grandparents and friends. For those remaining on the island, however, life became even more difficult.

Lachie Macdonald:

"Aye! I mean there was no hours when you weren't working then, you were working every time you could get; you'd to go with the tide; you had to go with the day, and so forth. Then the night in the winter time, you were doing the spinning, and carding, and making tweed. And when you think on it, the labour you were putting in there, and what you were getting out of it, wasn't much."

The pattern of work on the islands changed with the seasons, moving from the sea to the crofts and to the cliffs.

*Three generations of St Kildan women, Christina McQueen's mother wearing a white mutch (centre). 1900.*

Neil Gillies:
"They started the first sheep shearing in June, and went to Boreray, and were for a week in Boreray sheep shearing, and came back and started fishing with the long line for herring, and . . . and salted them and sent them to the mainland. And after that, they started to kill the fulmar on the 12th August, and took a week there, and after that, they started to cut the grass and dry it, and put it into the 'cleits' and after that they started to spin and weave. They were spinning, and they started to weave in the spring, it depends on how much wool you have. They started to weave and was weaving like that till about April, and then they started to wash that tweed and work it, and dry it, and roll it up, ready for sale. They used to sing songs, the women, when they were waulking the tweed. They used to get up at four or five in the morning, and first they tramped it. Then they waulked it, and from there they took it down to the river and washed it, in the running water. And then they spread it out on the wall to dry, if it was a good day. They got it dried and then they rolled it up. There used to be about 32 yards in each roll, and some had half a dozen, some had eight, some had only four or five, it all depends. They got about three shillings a yard for it. It was very good, they were all desperate for St Kilda tweed, 'cos they knew it was all woven, all done by the hand."

Just as the girls of the island acquired their skills by sharing their mothers' work, so the young boys would accompany the men on the fowling expeditions to the massive cliffs of Conachair, which fall well over a thousand feet sheer to the sea.

Lachie Macdonald:
"When you were five you went to school, so then if you grew up say to maybe 11 or 12, you'd go to school and you'd work at the same time. You'd be giving a hand to your father and mother and then when you grew up at the end, say maybe 12 or 14, you're away on the hills, looking after sheep, as soon as you get out of school, and then you went in the rocks after birds and eggs. My first memory was, maybe you'd be at the age, I'll say 12, and you'd be going up with some lunch to them and och, we'd be keen to get into the rocks ourselves, but it doesn't matter whether you're keen or no. There is a rope put round your waist you see, and if you were frightened you know, they would be near hand, you wouldn't be going a distance or that. You were just trained the same as what I would say, like the duck there, the way she took the young ones to the sea and all that. Well, on St Kilda you were just trained something like that, as soon as — just to put it in words — as soon as you are out of the egg you were taught to do the climbing — to do everything. We were more so for the young birds, the end of August to September, the fulmar — it was great. And you'd go down the cliff and you killed as you were going down. You just got a hold of it, and just drew its neck. So when they have a lot gathered, maybe two or three hundred, they would squeeze the oil into a drum. It was nice clear oil you see. If you were frightened you would get a telling off. If you were frightened to go to the birds you see, the birds would start spitting the oil — that's the only way he had to prevent himself . . . and when you were going to catch him, you would have to go just right down and catch him and don't let them spill the oil, and you kept the feathers and you used to send them to the factors for paying some of their rents and things like that."

Chrissie Cameron:
"He'd be about eleven and his father had a hold of the rope at the top. He'd fastened it very carefully at the top and we all gathered round to watch this performance. The little fellow tied the rope round his waist and when he was sure that Dad was quite in control, he went down. He stepped from crag to crag. He had to be very quick because the young fulmars' defence was a squirt of oil. And this oil was precious . . . he had a jar into which he was collecting it, it was used for their cruisie lamps and it was also used for the lubricating of the wool. When they were working with wool, they used to lubricate it, the wool, with it. And everything of course smelt of fish because that bird lived on fish. And when his rope was full, he pulled the bird's neck through the rope and gave a signal to his father and his father then gradually

pulled him safely to the top. And he was as proud as punch of his bunch of fulmars."

The St Kildan men would also undertake journeys to the neighbouring islands of the group, including the huge rock of Boreray, some four miles distant, to take the gannet and puffin. After leaping on to the rock wall of Boreray, the men would wait until nightfall and then climb the cliffs to find the sentinel bird among the sleeping gannets. When the bird had been despatched the men would be free to move through the sleeping colony, killing as they went, and the dead gannets — large birds with wing spans of between four or five feet — would be flung down to float on the sea. The soaking carcasses would later be piled up in the open boats for the return home. Other species of bird sometimes made a welcome addition to their diet.

Neil Gillies:
"The sheerwater was a good bird for eating, and they used to come in March, and the people used to go during the night and go on to Conachair, and you might be lucky enough to catch a few, two or three or four or five of them, and sometimes they're dazed coming down, vaulting down, and you might catch them then. Or if you got a wee dog, you were a good chance — he'll catch them. And sometimes you might catch them going to their

nest, and they're a great bird for eating. I've seen them making soup out of them, two or three of them made a big pot of soup, oatmeal and salt on it, and it was great."

Surprisingly, for a people surrounded by the restless Atlantic, and whose life was so interdependent with the sea, the St Kildans never learned to swim. Journeys to the other islands of the group or short fishing trips, were always undertaken with a wary understanding of the dangers involved.

Lachie Macdonald:
"Well, it all depends on the weather, you know. If it would come bad, it would be dangerous, it was just only open boats you see. So that was the way life was. We would go as far out maybe as three or four miles, and, what I used to do was, you know, a good night, dry night, I just slept in the boat, out there, on the lines, there. What they had was just a big, you know, wool bag, you'd go in there and sleep in the bottom of the boat, till such times, ach, till it got better, maybe three hours or so. Then you'd go haul the lines in and take the fish off them. Early in the morning you'd come back to the island. It's more ling we were after, more than anything else. You split them and cleaned them, and take the bone off, and you'd put them in a place to get salted."

*Finlay McQueen, snaring puffins with a fowling rod.*

*Before the small jetty was constructed, this was the method of landing all stores, or exporting the feathers, tweed or fulmar oil.*

The weather could never be relied on, and more often than not, it was something to contend with. Storms battered the island for nine months of the year. Even in summer, steamers might have to return to the mainland without getting a boat ashore.

Chrissie Cameron:

"One terrible day we lost one of our stacks. A gale just took it away from in front of our eyes and blew it out to sea . . . just dreadful. I was lifted completely off my feet one day, and thrown from hither to yonder, just completely off my feet; I didn't know why everyone was screaming, I was only aware of being carried, everybody was screaming, and then somebody grabbed me. But I have been terrified of being out in wind ever since, I always get the feeling that it is going to lift me."

On one occasion three young men, including Christina McQueen's two brothers, went to fetch some sheep from the island of Dun, a short distance from Hirta. There being nowhere to land a boat, getting ashore was achieved by leaping directly on to the rock.

Neil Gillies:

"The accident happened at the Dun. And when the people came back that night at around nine o'clock, they knew it happened when they could hear the dogs barking in the Dun, and they went over the next day and brought the dogs away from the Dun, and the boat that took them [the three men] over there was never touched and [they] let her drift away and get wrecked up. So, it was a

very sad island for about a fortnight and the funeral was on, and the minister, the missionary on St Kilda was Peter MacLauchlan, he was there for three years. He was the minister and teacher and all. So when everything was settled, they started as usual, to work again, but they never forgot, going to land there again. But they were there after that, 'cos it was an easy place to land. But they say they think it was a nail, a big nail, that was at the keel of the boat that caught the rock, and as my father said, if it had capsized on the way, they could've been all ashore. And if somebody had been ashore, they could have saved the whole lot, flung a rope and they could have drawn the boat right alongside of them. But nobody got ashore, so it was a very sad affair. I mind we were in school at the time, and a note came to the school and Mr Murray left, sent us all home, and he was going round the place and it was a very very sad affair altogether. Losing three boys, the two brothers and our next-door neighbour MacDonald."

Such a loss was obviously a severe blow to the community, which, nevertheless accepted such acts of God with a resigned fatalism. Christianity arrived on St Kilda early, probably brought by Irish monks on their journeys to Iceland in the sixth century. But the arrival of the Free Presbyterian Church of Scotland half-way through the nineteenth century heralded the acceptance of a religious orthodoxy that was to dominate the lives of the people, young and old, until the evacuation.

Neil Gillies:

"The missionary had three services on Sunday, an English and Gaelic and a mid-week service on

Wednesday, prayer meeting on Wednesday and a service once a month every Monday and there was no music of any description on St Kilda. No water was taken in on a Sunday and if you went on a Sunday to have a cold drink of water, on the hottest day, you had to leave the cup at the well not to take it back into the house till Monday morning. You had to stop work at 9.00 on Saturday night, and there was no more water until Monday morning. There was a family worship the first thing in the morning before you started work, and last thing at night there was a family worship."

Chrissie Cameron:
"Oh . . . there was never an empty pew in the church and the prayer meeting on a Wednesday was as well attended as the Sabbath services. And we went to Sunday school every afternoon. Every afternoon we went to Sunday school and they stayed on at the Sunday school until they were 15, 16, 17. They didn't leave just when they were teenagers, they stayed on. They wanted to learn more and more, and sing more and more."

Neil Gillies:
"Oh, there was lovely singing. I heard some of the ministers saying that the best singing they ever heard was in St Kilda when they would be there for

*A windy day at the grass cutting.*

communion. You couldn't marry there except when the minister went there once a year. They had marriages, communion or baptism. The minister did it once a year, and if you didn't make up your mind before the minister came, you'd have to go for another year. I've seen the minister marrying two or three at a time."

Early chroniclers of St Kilda emphasised the 'genius and enthusiasm' for poetry and song possessed by the islanders. By the 1900s, however, their love of music appears to have been sublimated in their religion.

Lachie Macdonald:
"You were just only working mostly, all the time. As you say, there wasn't such a thing as dancing music, or you know sing-song like that."

A social life did exist, but as it was carried out within the context of communal activities, the islanders made no distinction between work and play.

*Left to right: Finlay McQueen, Norman McKinnon, Finlay Gillies, his daughter-in-law, grandson and Neil Gillies, his son.*
*The wool was pulled from the sheep by hand, a penknife being used to cut free the stubborn parts of the fleece.*

Lachie Macdonald:

"You'd be away in one house to the other . . . they would come and help you, you would go and help them, and you'd be maybe mixing the wool to make colours. Well there'd be a good few in the one house, you'd be working there maybe till 12 or say one o'clock you see and you'd have a dinner that was made then, and you are getting maybe potatoes and a big bit of sheep. Oh it was very good right enough then well, if you'd a girlfriend

*Tourists wait to buy souvenirs and have their mail franked at the St Kilda post office during the summer of 1930.*

Lachie Macdonald:

"It's not a nice thing to say, but they were better off in war-time than they were in peace-time. They were getting boats and nets, if you had cattle or things you could get them away. And even the fishing part, you know, they were better off. The navy used to tow us out to the fishing grounds and they'd patrol there, and then they would tow you back in the early hours of the morning. So, it's not a nice thing to go and say, but we were better off in time of . . . war-time, but that is true."

The island was also being paid more attention by a new summer visitor, groups of tourists who came to

. . . you had to go and see her home and things like that. Oh there was plenty of that kind of activities going on, right enough." *(laughs)*

Life in the village was simple and frugal. Luxuries were associated with the arrival of ships, a not too frequent occurrence. Before World War One, when the army installed a 'Marconi' radio transmitter and trained an islander to operate it, the problem of communications could sometimes mean that months would pass before appeals for food in times of shortage or medical help in times of illness, could be answered. Messages in sealed containers flung into the sea from Hirta would sometimes be picked up, not in Lewis, but Shetland or even Norway.

view the 'Primitives'. They brought with them a host of alien values, subverting the economy and eventually bringing the natives to believe that their life on the island was untenable.

Janet Chalmers:

"They were just exploited by the people in the past who went out there on luxury cruises. And they would come to the island, and they would go around looking at all the things that the people had worked on all winter. They knitted socks, they knitted pullovers, they wove tweed. And this particular couple came to my mother, and she had been labouring all winter, and had made and spun a bale of tweed, and what she got in payment for that bale of tweed was an orange. Well, my mother had never seen an orange before, she didn't know what an orange was, and she put it on the dresser, and gradually, as time went on, as you know, it just went mouldy. And that was it. That was what she got for a full winter's work."

Neil Gillies:
"Oh, we took the tourists ashore from the boat, charged them a shilling return from the boat, and we used to get maybe a couple of pound, it depends on how many was on the boat, and we took them back and forward onto the boat."

Lachie Macdonald:
"We collected the coloured eggs. Och aye, white ones too, but, the coloured eggs was the best you see. You would get tuppence on these on the shells you see. This was, you know, boys when you were going to school you see. And we used to go round to the tourists and you thought it was great getting a few pennies you know and get things to buy on the boat the likes of biscuits. Even a loaf of bread, we hadn't got any loaf on St Kilda, it was all scones and home-made stuff you see, and then we'd get some sweeties and things like that. Oh, we thought it was a great day when the boat would come in."

Those childhood sentiments obscured the fact that the islanders' self-regard was gradually being eroded through contact with the more powerful, self-confident and affluent culture of the mainland. As the population dwindled over the next few years and fewer men were able to undertake the work necessary to sustain the life of the community, it became more and more obvious that evacuation could be the only solution. The problem of the St Kildans, when viewed in proportion to the economic depression which gripped Britain at that time, or the problems of administering the Empire on which the 'sun never set', may seem barely worthy of note, but the journals and newspapers of the period contained many articles, and much correspondence and discussion about what could be done for them.

The island community had long held a fascination for the mainlander, perhaps a symbolic one. Here was an island where there was no crime, where everyone was equal, and where the work and the fruits of labour were shared.

Neil Gillies:
"The only time a policeman was on the island was when there was sheep dipping, the policeman came to inspect. That was all, there was no such thing as crime on St Kilda."

Is it not tragic that the inexorable march of twentieth-century progress could not allow this little republic, which had over the centuries evolved unique solutions to the problems of living in that environment, to endure? There is a wren, that most common of British birds, that is found only on St Kilda. It survives

still, perfectly adapted, but the village is deserted.

By 1929 there were less than ten men capable of doing the work of the islands. There was severe hardship over the next winter and much talk of leaving, but like all problems on the island, nothing could happen until there was unanimity.

When the McKinnon family, with ten members, the largest on the island, eventually came to a decision, after months of provocation, to leave, it became obvious that there was only one course of action left.

Neil Gillies:
"The younger ones wanted away and the old people couldn't carry on with their rock climbing and the McKinnons went to the missionary and their nurse to see, and they put in a letter to the Scottish Secretary and they all agreed to go away, to evacuate it. Well, they say that we'll do our best but you'll be evacuated before the winter comes up. So that's the way they wanted St Kilda evacuated, and I think the government was quite well pleased to get them evacuated too because it would save them sending a doctor out there."

St Kilda was finally evacuated on August the 29th, 1930.

Neil Gillies:
"The *Dunara Castle* took all the cattle away and she stayed there until she took all she could, and the skipper of the *Hairbell* sent him a note over, thanking him for remaining there to see everything was OK. He were there all night that night till next morning. They were starting loading on his boat, all their gear, their bedding and all their other stuff. I left by the *Hairbell* by half-past on Friday morning and they landed at Lochaline at twenty-past six and they landed most of them at Lochaline then, and they proceeded to Oban with the rest. And I was on the boat right to Oban and we were all ashore round about nine o'clock at night. There were no reporters on the boat but there were plenty of reporters when we arrived in Oban and I landed at the pier at Oban. Alongside the pier, the crowds there, you'd be thinking you were going to a football match with the crowd waiting and I says 'What are you looking at? There's nae hairs on us.'

"Finlay McQueen and his daughter and son-in-law, they went to Kyle of Lochalsh. My uncle, Mr Ferguson and his wife, they went to Culross, and Mrs McQueen eh, she was in Lochaline. And Finlay, they were in Kyle of Lochalsh for about och, six month anyhow, and then they got a bigger house at Kincardine. And the whole family was put together again. Mrs Gillies, she got a house in Culross where the Fergusons was. The rest in Lochaline, there were my mother, my two brothers, the old Gillieses family, they were in Savouraidh, we were on Larraich-Beag, and the MacKinnons. Then the McKinnons flitted from Larraich-Beag to Black Isle."

The transition to mainland life was not an easy one. The habit of working for an employer in return for wages and to set hours was difficult for the men to adopt, and all the evacuees suffered in being separated from their own kind. Leaving their island home did not prove a solution to their problems, it merely exchanged them for others completely unforeseen. It was the very young and very old who suffered the most, the widows and the children. The McKinnon family, who had been instrumental in making up the community's mind to leave, and who stood to gain most from the new life, was cruelly stricken by diseases against which their isolated origin had provided no defences.

Chrissie Cameron:
"Some of them were like fish out of water but they were wonderfully adaptable really. The only snag was that they weren't fit for the work of the mainland and their health just gave way. And there was one family that was practically completely wiped out with TB, the McKinnon family. That little boy who went down the crags, nearly all his family, including his father, wiped out with TB. See, they were used to vitamins in the raw, raw eggs, raw birds' eggs. The vitamins they were getting in the fish-fed birds, they lived on the birds you see and these birds lived on fish, and it was rich in the natural vitamin, you see. And when they came to the mainland they had to buy butcher meat, and they just couldn't afford it. And they just went. And they just went . . . there was nothing to fall back on. It was all very sad."

Neil Ferguson:
"Fine I mind the evacuation of St Kilda. I was the last to leave the island, all the rest were aboard the steamer early in the morning. I was in charge of the post-office and made every excuse to remain as long as I could. I was threatened and pleaded with, but I always made the excuse that I wasn't ready yet, but excuses were of no use. I went for a last walk round the village. It was weird passing the empty houses, it was just like looking at an open grave."

*The coffin was for Mary Gillies, who died of TB at the age of 20, three weeks before the evacuation.*

NORMAN CHALMERS

## CUMHA H-IRTEACH
## A ST KILDA LAMENT

Slow

1 Gur a thall ann an Soà,
  D' fhàg mi 'n t-Oganach, clèusda';
  Urradh dheanadh mo thacar,
  'Slabhairt dhachaidh na spreidhe.

2 'Nuair a thainig do mhàthair,
  Cha do chàirich i'm breid oir,
  'Nuair a thàinig do phuthair,
  Bha sinn dubhach le cheile.

3 'S ge do chaidh thu sa chreig ud,
  Cha b'è'n t-eagal a leugh thu
  'S ann a rin do chas sraonadh,
  'S cha do d'fheud thu riamh éirigh.

4 Nuair a thàinig do bhràthair,
  Cha do chaomhainn, e'n èughadh,
  Bha sinn dubhach, a's craiteach,
  Gad amharc ann cèin uainn.

5 Bha t'fhuil air a chloich ud,
  Bha do lot ann dèigh leumaidh
  Bha thu 'muigh air bhàr stuaighe,
  'S muir'gad fhuasgladh' o chéile.

6 A sheachd beannachd nan càirdean
  'S a lon làdair na feuma,
  Tha mo chuid-s de na h-eunaibh
  Anns na neulaibh ag eughach.

7 Tha mo chuid-s' de na h-uibhibh,
  Aig a' bhuidhinn a 's treubhaich'
  'S ann thall ann an Soà
  D' fhàg mi'n t-Oganach clèusda'.

1 It was over yonder in Soa
  That I left my skilful young man
  Who was my provider,
  Who could summon home the stock.

2 When, distressed, your mother came
  There was no shawl to her shoulders.
  When your sister came,
  In grief we were as one.

3 Though you perished on that cliff
  It wasn't through fear.
  Your foot shot sideways;
  There was no rising thereafter.

4 When your brother came
  He spared no cries of grief.
  In anguish and sorrow we watched you
  Removed so far from us.

5 Your blood was on the rock
  Your wounds came from the fall
  You floated on the waves
  To be the sport of the merciless sea.

6 O seven fold blessing of friends
  And the stout rope of need,
  My share of the sea-fowl
  Are screeching in the air.

7 My share of their eggs
  Go now to the boldest.
  It was yonder on Soa,
  I left the skilful young man.

*The reeking lums of the jute mills on Lochee Road, Dundee.*

## THE JUTE MILL SONG

Steadily

1 Oh, dear me, the mill's gaen fest, The puir wee shif- ters can- na get a rest,

Shif- tin' bob- bins, coorse and fine, They fair- ly mak'ye work for your ten and nine.

2 *Oh, dear me, I wish the day was done,*
   *Rinning up and doon the Pass is no nae fun;*
   *Shiftin', piecing, spinnin' warp, weft and twine,*
   *Tae feed and cled my bairnie affen ten and nine.*

3 *Oh, dear me, the warld's ill-divided,*
   *Them that work the hardest are aye wi' least provided.*
   *But I maun bide contented, dark days or fine,*
   *But there's no much pleasure living affen ten and nine.*

# They Fairly Mak Ye Work

*Oh, dear me the world's ill-divided,*
*Them that work the hardest are aye wi' least provided.*

This quote by Mary Brooksbank, herself a Dundee mill lassie, could apply to the experience of many workers in many industries in the hungry 'twenties and 'thirties of this century. In Dundee, however, the worker's plight was drawn in bas relief, because of the domination exercised over the city by one industry — jute. In other cities where there was industrial diversification, the fluctuations of the market for one particular product would threaten the families of workers in that particular industry. Workers in other industries continued to earn, thereby cushioning the effect on the whole community. In Dundee, whole families, whole streets, even whole city areas depended on the jute industry for employment. When you read the accounts of the old spinners of Dundee, you realise that what the jute industry actually offered the working class was survival, and bare survival at that.

The jute industry developed out of the old linen spinning and weaving industry, which initially used locally grown flax, but gradually became dependent on imports of flax from Russia. When the blockade of Russian ports, during the Crimean War (1854-56), put a stop to Russian flax imports, the manufacturers turned to another fibre which could be spun and woven on the same machinery. The coarse Indian jute fibre which had appeared in the city in the 1820s fitted the bill and, with the Dundee whaling fleet providing the oil necessary for softening the fibre, jute soon established itself as the principal industry, while Dundee established itself as the jute capital of the world.

By 1881 the ratio of jute to flax workers was nine to one. The changeover from linen to jute also brought about a revolution in the structure of the city's work force, as it coincided with the introduction of power-looms on an extensive scale and mass mechanisation of the textile industry. The flax weavers were male and worked on hand looms. Fearing their political

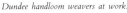

*Dundee handloom weavers at work.*

organisation, the manufacturers made sure that jute weavers would be female. Women could be paid less and had no tradition of organisation. It is likely too that the craft pride instilled in the hand loom weavers gave them little desire to work with an inferior fibre, in the foreign environment of the factory, in which they were relegated to the same status as the women. By 1900 women outnumbered men three to one in the jute industry, three-quarters of the working women in the city being employed there. The result was a unique reversal of social roles. Women were the family bread winners, while the men, doomed to crushing unemployment, looked after the home, or left the city altogether.

Sarah Craig:
"They used to say the men stayed at home and the women went out to work in Dundee. Well that's true in a way because there was work for women, no' for men, wi' the result the men 'boiled the kettle' as the sayin' is."

Mrs Cockburn:
"At that time, you got a wage when you started at fourteen, but when you come eighteen you'd get so much on your wages, you see. Well, rather than give you that, they paid you off and took a lad under eighteen 'cos that was sma' wages again for the boss, you see. Well, my man, his mother worked aside me in the jute works and his mother told me that he used to hae the hoose spotless when she come in, she says, an' ma denner a' made, 'cause he was gettin' nothing aff the broo, nothing aff a naebody an' it was only what his mother was giein' him on a Saturday tae gang oot wi' the lads tae spend. An' she told me hersel, the tears used tae be trippin' him — takin' that money frae his mother. But she said tae me, 'Ye know this, we dinna hae wir finger tae wet when we go in.' He wis doin' it for his bit food, an' his wee bit claes, ken. The same thing happened til a brother o' mine. My mother an' I was workin', an' he done the same an' he used tae, ken, be in tears when we were giein' him coppers gaen oot on Saturday 'cause he was paid awa' at eighteen."

James Daly:
"Oh the women was the workers at the time. They paid ye off at eighteen, you were too old — at eighteen. There was nothing else to do because when I was a boy of seventeen, I joined the army and I went to India — January 1922. There was no work, so I joined the army. I think the most of them done that, joined the Black Watch or the Gordons or something, so that was that."

As the ratio of men to women at this time was two to three, women had to be independent, as marriage prospects were bleak. It is no geographical accident that the folk song 'Auld Maid in a Garret' found great popularity in Dundee. Its relevance to the girls' situation there was immediate, while its humour served perhaps to exorcise the loneliness many of them must have felt.

*Oh, come Tinker, come Tailor, come Soldier and come Sailor,*
*Come ony man at a' that'll tak me fae my faither,*
*Come rich or come poor man, come wise or come witty,*
*Come ony man at a' that'll marry me for pity.*

*For it's oh dear me whit will I dae*
*If I dee an auld maid in a garret.*

*Noo I'll awa' hame for there's naebody heedin,*
*Naebody's heeding tae puir wee Annie's pleadin',*
*I'll awa' hame tae my ain wee garret,*
*If I canna get a man then I'll surely get a parrot!*

*For it's oh dear me whit will I dae*
*If I dee an auld maid in a garret.*

Mrs Cockburn:
"There wis too many women. There wisnae enough men, so when ye got a lad you had tae hing on tae him, or some ither body stole him! That's right enough."

*Mrs Cockburn (left), dressed up for the camera, as a young woman.*

For those who did get married there was little time to look after children, as necessity determined a quick return to the mill.

*Raw jute at a warehouse at Dundee wharf.*

Mrs Cockburn:

"When I got married an' athing, ye ken, ye were aff tae hae bairns, an' then ye were back again an' then ye bid aff tae hae anither bairn [*laughs*] — Bloody Dundee men was murder Polis! [*laughs*]. Meh God, ye worked tae ye were near fadin' awa. My grannie was near seventy an' she was still in the jute, an auld woman!"

A strong, assertive breed of women grew out of the hardship they had to confront throughout their lives. For many, life in the mills started when they were little more than bairns themselves. The poverty was so devastating that many mothers kept their children from school, so that they could put in a day's work in the mills — the 'puir wee shifters' of the song, whose job was to unload bobbins and fit new ones on the spinning frame.

Sarah Craig:

"Previous to goin' in when I was fourteen, I was goin' in an' workin' from I was ten-and-a-half on my sister's lines an' makin' out I was ma sister for tae earn money. An' so I went in as Nelly instead o' Sarah an' I saw the doctor that often, every seven weeks, he'd begin tae nod tae me instead o' sayin' 'Who are you?'. An' for that, from six in the mornin' to six at night, I get ten an' a penny. It's no' that meh mother wanted it, but it was a case of that extra money into the house was a sort of godsend."

Mrs Cockburn:

"The first mill I went in was Halley's, in the Ferry Road. And it was what they cried the rovins — shuftin' rovins. My mother was in what they cried 'the low mill' and of coorse I thocht, if I go in aside my mother I was a'richt; young lassie, fourteen, got in aside ma mother — wis okay — naebody would touch us, ye see. We aa worked in the jute, we were aa jute workers. Ye started at six in the morning till six at night, Saturday, six in the mornin' till twelve o'clock — an' when ye got aff for a fast day, that was a broken pay — ye didna get paid for that — no, no. An' the same wi' the holiday — when ye came off frae yer week's holiday, ye cam off wi' yer week's pay. Ye just had tae mak yer money dae ye, ye were glad tae get back tae work because ye were starvin' — ye'd nae mair money left, ye see."

Working conditions in the spinning mills were appalling, showing little change from the 1850s.

Mrs Cockburn:

"When they got it from Calcutta or wherever it come frae, it was dirty tae handle, dirty and stourie — ye never were clean, ye never were clean ken. Course, I often think this is what started like the TB in the lungs an' athing. It started that d'ye see, cause ye were bound tae be inhaling a lot o' that, but ye never thought nuthin' aboot it, cause that was yer job — ye just had tae like it.

"They were near a' women in the low mill. Oh, it was hard work, ye ken. We used tae tak in pieces an' hae cups o' tea an a' thing, but ye didna get them frae the work — if ye seen the gaffer comin' ye'd tae rin awa wi' the tea oot o' the road, or ye'd hae got the seck — no eatin' durin' workin' hours. Now they get served wi' teas, as far as I believe, in the works."

Mr Guild:
"The supervisor, he went about dressed up in his starched collar, his tie and whatnot, walking about with his hands behind his back. And if he didn't like somebody or thought somebody wasn't doing their job, then it was just, 'Your jacket on and out'. And all he had to do then was walk out to the gate where there was a crowd of people standing looking for jobs, pick one out and replace him."

Once the raw fibre had been treated with oil to batch and soften it, prepared, spun and wound, it was sent over to be woven at the factory nearby. The weavers belonged to a different social strata than the spinners. They seem to have inherited the pride of the old hand loom weavers, a pride reinforced by the higher wages they received. The actual job required no more skill than spinning, but being paid piece-work, their economic status reinforced their feeling of superiority over the spinners. Every spinner and weaver I spoke to emphasised this division among the jute workers.

Mr Guild:
"The weavers were the aristocrats of them all. I had a pamphlet in the house at one time, it was Cox's Mill in Camperdown, their annual picnic up to Perth. You travelled up the Tay on a boat, and it was laid down on the pamphlet, the order of procession from the mill down to the Craig Pier where they got the boat. And the Weavers' Band led the parade, then the weavers and it worked its way right back down until the sweepers brought up the rear. But, even at that time it was set. The weavers were the aristocrats of the mill. It all goes back to the song: 'If it wasna for the weavers, where would ye be', and they carried out the idea, that if we werena here, you wouldna have jobs. If there was nobody there to weave it, there's no point in spinning it."

*Weaving flat–Baxter Bros. Dens Works, c. 1908.*

Mrs Cockburn:
"They were aye that uppish like — they'd say 'I'm a weaver', ye see, which was a' rang. They were only a jute worker just the same as us. We had tae tak the dirty work — see, we went in at the start o' it. Oil an' a'thing, by the time they got it, it was a' kinda clean."

Sarah Craig:
"They were different frae us altogether. They were on piece-work, an' they wore a hat, an' they wore gloves. Whaur, the like o' us, we were low mill hands an' we used tae just rin wi' wir jeckits on — nae hats or gloves. An' they used tae walk past ye as if ye were something low, an' they were 'it' — an' if ye said tae them 'An' whit is your occupation?' — 'Oh, I'm a weaver.' Ye see that distinction wis there, even among the workin' folk there was a distinction."

Winnie Porter:
"I had no friends among spinners — nothing to do with the spinners. I was never in a mill in my life, I'd never even seen the inside o' a mill. When you went into your work, the factory was one side, the mill was on another side and you'd no occasion . . . the spinners were all mill workers, you see, and we thought we were a cut above the mill workers."

Annie Reid:
"We used to say 'snuffy spinners!' — because long ago they did snuff, you know, in the mills. They really had to do it, because at that time the

*'Back shift' leaving Dens Works, c. 1908.*

dust was flying across the place. No now, it's a' modernised now, but at that time there was nae ducts or anything to tak it awa'. Wi' the results it choked them and that's the reason they took snuff and they always got that name. We were the greetin' faced weavers and they were the snuffy spinners. If ye got bad work, they were moanin' because ye didna' mak the pay, you were on piece-work, and that was the term, a greetin' faced weaver, always was."

The petty rivalry between the two is contained in the humour of the city as well.

Jim Reid:
"Well, there was a lassie who was a weaver in Halley's, she was gettin' married, so she went doon to the Registrar to put her name down and everything, and the man was writing her name and all the other particulars on the form. So he says to her, 'Now — you're a spinster?' And she says, 'No, look I'm a weaver'. And he says, 'No, look lassie, doon on this form put — you're a spinster'. She says, 'Dinna ca' me a spinster, because I'm a weaver'. So he says to her, 'Look lassie, are you ignorant?' She says, 'Aye, fower month!'."

The actual job of weaving was much more agreeable than spinning, so the weavers rarely referred to conditions inside the factories, only the pressure of keeping the machines going to achieve a decent wage.

Annie Reid:
"My auntie was a weaver, it was through her I went to the looms. You got six weeks to learn them — that was your apprenticeship, six weeks, and we got twelve and six a week to learn on, and you got what we said, a weaving mistress and by golly, you had to learn or else, because well, you were on a pair of looms — if you hindered her, if you were a dud, you really hindered her and a' weavers are hungry! They're always on the bonus, you see. And you were never a weaver until you put two shuttles in a loom — and I did it! Everybody does it once in a lifetime, they do, and they meet in the middle, go right through and make a great big hole, and after this, she's got it a' repaired and everything, she said, 'It's a' richt lassie, ye're a weaver now!'. On the small looms you made bags. Now they could be all different kinds of bags, potato bags, sugar bags, onion bags, but on the big looms, the 90-inch looms, well in Halley's we did all the backing for linoleum, for Nairn in Kirkcaldy, well, that had to be perfect."

Winnie Porter:
"The job was alright, but the tenters — the mechanics, you know, these were called tenters. You'd to go to them, maybe something had broken down: 'I'll see it sometime', you know, and the longer your loom was off, the less money you were making, you see, because you had to make your own wages. And if you made two-pound-ten a week off a pair o' looms, that was very hard work. So the longer your looms was off, the more money you lost, you see. And that was the only thing I had against the weavin' — the tenters. You got one or two good ones, but most o' them were a lot o' rotten buggers, they really were."

Annie Reid:
"They're hard work, but — once a weaver, always a weaver. You never forget it. In fact, I had a neighbour one time — she'd been in Canada for over twenty years and when she came back, she got the loom next to me. And she just came right in, set it on and just started like she'd never been away from them you see. And I says, 'Mrs Anderson'. She says, 'You never forget them, lassie, you could be forty years off them and you never forget them'. Which is quite true. I bet I could go into a factory right now, just set it on, like I'd never been away from it."

For those unable to find employment in the factories and mills, the occupation which kept the people just above the level of destitution was that of sack sewing.

Sarah Craig:
"There was people at the West End used to go to the jute mills and get sackin' and used tae cleek it onto the walls outside their own houses and sit and sew the bags and take them back to the mills and get so much a dozen for them, the poverty was that bad in Dundee."

James Daly:
"I can go back to nineteen hundred and thirteen, and I'd be about nine year old then, eight or nine. And my father and my mother and his three brothers, and their wives used to sew sacks. Well, we got the sacks from Spalding and Valentine, and it was a sixpence a bundle, that's what we got, and we used tae get a hank o' thread, a 'clou' and we used to put it on the wall and there was two or three children there who used to thread needles and the women got hand leather, tied on the back, wi' a grill on the front to shove the leather through. Well anyhow, we worked all day there, and my job at the time as a child was to turn the sacks outside in."

Among the sack sewers, the home virtually became a factory, the wage being survival. But even for the mill and factory workers there was no escape from jute. Its stour and smell was on your clothes, you used it as bedding, your tenement flat was built for its proximity to the mills, and even if you escaped up on to the Law hill to get fresh air and admire the view, all you saw were jute boats sailing up the Tay. The strength of the people lay in the solidarity of helping neighbours and friends through hard times, despite the poverty which could have dehumanised them.

Mrs Cockburn:

"Oh my God, Dundee was a pair class o' people. Folk didna hae much, ken, long ago. We bid in an attic and there was my mother and father, and four o' us, ken, two rooms, that was a'. Beds were a' ower the place. Just a two-roomed hoose, through-going, ye ken, and toilets on the stairs. If you had a toilet in the hoose you were a toff."

Jim Reid:

"The houses were all built just round about the mill, and the tenements were mostly what you call 'Pletties', that was just like a platform — then there was an outside stair connected to these platforms — and then the houses were just two rooms, through-going from each other. The first room was a combination of a kitchen, a livin' room, and a bedroom. There was everything in that first room, you know. And then the through-going room, the other — the back room, was just the bedroom which the family lived in, if there was a big family there was a lot o' beds in it, you know. On the 'pletties' there was a pulley that you hung the washin' out on — there was a pulley with a rope stretching out to a big, what they called the greeny pole. And the pletties seemed to be a great congregatin' place, especially on a summer's night, you know, and all the women used to stand about, speakin' and we used to play round about and climb up the outside stair and everything like that. It seemed to be a great community spirit there, and old folk and people that werena well, always got a hand out, or maybe a plate o' soup or a cup o' tea and somethin' to eat. They always looked after their neighbours."

*A poverty-stricken household, in the Overgate, 1930.*

Sarah Craig:

"They used to go to the shop and get a tuppenny bit o' boilin' beef to make a pot o' broth, and they used to tell the butcher to give them a dirty bone. This was a bone with beef on it so that it would help to make the pot o' soup stronger and nourishing.

"I was away down the Hilltown lookin' for chipped eggs, bread that had been frae the day before for tae mak toast wi', and things like that. The woman next door tae me, she had somethin' less than what I had. We got that used to it — we'd nothin' in the hoose tae rin tae a pawnbrokers tae pawn, but maybe things that yer kids hid worn — they were no use, ye used to roll them up an' go doon and buy clothes and they needed altered and they would sit and sew night after night."

James Daly:

"During the sack sewin' time there'd be a big kail pot, you know, a big iron pot, well maybe a lippie o' tatties in that — a lippie — as we used tae say, a lippie o' tatties and maybe a pund o' mince, an' an ingin or twa an' that was a' stewed up thegither — well, we all got a meal oot o' that lot — an' the mair water, the mair dip — so ye dipped a piece in it, and ye, ye had yer fill o' bread. As long as yer mither seen ye eatin' bread an' that, dippin' up."

Sarah Craig:

"There were plenty of houses, but just if the rent was maybe four or five shillings a week, that was too much for them. They had to take a house where they could give as little as they possibly could and there was folk shiftin' their hooses, moon lightin' and maybe going from here. Some o' them shifted

The Pletties

Milne's Close, Overgate.

their house in the buildin' and when the factor called he'd say, 'Did you no live up the stair?'. 'No, I've always lived here!'. He got that mixed up wi' them shiftin' that he didna know who his clients were.''

In the 'twenties and 'thirties relief for the poor and destitute was scarcely developed. When the populace protested against their conditions, the reaction of authority was immediate and brutal.

Sarah Craig:
   "During the winter month, if you didn't have anything and applied what they would term as social security now, but it was the bread line, you might as well say. There was this Mr Allan that was here in the town. He run this lookin' after the poor, and if he came in and he looked round their house — 'Can ye no' sell this, can ye no' sell that?' — necessities. But eh, of course you would say I need that. They would even lift the lid of where you kept your coal — an' if you had one bit o' coal, you never got any coal. But they gave you a line, it would be for two pound o' jam, a loaf o' bread, a half-bag o' coal, it would come tae about a pound. You were well off gettin' that. Then the Means Test came in. That was in 1930 and I'll never forget it, they begun tae gather together people in crowds, and Albert Square wis the place that all the meetings was held. Ed Scrymgeour, he was an MP for Dundee and eh, all the Communist men, they come from Glasgow to hold their meetings there.

Well, they organised that they would have a big meeting and they would march the streets against the Means Test. Well, they marched from Albert Square. My man went up on the platform and he spoke and he told them, 'No vandalism, no breaking windows or things like that', and advised the people, what they had to do. Well, they walked from Albert Square in Dundee to a park in Lochee here, which was at that time called Maloney's Park. And had a great big torchlight procession — it was in the winter months — and they hid big meetings there and they walked back tae Albert Square again. They were goin' tae walk again and the people all gathered, when the doors in the Commerce Chambers opened — an' the policemen came on horseback and they were hittin' folk wi' their batons. They were hittin' the folk wi' their batons and chasin' them and breakin' up the crowds. And I remember, gettin' my girl and gettin' her outside the library door, and how I got out o' there I'll never know to this day, but the way I had to get home was going intae one close, as we termed it, into another, till I got up to Anne Street. What a feeling wi' seeing the policemen. And at that time it wasna like the lads that they have now, they were great big men frae the country. It was terrible. Well, the following day, we were sittin' in and I was pleading wi' him not to go out in case — and the knock came to the door, and it was the head man o' the detectives, the police force. And he says, 'It's me Peter, open the door. I want to talk to you.' Robinson was his name. And my man says, 'What have ye come up for?' 'Now look Pete,' he says, 'you gave them sound advice, which they didn't take.' My man said, 'You're a liar, it was your men that started it!' After they'd done that to the people then they started breaking windows, Birrell's the Shoemakers in the Overgate. They gave them cause for it. But he says, 'We've nothin' against you. But the boys that we have inside — they're for it.' But times went on, but when I got married and all the upheaval o' the Means Test and one thing and another, it just threw me back to when I was young and I faced up to it. I had a good man and he stood by me and him and I came through a lot, but we made it."

Given conditions in the city, one would have expected the workers to have veered left in their politics. However, Dundee housed a huge Catholic Irish vote, which in the early part of this century was more concerned with Home Rule for Ireland than local politics. The Liberal Party promised to deliver Home Rule. Their main candidate from 1908 to 1922 was a certain Winston Churchill. Following the 1916 Easter Rising when Churchill began his witch hunt of Sinn Feiners, the Irish vote turned against Churchill and embraced the Millenarian socialism of the local champion of the Prohibition Party, Edwin Scrymgeour. Churchill's last meeting in the city on 13th November 1922 is described by Sarah Craig of Lochee.

Sarah Craig:
"My father was always a Liberal, and he says, 'I must go,' he says, 'my man's standin' the night, you know.' So I says to him, 'Take me with you' and I went with him and it was held in the Drill Hall in Bell Street, and I'll never forget him comin' in and them that wasna supportin' him was booin' him. Churchill stood up. And the people that wasn't going to vote for him started singing 'Tell Me the Old Old Story' and he says, 'I will, and if you don't accept it,' he says, 'you'll be going on three to four days in your jute works and you'll know — you'll know, you should have put me in,' you know. And actually a fortnight after they put him out, the jute works went on three or four days a week. Oh, before he died he got — he told them he'd never come back to Dundee and they offered him the freedom of the city and he turned it down. He says, 'I said I'd never come back, and I won't', and he never. He was shattered, that the Dundee folk put him out."

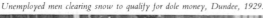
*Unemployed men clearing snow to qualify for dole money, Dundee, 1929.*

*Sarah Craig.*

Mrs Cockburn:
"Old Churchill was here. I mind just seein' him
ken, humphy backit man, I'm thinkin' to me he
looked humphy backit. He was a twister — he telt
ye he was for the workers and then when he was

speakin' to the other kind he was for them, two
timer — he wis."

For the majority of women in Dundee, however,
politics were a luxury they had little free time to
indulge in. In Mrs Cockburn's statement we have a
cameo description of the working-class woman's life in
Dundee, and elsewhere, during the first quarter of this
century.

Mrs Cockburn:
"I never voted for him. I never voted at a'.
Never did, I didna hae time! For washing bairns and
washing claithes, and looking after a bluidy boozy
man!"

*Churchill, shortly after an operation, is carried into a meeting, 1922.*

BILLY KAY

# Da Merry Boys

## THE BALAENA

Oh the no-ble fleet of wha-lers out sail-ing from Dun-dee, Well manned by Bri-tish sail-ors to work them on the sea; On the wes-tern o-cean pas-sage none with them can com-pare For there's not a ship could make the trip as the Ba – lae-na I de-clare.

CHORUS

*And the wind is on her quarter and her engine working free,*
*And there's not another whaler a-sailing from Dundee*
*Can beat the aul' Balaena and you needna try her on,*
*For we challenge all both large and small from Dundee to St Johns.*

2 *And it happened on a Thursday four days after we left Dundee,*
*Was carried off the quarter boats all in a raging sea,*
*That took away our bulwark, our stanchions and our rails,*
*And left the whole concern, boys, a-floating in the gales.*

3 *There's the new built Terra Nova, she's a model with no doubt,*
*There's the Arctic and the Aurora, you've heard so much about,*
*There's Jacklin's model mail-boat, the terror of the sea*
*Couldn't beat the aul' Balaena, boys, on a passage from Dundee.*

4 *Bold Jacklin carries canvas and fairly raises steam*
*And Captain Guy's a daring boy, goes ploughing through the stream,*
*But Mallan says the Eskimo could beat the bloomin' lot,*
*But to beat the aul' Balaena, boys, they'd find it rather hot.*

5 *And now that we have landed, boys, where the rum is mighty cheap,*
*We'll drink success to Captain Burnett, lads, for gettin' us ower the deep,*
*And a health to all our sweethearts, an' to our wives so fair,*
*Not another ship could make that trip but the Balaena I declare.*

*Arctic whaling ships in Bressay Sound, Shetland, c. 1900.*

Throughout the latter half of the eighteenth century until the opening decade of the twentieth century, the period from early March to mid-April in Shetland was known as 'da Greenland time'. Lerwick harbour was full of ships from Hull, Peterhead and Dundee, making up their crews with Shetlanders before setting sail on whaling and sealing expeditions to the Davies Straits and Greenland. To the crofter fishermen of Shetland, thirled to a subsistence economy in the control of the lairds, whaling offered the chance to earn hard cash, which could be used to pay their rents, boats or farming graith.

The business was lucrative enough to employ four different firms of agents in Lerwick, who recruited as many as 900 men a year during the 1850s. Profits and wages could be high but in a bad season, some of the men had very little to show for their work after they had paid off the agent for his provisions and the clothing required for an Arctic voyage. Indeed some men had to ship again with the same agent the following year in order to pay off their debts. The element of chance affected both the crews and the whaling companies. In the disastrous year of 1830, 19 of the 91 British ships in the Arctic were lost in the ice, while 21 of the ships that survived arrived 'clean' of oil, bone or skin. Years like this decimated the Hull fleet, and first Peterhead in the mid-1840s then Dundee in the 1870s became the principal British whaling ports.

In the eighteenth and nineteenth centuries, whale oil was used for lighting, soap, paint making and lubrication for machinery, while the flexible bone in the mammal's mouth was used in combs, brushes, umbrella frames and provided support in ladies' foundation garments. Whale oil was particularly important to Dundee where it was used to batch or soften the jute fibre for the city's textile industry. It was on board the Dundee whalers, the *Eclipse* and the *Scotia*, that Magnus Fraser and James Gordon sailed to

Greenland around 1910. Their reminiscences are probably those of the last Shetlanders to go to the Arctic whaling.

Magnus Fraser:
"Years ago in Lerwick harbour here, there were a hundred whaling ships one year and they used to pick up twenty or thirty Shetland men for crews, to make up their crews. They could come up here to Lerwick harbour and lie there for probably two or three weeks, pickin' up these men and then they would set sail for Greenland. There was the steam and sail — they were three masted barques."

James Gordon:
"They were all mostly Dundee and Tayport and that way. And then the old sailmaker, he was a Shetlander. And the boat steerer, he belonged to Bressay and the old harpooneer was frae Lerwick. That was the old men that had been at it for years. And there were one fellow — he sailed — and then he caught this Scotia comin' oot and God, he cam oot again, and he was been the year before, so he surely loved it!"

Tom Anderson of Lerwick recalls hearing tales of the Greenland whaling from the late Bruce Laurenson of Bressay.

Tom Anderson:
"He was on the old *Balaena*, the one the song is about. He was up there just as a boy, he went I think, first when he was sixteen. He went many years and he became one of the boat's crew for the actual killing of the whale, when it was hand harpoons. There were the harpooneers and then there was a man who stood by, when he got the harpoon into the whale, he had to stand by to keep the rope from burning the boat, because the whale would dive at a terrific speed you see. They would

let it plunge down, and Brucie's job, I remember him tellin' me, was to keep pourin' water on the boat, on the wood of the boat when the rope was going out because the friction could have set it on fire."

James Gordon:
"You see, when they . . . harpoon a whale, then he goes, ye see, an' the next boat hes to come up, the next whaleboat: yir lines is all into the whaleboat, coiled in the starn sheets o' the whaleboat, and the next boat 'at's there his to go and make fast his line on to this man that's fast. . . . Oh, the one [whale] that we had went out with three lines. . . . I was in the watch to come on deck the next time, and you see, if . . . you can get in a boat, get in a boat because you have an awful time on board the ship, gettin' up the tackles for to work the whale, so they tried to get in a boat. . . . They were four, or were they six pairs of oars and the boatsteerer; the boatsteerer hid to watch the line goin' out. Ye see the harpoon is fixed on the bow o' this whaleboat, and then there a cotton line that comes from it, and there a small tub that stands alongside wi' what they call the foregoer, and that's made fast to the main line, ye see. So when they fire

the shot then this soft cotton line, it disnae stop the harpoon, but ye had to be right on the whale before they fired the harpoon.
"But you see the Norwegians . . . hev the rocket on the point o' their harpoons. But the way 'at we hid to do, we'd to go in again an' kill her. . . . An' the way they know where the quhale is, all this fulmar petrels goes . . . works on top o'm, for the oil that's comin' out o' this wound, and you steer on where you see them, then you know where the fish is. I was into the boat that wis at the killin' o' him. They roll in an' he was lyin', ye see, within a round . . . just a round bit [in the ice] that could hold him. But . . . you hev to keep off his eye — if you come in on his eye he sees an' — oh, we were drenched, we hid to come in on his eye, but he put a harpoon within him for to push him ahead an' we got around his tail. They want to get this rocket in the left side . . . and they fire it into him and after it's been in you hear a 'bumm' and it's inside, an' that finishes him, he rolls over then. But before we would get in to kill him he put a harpoon in him so 'at drave him ahead a bit, an' we got in around his tail, but he saw wis comin' and his tail was goin' so we were drenched. . . . We came back, and when you come back to the ship then you get the tot o' rum. So the old steward wis aft, and he said to me, 'You're only a boy'. . . . But, I says, 'I'm been doin' men's work!'. So I got my rum."

*Preparing a harpoon before sailing.*

By the time these men went to the Arctic, whales had become extremely scarce in the region. Although successful whaling could bring in a fortune, with whalebone selling at £2,240 a ton, the few ships still working often had to rely on the sale of 'sundries' such as polar bear furs, seal skins and walrus tusks, to finance a voyage. This involved hunting the animals on the ice.

James Gordon:

"The way they tried to get the [polar] bears, they would put a piece o' fat or something in the fire, ye see, an' he got the smell an' came on the smell . . . the bogey fire. . . . They shoot them

Sometimes the sojourns on the ice were forced, and the killing of the bears was necessary for survival.

Magnus Fraser:

"Well, we had this storm an' we pulled the whaleboats up on the ice, the three whaleboats, and then we turned them on their sides an' put the sail over them, and we stayed there for five nights . . . a real blizzard . . . snow blizzard. An' we got a few seals, an' we got three or four polar bears. An' we ate them, a big part o' them, while we were frozen up on the ice. So we managed to carry on. And then at the end o' the fifth day . . . we could see the ship away down to the leeward, and she was

*Frontispiece of the 'Penny Magazine for the Diffusion of Useful Knowledge', May 1833.*
*'Harpooning the whale in the Arctic seas for lamp oil.'*

from the boat, ye see: he takes the watter, he can swim like anything. . . . An' they shot some o' them on the ice. I mind an old one . . . the old male, he ran away, and the old mother, she stood — and it was the bonniest sight ever I saw — she stood with a young bear under each side o' her, a half-grown bear, an' there she stood. Man, I thought it was a shame to shoot her, but they shoot her. But eh, it was a bonny sight, man, the old un standin' there. They just skinned them on a floe of ice, anywhere they got them."

come up after us, you see, and she was spotted us on the ice. And so that after that we were aa right: we got on board o' her, we got the boats laanched off the ice, and we were aa right."

Perhaps as an antidote to the cold and hardship, a cultural life was fostered amidst the ice, with most of the whalers hiring at least one Shetlander who could play the fiddle to entertain the men. As a result, many of the rhythmic, syncopated tunes we associate with Shetland fiddle music, such as 'Da Merry Boys o' Greenland' and 'Oliver Jack', were actually a product of Shetlanders mixing with other cultures at the Greenland whaling. Bobby Peterson, who later describes conditions at the Antarctic whaling, learned the tune 'Willafjord' from his father, who brought it back from Greenland.

Fiddle reel:                                                      WILLAFJORD

Fiddle reel:                                      DA MERRY BOYS O' GREENLAND

Tom Anderson:

"When you come up to Greenland or up to the Davis Straits you were meeting people from the other side, from Newfoundland and America and people from Scandinavia. So Greenland was really the top of the triangle, Greenland was the focal point, everybody met there. That was where there was a big exchange of culture. And actually where the Eskimos were learned to dance. You see they learned the Eightsome Reel there and they also learned the Shetland Reel. This was a strange thing because Jenny Gilbertson, who is now filming with the Eskimos, went a long distance about four years ago, two hundred miles, to film this Eskimo dance. She told me this, and when she came there she discovered that what she was filming was a cross between an Eightsome Reel and a Shetland Reel."

The music apart, life on board the barques must have been extremely hard. Today men who work on oil rigs live in cramped conditions far from family and friends, but at least they have good food to look forward to at the end of a shift. For the Greenland men, food was consumed for nutrition, not taste.

James Gordon:

[Ship's biscuits]: "It was, oh, big biscuit — they were aboot four inches square. But you hed — we got . . . cook's fat, dripping, an' we'd put it on the biscuit an' shove it in the oven an' hot it an' get them softened: then the biscuit was a bit softer an' you could get them broken — oh, my God . . . to try them any other way it was the same as the stone. They were lyin' aboard the ship, I believe, they jist hed them in the tank . . . a big oil-tank it wis, hed been kept for the job, an' the biscuit wis been pitten in there an' they were fae year to year. But I never seen any weevils aboard — in them. I'm seen the old fellows that wis at Greenland, they had been goin' years, they would take a piece o' the quhale blubber, an' how they ate it God only knows, but they hed a tin an' they would take a piece o' this an' they would cut it up in junks, small bits, an' put it in this tin and boil it, then they would eat it. An' I'm seen them eatin' it oot o' the hand an' jist the fat runnin' . . . God, you wad hed to have a good stomach!"

Yet despite the food, the danger, the chance of failure and the subhuman conditions the men had to cope with, one of the strongest impressions left in James Gordon's mind was the memory of the beauty of the Arctic.

James Gordon:

"It's a funny thing, men went there back year after year; an' I mind me sayin' tae an old fellow,

said, 'If I get oot o' this ye'll never see me here
again'. An' man, do you know 'at I believe if that
ships hed 'a' been goin' back a year or two efter, I
believe I would ha' gone: it's sort o' attractive. . . .
It opened one's eyes to see what wis . . . and
sometimes it comes on the television aboot them
bein' at the Sooth Pole an' the North Pole, an' I
love that — the ice, and the hummocks . . . I love
the look of that on television, pits it all back
again."

The whaling ships never returned to Lerwick again
as 1913 saw the last whaling expedition out of Dundee
on the ketch *Ernest William* which foundered in
Cumberland Gulf, and brought an era to its close.
   With the Arctic whaling in decline, new whaling
grounds were sought and in 1892 an expedition left
Dundee to explore the possibilities of whaling in the
Antarctic. Eventually it was a firm based in Leith,
Christian Salvesen and Company, which came to
dominate the Antarctic whaling industry. A family
firm of Norwegian origin, Salvesen had previously
acted as agents for Norwegian firms selling whale oil
on the British market. By the turn of this century, they
saw the commercial advantage of going to the whaling
themselves. Consequently they invested in purchasing
whale catchers, and fitted out stations both in Iceland
and Shetland which lay on the migratory routes of the
whale. The opening of Olnafirth station in 1904 was the
beginning of a long relationship between Salvesen and
the Shetlanders which lasted until the end of the British
whaling in the 1960s.
   At first the relationship was far from being amicable
as Shetland fishermen accused Salvesen and the
Norwegian owners of other stations at Ronas Voe and
Collafirth of polluting the sea with whale carcasses,
thereby forcing the shoals of herring away from their
traditional grounds. However, the fishing interests
could not prevail on the authorities to close the station
down and for 25 years it gave employment to local
men.

Tom Anderson:
   "I remember talking to one of the old whaleboat
skippers, and he said to me, 'You know, if we find
the Stream, we can find the whales'. Now the
Stream was the Gulf Stream and the Gulf Stream
passes by Shetland. Sometimes it would come in as
near as forty miles or maybe thirty miles, it would
vary from year to year and even from month to
month. On the edge of the Stream would be the
warm water where you'd get the cuttle fish, and all
the tropical fish would come up, whatever it was
the whale was feeding on. So you'd a chance of
getting the whale there, and that was where they
hunted the whale."

John Tait:
   "I stayed in the same place where the whaling
station was. We used to have bets on who would
have the most whales in the morning, you see.

Some of them was very good at it, and some of
them wasna so good. I was a boy working at the
school, you know, just — in the holidays from the
school, you see, and they employed half a dozen of
us to help discharge these empty barrels, oil barrels
off the ship that was in — that would be 1922."

*Catchers and whalers at Olnafirth, Shetland, c. 1920.*

Tom Anderson:
   "The whale catchers went out and could shoot
the whale with the harpoon with the bomb on it,
and when they were dead they just lashed them up
alongside the ship and towed them ashore. We had
a hotel in Hillswick which is about ten, twelve
miles from the whaling station. The visitors used to
come to watch this, it was a great sight, to see the
whale being cut up, you see, although the smell was
a bit overwhelming, the ladies didn't quite like that.
But they used to go back with huge chunks of meat
to the hotel where they would be served up as roast
and steaks of all description and this would happen
quite often, the man from the hotel used to come
and get an amount of whale meat to give his
visitors. This was a treat, something that was
different on the menu. I worked at Olna for two
seasons and eh, at that time whales were getting
scarcer and scarcer and they were having to go
further and further away. 1929, that was the last
year, it was closed down."

Fortunately for those willing to travel and be away
from home six months at a time, employment was
available with the same company in the Antarctic,
where Salvesen had constructed a whaling station on
the island of South Georgia in a place they christened
Leith harbour.

John Tait:
   "There was an old Captain Sinclair, a Shetland
man, he was skipper of the whale factory ship that

went on to Graham's Land in the Antarctic, you know, and he came up to the whaling station to engage so many men and boys, you know, for the ship. And you were in a great state in case you didna get a job. The first year I put my name down, and I asked to get a job. I came home and of course my mother and my sister stopped it. I was too young. I was fifteen or sixteen or thereabouts — just rather young for to go to the other end of the world! And I can remember I was crying because I couldn't get! But I knew, ah well, I'll get next year. So I got the next year alright."

For boys who had grown up hearing tales from sailors of far distant lands, the journey to the other side of the world held no great terrors for them. However, the first trip did leave a vivid impression and a fascination for the exotic.

John Tait:
"We joined the whaler at Leith and she was all ready with whale catchers and all, with her, and left there and went to Las Palmas, for bunkering . . . our next port of call was Rio de Janeiro. It's funny, I can remember more about that first trip. It was a great sight to see the Sugar Loaf Mountain there, and Rio de Janeiro."

Bobby Peterson:
"We just had the one stopping place, and that was the bunkering port — for taking the oil, you see, to drive the ship. I'll tell you, when we come into the bunkerin' port, Aruba, then it was monkeys. Oh, they were keen on the monkeys, man, especially that Western Isles boys. They would tak them aboard, there was some from St Abbs Head too, boys frae there. I mind there was two brothers fae there, one Alec Crow and one Charlie Crow, ah, they were two fine fellows. Charlie, he got this monkey. Man, you see he had it in his room, and there was maybe six or eight in the room he was in, it was a big room. And you see, they're tricky things, man, he was tearin' all their clothes, man, just chewing up the best suit or anything. Never should have been allowed on board — never should. There was none in the room that I was in but we were going along Charlie's room and this thing was sittin' in there, man, just kicking up the devil, man, and Charlie's lyin' there laughin', [laughter] just thinkin' it was good fun! And I hae mind, an old fireman coming aboard with one and he gaed to take it in one night and he'd a rope on it but of course the monkey snapped off the rope as fast as he could put it on. So he got a piece of wire, electric wire, and he was going to handle it with this and man, didnae it nip him, catch him by the hand. He gave him a dirty bite. Oh man he took it by the end of the rope and he threw it three or four times around the rail of the ship like that and then he tossed it over the side. We were lying in at Aruba at the time. And man, the monkey lay on top of the water for a while absolutely still. 'Aye well', he said, 'that's put paid to you', and he threw the rest of the wire over the side. However, no time after we saw the monkey coming to, you see, and looked around it, man, and swam doon along. Somebody was clever and nipped around the other side you see, and somebody threw a line to her wi' a knot in the end, then he took hold of the rope and he pulled it up the stern of the whaler. . . He could never understand how that monkey got aboard, and it was something he never found out! Ha ha, he never found that out."

The journey down to South Georgia was a slow one taking altogether five to six weeks. When they got to within reach of the island, the smell of the whaling station came out to greet them.

Jimmy Mann:
"I remember the first time we got there, the mate, he was a Shetlander, was standing on the foredeck of the ship and everybody was complaining of the smell coming off the shore in the guano factory. And he said — he was standin' there lookin', he'd been down there about half a dozen times before that. and he said, 'That's the stuff that makes men o' ye — oh, smelly! Put it like that!'."

*Leith Harbour, South Georgia, from Coronda Peak.*

Bobby Peterson:

"When you see South Georgia first you would just see nothing but the white mass of Coronda Peak. It's the highest mountain in it, you see. She was all snow covered, but a beautiful sight to see. And of course the first you meet is the icebergs standing up, huge, some of them huge, and then of course South Georgia is a beautiful island, you ken. And you saw some of the loveliest scenery I think you'll ever see again — sunsets for one thing, sunrise for another. Oh man — and lovely weather. I mean there was bad weather, but there was some lovely weather . . . it froze down solid and lay with not a breath of wind, then you could get a terror coming up all of a sudden, wet snow and flying gale, a blizzard, and that sort of thing. But ah, man, you can get some lovely weather, and as I say — as for a sunset in the sky at night, it made you look sometimes, made you wonder. The beauty was really . . . and that red sun going down into the water ye ken, shining on the icebergs, and these great big seals lying there looking at you, with their great heads [laughs] and officers on the bridge cracking at them with a point-22 [laughs]. It has as much effect on them as . . ." [laughs].

In South Georgia the Shetlanders were mainly employed in the various stages of processing the whale's carcass on the deck of the factory ship. The highly paid job of killing the whale was jealously guarded by the Norwegians. Their countryman, Svend Foyn, had invented the first steam whale catcher and the explosive harpoon which revolutionised the industry and insured its domination by the Norwegians. Two Shetlanders recall witnessing a kill from a Norwegian whale catcher.

Tommy Laurenson:

"I was on a whale boat, a catcher called the *Sleuga* and Albert Jacobsen was the gunner, and he was lucky enough, he got two whales on that expedition. Well, we set off on the hunt, you know. And the man goes up on the crow's nest, he would look out, and just chasing around and when we would sight the whale, or when he sights her, then he sings out where she is and directs the boat accordingly, and then you just chase around and sometimes you have a very long chase, and sometimes you're lucky, you may just harpoon the whale right away."

Jimmy Mann:

"He just fires the harpoon as soon as he spots the whale going to surface and the harpoon hits the whale and there's a delay action on the charge and this explodes a second or two after it goes into the whale, and hopefully it kills it quickly, but sometimes doesn't, depending on where the whale gets hit. If it's quite near the head it dies quickly. But if it's hit further back it's quite full of fight for a while and then it's just a case of following. As soon as it's hit, the whale sounds, that means it runs

as deep as it possibly can. And you have to pay out the line as quickly as possible and then, just as you'd play a fish on the end of a rod, you play the whale on the end of the line and you tire it out. If it doesn't die very quickly then they put another harpoon in, when they ever have a chance, that one is usually a killer. It usually dies quite fast after that. It's dramatic in the sense that you see an awful lot of blood floating around — and when the whale's blowing, the first time you see it blowing, it's nice and frothy — the water's nice and white, he blows out the vapour. But if the whale's got a serious hit, the next time you see it blowing it just spouts blood. You're very much aware it is a living animal, as you would say, a living thing, and I was sorry to see them killing the whale, but at the same time, you had to earn a living and this was the thing. What we were sorry for and what occasionally happened was a mother whale and a baby alongside and they shot the mother by accident — not intentionally. But sometimes with heavy seas running, the gunner just didn't see the baby, and shot the mother and then that was a tragedy. A beautiful animal, but, as I say, you hated to see it being killed but there you were, you had to live."

Tommy Laurenson:

"After it was harpooned and killed it was heaved in alongside and then there was air pumped into it because a dead whale sinks and they have, oh, it's a pipe with holes into it and a spear end, with an air compressor and they pump air in, and it just practically goes under the blubber more or less and they — when they think there's sufficient, then they just pull it out and flag it — they put a flag, a big red flag, and away chasing again. And at night-time they put a light on the whale — a battery light so the boat again when they've finished for the day, they can come back and see the light and pick up the whale again. And they take them into the stern of the factory ship, deliver them there and then they're hauled up."

*Drawing whales up the slip of the* Southern Empress, *later sunk during the Second World War.*

*Flensers at the station, Leith Harbour.*

In the early days of the Antarctic whaling, the whales had been flensed at the side of the ship. By the late 'twenties and early 'thirties, however, all of the new factory ships had a stern slipway and a Gjelstad's steel claw which clamped on the whale's tail and drew it on to the plan or deck of the factory ship. There the carcass was stripped of blubber by the flensers, stripped of meat by the lemmers and along with the bones, these various products were sent to different parts of the ship where they were reduced to various grades of oil, for soap and margarine, meat meal, and guano for fertiliser.

Robert Watt:
"I always recall the day when the first whale was up on the deck and I looked at it and it was *enormous* — after being used to small haddocks and whitings, you know! — it was enormous!!! The three flensers commenced cutting. One jumps on top o' the whale and the other two is on either side and they stick — the two that's on the plan — they stand still where they are, they don't move — but they stick their knife in, into the whale and as the whale is hauled for'ard their knife cuts all the way along — all the way along, and as the spick is cut there's so much pressure on the meat inside that this — the blubber, it comes apart and the flenser can see how deep he's cuttin'. Now that carries on all the way until the whale's up, but, the one, the poor one that's on top, the flenser on top, he has to walk — but all the whalers have got special instruments on their heels to prevent them from sliding, which is spikes in their heels. Therefore this one on top of the whale has got the spikes on his heels and it

holds him and he starts cutting in the centre of the back, right up to the head. And it falls off, it falls on the deck, then the spick cutter takes over — the spick cutter takes over and cuts it up into small sections and puts it into the kettle to be processed to be made into oil."

The work was often tedious, not unlike the slow grind of the assembly line in a car factory. However, there was always a character on board who would do something outrageous to prevent weariness from setting in.

Bobby Peterson:
"I mind the smallest man I ever saw, frae Leith, and they called him Walter, and he had a long black beard. I mind this day the kettle of meat was coming pretty, pretty high up, and it was a silly thing he did because it was coming high up you see, with great chunks of meat in it, and somebody happened to drop their meat hook, you see, what you dragged this meat along the deck was a hook just like an old-fashioned stove poker. You see you just dug in the hook and worked away wi' it, it had a handle on't and somebody's hook of course went with the piece of meat they were dragging in, you see, and they said — Oh that was their good hook gone. 'Oh,' Walter said, 'you wouldn't say that' — and all of a sudden he just booled right in, right in among the meat and man, you never saw him for a while. If ye wir looking down you saw the black beard stickin' up, [*laughs*] he dived into the whale meat that was down in the kettle, it was all cut up, the whale was just in pieces, you see. But somebody threw in a rope and Walter got a hold. And Walter came just in blood,

slush and muck, man, you never saw such a picture
— the very beard was thick — man he just laughed
and went away and got a shift and was back on
deck in no time. He got the hook — oh, trust him,
he got the hook alright. But you see he sank in it,
just like going in a bog, just the same, blood and
. . . oh my that was a laugh — no' everybody
would ha' done it!''

---

*Lemmers cutting out whale bone from the jaws of a flensed whale.*

With the men working 12-hour shifts there wasn't
much time or energy for recreation, but the
Shetlanders always carried their music with them.

Jimmy Mann:
"Oh, everybody played that could play, you
know, but it was mostly Shetlanders, I must say,
that carried the musical instruments."

Bobby Peterson:
"Goodness yes man, we had a concert every
week. All the drink you got was a tot o' rum every
Sunday, that was all and anybody that didna drink
it, well, you could give him something and get that
one if you wanted [laughs], if you wanted an extra
one.''

Tommy Laurenson:
"Well, the only recreation there when the station
was working — they had football teams, you see.
There were Stromness, that was one station, and
Husevik was another one and Gratevicken
was another one — belonged to the
Argentine Di Pesco. And every summer when
the whaling fleet was down there, they had the
competitions. And then they had the sports, ski-
jumping and all this carry on. So that's the only
enjoyment that was on there, and they had, of
course, the cinema. It was the silent pictures when I
was down there but later on then the talkies came.

And then in the winter time there was — that was
in the war years, of course, when I was there, we
went reindeer hunting. But the reindeer meat was
very good and in the summer time we went
for penguin eggs, went and collected penguins'
eggs, so many — oh, by the thousands, it
wasn't just a few dozen there, no, no, and we
preserved them in waterglass. They took back the
penguins and they're in the Edinburgh Zoo. That's
the ones, Ivor Salvesen, Captain Salvesen, he took
them home, and that's the offspring of them yet
that are in Edinburgh Zoo."

There was more than the penguins happy to reach
Leith safely. Like the Shetlanders at the Greenland
whaling, the South Georgia whalers could return with
money to put into their crofts at home.

Bobby Peterson:
"Oh, it paid well. I canna mind, remember, how
much it was a month, but then you see it wasn't so
much what you got a month, it was what we got
for *bonus*, you see, and when the oil went up or
down. You see when I paid off with something like
a hundred and twenty pounds, well, you see, for six
months, you see — that was good money then, yes,
good money then, £120, and you see you had your
bonus and if the oil went up, which it did — you
see, at the beginning of the war, it was sold for
more then. You see we got a sliding scale, so we got
a cheque again maybe in the month of July or
August, we got another cheque for say maybe £70
or £80. I canna mind just now, it was too long ago,
how much — oh, but it was a great thing, ye ken.
It wasna easy earned money, but it was very good."

Their hamefarin was celebrated with one of the
grand occasions in the Shetland social calendar.

Tom Anderson:
"The Whalers Ball was the — *the* thing of the
season when they came home because everybody
turned up there, all the whalers, old and young.

*Whales astern* Southern Empress, *1940.*

*Bobby Peterson, 1937.*

There was no drink inside the hall, you see — there were plenty o' drams flowing outside, I mean everybody had his bottle and at that time, well the police wasn't so strict wi' cars or that. But, whatever, there was any amount o' drink flowing and they were very generous, and of course, all the stories were goin' and all the dancers were goin'. It was just one o' the things of the season, you looked forward to the Whalers Ball."

Mrs Mann:
    "We were terribly excited. When the night — the night arrived, we all had to get new dresses. And we had some great nights — some of them slightly nightmarish — because the boys took too much to drink! [*laughs*]. Well, they fought, some of them, especially over girls!" [*laughs*]

Tom Anderson:
    "Oh that was just a unique occasion. And it would last till — well, it started maybe eight or nine o'clock and it would last till four or five in the morning — we were never home before five or six o'clock any time."

The 'ball' that the European whaling companies celebrated from the profits derived from the mass killing of the whale ended in the early 'sixties. The reason for the decline was the same as in Greenland— overkill. Salvesen terminated its whaling operation in 1963, and to the company's credit, set up a fund in Shetland to help the men in their transition back to the work of the islands. Many used the money to help buy boats and equipment for their crofts. After over 200 years at the whaling, the Shetlanders returned to their traditional role as crofter fishermen.
    But for the Antarctic whalers, something of South Georgia lingered with them, even after the last long voyage home and a night's carousing at the Whalers Ball.

Jimmy Mann:
    "We thoroughly enjoyed ourselves [going home] but when you opened your sea-bag — everybody carried a sea-bag at that particular time, because you had to carry everything — blankets, pillows, everything to sea you had to carry it. So you'd a huge big bag of clothes you had to carry around wi' ye all the time; and when you got home and opened the sea-bag, the first thing that met you was the smell — South Georgia smell [*laughs*] and that was a reminder of where you'd been."

                                                    BILLY KAY

*John Maclean, emigrant bard from Balephuil, Tiree,*
*on whose departure for Canada the Balemartin Bard composed 'Manitoba'.*

## MANITOBA

Refrain 'S nach mu-la-dach mi-se bhith 'seo gun duin id-ir

A thog-as, no thuig-eas, no shein-neas leam dàn!

Le dù rachd mo chri-dhe soir-idh slàn leis na gil-lean

Á sheol air an t-sli-ghe gu Ma-ni-to-ba.

Refrain *How sad I am here without a single companion*
*To raise a chorus, or understand or sing a song with me!*
*From the depth of my heart I send a farewell blessing to the lads*
*Who sailed on the voyage to Manitoba.*

O's bu ghrianach ar maduinn 'nuair bha sinn 'nar balaich,
Gun chùram, gun ghearain, gun teannachadh màil,
Ach sunndach, làn aigheir, cha laigheadh a' smalan
Air a' chomunn a bh' againn am Baile nam Bàrd.

How sunny was our morning in the days of our boyhood,
Carefree, uncomplaining, unoppressed by the rent,
We were light-hearted and joyous; no cloud overshadowed
The good fellowship that was ours in Baile nam Bard.

'S 'nar a ràinig a' mhaduinn gu dol air an aineol
'S a thionail gach caraid a bh' aca 's an àit',
Chan urra mi aithris am bròn a bh' air m' aire
'S an cùl ris a' bhaile 's a' mhaduinn Di-màirt.

When the morning came when they were to set out for a strange land
And every friend they had in the place had gathered together,
I cannot express the sorrow that weighed me down
As they turned their backs on the township on that Tuesday morning.

'S chan fhaic mi 's an àm seo ach caoirich air bheanntan:
Chan eil as a' ghleann ach fear Gallda no dhà:
Am beagan a dh' fhan dhiubh air rudhaichean mara
'Gan iomain gu cladach 's 'gam feannadh le màl.

I can see nothing now but sheep on the hillsides:
There is no one left in the glen but a stranger or two:
The few of them who are left are on headlands by the sea
Driven to the shore and flayed with rents.

Tha luchd-fhearainn shaoir as an àm seo ro ghaolach
Air stòras an t-saoghail a shlaodadh bho chàch;
G' eil innleachdan baoghail 's a' Ghàidhealtachd seo daonnan
Air fògair nan daoine 's chur chaorach 'nan àit'.

The land-owning proprietors at this time are all too eager
To grab for themselves the worldly possessions of all the rest;
Cunning schemes are always being used here in the land of the Gaels
To drive the people out and make room for sheep.

'S e faileas na daoine; 's nach sgarach an saoghal—
'S e 's fasan dha daonnan bhith caochladh gach là.
'Nar coigrich air 'uachdar, cha mhaireann 's cha bhuan sinn
Is mìltean de thruaghain 'gam fuadach far sàil.

The people are but shadows; how fickle the world is—
It is ever its nature to change day by day.
We are strangers upon its face, we are fleeting and impermanent,
With thousands of poor wretches being driven overseas.

Luchd fhéilidh is osan, fo bhonaidean cocte,
Bha riamh air am moladh air thoiseach nam blàr,
Tha 'n diugh 'gan cur thairis gu dùthaich neo-fhallain
'S gun nì air an aire ach a' fearann chur fàs.

The wearers of the kilt and the hose and cocked bonnet,
Who were always renowned in the forefront of battle,
Are today being driven abroad to unwholesome countries
With no other object but to lay waste the land.

Cha labhair mi tuilleadh ma euchd nam fear duineil
Ach ruigidh mi Ruisia 's mullach Alma:
'S e daoiread an fhearainn chuir na Gàidheil an tainead:
'S gun chuimhn' air Sebastopol 's Balaclava.

I shall say nothing more of the deeds of the brave men
But only mention Russia and the Heights of Alma:
It is the weight of the rent that has left the Gaels few in numbers:
Forgotten are Sebastopol and Balaclava.

# Poets And Pioneers

In the nineteenth century, many hundreds of people, whole families and individuals, left the small, low-lying island of Tiree, the outermost of the Inner Hebrides, for new homes in Canada. There were two main periods of emigration from Tiree in the century. The first occurred from the mid-1840s to the early 1850s, when the small crofts which had replaced the traditional joint tenant, run-rig farms at the beginning of the nineteenth century could no longer continue to support the island's rapidly increasing population — almost five thousand in 1841 — and when the potato crop, on which so many depended, failed in a series of disastrous years. The second took place in the late 1870s and 1880s, when the prospect of free homesteads in the Canadian West, then being opened for settlement, offered an attractive alternative to an island where, as throughout the Highlands, security of tenure for crofters was yet to be established and the claims of the landless still to be met.

Life in nineteenth-century Tiree was precarious in economic terms. But this did not mean that existence as a whole was bleak or unrewarding. In the thirty crofting and fishing townships of the island, the community was a close-knit one, the oral culture lively and creative. Ties of family and neighbourhood were strong, and mutual aid and communal work were activities characteristic of every season. Special respect was given to those with certain gifts: the local

*Log home of Laughlin and Catherine MacFadyen, Brock Township (7th Concession), Ontario.*

bards — and there were many of them, men and women — who could compose songs describing people and events, satirising anti-social behaviour, and in general reflecting the values of the community; those who were skilled at story-telling or who could relate the history of the island's townships and the genealogy of local families; those who were adept at curing illness in animals or in people with traditional remedies including herbs and charms.

It was an island that was undergoing change. Not isolated from national or international events, it had sent men to fight in the Napoleonic Wars, and its economy fluctuated according to wider markets and demands, and decisions taken far away. The Baptist and the Congregational or Independent churches were established there in the first half of the nineteenth century, under the leadership of evangelical, Gaelic-speaking missionaries who were themselves composers of secular songs as well as of hymns. And while seasonal migration to the Lowland harvest had become a feature of island life, by the middle of the nineteenth century the expanding industrial and mercantile centres of the Clyde were offering the prospect of permanent employment to the young men and women of Tiree.

Only a handful of individuals and families had left the island for overseas destinations before the 1840s, but among these was Tiree's most famous emigrant of all, the poet John Maclean. Called *Iain mac Ailein*, John son of Allan, in Tiree, he was known more widely as *Bard Thighearna Cholla*, for before his departure he was bard to the laird of the neighbouring island of Coll.

With his wife and children he left Tiree for Nova Scotia in 1819, settling first in Pictou County at *Baile Chnoic* near Middle Barney's River, and moving later some six miles west to a spot which came to be known as Glenbard, in Antigonish County. It was during his early years in the woods of *Baile Chnoic* that he composed his *Oran do America, A'Choille Ghruamach,* 'The Gloomy Forest'. The words of this song, expressing so eloquently the hardships he had experienced and the loneliness of an existence far from the congenial society he had known at home, must have been in the minds of the mid-century emigrants as they left Tiree for Canada.

[Translation]

> *When summer comes and the month of May,*
> *The heat of the sun makes us feel faint;*
> *It gives new life to every creature*
> *That is lying dormant in its hiding place.*
> *The roaring bears wake from sleep*
> *To prowl among the flocks, and great is the*
> *    destruction;*
> *And the sharp-nailed mosquito, vicious and*
> *    venomous,*
> *Covering me with wounds from the point of its lance.*
>
> *When the winter comes, and the time of bad*
> *    weather,*
> *The snow lies thick at the back of the branches.*
> *Deep and dense, it goes over the knees,*
> *And however good the trousers, they are of little*
> *    use*
> *Without double stockings and furry moccasins,*
> *Laced tightly with thongs.*
> *It was a new fashion for us to wear it with the hair*
> *As it was stripped from the animal yesterday.*

Shortly after he left Tiree, cousins of the bard, MacFadyens from the township of Salum there, were among the first to take up land many hundreds of miles inland, in the newly-surveyed township of Brock in Upper Canada, or what is now the Province of Ontario. There, not far from emigrants who came from other parts of Argyllshire and who gave names such as 'Argyle' to their settlements, they and their relatives and in-laws established a small Tiree community in the seventh concession, the name given to the parallel ranges of land, divided into lots, which formed the gridiron pattern of the land survey.

There can be no underestimating the psychological and social impact of emigration both on those who left and on those who stayed behind. But the total isolation from the familiar faces and ways of Tiree which the bard experienced in his early years in Nova Scotia was not to be the lot of the Tiree emigrants of the mid-century. Large numbers of them travelled together aboard the ships that took them across the Atlantic, and they continued to journey in company to their places of settlement. Many of them made as their initial destination the already-established Tiree community in Brock, where, in addition to the warm hospitality of friends and relations, amid people of a common origin,

they were able to acquire valuable instruction and advice from those with a generation of expertise in dealing with the new environment.

By the middle of the nineteenth century most of the good arable land in Brock Township had been taken up, but new lands were being surveyed in Grey and Bruce Counties to the west, and as these areas were opened for settlement groups of emigrants moved on from their temporary bases. They took up land on adjacent or neighbouring lots in several localities or townships in a line between Brock Township and Lake Huron. One of these settlements was in Osprey Township of Grey County, around a spot on the Blue Mountain called 'McIntyres' Corners' after four McIntyre brothers from Tiree who each bought a farm at the crossroads. Another, also in Grey County, was south of the Old Durham Road near Priceville. A third was created in the Townships of Bruce and Kincardine in Bruce County.

For settlers from windswept, tree-less Tiree, the virgin forests of Canada, which provided the title for John Maclean's song, must have presented a daunting prospect. But they were versatile people, able to turn their hands to many tasks, skilled at building their own boats and constructing their own houses. And the habits of home, of working together and offering support to each other, 'making a bee' as it was called in Canada, and of enjoying recreation together, instrumental music, song, and the visit or *ceilidh*, were readily adaptable to the new situations.

---

*Ann Maclean (Mrs Sandy Lamont).*

Alex Lamont:
    "I heard, I often heard my grandmother talk about lightin' fires at night to keep the wolves away. The men would build a brush shelter, you know, as they went along the road, and they had to light these fires to keep the wolves away. When they got to McIntyres' Corners at the Blue

Mountain — they really didn't know where they were goin', she said they just kept goin' until they came to a place that looked like home, and the Blue Mountains looked like Scotland, you see, and there was lots of fresh water, springs and everything like that. So they settled there. The first year they lived there they lived in brush houses, just that they made out of brush, 'til they got their log houses built and then they had their log houses. Got a bit of land cleared and just went from there. They'd make bees to clear the land and these old pipes, this Sandy McFadyen — they had a dance every night after there'd be logging bees and he'd play the pipes at night and they all danced to the bagpipes. My grandmother she was just a girl in her 'teens then, and they said that she used to dance the highland fling every night to the bagpipes after binding sheaves all day."

These bagpipes are still owned and played by the descendants of the family that brought them from Tiree in the 1840s.

Alex Lamont:
"Well, my great-grandfather brought them over in 1846 from the Isle of Tiree and a cousin of my grandfather's, a Sandy McFadyen, played them, played them at all the clearings, log clearings in Osprey Township where they settled, and when they moved from Argyle up to the Blue Mountain, he played them goin' through the bush on the way up there."

The provision of shelter and food were the immediate necessities:

Mrs Jean Schroeder:
"At first they would just clear a little clearing and build a log house . . . and plant a bit of grain just to keep them going through the winter. And they had a few cattle that provided milk and so on. They built houses close to each other in the beginning, and then as they got the land cleared they went farther afield, you know, the different families did. . . . They more or less were in one small community."

The earliest crops were sown among the stumps of the felled trees:

Alex Lamont:
"I heard my grandmother say that they could put a hill of potatoes in around a stump and they'd get a whole pail of potatoes off one hill and they'd be just as white as snow — that new land, you know. They grew an awful lot of stuff on a small — you know — it took — they would be there maybe three or four years before they'd get any more than four or five acres cleared."

Mrs Jean Schroeder:
"Wood was so plentiful here, it was really a burden to them to get rid of the wood. They would

have huge fires going all the time trying to burn it up. . . . And you know, they used to have stump fences around their fields and they were very effective. Usually pine stumps, because they seemed to last, they didn't rot, the pine seemed to be their favourite. 'Old pine stumps' — I've heard them talking about them. But even that wouldn't keep the wild animals out of their crops. I've heard of Laughlin driving the bears from his field with a pitchfork."

_Laughlin and Catherine MacFadyen._

Along with the difficult tasks of clearing the land of trees and preparing it for cultivation and erecting their buildings, the Tiree emigrants had to become accustomed to the extremes of climate which John Maclean had described in his song and to the crises which these could bring:

Mrs Jean Schroeder:
"The first winters were all hard because they were not used to the weather that we have here in Canada or the snow, and they didn't have enough land cleared to provide feed for their cattle all winter. So the cattle used to have to browse the trees, like the deer do — those are the little buds that form the leaf later on in the spring, they eat that. But the cattle didn't seem to be able to get their cud up from just eating the browse. So I've heard of them having to open their straw mattresses and feeding the straw to the cows so they could get their cud up. They had to have more bulk in their stomach before they could get their cud up. So you know, times were very hard."

*John McMillan and some of his stock.*

Gradually the land began to yield a return for the labour of the settlers. By 1861, John McMillan, who had left the Tiree township of Balephuil a decade earlier and settled on a lot near Priceville, had nine of his fifty acres cleared for cultivation and in the previous year these had produced fifty bushels of spring wheat, thirty bushels of oats, and two hundred bushels of potatoes. The remaining forty-one acres were still under bush. He had four steers or heifers, one milch cow, and four pigs, and his household had produced eighty pounds of butter, a hundredweight of salt pork, and twenty pounds of maple sugar. In the words of one of his descendants, "They worked together and helped each other a lot".

Alex Lamont:
"They never did too much work alone. There was lots of them and they were all like one family anyhow. There was just the settlement there and maybe, well you'd go all the way across the Collingwood mountain before you came to another settlement. The other settlement was from the Isle of Islay. No, in your own settlement you more or less worked together. I don't remember of my grandfather doin' much alone. Only tappin' trees. And my grandmother used to have an awful time to get him to do that, to get him started. She'd have to go out and tap the first tree, and then after she got started he'd go at it."

Tapping the maple trees for sap, which was reduced by boiling to make maple syrup and, by further reduction, maple sugar, was one of the many skills which the first European settlers in Canada learned from the original inhabitants, the Indians. Like the Indians, the Tiree emigrants were accustomed to the use of plants for a variety of purposes from dyeing wool to curing ailments, and when they came to Canada those settlers with a special interest in these matters were anxious to discover the properties of the plants growing in their new localities.

Mrs Jean Schroeder:
"Old Mrs MacFadyen . . . was the 'doctor' of the community and the old Indian lady took her around, showed her all the different herbs and roots that they used for medicine."

Traditional work techniques such as using the flail, winnowing the chaff, singing while milking, and raising the nap of handwoven woollen cloth by rhythmic pounding on a board to the accompaniment of song continued to be practised in the Tiree communities of Ontario. Fortunes were cast at Hallowe'en and the last sheaf to be harvested was kept until the following spring. Many of those who left Tiree in the mid-nineteenth century were members or adherents of the Baptist and Congregational denominations, which were strong in Tiree in the pre-emigration period and with their emphasis on lay participation were ideally suited to the needs of emigrant communities. But in addition, many beliefs continued to be held in omens, signs of luck or unluck, second sight, the evil eye, and the supernatural.

*Alexander (Sandy) Lamont.*

Alex Lamont:
"Up in Osprey they believed in ghosts, really believed in them."

Mrs Jean Schroeder:
"There were people that saw lights. . . . It bothered them; it was an omen of, a bad omen, it wasn't a good thing to see."

*Congregational Church on Tenth Concession of Kincardine Township.*

Alex Lamont:

"There was a family in Osprey from Tiree, their name was . . . MacPhail, Archie MacPhail and Neil MacPhail. They were brothers. And this Archie MacPhail and Neil MacPhail, they were great fellows for collie dogs and they talked to them in Gaelic all the time. And this Neil MacPhail went to the States, to the lumber camps, and one night this dog — he had left his dog at home — and this dog went up on the hill by his house and he stood there and he was howlin', cryin'. Cried all night. And Neil MacPhail's mother said, 'Something happened to Neil. I know by the dog that something happened to Neil.' And they found out later that he was murdered, in a lumber camp. And his dog knew it, you see. Then this Archie MacPhail, he was a big man, he was a regular giant, and strong. He went to Badjeros with a team and sleigh, with the oxen and a sleigh. I guess it was a straight sleigh at that time they had. And he bought a barrel of salt. That weighs three hundred and fifty pounds. And he picked it up and threw it in the sleigh, so that shows you how strong he was. But on the way home the sleigh upset, and the barrel of salt and the sleigh was on top of him in a snow bank. It was a real cold night. These two dogs came to my grandfather's place and woke my grandfather up. My grandfather got my father up, and he said there was something the matter with Archie or the dogs wouldn't have come. So they went back and found him and that's where he was."

Mrs Marjorie Stewart:

"My grandmother Cameron . . . she didn't like rabbits. She always said anybody who had rabbits, tame rabbits, you know, always had bad luck."

Alex Lamont:

"She used to tell a story and this is a true story too. There was a little girl was drowned in a crick [creek] down from their place a piece, maybe a few miles away. And they hunted along. The ice was on the crick and they couldn't find her; they broke the ice and broke the ice and they couldn't find her. And one night my grandmother dreamt where she'd come up in a hole in the ice where some people was watering cattle, and this was about, oh, it would be

ten or twelve miles from their place. So my grandfather took the horse and cutter and he went and drove down to this place and he told them. And they went back and they found this little girl right where she'd seen her. And that's a true story. . . . But they believed in, oh, they believed in so many signs and everything. . . . And a lot of them were true. They'd come true, you know."

In the early days Gaelic was the language of all the Tiree households and communities in Ontario. Some of the emigrants of the mid-nineteenth century were able to read and write Gaelic as well, possibly as a result of the existence of Gaelic charity schools in the island in pre-emigration times. But there were also settlers who did not speak Gaelic, many of them from elsewhere in Scotland, in the districts in which the Tiree people made their homes, and a sense of neighbourliness transcended linguistic boundaries.

Miss Mame Bell:

"On the ninth of Kincardine this lady came and she couldn't talk Gaelic. . . . She was living on a farm and this other woman was over here. And they used to go out and bind, you know. The men would cradle the crop and they'd bind it, and about four o'clock they always made afternoon tea. So she went home to make the tea and she brought it to the field to the men. And she brought this little extra jug and she said, 'I'm going over with Mrs Robinson.' 'Ach,' they said, 'you can't. She doesn't know what you're talking about.' 'Well, I'm going over anyhow,' she said. So she did, and they had their tea together. She said again, 'You know, it's surprising what a conversation you could keep up with signs and smiles.' Was too. They were friends ever after."

As long as the emigrants of the mid-century, and their children, were alive, Gaelic was heard regularly. But by the time of the First World War the language was in decline. Nevertheless, individual words and phrases such as greetings and farewells continued to be known and used, and people continued to be identified, if in translation, in the traditional manner, by patronymics, nicknames or by-names.

Mrs Jean Schroeder:

"So many people had the same name, especially the same Christian name, that they had to distinguish them some way. So they'd call them 'Red this' and 'Black Dan' and 'Big Laughie' and so on. Or maybe they would say his father's name and then his, you see. It'd be like 'Laughie's Dan' or that way."

Neil Aldcorn:

"Oh, everybody had a nickname . . . Long John and Black Archie, White Archie, Squealin' Archie. Oh, hundreds. Big Dan and Long Dan."

*Tiree men of the Tenth Concession of Kincardine Township.*

Miss Mame Bell:

"They had to nickname them because they were all the same names — so many in the same family with the same name. They didn't nickname them to be mean. No, it was just to show who they belonged to."

The bonds of kinship and neighbourhood manifested themselves throughout the seasons in the Tiree communities of Ontario, and throughout the cycle of life. When a death took place, the whole community mourned and supported the bereaved with their presence.

Alex Lamont:

"Oh, you'd see a funeral procession a mile long. The whole section, like that McIntyres' Corners, the settlement, they'd all go to the funeral. Quit everything, never think of working, head for the funeral. They mostly would go to that house, like the night before they'd have a wake, they called it a wake. And the house would be full of neighbours. I don't know how they'd all get in but there'd be, oh, an awful gang around. I've heard them talking about them. No matter what happened, they'd have something to drink. A keg of whisky and a dipper would be sittin' on the kitchen table and they just went and helped themselves. . . . Just sitting around visiting."

In the mid-1870s the rich lands of the Canadian West were opened for settlement, and the government offered homesteads of one hundred and sixty acres free providing certain conditions were met. In each of the first three years a stated number of acres had to be 'broken' or prepared for cultivation, stock acquired and buildings erected. For many in Tiree, where crofters were not to gain security of tenure for another decade and where those without land were to have a longer wait before their claims were recognised, the prospect of farms in Manitoba, the richest agricultural land in the world, was compellingly attractive.

By this time too the farms of Ontario were proving too small to accommodate the new generation in the Tiree settlements formed in the 1850s, and many of these decided to go west as well. It became a common practice for the Tiree emigrants of this period to leave the island once the harvest was in, to spend the winter in Ontario with friends or relations in the Tiree communities there, and to continue west to stake a claim in the following spring, often in the company of descendants of the earlier settlers. The Tiree households of Ontario, particularly those in Bruce County, fulfilled for the emigrants of this period the role which the Brock Township households had fulfilled for them a generation earlier.

Such was the case of John and Charles Maclean, brothers from the township of Balephuil, who left for Canada in 1878, taking with them their nephew Hector. The croft they left is known to this day as 'Manitoba'. John was one of those local poets who earned for Balephuil the nickname *Baile nam bard*, the township of the bards, for most households there could boast at least one member with this talent, and many more than one. The Macleans' decision to emigrate prompted the pre-eminent bard of the neighbouring township of Balemartin, another John Maclean, to compose a song which focused first on his own grief at losing a close friend and bardic companion, and then turned to the causes and impact of emigration in the Highlands as a whole.

[Translation]

> How sad am I here without a single companion
> To raise a chorus, or understand or sing a song
>     with me!
> From the depth of my heart I send a farewell blessing to
>     the lads
> Who sailed on the voyage to Manitoba.
>
> When the morning came when they were to set out for
>     a strange land
> And every friend they had in the place had gathered
>     together,
> I cannot express the sorrow that weighed me down
> As they turned their backs on the township on that
>     Tuesday morning.
>
> The wearers of the kilt and the hose and cocked
>     bonnet,
> Who were always renowned in the forefront of battle,
> Are today being driven abroad to unwholesome
>     countries
> With no other object but to lay waste the land.
>
> I shall say nothing more of the deeds of the brave
>     men
> But only mention Russia and the Heights of Alma;
> It is the weight of the rent that has left the Gaels
>     few in numbers:
> Forgotten are Sebastopol and Balaclava.

Minnedosa main street, before 1905.

After spending the winter in Ontario, the Tiree emigrants of this period would travel west, an arduous journey by boat to the head of the Great Lakes, from there by train through the States to the Red River, along the Red River by flat-bottomed river boat to Winnipeg, and from there by foot or ox-cart to their chosen district of settlement. In 1879, John McLean from Urvaig, Caolas, his wife Christina MacDonald and their children took this route. "They said they wanted to get to the west side of the Little Saskatchewan River, where the soil was good", and they made their way to the Cadurcis district west of the present-day town of Minnedosa over the Portage Plains, which that spring were very wet. The woollen stockings of the children quickly became sodden. "They talked about holding them up on a stick and drying their socks that way."

Mrs Christie Dickie:
"They stopped somewhere along the way and grandmother either baked bread or bannocks or something on the way. They . . . made a little fireplace and she baked something when they were running out of food, I suppose, by the side of the road, well no, it would only be a trail. . . . They got to this Hare's Crossing on the Saturday, and so they camped there over Sunday and went on Monday. They wouldn't be more than two-and-a-half or three miles from where they were going to settle. They wouldn't travel on Sunday."

Among the possessions the family brought with them from Tiree was a spinning wheel.

Mrs Maggie McNabb:
"They brought it from the Old Country with them. I think I heard my mother say my grandmother put it between two feather ticks and that was the way it came here."

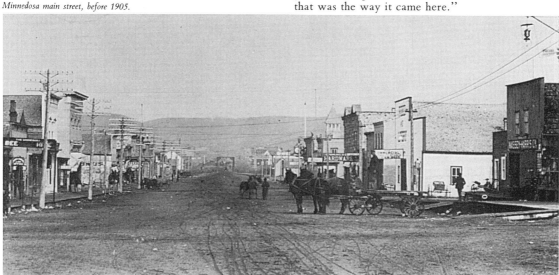

John MacPhail from Kirkapol found his homestead further west still, beyond Shoal Lake in the Vista district.

Alexander MacPhail:

"I understood afterwards that they wanted to be where there was water and wood, because if there was both there would be wild fowl and there'd be wild meat."

This was not the dense forest of Eastern Canada, but stands of light trees such as willows and poplars, often fringing the shallow alkaline sloughs which were such a feature of the Western Canadian landscape.

The land was surveyed in sections of 640 acres, with the homestead unit a quarter section. John MacPhail's homestead was on the south-west quarter of section ten, township nineteen, range twenty-four, west of the First Meridian.

Alexander MacPhail:

"He had to go to Brandon, so he had to walk to Brandon in order to register for this homestead, which he did, and apparently was successful because sometimes some of the men that went, they were a little late, somebody else had filed a claim for the same quarter section. So in that way ours was got."

Some Tiree settlers went to the Brandon Hills, and others to the Wapella-Red Jacket district in what was to become the Province of Saskatchewan.

Mrs Hughena Ellis:

"Well, of course, when they gets out to Canada and see, you see, you could have a hundred and fifty, sixty acres of land. You prove it up, you see, for three years, you have to have so many acres of land, you see, ploughed. Well, you see, the average person would do that, and quite a few would give up, because they thought that was an awful hard deal to do. But it's a very good way to get a start. You might put up a log house, a sod house is what they first were putting up here. Did you ever see a sod house?"

Dan McFadyen:

"They ploughed the sod in the slough and they cut it in squares . . . and you put it on the poles on the roof, and they put it on like shingles, one overlaps the other, and then if that got sand perhaps on it or something to fill in the cracks, then the weeds started to grow on it, you had quite a good roof. That's the way they used to make hen houses and their cow and horse stables. They had three or four horses at the finish, they were pretty good farmers then, and maybe six cows. . . . But they'd build a shack with the sods, you know, put something like shingles up the sides, all around. I don't know what they had for windows in the early days, just had a curtain or something hung over. Well, they'd put a wall of poles and then bank it up all the way up with the sods. Oh, it made quite a

warm building. They'd start ploughin' you see, but they generally got the tougher, at least I remember my Dad taking them out of the slough, a dried slough. And there'd be tough roots of grass in there and they sort of held it together better. We had lumber in it eventually, but most of them early shacks were just earth levelled off good and clean. They'd have bedrooms, but they'd have curtains, mostly curtains, because they hadn't the lumber to put up. They didn't want to put sod in because it took too much room, no, you generally had curtains. But a bachelor shack, he just had a bed in a corner, a bunk of some sort in a corner."

In the hot, dry summers, prairie fires could cause devastation, and though John Maclean in Nova Scotia and the Tiree settlers in Ontario experienced harsh winter cold, its intensity cannot have approached that of the Western Canadian winters, where temperatures might drop to 60 degrees below zero, and where blizzard conditions often prevailed. The vigilance of friends and neighbours in these circumstances could sometimes make the difference between life and death, especially for those who came out initially not with families but on their own as bachelors, 'batching' as John MacPhail did.

Alexander MacPhail:

"Well, he was drawing out logs for an addition to the stable. And apparently he thought the ice was all right over this slough, lots of snow then, and he went through and got his feet wet. Well, by the time he got home — it was only a mile or a little better from where he got wet 'til he got home — it was quite a problem, and I guess the fire was out, the house was cold, and I don't know what he might have suffered in the meantime. But anyway, he was supposed to go some place that night and didn't, and the neighbour came to see what was wrong. I guess they did in those days. If you said you'd go, you went. So he came over to where he was and sure enough, he could not get out, and he was taken down to a Dan McKinnon's at Culross, and Dan McKinnon and his wife, they looked after him 'til spring, 'til his feet got quite all right. And they did, although they did give him considerable trouble at times. But that was just frozen. . . . I think it was always in those days, I think one looked after the other pretty well, and they were a good distance apart in some cases, you know."

John Maclean, the bard from Balephuil, settled in the Brandon Hills district with Charles and Hector and the wife, Flora, he had married in Ontario the previous winter. There were other Tiree families in the area, including the Lachlan Macleans from Cornaigbeg, with whom they would ceilidh regularly.

Mrs Annie Baker:

"He was a pleasant little man and loved to sing. He always sang a Scottish song, Gaelic song for grandfather before he went home and then they'd toast, they'd drink this little toast to their health."

On his first New Year's Day in Manitoba, January 1st, 1880, John Maclean composed a song to send as a letter describing their early days there to friends and relations in Bruce County, Ontario and in Tiree. The size of the western homesteads, the more dispersed pattern of settlement, and the long winters brought a sense of longing in the Tiree homesteaders for the

fashion. In the early years this might mean long journeys on foot, while later, sleighs came into use in winter weather and 'democrats', light, two-horse spring wagons, when the roads were clear. The Tiree homesteaders were noted for their skill with horses, and one of them, Dougall McKinnon, even did his courting driving a team of young, trained moose!

Dougall McKinnon and team of moose.

congenial companionship known at home and in the Tiree communities of Ontario. But they kept up their old customs whenever they could, and retained the hope that the land would be fruitful and that more Tiree people would join them.

[Translation]

*Wandering I am now in this new place,*
*Which has never been cultivated, or had crops taken*
*from its soil;*
*But what is really causing me to be low in spirits*
*Is that I won't see my people on New Year's Day.*

*Last year in Ontario things were fine for us—*
*Our friends and fellow countrymen were nearby;*
*But now we are wandering in an uncongenial land,*
*Out of reach of loved-ones and friends.*

*It is seldom one sees the like of this land of ours,*
*Without a stick or a stone to hinder the plough;*
*As long as we, as Tiree people, stay here,*
*We'll call the place "Maclean's Hillock".*

*Although at the moment we're far from our friends,*
*If they live the rest will come of their own accord;*
*And when we get the place cultivated and in use,*
*We won't dwell on the days we've left behind us.*

Whenever possible, the Tiree families in Manitoba tried to overcome the distances and visit in the old

Mrs Marion MacCormick:
"But it was the isolation, I think, and so far away from their own people, although there were people from Iona and people from Tiree in the area and they certainly kept very much in touch with each other. The only means of conveyance of course were horses and democrat, but they did visit back and forth and there was a friendship that existed all through there, and if anyone was ill they just, you know, they were right there to do whatever they could."

Alexander MacPhail:
"I remember going places with the team and sleigh and the box. And you put straw in the box and put blankets in and everybody got into the sleigh, and you went to wherever you were going. There was no telephone to let them know you were coming; you went."

Mrs Marion MacCormick:
"It seemed to me they just enjoyed visiting and talking about news they got from Scotland, or discussing politics, or discussing just current events. . . . I can always remember these occasions, even as a child, being such a happy time. We were always, we were happy when people came because our parents were happy to see people coming. And then of course we visited at their homes too. . . . My father was very good at telling ghost stories, and we just would love to hear them. But it seemed to

*Mrs John McLean (Christina MacDonald), Cadurcis District, Manitoba.*

me that the ghost stories would be told often when we had company and in the evening and I think my mother was concerned in case we would have bad dreams. . . . Oh, when people came in they discussed happenings, things that happened years before on the islands. They just, they loved to exchange views and exchange stories. That seemed to be something that they really enjoyed."

John Maclean of Balephuil was by no means the only Tiree bard in Western Canada. Donald MacDougall, another gifted bard from the same township, composed Gaelic songs about events in the Red Jacket district, and the song of a MacKinnon bard in praise of the Massey-Harris reaper was enjoyed and quoted for many years. While increasing mechanisation altered the types of occasion on which communal labour might be required, it continued to be a feature of life for the Tiree people in the West. They depended on each other, and enjoyed each other's company for visiting, dancing, music and song.

Mrs Maggie McNabb:
"They thought nothing of driving a few miles to visit. Well, I guess that was their only entertainment. They'd have a dance or something, you know. They were good dancers, a lot of them. In their houses, in their homes. They'd clear out a room and have a great time. Scotch music, mostly. Fiddles, violin. Yes. Well, I guess they used to use

the mouth organ a lot too. Uncle Hector would play the fiddle, he played the fiddle a lot. He used to play for dances."

Alexander MacPhail:
"New Year's was the holiday. Christmas was the religious holiday, and it was generally very quiet — some of the friends in. But New Year's, you enjoyed New Year's, went out, visited your neighbours. And usually there was always a dance, and the old year out and the new year in."

The possibility of regular communication with Tiree, of corresponding with friends and relations and of receiving news of the island, was much greater for the Tiree settlers in Manitoba than it had been for the emigrants of the earlier period.

Mrs Marion MacCormick:
"If somebody got a letter from Tiree, from their people, they came to tell the news. You had a visit. And it was the same when my people got a letter. The news was relayed. . . . The *Oban Times* was sent, the *Oban Times* had news of the islands you see. And when an *Oban Times* came it was shared with everybody. And it didn't matter even if it was months old, because in those early days when the mail came by ship it was months, certainly weeks old anyway, before they received it."

As time went on, mobility increased as well. Some young men would come out from Tiree not to homestead but to work on the farms or get employment in Manitoba as craftsmen for a period before returning to Tiree permanently, inheriting a croft or settling down in marriage there. But for the most of the settlers there was no opportunity to see Tiree again.

Although many of the experiences of their early years in Canada were ones common to all settlers, of whatever origin, the Tiree people retained certain ways of life which reflected their own particular home community and its oral traditions, its *bardachd*, its beliefs and its religious history. And they passed on to their descendants a sense of identity with that small island in the Hebrides. Some of those descendants have visited Tiree, and have seen for themselves the places their people often talked of and fondly remembered.

Mrs Marion MacCormick:
    "Oh, they were interested in everything that went on 'at home', as they said, although they were many miles away. And I must say that the first time I went to Tiree I felt, I stood on the pier there and looked out at the *Claymore* coming in, and I thought of the day — there was no pier there when my father left and I know he must have gone out in a little boat to get on the vessel — and I thought to myself, I wonder if he ever thought he would see the shores of Tiree again? They knew they couldn't go back, they didn't have the money to go back, but the island was, that was a special spot."

MARGARET A. MACKAY

*The historical background to land raids in Knoydart and elsewhere – a ruined croft, and once cultivated land gone back to scrub in the depopulated Highlands.*

# The Seven Men Of Knoydart

In the autumn of 1948 the last land-raid in the Highlands of Scotland took place. It was a small event by earlier standards, and yet it has been remembered better than many of the great raids of the late nineteenth and early twentieth centuries. The tactic of land-raiding had been pioneered in the 1880s, in the course of the anti-landlord mass-movement of crofters, organised around the Highland Land League. Land-raiding simply involved the crofters of a locality in trespassing upon the arable or grazing land of their landlord, and then refusing to move while they commenced or continued cultivation of that land. In that decade the people of the Highlands had gone on the offensive against landlordism with remarkable unanimity and had made widespread use of the tactics of rent-strike and land-seizure, forcing from the government of the day a Royal Commission to enquire into their grievances and conditions. The commission's report did not contradict the complaints of the movement, and it continued on the offensive, winning in 1886 the great victory of the Crofters' Act. Throughout the agitation, direct and often illegal action had been a characteristic tactic of the movement — and that continued as a feature of land-agitation in the Highlands right up to the 1920s, by which time the authorities had conceded further half-hearted legislation in the form of the 1911 Small Landholders' Act and the 1919 Land Settlement Act.

The 1948 raid took place on the peninsula of Knoydart in western Inverness-shire, a wild and mountainous land, roadless and remote, bound on one side by the eastern hills and on the other three by the Sound of Sleat and the lochs of Hourn and Nevis. In 1948, much of Knoydart was a wilderness; and yet, until the 1850s, Knoydart had been a populous district, untouched till then by the shadow of the Highland Clearances. By the middle of that century the worst period of overt and forcible Clearing had passed — but in 1853, without warning, the pursuit of landlord wealth was to have disastrous consequences for Knoydart's native people.

In the previous year Aeneas MacDonnell of Glengarry, sixteenth chief of that name, was buried beside his father at Kilfinnan, and the administration of the estate of Knoydart passed to his widow and his young son's trustees. With his estate, the young chieftain had inherited a mountain of debt — and as usual, the tenants were to be made to pay for it. Due to the potato famine of the late 'forties, most of the people were in arrears with rent and though the total amounted to a tiny sum, this was as convenient an excuse as any to evict them, and sell the estate as a sheep-farm. The people heard of the plan, and in early 1853 petitioned the landlord, for the second time, that they be allowed to remain on their native soil. But by then negotiations were well advanced for their removal and that summer the government transport *Sillery* came to Isleornsay to take the people away. Over 300 of them went peaceably, across the sound in the *Sillery*'s boats and off to the colonies, while their houses were destroyed behind them.

Some, however, refused to go and in the autumn they were forcibly evicted, and their houses torn down. An eye-witness wrote later:

"From house to house, from hut to hut, and from barn to barn, the factor and his menials proceeded carrying on the work of demolition, until there was scarcely a human habitation left standing in the district . . . while all this work of demolition and destruction was going on, no opposition was offered by the inhabitants, no hand was lifted, no stone cast, no angry word was spoken. . . . The Strath was dotted all over with black spots showing where yesterday stood the habitations of men. The scarred, half-burned wood — couples, rafters, and cabars — were strewn about in every direction. Stocks of corn and plots of unlifted potatoes could be seen on every side, but man was gone. No voice could be heard. Those who refused to go aboard the *Sillery* were in hiding among the rocks and the caves. . . . When I looked in upon these creatures last week I found them in utter consternation, having just learned that the officers would appear next day, and would again destroy the huts. The children looked at me as if I had been a wolf; they crept behind their father, and stared wildly, dreading I was a law officer. . . . These are facts as to which I challenge contradiction. I have not inserted them without the most satisfactory evidence of their accuracy."

By 1855 there were still some people existing in such circumstances in Knoydart; but two years later, when the estate was sold to a southern coal-king, almost all of it was under sheep, and only a dozen impoverished 'clansmen' and their families starved on the shores of the Sound of Sleat.

By the early 1930s Knoydart and its small population was in the hands of the Bowlby family, during whose ownership Knoydart became known as one of the best salmon-fishing and deer-stalking estates in Scotland. The Bowlby's reign in Knoydart was a benevolent one, remembered with affection by those who knew it. Duncan MacPhail, one of the land-raiders in 1948, recalls:

"Oh, it was marvellous, it was great, it was a wonderful place, Knoydart, in those days. It was a very happy community, you know — we had a really good time. I must say, it was a lovely place Knoydart in my young days."

Annie MacDonald, sister of another of the 1948 land-raiders, remembers how the people welcomed the annual visit of the Bowlbys, and their yacht, the *Vanessa:*

"They were there for the shooting-season, and then they went away in October. And then the ghillies' Ball came on, and that was something to look forward to. It started early, about nine o'clock, and kept on till daybreak, because the musicians came over the hill, they came from Li and Inverguseran. They were good musicians too; the Inverguseran boys, Jimmy and Roddy, one played the violin and one played the melodeon. And the Li boys, they came right over, they walked miles right over the hill. Oh, they were good musicians too, there were three of them and they used to come."

But things changed in the 1930s, when Knoydart suddenly passed into the tenancy, and soon ownership, of a southern millionaire brewer and landowner, one Arthur Ronald Nall Nall-Cain, Lord Brocket. His was not an old title; but Lord Brocket, just 30 years of age in 1934, conducted himself as if it dated back to

*Lord Brocket, 'a particularly convinced pro-Nazi', shakes hands with Hitler at the 1938 Nazi Party rally at Nuremberg.*

antiquity. His credentials for ownership of a Highland estate were impeccable — he had attended Eton, played golf for Oxford University, and spent some years as a barrister and Conservative Member of Parliament. Apart from his brewing interests, and Knoydart, he also owned land and properties in Hertfordshire, Hampshire, and Maynooth, near Dublin. His political interests extended beyond the Conservative Party; he was closely connected with the Anglo-German Fellowship, "a loose association of Conservative and other well-wishers of Hitler", and by 1939 was vice-president of the Fellowship. It was highly approved of by the Nazi leadership in Germany —leading guests of the Fellowship, and of its individual members, included the S.S. Adjutant to Himmler, and Herr von Ribbentrop.

Lord Brocket was especially welcome in Nazi Germany.

*The Times*, London, 12th September 1938
"The Parteitag is drawing to a close in an atmosphere of indescribable tension. Herr Hitler today was speaking to 120,000 of his Storm Troopers and S.S. men, paraded before him. Sir Neville Henderson, the British Ambassador, remained here until this evening. He attended the parade of the Youth Movement yesterday morning, and in the evening was the guest of Herr Himmler,

Reich Leader of the S.S., at supper in the S.S. camp on the outskirts of Nuremberg, at which Herr Hitler had a friendly conversation over the tea-table with some of his English guests of honour. Those at the Fuhrer's table were Lord Stamp, Lord McGowan, and Lord Brocket.

*The Times*, London, 16th February 1939
"Sir Neville Henderson spoke on Anglo-German relations at the annual dinner of the Deutsch-Englische Gesellschaft in Berlin tonight. Lord Brocket, from the Anglo-German Fellowship in London, also spoke."

*Glasgow Herald,* 20th April 1939
"All Germany is tonight celebrating Herr Hitler's birthday. One important feature of the birthday celebrations is the swearing-in of 10-year-old boys and girls as members of the Hitler Youth. It is believed that with the addition of this year's class, membership will reach 8,500,000. Major-General Fuller, and Lord Brocket, vice-president of the Anglo-German Fellowship, are the private guests of Herr Hitler."

Shortly after becoming owner of Knoydart, Brocket had visiting him there none other than von Ribbentrop, Nazi ambassador to Britain. Some of the people in Knoydart knew of Brocket's apparent admiration of Nazi Germany — on occasions he would tell some of his employees of "the great job Hitler was making of Germany".

When Brocket got Knoydart, high hopes were entertained that he would continue to administer it in the Bowlby tradition. But instead, things began to deteriorate quickly.

Annie MacDonald:
"Oh, he was awfully plausible. He was going to do wonders to the estate and to the people —. but it became a sort of second Clearance during Brocket's time."

Archie MacDougall, another of those involved in the land-raid, remembers:

"When he came to Knoydart at first it appeared that he was going to carry on the work of the man before him — but eventually things began to change, and he seemed .to turn against the people. He had big shooting-parties. He used to come twice a year. He used to come there about Easter. And then they used to go off and come back again in June, and they were there until maybe September or October, and during that time they had plenty of guests. In fact, quite influential people — I can remember Lord Woolton there, and also people like Chamberlain, who was there — the Prime Minister, Neville Chamberlain.
"He started evicting people, especially the older employees here and there, and this went on from time to time, and restrictions put on the movement of people. People weren't allowed near or around Inverie House, where he lived, and such things like that. And this led on that way right up until the war started."

When World War Two came, Duncan MacPhail volunteered for service and joined the Royal Artillery. Knoydart was requisitioned by the government and, as it lay at the centre of the huge wartime restricted zone in which the Commando units and Special Operations Executive trained, was turned over to military use.

Duncan MacPhail:
"Brocket had this bad name you know, being friendly with the Nazis. Of course he was friendly with them; he had some of them visiting in Knoydart before the war; he was very much in favour of a lot of Hitler. He was well-watched during the war. There was always somebody watching him, Brocket; yes, they were keeping tabs on him. He was watched by the Secret Service; there was no doubt about it, he was on the side of the Nazis."

James Dewar, a gardener in Knoydart in the immediate post-war years, adds:

"Brocket was a German sympathiser. Ribbentrop was one of his personal friends. He used to come to Knoydart on holiday. That was a fact, that wasn't folklore. What caused part of the resentment was Lord Brocket maybe being interned during the war."

After the war, with rather less friends in Germany than previously, Lord and Lady Brocket again turned their attentions to the affairs of Knoydart.

Duncan MacPhail:
"Things changed rapidly after the war. You couldn't call him a man you could get to like or anything like that."

John McKie, farm manager in Knoydart after the war, adds:

"Oh, he was Lord Brocket and Lord Brocket only on the estate. Made it very obvious when he was there. Lord Brocket wanted all things just to suit himself, not to suit other people.

James Dewar:
"He was a man, I would say, who looked down on working people. In fact, if there was one of them coming along the road smoking, he would stop them and tell them to put their pipe out, their cigarette out, or something like that. There was a tradesman from Glasgow working in the big house; he came up when Lord Brocket was speaking to someone, and he was smoking his pipe. Brocket

*'All sound and solid Scotsmen'–four of the land-raiders at Knoydart, November 1948.*

stopped him and asked him to put his pipe out — well, *told* him to put his pipe out.''

Soon enough Brocket's intentions for Knoydart became clear.

John McKie:
"He was running it all for his own personal benefit, not for the benefit of the community. The shepherds weren't allowed in the hills to look for sheep when they were shooting stags — maybe just as well in case they got shot too. He didn't like visitors coming about the place — his standard of living was great. Even the piano was painted white, just an idea Lady Brocket had. She wasn't popular with the local people, no, I don't think so. I don't think she was popular anywhere."

Archie MacDougall:
"Even hikers were turned back, mountaineers and such like were all turned back. An order was given by Lady Brocket herself that local children were to keep away from the front of the house, and not walk along the beach in front of it. The idea was to get the native people out of the place."

Duncan MacPhail:
"All he wanted was the deer and, well, people began to realise that he wasn't very interested in them — that it was going to be a question of getting them out, bit by bit. There's no doubt about

it, he wanted to get rid of all the locals, he just wanted it as a big estate for deer-shooting. His idea was to get rid of everybody except the few that would be handy for himself, for this deer-forest. I always thought that, and I always will think it. That was the whole thing, to get rid of the locals."

In June 1947, Father Colin MacPherson, the young parish priest in Knoydart and the estate's resident clergyman, submitted to the appropriate government authority a development plan for Knoydart. A century before, the plan argued, there had been perhaps 1,500 people on Knoydart; now there were just 80, and 12 usable houses were lying empty. The plan proposed a development which would increase estate population to 500 in five years, and provide a welcome increase in domestic production of foodstuffs for hungry and rationed post-war Britain. Brocket blocked the plan; within a year, another 15 families had left Knoydart, and the plan with which Father MacPherson was associated had been forgotten. He explains:

"When the war was over and things returned to normal, it became obvious what the estate's intentions were. This was to further reduce the crofters' holdings and to reduce the number of cattle and sheep on the estate. The obvious outcome of this was that many of those employed on the estate would lose their jobs and therefore their homes. When the native population realised they were losing their work, they began to think of ways or means of staying in their own homes and country. They realised that the only way was to take over land for themselves where they could live in peace and security. They decided to write to the Secretary of State, and since I agreed with them, and disagreed with seeing people leaving their friends and relations, without knowing what was ahead of them, I decided to give them every help I could. A letter was sent to the Secretary of State, stating that they wanted their own crofts in Knoydart. The letter was acknowledged, but very little happened after that. As time went on it became obvious that letters were of no effect."

At this point, in the summer of 1948, some of the people of Knoydart conceived the idea of resorting to the tactic pioneered in the days of the Highland Land League, and staging a land-raid.

Duncan MacPhail:
"We put our heads together and thought, well, all this lovely ground and everything going off, he was keeping on putting off all the stock — it was obvious he was interested in one thing, and that was the deer. We thought, why not have a crack at getting some of the land? I was very keen — after all, I had served six years and four months in the

*Father MacPherson and land-raiders discuss the interdicts from the Court of Session.*

war, and most of that abroad, and I thought it was dash hard lines that after all these years fighting, if you weren't going to get something out of it for yourself. Probably we all had the idea at the back of our minds that we were going to be put out — and we thought, well, we're entitled to a bit of our own land. So one thing led to another, and that was really the beginning of what started the land-raid."

And so, on Tuesday, November 9th, 1948, the Knoydart land-raid began. The raiders' spokesman was Father MacPherson, who was just old enough to remember hearing about the last of the great land-raids in his native Hebrides; and the six — and later seven — raiders were all men that John McKie, who had by then left Knoydart, describes as "very sound, solid, good Scotsmen. Well-seasoned Scotsmen." The following week was a busy one in Knoydart. On the 9th, each man staked out 65 acres of arable land, and preparations were in hand to also raid the hill-grazing land. Brocket was in Knoydart that same week; and the next day he petitioned the Court of Session for interim interdict against the raiders. The petition claimed:

"On or about 8th November 1948 the Respondents entered upon cultivated parts of the said farms of Kilchoan and Scottas to which they

*Land-raiders clear a site above Inverie village.*

have no right title or interest whatsoever and staked out claims to small-holdings thereon. Each claim was pegged out and contained a post bearing the name of the person who alleged that he was the owner of that particular small-holding. As the action of the Respondents in staking their claims was well-organised, carried out in concert, and with the Press having been duly informed beforehand, the Petitioner believes that for some unknown reason some of the local people object to the Petitioner's ownership of the estate of Knoydart and that further action may be taken."

Interim interdict was granted that same day by an obliging Lord Strachan; at that very moment the raiders were clearing the land they had seized and getting it ready for cultivation. Brocket left Knoydart that day too, but though he passed the raiders on his way to the boat, he pretended not to see them. An hour later, once clear away from Knoydart, he told enquiring Pressmen that, "Knoydart is not suitable for many people, as there is too much rain there." On the following Thursday, "in the tiny post-office telegrams pledging support flowed in from all over Scotland". The following day, however, the interim interdicts arrived from Edinburgh. The raiders had already decided to engage a lawyer, and after discussion, it was agreed to temporarily recognise the order of the court. The following week there were further expressions of support from many quarters in Scotland; on the Monday the Chief Constable of Inverness-shire wrote in secret to the Secretary of State:

*Intelligence Report:*
*Land-raiding in Knoydart*
The raid appears to have been well-planned, press reporters and photographers from far afield being on the spot in advance. It is understood that for some years, the raiders have been agitating with the Department of Agriculture for occupation of land. The parish priest, Father Colin MacPherson, is playing a leading part in the effort of the raiders to draw public attention to their desire to obtain occupation of land. It is believed that the raiders will persist in the raiding.

At the end of that week, Father MacPherson addressed a meeting in Glasgow in support of the raid, where he spoke on "the past 150 years of Knoydart, depopulation there, and the need for re-populating the Highlands". But by then the dispute was in the care of lawyers and career politicians, and Brocket was masterminding a vicious campaign against the raid. Later, he would claim to the Court of Session that Father MacPherson had "induced and persuaded" the raiders "to take the action they have taken and has persuaded them to trespass upon the said lands, and has since his appointment to Knoydart consistently worked against Lord Brocket". Others observed at the time that, very clearly, anyone working against Brocket was working for the interests of Knoydart and its native people, and the interests of the Highlands as a whole. Meanwhile, the government prevaricated, setting up a Court of Enquiry under an "independent expert". A public meeting was held to hear evidence; everyone concerned came, except Brocket, who despatched his lawyer to say that he was not feeling well. The Secretary of State announced that he had visited Knoydart; in fact, he had simply sailed up Loch Nevis on a government ship, inspected the estate through a pair of government binoculars, and then sailed away again, without having set foot ashore. The "independent expert" reported that winter — against the raiders. They appealed to the Secretary of State — Arthur Woodburn rejected their appeal. The depopulation of Knoydart went on. The land-raid had drawn great publicity to the question of Highland land-use and the problem of Highland landlordism; otherwise, it did not achieve anything concrete. But Brocket was beaten too, in spirit if not formally — within a short time, he sold out and returned to his English estates, and his going was not regretted in the Highlands.

Once in the hands of lawyers and politicians, the raid was doomed.

Duncan MacPhail:

"Well, I was in favour of sticking on the land, you know, sticking on, like in the olden days they did, but this lawyer got round and he said that in these modern times these things wouldn't need to take place, to do it in the legal way, you know, and that it would work out pretty good. But I'm afraid that was our downfall — we would have been far better to have done what the old boys in the olden days did, stick on the ground till they put you to gaol. We all thought it was a very good idea, that it was going to be legal — but afterwards when we saw the whole thing, and you look back on it, you realised it didn't pay to be doing it the modern way. Oh yes, it would have worked — if we had got the ground I'm sure we would have made a go of it. Anything was better than the way it was. It was getting less and less used, Knoydart — plenty ground in Knoydart and good ground, but all that Lord Brocket was interested in was the deer. That's all he lived for, to come up and shoot the deer, and I always said, to get rid of the locals."

And so ended the last land-raid in the Highlands. As a publicity gesture, it was magnificent. As a land-raid, however, the Knoydart raid was a defeat. But it will be remembered, and remembered in the spirit in which it was intended. And Lord Brocket too will be remembered, though not, perhaps, in the spirit which he himself would have wished.

IAIN FRASER GRIGOR

## BALLAD OF THE MEN OF KNOYDART

By Hamish Henderson                    Tune: 'Johnston's Motor Car'

'Twas down by the farm of Scottas,
Lord Brocket walked one day,
And he saw a sight that worried him
Far more than he could say,
For the 'Seven Men of Knoydart'
Were doing what they'd planned–
They had staked their claims and were digging their drains,
On Brocket's Private Land.

'You bloody Reds,' Lord Brocket yelled,
'Wot's this you're doing 'ere?
It doesn't pay as you'll find today,
To insult an English peer.
You're only Scottish half-wits,
But I'll make you understand.
You Highland swine, these Hills are mine!
This is all Lord Brocket's Land.

'I'll write to Arthur Woodburn, boys,
And they will let you know,
That the Sacred Rights of Property
Will never be laid low.
With your stakes and tapes, I'll make you traipse
From Knoydart to the Rand;
You can dig for gold till you're stiff and cold–
But not on this 'ere Land.''

Then up spoke the Men of Knoydart:
'Away and shut your trap,
For threats from a Saxon brewer's boy,
We just won't give a rap.
O we are all ex-servicemen,
We fought against the Hun,
We can tell our enemies by now;
And Brocket, you are one!'

When he heard these words that noble peer
Turned purple in the face.
He said, 'These Scottish savages
Are Britain's black disgrace.
It may be true that I've let some few
Thousand acres go to pot,
But each one I'd give to a London spiv,
Before any Goddam Scot!

'You're a crowd of Tartan Bolshies!
But I'll soon have you licked.
I'll write to the Court of Session,
For an Interim Interdict.
I'll write to my London lawyers,
And they will understand.'
'Och to Hell with your London lawyers,
We want our Highland land.'

When Brocket heard these fightin' words,
He fell down in a swoon,
But they splashed his jowl with uisge,
And he woke up mighty soon,
And he moaned, 'These Dukes of Sutherland
Were right about the Scot.
If I had my way I'd start today,
And clear the whole dam lot!'

Then up spoke the Men of Knoydart:
'You have no earthly right,
For this is the land of Scotland,
And not the Isle of Wight.
When Scotland's proud Fianna,
With ten thousand lads is manned,
We will show the world that Highlanders
Have a right to Scottish Land.'

'You may scream and yell, Lord Brocket–
You may rave and stamp and shout,
But the lamp we've lit in Knoydart
Will never now go out.
For Scotland's on the march, my boys–
We'll think it won't be long,
Roll on the day when The Knoydart Way
Is Scotland's battle song.'

*Alex Small and Bob Grieve on Douglas Boulder.*

# Mountain Men

Before the 1930s mountaineering was the sport of a minority of middle-class intellectuals — usually Oxford or Cambridge dons who had long vacations and no financial worries. From around 1880-1890, it became the custom for these men to pioneer routes in the Alps and in Britain and write about their experiences. Mountaineering was a gentleman's sport and after a hard day's climbing their nights were spent in comfortable hotels or inns with a good dinner to end the day. In the 1930s in Britain a very different kind of mountaineer emerged, men from the industrial cities such as Glasgow. They were men from working-class backgrounds who worked in the shipyards, in shops or as apprentices, but all had in common the uncertainty of unemployment and the bleak prospect of being young in a large industrial city at a time of dole queues and recession. For many of them getting out of the city was the great escape.

Alistair Borthwick:

"You have to understand what Scotland was like in those days. It was a grim place. There were a million people in Britain out of work and more, was it two million? People were on the dole, there

*Nearly two million people were out of work.*

was absolutely no hope at all. It really was grim and you were a youngster in this and you accepted this, you had been brought up to this, this was normal, this grimness, then suddenly to find this escape route, this climbing thing and it absolutely bowled you over. Here was an entirely different world where it was alive and things were happening. And the people in it were all young and full of enthusiasm and so on. And the escape from the city at the weekend, it's something that I don't think any youngster today could possibly believe. I mean, today they go off and they hitch-hike to Istanbul and nobody thinks anything of it, but in those days, the idea of simply getting out of the city, even as far away as Glencoe, people just didn't understand it, they didn't realise that this could be done. It was an explosion, it was a wonderful thing."

Bob Grieve:

"I lived near the centre of the great industrial city and it was a kind of escape from that. It wasn't really a very pleasant environment I lived in, it was all right when one was a child and could play marvellous games, but later on as you moved into adolescence, there were other things that you

*Glencoe, a favourite rock climbing area.*

required and couldn't really get in the stone jungle. But the escape was a necessity and even to this day at my age, nearly seventy, I still walk on the hills and I still get from them what I got then. And what is it that I get? A kind of lowering of the temperature; a falling away of neurosis; an ability to think about problems more easily with a saner view possibly at the end; health; and peace. Yes, all these things and of course I would never have seen the splendour of sunsets from the tops of mountains or dawn across Loch Lomond from one of the upper islands, if I hadn't done that — and what then would I have missed?"

In Glasgow they were lucky to have some very fine countryside nearby, Loch Lomond, the Arrochar hills and a little further on, Glencoe, but they were limited.

Bob Grieve:
"We used to describe it this way. We had slept in every barn or bothy and climbed every mountain within 2/6 of Glasgow, that was the kind of expression we used, in other words, as far as we could afford to travel. And that meant, Ben Vane, the Cobbler, Ben Lomond, Ben Vorlich, all the mountains round the top of Loch Lomond, that kind of thing. A lot of them, there were many . . . but of course there were limitations, money was the limitation and time."

It was a new idea for people like this to walk and climb in the hills, so how did they start at all? In the 1920s hiking and cycling had become popular amongst ordinary city people. Out of every city, including Glasgow, people would walk out in large sociable groups, often dressed in funny hats. They walked on roads or on paths but they rarely went off the beaten track. These groups formed themselves into clubs and it is out of this tradition that the climbers emerged. To begin with most of the men who became climbers started on their own.

Alex Small:
"The thing to remember about me is that I had polio and therefore couldn't take part in team games and I was distinguished through most of my youth by the fact that I wore bandages on both my left and my right knees as I was constantly falling. But about the age of fifteen or thereabout I found that I could walk reasonably well, reasonably far. And then I found this book by T. C. F. Brotchie of the walks that you could do from the tram terminii round about Glasgow. And having done a whole lot of these, in due course I found myself out on the Campsies, and there to my astonishment, one weekend, I saw three gentlemen tied together with a rope climbing a piece of rock. And one said, 'Would you like to come on the rope?' And I said, 'Sure.' And he said, 'I'm Andy Saunders.' And of course he was later the founder of Craig Dhu."

*One way of getting to the hills.*

The Craig Dhu was one of the first mountaineering clubs to be formed in the early 1930s. They still exist, always maintaining the reputation for hard climbing and rough living. But you did not have to belong to a club to become a climber. At that time most people just bumped into each other and the clubs were formed later.

Tom Weir:

"For me, I think it was because I lived in Springburn that took me to the hills because in those early days, Springburn had space, good countryside. That's swallowed up in housing schemes and high-rise flats now, but from where I lived in Springburn you could see Ben Lomond, Ben Lui, you could see the Arran hills. And of course although I didn't really think of them all that much, but because I had always had a tremendous love of the snow, what I'd noticed was that when everything was green around us, out there, the snow was on the hills. And that's what really took me to them because I loved the snow and the bus to Campsie Glen passed our door, 6d half fare, and for me that was a great discovery because up on the tops of the Campsies there were other ranges of hills and these were my Himalayas. Beyond Ben Lomond the great ranges.

"How did you get to them? I didn't know anybody who was a climber but what I did know was that out there, there was adventure for the easy asking and I won it when I bought my first bike. 2/6d. Somebody had bought a new bike, I put my leg over this one and said, 'How much do you want for it?' 'Half a dollar.' 'Right!' So in the evenings I could be away in the crags. Nobody had taught me anything about the hills but I saw the cliffs above Lennoxton and I'd read books like *First Steps to Climbing*, so I made routes up these cliffs.

"Little did I know in fact that I was dicing with death because that's some of the rottenest rock

in Scotland. And years later when I reckoned I was a pretty good rock climber, I was shocked to see what I'd been climbing on."

Tom Weir also describes how as a young boy he walked out of Glasgow 'up the pipe track'. The pipe track was the route of the Corporation water pipe, running to Glasgow from Loch Katrine and along it were built several wee bothies from the time of its construction. Here the men who Tom Weir called the 'outdoor men' would gather to spend the night.

Methods of getting to the hills were varied, by foot, bicycle, bus, train and other more ingenious methods.

Jock Nimlin:

"Some of us in those bad old days when jobs were hard to find were working in shops and when you were working in a shop you had to work a six-day week until 9.00 p.m. on a Saturday. The lucky people only worked a five-and-a-half-day week, they got off at noon, and they could catch trains and buses going away out into the Highlands.

"But those of us who worked in shops and quite a lot of my friends did, would have to take late trains and late buses to some point in the countryside as close as you could get to the mountains. If you were going to Arrochar, for example, you got as far as Balmaha and Loch Lomond and we had an arrangement with the boat hirer there to leave out a boat and two sets of oars and we would board the boat perhaps eight of us, sometimes ten of us, we sometimes had the boat overloaded and off we would go about midnight from Balmaha and we would row fourteen miles up to Tarbet.

"Then we would pull the boat ashore, snatch a few hours' sleep under trees until daylight and then we'd have a very early breakfast and walk across to Arrochar and from Arrochar we would climb the Cobbler, Ben Ime, Ben Narnain, any of the mountains in that vicinity, and in the early evening, we would make a point of getting back to the boat, back into the loch again and we had that fourteen miles to row, back to Balmaha. Of course we always tried our best to get the last bus at Balmaha but on one or two occasions we were held up by headwinds and we missed the last bus at Balmaha which meant that we had to walk from Balmaha right back into Glasgow again to start work on the following morning. And some of these weekends were super-strenuous, we were absolutely exhausted when we got into work on a Monday morning and I can always remember the manager of the music shop I worked in at this time, he met an acquaintance of mine, he didn't know this man was a friend of mine, and he met him because he had a rucksack on. He spoke to him and he said that he had a youth working in his music shop who went away climbing at weekends and came back so tired that he didn't wake up until Wednesday of the following week, which I think was gross libel because I used to be fully awake by Tuesday!"

For many people, unemployment enabled them to discover more about mountaineering than might normally have been possible.

Bob Grieve:

"I was serving an apprenticeship and when it expired, which was early '32, the Depression was coming to its peak and I was dismissed because the office I was in was only keeping married men — quite rightly so but very tough on me. And therefore I was on the dole for a period. About nine months. And I spent quite a lot of time moving about on hills and I met some curious and interesting people, living on very little. Chaps from the shipyards, engineering shops of Glasgow, not

"We made flapjacks with water and sugar, we had sugar and tea of course, and we had flapjacks and tea. It was very Robert W. Service."

If you were employed, the time for exploring further was during the fortnight's annual holiday. It was only then that they could get as far away as Skye and the Cuillins.

Bob Grieve:

"It is not too much to say that Skye to us was the kind of Himalaya of the mountaineer today. It was as remote, as legendary, as marvellous as the Himalaya."

*Climbing on the Cobbler in winter.*

many but I knew them, I got to know them all and it was during that period that the first democratic or proletarian climbing clubs were formed, like the Craig Dhu, the Lomonds and so on and I met some of them of course. They were very interesting characters, I must say, and I remember for example sleeping on the shores of Loch Lomond one night beside a little fire and a man came up through the gravel of the shore, crunching to the circle of firelight and said, 'Are you alone?' and I said 'Yes'. And he said, 'Well, I've got a wee hut up the burn here' — which he had made for himself — 'Come and spend a night there.' So we slept there that night and between us we had a bag of flour, I think that's all we had.

Jock Nimlin:

"We had never been in that part of the country before and I can always remember I had one friend with me, Bill Duggan, and we both had new boots, they were great big climbing boots with heavy iron nails, we called them clinkers, all round the edge, we didn't have the rubber-soled boots of today, but they were ideal for climbing.

"And we spent a lot of our time rock climbing in the Cuillins. We were travelling light as usual, we didn't have a tent, but we landed at Sligachan and at Sligachan then as today there was only one hotel set among the hills with moors all around. And we had to find some kind of shelter because this was going to be our base for more than a week.

"Well, we found a pile of builder's rubble lying quite close to the hotel and we found two wooden trestles and we carried them across the moor to a little peat shed. It was locked, the peat shed, and we put the trestles against the side of the peat shed and then we collected some planks and we laid them across the entrance and we slept on the ground but we had a pile of heather underneath us and we stayed there I think for about eight days, sleeping under what appeared to be a pile of rubble."

Sligachan Hotel in Skye was one of the hotels in which the earlier climbers had lived. Many of the Glasgow climbers remember seeing a very old Dr Norman Collie who lived out his latter years there within sight of the Cuillins. They had read his books but they didn't dare speak to him. There was even a peak in the Cuillins named after him, *Sgurr a' Tharmaid*, Norman's Peak. One wonders what this academic old man would have thought of this new generation of climbers, who lived in caves or barns when they were available, slept under trees or wrapped themselves in newspapers. One of the best known caves was Bruce's Cave near Arrochar.

Alistair Borthwick:
"The first time I realised the wonderful kind of society that I had landed in was one weekend early on, we went up to investigate Bruce's Cave in Glen Loin, that's just above Arrochar. And the advice I'd been given was to go beyond the hostel and there were various other instructions about where to turn off.

"And after that I was told to wait until I smelt kippers, and then to follow my nose and we did this, and we came to a place where a cliff had collapsed and there was a great jumble of boulders and sure enough half way through this, I smelt kippers and I followed my nose and there was a hole in the ground and I dropped through this hole, about six feet down onto the floor. This took me under the boulder which was the size of a church and there was a great room inside, speaking from memory perhaps twenty yards one way by a roof maybe fifteen feet high. There were a dozen chaps in, sitting around in among the rocks and there was a fire going with kippers. And in all stages of dress and undress, we sat that night and discussed anything from football to philosophy.

"And every ten minutes or so somebody else would drop in through the door because you see they were all hitch-hiking and some had got a lift early in the day and some hadn't managed to get one and they were still coming through the door at midnight."

The cave was a very sociable place where everyone was made welcome. Many a night large companies gathered and sing-songs started. The songs they sang were all hill-billy songs like 'The Brave Engineer', the kind of songs that described the great open spaces of America, pioneering, the gold rush and adventure. They identified themselves with these songs and the

poetry of Robert W. Service whose tales were of the hard men. Amongst all of these Glasgow men was a desire to live like a hard man or a tramp.

### THE BRAVE ENGINEER

*'Twas a cold winter's night
Not a star was in sight,
And the north wind came howling down the line;
With his sweetheart so near,
Stood a brave engineer,
With his orders to take out Number 9.
He kissed her goodbye with a tear in his eye,
'Though the joy in his heart he could not hide;
And the whole world looked bright for she'd promised that night,
That tomorrow she'd be his blushing bride.*

*Now the wheels hummed a song,
As the train rolled along,
And the black smoke came pouring from the stack;
And the headlights agleam,
Seemed to brighten his dream,
Of tomorrow when he'd be going back.
He sped round the hill and his brave heart stood still,
For a headlight was shining in his face;
And he murmured a prayer as he threw on the air,
For he knew it would be his fatal race.*

*In the wreck he was found,
Lying there on the ground,
And he asked them to raise his weary head;
As his breath slowly went,
This message he sent,
To the maiden who thought she would be wed.
'There's a little white home that I built for our own,
Where I dreamt we'd be happy by and by,
And I leave it to you for I know you'll be true,
Till we meet at the golden gates, goodbye.'*

Jock Nimlin:
"We stayed in some of the most enchanting places you can imagine. We stayed in what we called 'howffs'. It could be an old Scottish word, but I'll tell you how we came to use this word: a group of us in the late '20s were sleeping under an overhang on Loch Achray. It was a sort of cave which had been formed perhaps thousands of years earlier when the loch had a higher level and during the 1926 strike, miners fed up with no work had gone out into the countryside to fish and possibly to do a bit of scrounging of potatoes and turnips from the fields. But anyhow, you used to meet quite a lot of miners at that time in the countryside and they had improved this overhung section of the bank and they had put in one or two wooden shores they had collected from the driftwood of the loch and we were all sitting here one night with a fire going and a bit of smoke coming out when an old tramp wandered in.

"And the tramp told us he wasn't staying the night, he was going to a meeting of tramps in a barn a few miles further along the road but he asked if he could boil his can on our fire and of course he did and just before he left, his last words were, 'Ye've a real guid howff here.'

"So we got onto this word 'howff' and we looked up the Oxford Dictionary and we found that it had quite a number of meanings. One being a resort or a haunt; it could be a tavern; it could be a graveyard; in other words, a resting place. So all our resting places were known as howffs and we applied them freely to old bothies in the mountains and sometimes under bridges — some bridges were favourite howffs — you got shelter from the weather to some extent and when I go through the Highlands nowadays with friends, I'm always pointing out the howffs I've slept in and sometimes I'm still able to point out the trees I've slept under.

"I know some of our members joined youth hostels eventually, some of them became more civilised, but some of us kept to this old business of hunting for howffs and we still do."

Living simply and cheaply was a challenge but there was also a challenge in the actual climbing. They had a great pride in their fitness and stamina and their ability to do without equipment.

Hamish Hamilton:
"Ironmongery in these days was frowned upon, you know. If you carried a piton with you, you were regarded as a softie. But now the whole approach has changed and unless you go about bristling with pitons, you're really not supposed to be a man at all. Which I think is a pity, because I think free climbing had much more to offer than the present sort of mechanised approach but then I'm one of the older school and this is understandable."

Alex Small:
"It was quite a triumph for you in the earliest days when you actually got a hemp rope, particularly a hemp rope with a red thread through the middle, that was quite something to get a rope like that, that was really doing things in style.

"It had never occurred to us to use runners or anything similar to that, we merely belayed on what was available within reasonable distance of us. We used to tie onto 120 feet of line and when we were in form, I would climb up until the rope was practically tight, Jim would give me a shout and I would belay on whatever was near it and I would just bring him up. When Agag's Groove was done, there was no slings, nothing, I mean it was just literally free climbing, you had to go on and run out a very, very big distance with no support and you knew if you came off it was going to be quite rough."

Alex Small has described how he often found climbing on an ice face much easier in his stocking soles as they gave a better grip. The heat from the foot melted the ice a little and thereby gave you a greater

*Jock Nimlin on Buttress Pinnacle, Glencoe.*

adherence. But it was not just the ability to climb difficult rock faces that they found a challenge. Battles with the elements were quite common.

Hamish Hamilton:
"We went for a weekend at New Year to the Cairngorms, at this time, of course, Aviemore hadn't been developed, it was just another fairly simple place and the first day we walked across the Lairig Ghru to Carrour Bothy. Carrour Bothy has limited floor space and it was a wild night and twenty-two people turned up and the result of this was that we had to sleep on our sides because if you slept on your back it was undoubtedly an anti-social move.

"The next day we crossed over Ben Macdui and we went down that night to the Shelter Stone. The conditions were pretty rough, very frosty, very cold and the Shelter Stone has quite a limited area so it was quite a tight squeeze with five people but it was really quite a haven in comparison with the conditions outside.

"The following day the weather was even worse and instead of taking a safe route out by the Saddle, we decided just to carry on over Cairngorm down to Aviemore. Unfortunately on top there was a high wind blowing and there was a white-out and spindrift and it was impossible to see anything at all, you literally couldn't see your feet.

"And because of an error of navigation, instead of being on top of Cairngorm as we assumed, it transpired that we were on Cairn Lochan. Now Cairngorm has a summit plateau from which it would be impossible to fall, but Cairn Lochan is quite different because there are steep crags immediately at the cairn and because of the conditions of white-out and because we assumed that we were on Cairngorm, two of us stepped off in the conditions of nil visibility and walked over a cornice.

"Now this was really quite a surprising thing to do and we fell literally hundreds of feet through the air bounding and sliding and bounding and sliding and by great good fortune we landed in deep snow and neither of us was seriously hurt. We were able to walk down to Aviemore and our friends of course looking downwards through the hole in the cornice and seeing us disappearing into nothing, had written us off, and when we joined forces later on it was great rejoicing."

Tom Weir:

"I think one of the most violent storms that ever I was out in occurred at New Year time. New Year's Day was a holiday and we were going to go up in the early morning train to Fort William, it

*Many a night was spent under Shelter Stone in the Cairngorms.*

leaves at ten minutes to six in the morning so Matt walked in from Dennistoun and I walked in from Springburn to catch it. We'd no idea what to expect. You start in the dark, and daylight breaks as you're on your way up Loch Lomond. Oh boy, what a wintry morning this was and when the dawn came I saw the most extraordinary sky I've ever seen in my life, everything had a ghastly green pallor. The snow was right down to the railway train, the two engines were groaning their way up to Bridge of Orchy and when we got off it was a violent wind that met us and no mistake.

"If the train had been there in the siding, I think we would have shrank back into it. Anyway we had come to climb Ben Dorain and away we went. And about half-way up the hill there was a big waterfall coming down a gorge and the smoke, it looked like smoke, but it was the waterfall going straight into the air blown upwards.

"By this time we were nearly going upwards as well, we were down on our tummies at times because we couldn't stand and believe it or not we crawled right to the summit of that peak. Hands and knees stuff. I'll never forget the noise of the wind round that pointed top of Ben Dorain and after a bit we kind of bawled in each other's ears that we'd better crawl.

"Well, we crawled for quite a bit, it was freezing down there and we were getting colder and colder so we got to our feet and a big gust lifted me off my feet and banged me against Matt,

*Jock Nimlin on Birch Wall.*

been dipped in the Orchy and it wasn't till we got back to Glasgow that we discovered that, the facts about that particular day because the Glasgow tramway clock in Bath Street was blown down in gusts of over 120 m.p.h.

"And two young climbers lost their lives on Ben Macdui that day. They just couldn't make it. Well, we didn't know any better, all we can say is that we had the stamina to get up and down but it wasn't a wise thing to do and I don't think, armed with the knowledge I've now got, that I would do it again but that's how you get your experience. You've got to walk the tightrope."

To the non-mountaineer many of these stories may seem acts of sheer madness but to these early climbers the mountains were a release and a challenge. From these early beginnings many of these climbers became well acquainted with the Alps and have even been to the Andes, the Himalayas and Turkey. The Highlands of Scotland could offer a practice ground for many more adventurous expeditions. Also from these beginnings the clubs were formed, the Lomonds, the Ptarmigan and the Craig Dhu, and many of them exist to this day. Many of our great Scottish climbers started off in this tradition. Dougal Haston who reached the highest summit in the world, Mount Everest, started climbing one day in Glencoe wearing a pair of wellingtons with socks over them to prevent him from slipping. The tradition of getting out of the city lives on. I recently met two 14-year-old twins on the

*Old clothes were worn—note the nailed boots.*

the two of us were bowled over and went rolling down for a bit and incidentally we had two flasks of tea in Matt's bag and the collision of me with him meant the flasks were broken. So were our dry clothes soaked.

"Believe it or not, we were still going to climb another peak, Ben Dothaidh, but that was impossible, we could hardly stand even at 1,000 feet above Bridge of Orchy and we were now so wet with this wet blizzard that was blowing down there that we were glad to cram into the navvies' huts because they were building the new Glencoe road at that stage of the mid-thirties, aye, it would be about the mid-thirties.

"And the navvies lent us some clothes and we got them to a stove, got them dried off and got absolutely soaked walking back to Bridge of Orchy to catch the train about six o'clock. It was about an hour's walk to the station and it was as if we'd

Cobbler who were planning to sleep under boulders without a tent near the summit for four or five days, having hitch-hiked there from Glasgow. They told me that they went to the hills like this every weekend and picked up their tips about rock climbing from older climbers.

To all these generations of urban climbers the Scottish Highlands offer adventure and freedom. Jock Nimlin very simply sums up what it meant to him.

Jock Nimlin:
"It did you a lot of good. It was a marvellous tonic to get away from Glasgow, to escape from Glasgow if you like. A friend of mine once implied that the word escape meant fear. Well, I agree with that. I did at that time fear the city. You could have your imagination completely stunted if you lived all your life in a city surrounded by buildings. And the antidote to this situation was to get away at weekends as we did. A wonderful tonic."

*It was a great tonic to get away from Glasgow.*

ISHBEL MacLEAN

*An Auchmithie wedding—the village procession with fiddler.*

## BIRNIE BOUZLE

Gin ye'll mair-ry me, las-sie, At the kirk o' Bir-nie Bou-zle,

Till the day ye dee, las-sie, Ye will ne'er re- pent it.

Ye will wear when ye are wed A kir-tle an' a Hie — land plaid, An'

sleep up- on a hea-ther bed, Sae cou-thy an' sae can- ty

2　Will ye gang wi' me, lassie,
　　Tae the kirk o' Birnie Bouzle,
　　Till the day ye dee lassie,
　　Ye will ne'er repent it.
　　Your wee bit tocher is but sma',
　　But hodden grey will wear for a',
　　I'll save ma siller tae mak' ye braw
　　An' ye will ne'er repent it.

3　Gin ye'll mairry me, lassie
　　At the kirk o' Birnie Bouzle,
　　Till the day ye dee, lassie,
　　Ye will ne'er repent it.
　　We'll hae bonny bairns an' a',
　　Some lassies fair an' laddies braw
　　Just like their mither ane an' a',
　　An' your faither he's consented.

4　Gin ye'll mairry me, lassie,
　　At the kirk o' Birnie Bouzle,
　　Till the day ye dee, lassie,
　　Ye will ne'er repent it.
　　I'll hunt the otter an' the brock,
　　The hart, the hare, an' heather cock.
　　I'll pu' ye limpets frae the rock
　　Tae mak' ye dishes dainty.

# Will Ye Gang Wi' Me Lassie?

The rituals of courtship, betrothal and marriage have always been associated in Scotland with a rich variety of customs and traditions, their origins often lost or forgotten, but with some of their roots seeming to relate to pre-Christian belief. Scots marriage laws have always differed from those of England, and the involvement of the Church in the actual ceremony has not always been essential.

Before the Reformation, a practice known as hand-fasting or hand-in-fist, was generally accepted. Then, a local annual fair was commonly the appointed time for unmarried couples to choose a mate with whom to live until that time next year. If, at the end of a year, the couple were still happy with one another, they remained together for life. If not, they separated and were free to choose another partner. Hand-fasting was deemed a social irregularity by the reformers, but the custom was still in evidence in Eskdale in 1772.

In the eighteenth century also, it was accepted practice that if two people desired to marry, they could do so straight away, without proclamation of banns, blessing of priest, or formal legal registration of the ceremony. This was, of course, at variance with the English law of 1754, and from that time, runaway marriages between young couples became common in the Scottish borders, centred mainly at Gretna where ceremonies were conducted over an anvil, by a self-appointed priest.

In 1854 an Act was passed making legal registration of a marriage compulsory, but young runaway couples still came to Scotland to be wed legally here without the necessity of parental consent.

Most weddings, however, have traditionally begun with a church ceremony of some kind, with celebrations before and after the marriage involving the family and community as a whole. In lowland Scotland in the seventeenth and eighteenth centuries it was customary for everyone intending to be present at a marriage to give a penny Scots to the young couple; these celebrations became known as Penny or Paying weddings, and the festivities often extended over several days.

*'Penny Wedding' by David Allan.*

*Marriage ceremony at Gretna Green Smithy.*

Courtship and betrothal were, until very recently, always dominated by parental and extended family involvement, and since the events of everyone's own wedding day are usually happy, out of the ordinary and something of a milestone in life, the memories and recollections I have recorded are almost always clear vivid and treasured, and involve the natural use of the Scots and Gaelic languages to recall the names of particular ceremonies and customs.

Since wedding traditions vary so widely throughout Scotland, I decided to look mainly at customs in rural Gaelic-speaking and lowland urban areas, although of course Orkney and Shetland have their own highly individual wedding traditions. What has emerged from the recorded memories of people recalling weddings of fifty to sixty years ago, is that the customs of the Western Isles and the Lowlands are obviously linked and go beyond simply the religious solemnizing of the marriage vows. Rites such as the breaking of oatcake or shortbread over the bride's head; blacking of faces and hands of bride and 'groom before the ceremony, and shooting of guns to ward off evil spirits are still in evidence, and are perhaps remnants of pagan belief.

In our recent past, courtship and betrothal were events which the whole community shared and in the Western Isles the *Réiteach*, a formal arranging or 'clearing the way' for a marriage had to be organised before the wedding could take place. It was originally a form of bargaining ceremony, where an older man friend of the 'groom would speak for him to the bride's father, asking indirectly for the girl's hand, often referring to her as a sheep, or boat, or a piece of wood needed to finish the home. (The bride-to-be never entered into the discussion at this point!) Eric Cregeen

of the School of Scottish Studies at Edinburgh University recorded this memory from Donald Sinclair of Tiree.

"A good while ago this wedding was on and it was a man from Islay in Tiree. MacPhee was his name: his daughter was getting — going to get married to a certain Campbell from Mannel. And it was an old poet of a postmaster that came with Campbell to ask the hand of the bride. And when they arrived at the old man's house down at Balemartin, this old poet he turned round and he says, 'Well, I wish you would help me, Mr MacPhee.' 'Well,' says the old man, 'I'll do anything at all I can to help you.' 'Well,' he says, 'I'm putting a roof on a barn and I am short of one bit of wood. I wonder will you supply me with it. There's so many couples of the house, but I'm short of one piece of wood to make the other couple.' 'Yes,' he says, the old man of the house, 'I will help you with that, and I'll give you that bit of wood, and I'm almost sure that you'll never see dry rottin' in it.' And so then the girl was asked, and everything was OK. They got the consent of her father. And then there was a big party on. Plenty of drinking. Whisky was cheap then."

Mrs Marion MacLeod of Brue on the island of Lewis, recalls a *Réiteach* there.

"Well, sixty years ago, courtship was generally carried on in secret, although everybody knew that it would be more or less denied by the courting couples, but it became official when the *Réiteach* was announced. The *Réiteach* is the official engagement party in modern terms. At the *Réiteach* the prospective bridegroom chose a speaker from the community, usually a friend, to ask the bride's father for his daughter's hand in marriage. At the actual *Réiteach* a long table was prepared which stretched the whole length of the house. The prospective bride and 'groom sat at opposite sides of the table at the head. After grace was said, the prospective bride and 'groom were told to stand up and clasp hands across the table while the *gille-suiridhich*, that was the man who spoke for the 'groom, addressed the bride's father asking him if he had any objections to the marriage taking place. On being told that everything was approved there was great applause."

In Scalpay, where the tradition of the *Réiteach* seems to have survived longest, there was also apparently an element of the chase in the proceedings, with the 'groom having to catch his bride from all the young women in the room, who were often pushed in his direction. Mrs Jessie Nicholson of Braes, on the island of Skye, remembers how the custom was carried on there.

"The Friday before the wedding, all the old men and women gathered together in the bride's home.

And the bride and the bridesmaid was in the bedroom, hiding in the bedroom, and all the old men were cracking away and in about half an hour they would say 'Oh well, we'd better see about this *Réiteach* in the house'. And one of the old men would get up and go down to the bedroom and get a hold of the bride to be and the bridesmaid would follow her. And the bridegroom was sitting along with the old men and one of the other old men would get up and say 'Well, I think this bride will be well fixed to this one'. And they would try and get a hold of one another's hand, you know the bride and the bridegroom. And one of the old men would say that's fine, they're nailed together now. They would carry on and sing songs and have tea until about one or two in the morning. And then the wedding would be the next Thursday — it was always a Thursday in my young days. Always on a Thursday."

*Tinkers' wedding; Barrie, Angus, 1936.*

*My sweetest May, let love incline ye,*
*Accept a heart which he designs ye,*
*And as you cannot, love, regret it,*
*Syne for its faithfulness receive it.*
*'Tis proof as shot to birth or money,*
*But yields to what is sweet and bonny,*
*Receive it, then wi' a kiss and a smiley,*
*There's my thumb, it will ne'er beguile ye."*

Extract from *Old Scottish Customs—Local and General,*
E. J. Guthrie (1885)

John Provan, a retired miner, originally from Coaltown of Balgonie in Fife, remembers that, forty-seven years ago, permission to marry had always to be asked of parents, and very long engagements were quite common in those days.

"I would say we were engaged — what five years aye, and saved hard. Of course the wage at that time was two pounds ten a week, so you can imagine, you had to save every penny that you

Lowland Scotland has its own betrothal customs. Traditionally, parents' permission had always to be sought, but after the engagement there was often a gap of several years before the wedding. Looking back to last century, however, there seems to have been a lowland tradition of public betrothal in existence at this time.

"When a young man went to pay his addresses to his sweetheart, instead of going to her father and declaring his passion, he adjourned to a public house, and, having made a confidante of his landlady, the object of his attachment was at once sent for. The fair maiden thus honoured seldom refused to come; and the marriage was arranged over constant supplies of ale, whisky and brandy! The common form of betrothal on such occasions was as follows: the parties linked the thumbs of their right hands, which they pressed together, and vowed fidelity.

could possibly save. However, we made it and managed to get a house of our own and get married and we were able to furnish it to our likin' and that was quite nice we thought."

Mrs White of Markinch in Fife, married for fifty years, courted for five years before her engagement and wedding, three months later.

"Oh yes, we went for a long time together and as I was telling you I always got a quarter of sweets on a Saturday night. But after a year or two when we were really courting, we stopped buying the sweets to save that money. We had money to furnish our house. We had a bedroom suite and a dining room suite, we got two chairs from the co-operative, the workers, and that was our big chairs. And then we had five pound in the bank clear to start away with. Every penny was saved. And we did without lots of things so that we could always put money in the bank, for our home."

Once the permission of family and approval of friends had been obtained, and the money saved up, the wedding preparations began in earnest and several important traditional rituals had to be observed by both bride and 'groom. In the Lowlands, the week before the wedding was devoted to small parties for friends of the bride to show gifts, and wedding clothes. These parties, known in parts of Fife as 'the joobles', were mainly all-women affairs, as is the ceremony of 'bottling', common throughout Lowland Scotland, though not in the islands. Mrs Provan of Coaltown remembers the ceremony of 'Benjy on a box'.

"Four got hold of ye and ye got bumped on a box at that time. And then I was dressed up also and they come with the bell. Somebody at the side ringing a bell. You walked from Markinch to the Coaltown all done up with paper. I had a hat on also, I'm sure. They were singing a' the way doon."

Ellen Stannage of Ruchhill in Glasgow vividly recalled her sister's 'bottling' for us.

"Do you know what happened to my big sister last night? Well, all her pals dressed her up in jumpers and old skirts, a bra and knickers singing through the streets.

> Hard up, kick the can,
> Rita Muir has got a man,
> If you want to know his name,
> His name is Ian Wilson.

Pots and pans hangin' a' aboot her. Intae the pub she went. 'Any spare coppers? We'll gie ye a wee song.' We made a coupla bob, screaming all the way. The wee weans trailing after us sayin', 'Haw Missus that's rare'. Thank God we didnae dae that a' the time but it's done before the wedding night. Laugh wisn't it?"

Dundee jute weaver Winnie Porter remembered similar celebrations.

"Well supposin' somebody was gettin' married, word would go round that she was gettin' married in a fortnight or three weeks' time, so we'd get a book and you'd go round all the weavers, put your name on the book — you'd may be get sixpence from everybody. So you'd buy a present for the bride then, you see, and it usually was a clock — that's what I got myself, a clock when I got married. But I mean that was about all ye got, sixpence at the most from every worker there, that was to buy a gift for the bride, and then the night the bride was leavin', you used to dress her all up

and take her along the streets and sing, 'Hurray, Hurro, Maggie's gettin' married'. Somebody would bring in a lace curtain and somebody would bring in a bit veil and a big chamber pot, and you filled that wi' salt and you stuck a wee dolly in it, one of those celluloid dolls, you know, and the bride had to carry that home, and maybe another one o' the girls would dress up as a man, get a pair o' trousers and maybe a tile hat, collar and tie and walk all up the road — all the back ways if she lived quite near, you'd walk a bittie before you got home, and you got into the bride's house and then you got a cup o' tea, maybe a sherry, something tae eat, and that was the bride on her way then."

Young men had their own initiation rites before the wedding day; it was common for them to have hands, feet and face blacked with soot, oil, or polish, and in Glen Clova as recently as 1975 all-male pre-wedding 'blackening' ceremonies took place.

On the day of the wedding an unusual ceremony used to be observed in parts of Fife, although it now seems to have died out.

John Provan:
"Well, the tradition at that time was that, there were usually two men that did this regularly. They would climb on the roof of the bride's house and fix a flag on the chimney pot, then they had a double barrel gun and they fired two shots out o' this gun which was supposed to bring good luck to the married couple all the rest of their life. They were presented wi' a bottle o' whisky and of course it maybe only cost aboot five shillings a bottle at that time, but I suppose the spirit of the thing would be the main thing aboot it."

In some parts of Lewis, white flags or cloths are hung from the houses in the bride's home village, and in Eriskay, guns are still fired for good luck, or to ward off evil spirits.

## AN ERISKAY WEDDING

The Parish Church of St Michael, Island of Eriskay, was filled to capacity on the afternoon of Thursday, 31st July, to witness the marriage of Margaret Ann MacInnes to John Alick Campbell, son of Duncan and Mary Kate Campbell of Bunavullin, Eriskay. The bride, who was given away by her father, Hector MacInnes, looked radiant as she emerged on the arm of her husband into the beautiful summer sunshine. Greeting the bridal party and guests at the church door was Pipe Major Roddie Gillies, Smerclait, South Uist, the school's piping instructor of South Uist and Eriskay, and in traditional style playing 'Highland Wedding' and with shotguns firing (to ward off evil spirits) piped the wedding procession to the nearby school meals restaurant where *righle na bainnse* (the wedding reel) was danced *Air a' starsaich* (on the threshold). Thereafter, the sumptuous wedding breakfast, beautifully prepared and set out by ladies of the Eriskay community, was served. . . . Throughout the evening, refreshments were available, and not until the waning moon was sinking slowly into the haze beyond Beinn Stac and daylight had broken above the hills of Glendale, South Uist, were the last of the 360 guests piped from the hall.

The following day, 1st August, the *banais-tighe* (house wedding) took place and later the children on the island were entertained to a party in the Community Hall. The bride and 'groom left for their honeymoon, touring the North of Scotland.

From us all in Eriskay and beyond — *Gur iama latha sona dhaibh.*

*The Stornoway Gazette,* August 16th, 1980

In most parts of the Lowlands, as the bride left the house for the church, a 'scatter', 'poor oot', or 'scour oot' of coppers was flung to the local children, although often adults were just as eager to scramble for the 'lucky' pennies. John Provan recalled a 'scour oot' with a difference.

"After the couple was married you had this old tradition also which was called the 'pour oot' or the 'scour oot'. That was the bestman's duty. He had a pocket full of coppers and they were thrown to the children and the children always knew if there was a wedding on there was bound to be a 'poor oot'. If there were no sign o' money comin', they got kind o' impatient and you all started in one voice singing, 'Hard up, Poor oot — cannae buy a washing cloot'. One o' the times, at one o' the weddings when I was a boy I could remember this quite clearly. We were crying, 'Hard up, Poor oot, ye cannae buy a washin' cloot', and, eh, we were waitin' and waitin' and eventually they did come out and threw the money off a shovel which didnae mean much tae us but they'd heated the coins on the shovel on the open fire before this and there you were, scrambling and pickin' them up and droppin' them — rakin' them in wi' yer feet so that ye would have some between your feet when they got cooled doon and stamped on them and there it wis. But it was quite funny but quite painful."

Fifty years ago in the Lowlands weddings generally took place at home, in a hall or in the manse. Church weddings were not so common then, although in the islands it was more usual for the ceremony to be conducted in the local church with everyone in the village present. Mrs White recalls her wedding in the co-operative hall in Cowdenbeath in 1930.

*Nan and John White—married in Cowdenbeath, 1930.*

"It was in the Co-operative Hall and we had about a hundred and twenty guests there. We were married in the hall in front of all the people, you know. John was at the bottom of the hall waitin' till I walked down and the minister was there waitin' on us. They played the Wedding March and I came down the hall with my father and the people all stood — they were sitting before because they all sat in the places where they were to eat, you see, to wait on me coming in and then they all stood when I came in. After the wedding, we went round and shook hands with every person. And I was so pleased when there was one man congratulated me as Mrs White. That was the first time; I've always remembered that."

Jessie Nicholson of Skye remembers the events of a wedding on the island before the Second World War.

"On the wedding day they would all gather to the bride's home and there were couples there, boys and girls were partnered and they would go arm in arm to the church for the marriage and when it was over, they would walk home together again. There was no wedding cakes then, but they had oatcakes and at that wedding I was at, it was my old mother who made the oatcake. And it was all made fancy and when the bride and bridegroom were to come to the door, the woman who made the oatcake was breaking it up over the bride and bridegroom's head and all the young ones would come to get a bit of the oatcake. And that was the wedding cake. And you took that home and put it under your pillow for three nights and dream, but the one you would dream of would be the one you were supposed to marry. Then there was supper and in them days it was broth and tea and a bit of fruit cake, they would have tea and home-made scones and oatcakes and that. And after that they would sing songs and dance and drams going round until all hours of the morning. And there were sweeties, even at my own wedding. They would get pounds and pounds of sweeties and all the young children would be out at their doors. One of the old women would go out with the sweeties and throw all the sweeties at the children and the children would be, oh fighting and gathering the sweeties you know. Pounds of them. I had seven pounds of sweeties at my own wedding. When I came into this house. But of course there's not such a thing now."

Marion McLeod of Lewis recalled how elaborate and important the preparation of the wedding food was, and how everyone contributed to the celebrations, which extended over two or three days.

"Well after the Réiteach everybody more or less joined in to help for the wedding feast. On the week before the wedding, the bride's father would kill at least four sheep and prepare them for the feast. All the neighbours and cousins and friends from many miles away who had been invited to the wedding would all contribute a fowl. The day before the wedding, these fowls would be prepared, cooked and also the meat, mutton, from the sheep, in great big cauldrons outside, usually because the houses were not big enough and there were so many helpers around that they had to do a lot of the cooking outside. The baking was done inside because they had to make a bowl of flour, a bowl of oatmeal into scones, pancakes and bannocks. The day of the actual wedding a piper came along and the piper preceded the procession to the church. The bride on the way to the church was led by a 'groom's man. On the way back home, the bride and 'groom led the procession, after the piper. On the arrival at the house, the feast started with what was called the dinner. The dinner consisted of broth, and mutton, potatoes and vegetables, followed by tea, scones and pancakes. The people were taken in to the wedding table in relays after which they would go out to the barn where the dancing went on till two in the morning. The bride took off her costume jacket and replaced it with a white shawl and instead of the hat she wore at the church, she wore a coronet usually of white flowers, on her hair; no veil. But the bride and 'groom had to sit it out at the head of the table while the relay after relay of guests sat at the table and toasted their health. Now the toasts were

*Colin and Catherine Macleod–married at Barvas Free Church, 14th October 1915.*

*Wedding at Luskintyre, Harris, early twentieth century.*

individual, so it took quite a while. About two o'clock in the morning they started what was called the supper and this is where the chickens came in. They had chicken, tea, pancakes and scones and the rest, while the dancing went on all the time. Now two days before the marriage, two men were nominated to look after the guests and see that everybody had their meal. It would have been a terrible disgrace if someone had gone away and had not taken of the meal that had been prepared. The following night they had what was called the *Banais-tighe*. Now that meant another celebration in the bridegroom's house, for the elderly and for the people who just couldn't sit it out the night before."

The custom of 'kirking' on the first Sunday after the wedding was an island and Lowland custom, and was the first appearance of the bride and 'groom at church after the marriage ceremony.

Marion McLeod:

"And on the following Sabbath, they had what was known as the Kirking. This meant going to church, the bridegroom and his bride, the best man and the best maid, and in this case, the best man went into the church followed by the bride and the 'groom and the best maid and they sat in that order in the pew. The best man led the way into the church. He stood at the end of the pew while the bride and 'groom and the best maid went into the pew and he took his seat at the end of the pew, that was the Kirking. They never had a honeymoon. It was a case of going straight back to work the following day. And, generally, in those days, they went in to live with the 'groom's parents, that was the general way it was done in those days. In two or three years' time, if there was any money available, or time available, they would try and

build a home of their own on part of the croft, but very seldom did a 'groom in those days have a house of his own to bring his bride into. It did happen, but it wasn't the general trend, because there was not enough money around for people to do that in those days. I've known houses where there were three couples staying at the one time. The elderly couple, the father and mother, and two brothers and their wives."

Although in the 1920s and '30s money was scarce, and couldn't be spared for elaborate 'wedding braws', everyone I talked to remembered their own outfit with pleasure and pride. Men had 'fifty-shilling' suits made to measure — and some still hang in wardrobes today. Spats were worn over good boots and grey gloves on hands that were used to rougher treatment. Wedding dresses were not always white, but were made with care, to be worn for best afterwards. Jessie Nicholson remembers hers.

"I was wearing a pale blue dress with a salmon pink bodice and a wee coat that was all done in gold on the front. The dress had a flared skirt, pale blue, quite nice. And round my neck I had a string of pearls. Not Woolworths! I didn't have a veil, I just had a hat. And the front of the hat was done up with every colour of the rainbow to match my dress."

Mrs Rae of Aberdeen was married in 1921 in blue velvet.

"It was chiffon velvet, a very pretty blue, and I got it made at the dressmakers, and I really loved that dress. It was really beautiful. It was a dress that you could wear — you couldna buy a dress in those days that was going to do for a day. I had a veil — I borrowed my cousin's veil — I was her bridesmaid and the day I got married she was up at my wedding and she brought her wedding veil with her."

*Mary and William Rae—married 21st January 1921.*

Although weddings fifty years ago may not have been such costly affairs as some are today, gifts were given by everyone who knew the couple. They needed to be practical and, in the main, inexpensive.

John Provan:
"Well, at that time you knew everybody and everybody knew us, and there were very few houses in the Coaltown that didn't come along with a present. But not the elaborate presents that they get nowadays. There were no fridges and deep freezers and washing machines and things like that at that time. It ranged from two butter dishes, a cake stand, a clothes rope, a clothes basket, a bread bin and things; an' cutlery of course, china. Well ye'd always yer set o' china from the bestmaid. She always provided a full set o' china for ye. And, the bestman, he usually gave the bridegroom a clock. That's it sittin' there. But these were all things that ye needed; boot polish and brushes, brown and black and a' these little bits o' things that if ye had to buy them — if they'd just given ye different presents and ye'd tae buy all these things — it would have cost ye a wee fortune at that time to buy a' that stuff. Everybody helped."

Mrs Mason was married sixty-six years ago in Aberdeen.

"It was hard-up times in those days. 30th January 1914. I was married in my grandmother and grandfather's house. My husband was a cleaner on the railways and we just had a pound a week, two pounds a fortnight. One of my wedding presents was a black kettle and three jugs of different sizes and my grandmother gave me a zinc pail and a clothes rope and pegs. A'thing I would need for the washhouse and I never had to borrow from anybody. I wore a tailor-made suit and a nice hat with a peacock feather right on the front. I was a tailoress. The wedding was a Friday night, just a few friends, we'd no money and our folks had no money."

In 1980, gifts are more elaborate, wedding clothes are costly, and starting married life in your own house is the norm; but the proposal and the buying of a ring as a pledge are still very important. Fifteen-year-old Debbie from Wester Hailes in Edinburgh told me:

"Well we were sitting in his house and his Mum and Dad were out, and he just asked me if I wanted to get engaged and so I just says yes, and we went

*Betty and Francis Ford—married in Markinch, 1934.*

up town and at that time I says to myself should I or should I not, because my parents didn't know about it and I mentioned that fact to him and he says well it's up to yourself, so I just went along with him and we bought the ring and I think it was at Bobby's of Greyfriars and we just went in, we didn't look in the window, we just went straight in and there was the glass cages and we had a look in there, and I picked my ring. It's gold and it's silver in the middle and it's got a small diamond in it."

If the tradition of 'getting engaged' hasn't changed over the years, it seems too, that the qualities required of a good partner for life remain the same.

Marion McLeod:
    "Well, I think a good husband would be a person who could build his own home, be a good joiner or be a good all-round sort of person, a dependable person, a person you could trust, a person who could more or less earn his own living at anything that was available at the time or in the circumstances."

Mrs White:
    "Looks doesn't count, but I would say, kindliness and thoughtfulness — if that's there and love's there — that should be all right, and I feel I've had that, all my time."

MARILYN IRELAND

### ORAN D'A CHEILE NUADH-PHOSDA

*A Mhàiri bhàn òg 's tu 'n òigh air m'aire*
*Ri m'bheò bhith far am bithinn fhìn,*
*Oh fhuair mi ort còir cho mór, 's by mhath leam*
*Le pòsadh ceangailt' o'n chléir,*
*Le cùmhnanta teann 's le banntaibh daingean,*
*'S le snaidhm a dh'fhana, nach tréig.*
*'Se t'fhaotainn air làimh le gràdh gach caraid*
*Rinn slàinte mhaireann am chré.*

*'Nuair bha mi gu tinn 's mi cinnseal leannain,*
*Gun chinnt có theannadh rium fhéin,*
*'S ann a chunna mi'n òigh air bòrd taigh-leanna,*
*'S bu mhòdhar ceanalt' a beus,*
*Tharraing mi suas rithe 's fhuair mi gealladh*
*O'n ghruagaich bhanaeil bhith 'm réir.*
*'S mise bha aobhach t'fhaotainn mar rium.*
*'S crodh-laoigh a'brarain ad dhéidh.*

*Dheanainn dhuit ceann is crann is arachd,*
*An am chur ghearran·an éill,*
*Is dheanainn mar chàch air tràigh na mara*
*Chur aird air mealladh an éisg;*
*Mharbhainn dhuit ghèoidh is ròin is eala*
*'S na h-eòn air bharraibh nan geug,*
*'S cha bhi thru ri d'bhèo gun seòl air aran.*
*'S mi chòmhnaidh far am bi féidh.*

*le Donnchadh Ban Mac an t-Saoir*

### SONG TO HIS BRIDE

*You, fair-haired young Mary are the girl I wish*
*To be with all my life,*
*Since I won a right to you as I wished*
*By nuptial ties from the clergy,*
*With firm covenants and strong bonds,*
*With a knot that will last, and not yield,*
*It is winning your hand with all our friends' goodwill*
*That has given my body lasting health.*

*When I was sick and desiring a sweetheart,*
*Not sure who would draw towards me,*
*Then I saw the girl at an ale-house table,*
*And her manner was calm and refined;*
*I became acquainted with her and got a promise,*
*From the gentle girl to be mine;*
*Joyful was I to get you beside me,*
*With the baron's calves as dowry.*

*I would lead and plough and till for you,*
*At the time of yolking the horses,*
*And I would do as well as anyone else*
*On the sea-shore, luring fish.*
*I would kill for you geese and seals and swans*
*And the birds on the trees;*
*And as long as you live you will never lack food*
*While I live in the land of the deer.*

Duncan Ban Macintyre

*The bothy at Gagie, Angus, before the Great War. On the left is the form or seat, and to the right one of the men's kists also serving as a seat. A man had his mealer and claes kist which went with him from farm to farm. Besides the loaf, the men are supping porridge or brose from the large bowls. The bothies perpetuated old-fashioned habits – for instance eating round the fire from bowls held in the lap.*

## SLEEPYTOON

It hap—pened at last Whit—sun day, I tired o' my place, And

I gaed up tae Insch to fee, My for—tune for to chase. And sing

air—rie erritie a—die, And sing air—rie erritie an.

I met in wi' Adam Mitchell,
Tae fee we did presume.
He's a fairmer in Kinnemonth
And he lives at Sleepytoon.

If you and I agree, he says,
You'll have the fairest play,
For I never bid my servants work,
Above ten hours a day.

If a' be true ye tell tae me
I think the place will suit;
Guid faith, I think I'll gang wi' ye,
Though ye're an ugly brute.

So 'twas on a Monday morning,
I gaed hame tae Sleepytoon,
And he ranked us in good order
And we laid his turnips doon.

I was sent to drive the dung,
Likewise my neighbour Knowles,
But soon the rain it did come doon,
And the order cam tae lowse.

The rain it still increased;
The son was at the mill,
For meal, auld Adam Mitchell said,
Oor bellies for tae fill.

The rain it soon went over,
And the day began to break,
And oor next orders were to scrape,
Oor dinners frae the secks.

We'll ne'er refuse yer orders,
Whate'er ye bid us do,
But eat the scrapins' o' yer secks,
Is a thing we'll never do.

Do ye refuse what I command,
Ye scoundrels that ye are?
Ye bargained for ten hours a day,
Refuse then if ye daur.

But if the one thing winna dee,
The ither I can try,
I'll go and get the kitchen maid,
Tae mix it through the dry.

The order was to bed at nine,
And never leave the toon,
For every time we left it,
We'd be fined half a croon.

We never heeded Adam,
But aye we took the pass,
Sometimes tae buy tobacco,
Sometimes to see a lass.

But noo the term's come roon at last,
Oor money's safely won,
And we'll awa tae Rhynie Muir,
And there we'll hae some fun.

When we're a' ower in Alford,
We'll gar the glass gae roon,
And we'll tell them o' the usage,
That we got in Sleepytoon.

We'll maybe see auld Adam yet,
Suppin' at his brose,
And we'll gie him a lend o' oor hanky,
Tae dicht his snottery nose.

# A Weel Plou'd Rig

Many parts of the Lowlands of Scotland have been cultivated for thousands of years, yet during that time the horse has drawn the plough for a little over a couple of centuries. The pack-horse had long been the beast of burden in the Lowlands, and in the Highlands and Islands the horse served both for transport and cultivation. But in the Lowlands it was the ox which once drew the plough.

As the name implies the great race of Clydesdale horses came out of the Western Lowlands. Bred of stock imported from the Low Counties, during the eighteenth century they spread East and North, replacing the great teams of oxen at the head of the plough, and hauling the new generation of carts that came in then.

These horses are symbolic, for they coincided with a way of life that is only now passing out of memory. They were part of the Agricultural Revolution, or farming improvement, where the old-style medieval

farming was changed for the basic methods of land-use we still recognise today.

This was a new commercial farming working not for a simple subsistence, however comfortable, but a cash return. More intensive and productive, it turned the whole countryside upside down, with dykes, new field layouts, roads, new steadings and housing. The Clydesdales were part of this new pattern. As the ground was cleaned and drained, they headed the new light swing ploughs that came with a new technology. They were faster, more intelligent and biddable than oxen, and could hold a shoe on the new metalled roads where the soft cloven hoof of the oxen could not. The old-style ploughs, with their teams of up to six pair, could hardly be worked by less than three people. With the new horse-drawn ploughs, one man was out in the parks alone, both guiding the plough and driving his pair of horse.

Thus farming improvement dictated new patterns of work. Before, to make a living most people sought land on which to raise stock and a crop. At that time the countryside was peopled with small farmers, holding their land in joint tenancy, sharing their fuel supply and grazing. With improvement, the ground was let out in much larger units to a greatly reduced number of

*Tom Robertson at the East Fife ploughing match, at Bonerbo. The horses are in decorated show harness. The draught chains run from the hames to the swingle-trees held up by the back band, and are in turn attached to the yoke, and thence to the plough bridle at the head of the beam.*

newstyle farmers. They in turn took people on not as subtenants as of old, but farm servants, to work their ground and do their bidding for a fee. Feeing markets or hiring fairs grew up where people could sell their labour.

Andrew Law:
"The feein' markets? Ye juist gaed in an' ye wandert about. The fairmer 'ad speir, 'ye feeing laddie?'. He'd need a little bylie, or an under cattleman, or an orra loun or somethin ye ken, a boy for the second pair, ein for the third, ein for the fourth, ein for the fifth — I was feed for fift at Mains o' Melgin. Five pair on it. Nou there's twa fairms and there's ainly twa men.

"A'body juist wandered about. Like Freik market. Ye ken there's only houses at ae side of the street at Friockheim. Fan ye gaed intil Friockheim market ye had a strae an' sitted on the dyke an' the fairmers had a walk up an' doun an' they come an'

*The bothy door at Lundie Castle, Angus. The posed bothy pictures were taken by local photographers who went round the farms on their bikes with their three-legged cameras. The pictures often show the men's own humorous notion of themselves. Here Robert Buick stirs the porridge pot, H. Scott cuts the loaf, and J. Martin plays the squeeze-box. An old garden seat has been requisitioned as the bothy form or seat. The milk can and sack of meal indicate the basic diet.*

seen a likely lad for somethin, he wald hae come an' feed ye. Ye'd spit out yer strae an' gae ower tae the pub and there ye was. Ye got a shillin — ye wasna feed until ye got a shillin. I kent one o' the boys, he was feed, he was at Bogie o' Fern, he gaed doun wi another lad tae hae a day at Perth Market like, and I think he feed about a dozen times, he had a guid day's pye onywye!"

Although something new, the improved farming soon developed its own set patterns and its own brand of conservatism. Although constantly developing and changing through such new phases as subsoil drainage and horse-drawn field machinery, its efficiency was always informed by a fierce providence and dislike of waste, and high standards of work that were their own reward.

Andrew Law:
"If they'd tae get up at five o'clock an' sort their horse nou, well — they'd be finished, they juist waldna dae't. But they did it then, lookit eftir their horse and harness an' a'thin, Christ ay. I've kent them gaein back eftir lowsin time at nicht an' cleanin harness for about mebbe twa or three hours in the evenin, ken — tae keep it richt. But they niver wash a bogie [cart] nou, they leave it outside an' let the rain dae't."

The horse-worked farms developed a considerable regional variety in the organisation of their workers. In the Borders, Mid and East Lothian, a man was hired as much on the strength of his wife and daughters as outworkers as his own labour. In parts of Buchan and Stirlingshire it was common for small family farms to put up a servant above or beside the stable in the chalmer and feed him in the house. Besides the married cottar-man (married farm servant, provided with cottar-house), in Fife, East Perthshire, Angus, Kincardineshire, Moray and Easter Ross, the bothy was common. There unmarried ploughmen did for themselves, in accommodation which was usually part of the steading.

Andrew Law:
"Ye bocht yer breid an' tea fae the baker like. Ye aye got yer meals, dived in wi the bothy lads, there was aye plenty o' meal about a bothy. I gaed intil ein eince an' opened the door an' met the ashes at the door. They niver pyed nane o' the wummen tae clean out the bothy ye see, and the boys juist tuik a shovel and throwit the ess back. They hakit aye a week's sticks. Every man had a week on the pan as they ca'ed it. He had sticks for the firewuid gaein. On the Setturday efternuin he'd 'ae hackit his sticks, cairrit them aa in and juist cowped them lowse in a corner o' the bothy. There ye was. The foreman in the bothy sat on his kist at the left hand side o' the fireplace and the next lad, he sat at the richt hand side. And there was a form faur three fower o' ye sat, like. And there was a table that

*An attractive group at Chapel of Segget, Aberdeenshire, 1909. They are posing for a horseman's picture.*

was shoved awa up against the waa. And well, the meal bag sat there, an' ither things like. Weil, there was the orra loun, he made the porridge an' the tea in the mornin, that was his job. And fan the milk flagons was emptied he tuik aa the flagons up til the fairm hous and then come doun tae get his orders from the fairm. And then denner time, made a lot o' porridge. They yissed tae slice it up and eat it cauld at dinner time or sometimes some o' them fried it. If they didna tak that they tuik brose.

"The wumman then cleaned the bothy, she come and tuik awa the spare milk and poured it intil the bucket, the porridge was pitten intil the bucket, and she tuik it hame and fed her pig wi' t ye see. Mostly it was juist loaf bread, butter, seirup and cheese for their tea, then awa til the pub at nicht.

"They walkd hae gotten awa about seiven o'clock, they'd been on the bike and awa doun the road like onythin."

Perhaps the bothies are remembered better than the other patterns of farm servant employment because they developed something of an independent sub-culture more than the others. A slight edge of financial advantage lay with the single men.

Andrew Law:
"Takin it aa ower, the single boys had the benefit. Weil, they got bigger pye. Ye see the merriet man he got mair meal, mair milk an' then he'd tae buy his fire. But, say the foreman was merriet at a fairm, the second boy was single in the bothy, he got half meal, half milk, but he got his fire, ye got yer soap an' yer salt. The wages was practically the same. The second lad micht hae a pound less in the six month. But he'd naethin tae

buy, hardly onythin bar his grub ye see. The foreman had fowerty five pound but eftir 1920 the wages come doun."

However, there was also a sense of independence which counted for as much. The bothy men had a confident notion of their identity which often put them beyond the normal means of social censure and control. They could act in unison in the face of a mean or bad employer. If the foreman left at the end of the six-month term at May or November, so did the other horsemen, leaving the farmer with a clean toun and a whole new team of horsemen to be sought at the feeing market. The bothy songs served to stick names on whatever bad dogs were on the go. The farmer of Sleepy Toun in Aberdeenshire went to fee men at the market:

> If ye'll agree to work for me
> I'm sure the place will suit.
> Indeed, quo I although I think
> Ye are an ugly brute.
>
> Sae early next morning
> I gaed out tae Sleepy Toun.
> And he ranked us in guid order
> Tae lay his turnips doun.
>
> The orders were tae bed at nine
> And nivver leave the toun,
> For every time ye left it
> Y'd be fined half a croun.
>
> But we nivver did tak heed o' this
> And often tuik the pass,
> Sometimes tae buy tobacco
> Sometimes tae court a lass.

[Traditional]

The independence of the bothy men gave them a kind of style not open to a cottar man, or married farm servant.

Andrew Law:
"Ye ken yon lumpers [baskets] they yissed til gaither tatties intil? At nicht, eince the cauld weather come in at nicht, the boy gaed out, filled ein o' yon lumpers wi' coal, come in and juist set it on the fire, lumper an' aa! The hail lot gaed up! That fire was burnin next mornin."

In large parts of the East Coast the bothy system was in full swing from early last century to Hitler's war, when it was broken up largely by powered mechanisation and the weekly wage. During that time, particularly during the middle of the last century, it was subjected to much criticism. This was partly out of a genuine philanthropic spirit, directed at the spartan and barrack-like conditions that often obtained then. It could also include a good measure of moralising interference directed at the independent spirit of the bothy men. Social commentators saw in the bothy men a restlessness and wayward whims that ran counter to their visions of an Arcadian contentment. There was also the unruly insolence that had to be endured.

*A binder about to start another bout at Grahamstone, Kinross-shire, about 1920. It was common to have a three-horse yoke on the binder, as harvest was a heavy job that came when the horses were often soft from want of work.*

Andrew Law:
"They was aye gettin at the fairmer's wife some wye. I min' whyles this boy yissed tae catch 'er hens. He'd sit at the door o' the bothy wi' a bit tow [string] and a heuk baitit wi' breid at the end o't. Hou did ye cook it? Ye tuik the heid fae it, rowed it in clay, about twa inch thick, feathers an' aa, pit it intil the fire and left it till the clay glowed reid, like ye could see through it. Ye lat it cool, broke it open and the feathers come awa wi' the clay. Ye gied it a shak and the puddins come out, and there it was, ready."

However, such occasional pranks did not affect farmers' own judgement as to where their best interests lay. If the bothy system had its conventions it also maintained its own fierce internal discipline which produced a very high standard of work, and provided a substitute for the stability provided by the patterns of family employment found in other areas. But whatever the system, in places as different as East Lothian, Angus or Easter Ross, there was always a strong element of hierarchy.

Willie Urquhart and Willie Murray:
"There was a place that I was at. There was a grieve and he telt ye what tae dae. Oh, he was gey fu' o' himself. There was ae day he come into the stable. He says 'Hou lang are you supposed to get to put on a horse harness?' Says I: 'I dinna ken, I've nae idea. I ken it's nae use gaun out without the

*James Brown with Bob, carting neeps at Traquhair Knowe, Innerleithen, Peeblesshire, about 1923. The collar bears on the horse, the steel hames bear on the collar. Chains connect the hames to the slider on the cart shafts. The back chain carrying the weight of the shafts runs in the brig on the cart saddle. The britchen over the horse's hindquarters is connected to the slider by a chain. This prevents the cart running into the horse's hindquarters. The capacity of the cart is increased by the addition of shelvins.*

harness on if you're gaen awa tae plew or cairt.' So he didna say nae mair — ha! Na, it was nae use wi' out the harness!"

Standards of work could be as important as pay, and could either attract men or drive them away.

Andrew Law:
"Mains o' Melgun — there was a braw grieve there ye ken. He didna hae much say ava the fairmer — an affa boy at the boose. He'd twa load o' sand cowpit at the back o' the garage sae's it stopped the car fan he come hame drunk.
"The grieve — he moved too — a lot o' them did, it dependit on the fairmer. I mind o' the grieve — there was a bit o' a Bisset binder [harvesting machinery] broke — ye know the packers at the front o' the binder — weil the pinions broke doun below like, that and above the packer and they were pittin them in, and the grieve was pittin this shaft doun through, and they were workin' awa at it, and auld Arthur the fairmer picked up the haimmer an' hit the tap o' the shaft and burst the pinions baith tap eins an' bottom eins. And he said, 'Ah, damn it,' he said! Na, he was aff his bluidy heid. Sae the gaffer sayed 'Aw weil, if that's the bluidy style o' ye, ye can get it duin ony wye ye

like, I'm feinished. I'll bide wi' ye til November term but that's aa. I'll be off.' He's a rare boy the gaffer ye know!"

However, one cardinal skill dominated all others, and that was how to work with and manage a horse.

Willie Urquhart:
"Well, you've a bridle, collar and hames you see, back band and theats for ploughing. Tae cairt ye had a bridle, collar and hames, saddle and britchen, for a cairt you see."

Willie Murray:
"Oh aye, there's just a way in it, juist ay. If you hae nae a wye with them they hadna a wye wi' you, you see. You ken, you've got to get the humour . . . you've got tae be boss."

Willie Urquhart:
"There were a lot of different methods, you see. If you were ploughing stubbles, you threw out two furs, opened it up like, then ploughed it back in, but when ploughing grass lea you made two very small scratches and then you closed them up, you see. But there was still a bit in the middle of the lea that was never ploughed. It was the idea of it."

Willie Murray:
"Ah weil, if ye was a horseman you didnae like tae dae orra work. Ay. Orra men tae pu in neeps and that, ye didnae like it if ye was broken awa fa your horse work to pull neeps or onything o' that kind — orra work or clearing ditches — ye worked your horse if ye was horseman, ye see."

This pride was that of a skilled craftsman. It was one of the differences that came with farming improvement. Despite the notable richness of areas such as East Lothian, the Carse of Gowrie and the Laigh o' Moray, the old-style farming was generally a system of low productivity sustaining a thin scatter of

*Lifting and carting tatties at Easter Kellie, Fife, 1920s. On the right is a potato digger with a three-horse yoke, driven by Alex Dickson. The box cart has shelvins on to increase its capacity.*

population over a wide area. When that population increased and resources were put under pressure, it became a hand to mouth business. The principal satisfaction then open to most people must have been relief — relief when the harvest was in, and relief when stock survived the ravages of disease and winter starvation. The sure-footed success of improved farming pushed back this threat of famine and allowed people to contemplate their work in a different light, and take a satisfaction in it for its own sake. Improved farming produced a tremendous differentiation and specialisation of skills, including that of the ploughman. The man who could build and thatch a stack well, turn out good show harness or do well at the ploughing match enjoyed great prestige in his district. But how did men start on this path?

Willie Murray:
"It wasnae leaving time but my father had a place. 'Och,' he says, 'you'll be mair use to me here at hame than ye are at schuil.' So I just left when I was fourteen . . . took hame all ma books and I mind, I made a bonfire of them, you see and burnt them. In 1924 I fee'ed to White Rashes . . . Smith o' White Rashes 1924, and I was a year baillie kinna loun an' syne I gaed on for second. There was twa pair working an' I was second for half a year. Syne I got to Brakens, Cowie's o' Brackens for third horseman there."

A laddie was shoved into compulsory manhood at an early age, often a fully fledged horseman by the age of sixteen. Much of the knowledge was picked up from the example of the older men.

Archie Webster:
"The vera first day, the fairmer says 'Ye'll be wanting to bring your kist hame son.' And he says 'Just yoke a cairt and gang hame and get your kist,' for I was gaein bidin in the bothy wi another twa plew boys. And he says to me in a surprised kind of wye 'Are ye taking that horse?' An' I says 'As well him as ony other yin.' I got the harness on him aw richt but whan I put him between the shafts he kicked like the blazes. He would kick when ever he got the chance. So I kent it was a wee bit out o' my depths, this, and I asked help fae an uncle o' mine. He came ower. Wi a plough line tied round his [the horse's] lower jaw leaving out the tongue, put them ower the neck line, ower the hames and through the britching and tied them doun on the shafts and deliberately made him kick. He tried it three times, and that was aw. He was the best carting horse we ever had efter."

Knowledge could also come through the fellowship of the horsemen's societies. There could be a fair element of ritual and pranks in the initiation ceremonies.

Archie Webster:
"Well, there was different things, things that wasnae much in connection with horses at all. But yet, it was more for tae test the reflex of intelligence such as 'Whan did you lowse yer plough?' The answer being — beneath the muin on the tap o' a stane at the heid o' a weel plou'd rig. Another one was 'How long is a plough line?' the answer bein' fae hand tae mouth. Well it was from the hand of the driver to the mouth of the horse and another 'Where did you leave your horse?' or rather 'How did you leave them?' — with their head to the waa and their tail to the waa, and eatin their feed when we came awa. 'How high is a stable door?' — higher than a fool could reach or a cuddy could kick."

However, there was also a mystique of power and knowledge that extended to the control of horses.

Archie Webster:

"I could aye remember it, we started to work,
the farmer sent me out with the foreman to cut the
thistles in a field and as he was goin out he says to
John Mac, the foreman, 'There's a chap coming
here wi a double cairt for turnips, he should be
here round about 9 o'clock. Show him whaur the
pit is.' 'That's aw right sir.' And away out to the
field we went, and we cracked awa. And in the
distance we heard the cairt approach, it was afore
the time o' the rubber tyres, then suddenly a great
commotion. 'In the name of God, John,' says I,
'what the devil's that?' He says, 'Oh, something's
feared his horses.' And just wi that we saw them,
they appeared, comin doun the road in full gallop.
The cairt turned, the tracer streaked out in a
gallop. Jack says, 'Archie, I'm going to stop this.'
He says, 'Stand back a wee bit Archie, my lad.' I
stood back, but yet was near enough to feel this
strange uncanny influence which he projected. The
horses come abreist wi him and they stopped in full
gallop, stopped dead in their tracks. We walked
forrit tae the fence, we put our jackets ower the
tap o' the barbed wire and climbed ower into the
road. Just wi that, their driver come runnin up.
'Thank God, you've got them stoppit,' he says.
'They were clean away fae us, I couldnae haud
them.' 'That's all right son,' he says, 'here's your
horses. They winna run awa fae ye again. The neep
pit's at the other side of the farm on the richt hand
side o' the road.' The man taen his horses and they
were never kent tae run awa again. Says I, 'Jek,
what the devil did you dae the nou?' 'Listen sonny,'
he says, 'your faither wes a horseman, and aa his
brithers, an' you speir at me a question like that!
Haud your tongue and sae nae mair about it and get
on wi your work'."

This knowledge also extended to various tricks.

Archie Webster:

"Well, there were a trick played on me,
somebody had rubbed the seat o' the britchin wi
fiddle resin. Well that's a sure way to mak a horse
kick. Of course, we had this to scrape aff. But
fiddle resin on the seat of a britching, cannae be
seen, but can be felt by the horse. It pu'd on the
hair of his buttocks you see."

This was all part of the fun that offset the long hours of
hard work.

Willie Urquhart:

"Well, the first of March you went on to ten
hours you see, six in the morning to six at night.
Aye, there was four pair, and my pair and foals,
and the three pair, and the courts had to be tuimed
o' muck and there was ae pair got out and another
horse come in, just grinding away. Oh ay —
astonishing what they covered. They were aye
gaun, just grinding away. Oh — but it's different
nou, a'together see."

After the Great War, the wages dropped, often quite
drastically.

Willie Urquhart:

"Oh, there was worse times. In 1933 . . . my
God, a pound a week you hadnae mair 'n a pound a
week. Oh ye had your house like, and tatties and
meal."

The payment in kind was important. Besides his pay,
a single man might get 12 gills of milk a day, 35 lbs.
meal every fourth Saturday, besides accommodation,
fire and light. In practice, the milk and meal were
plentiful enough.

Despite the work, there was time enough for
entertainment.

Andrew Law:

"Discussion o' politics? Nae very often. Na na. It
was mair get the melodeon or the fiddle out —
mair interestin! Summer time, thrawin the
haimmer, capers like that. Doun the burnie,
guddlin trouts, comin back an' fryin them up for
yer supper. Oh, there was some pretty good
fiddlers, ay."

Besides that, famous characters such as Dancie Kidd,
who ranged from the middle of Strathmore to the
Mearns, taught a wide range of dances.

Andrew Law:

"Fan I was at Mains o' Melgun he had a class at
Aberlemno school. Mebbe fowerty fifty in his class.
Ye'd mebbe be in Dancie Kidd's class one winter.
Ye stertit at the end o' hairst. Twalve weeks then
ye'd mebbe gae intil Brechin. There yissed tae be a
lot o' dancin classes in Robbie Paterson's place —
mind the Turra Coo mannie — in his laft. There
yissed tae be a lot o' dances held in his laft, dancin
classes an' that."

Although mostly decorous affairs, the dances could
also be the sources of boisterous fun.

Andrew Law:

"I mind o' ein at Fyvie, there was some lads gaed
ower there, they waldna let them in. Oh, they were
a wild bluidy lot! And they tied the door, fowk
couldna get out, and they opened the window to let
air in. And they gaed intil the minister's hen hous,
they tuik the hens an' heaved them through the
window — they were fleein' about half the nicht!
But mostly they were pretty decent."

Many marriages started at the local dances. Yet in
the end it was the demands of work that dictated the
shape of things.

Andrew Law:

"If a lad got merriet, instead o' gaein til the feein
market at the term, he gaed til the cottar market
eince a year. I mind ma brither, he was cottared,

*Fiddle and squeeze-box, Angus, before the Great War. The fiddle is played in the old-fashioned way, without a chin rest. The men are wearing slopes – striped . overshirts.*

fee'd for a cottar man in the mornin at Inverurie market an' he was merriet eftir denner time, about ein o'clock. But aa the waddin was set up. A lot o' them gaed til Bell's Fair [a feeing market] in Dundee, and they cottared there [were taken on as married farm servants].

*A cottar man and his family in Angus before the Great War.*

The well-populated countryside which people recall with pleasure was in a large part dependent on the labour-intensive nature of horse working, and the trades that serviced these skills and that population. Powered mechanisation was to change all that. Although the tractor appeared during the Great War, its first real impact came in the time of the grass sickness.

Willie Murray and Willie Urquhart:
"I would say the grass sickness put out the horse; a lot of them died with grass sickness, the disease. Some places lost them all wi the grass sickness. It's a mystery disease, I've never found the cause o't yet. Some of them was acute, and the ein next lingered on like enough though they were just a skeleton, skin and bone. An antrin ein got ower but, oh no! — very few could beat her. Well, I just counted loosing two every year yet. It started, the Barry camp in Dundee in 1919 when the horses came back from the First World War. And it wore up through the Mearns and it wore up here. It never was doun in England . . . but a few year. They're doing research on it like, that's where it

was first known to be. At the Barry camp in Dundee after the war. And they've spent thousands on research, it's like cancer like. They canna get a cure, you see. The acute kind, the horse micht be weil that day, an' deid the next. Ay, quick. The next ein could hae lived six weeks but he eventually died you see. So that's what put the horses out quicker than they were going out like. See everybody was losin."

Norman Strachan:
"My father lost quite a few horses wi' grass sickness, some good horses too. Ay, there was a big loss when a fairmer lost two or three horse . . . juist during the summer before the harvest started. He had to go to look for other horses to get into the binder . . . it was a big loss that time of day when there wasnae so much money going about as there is now."

The worst affected area was Buchan, and in consequence the tractors made greater inroads there than any other part of Scotland between the wars. Mechanical skill was also building up in the country towns.

Andrew Law:
"They was maistly the same, the bothy lads, aa country louns. They juist followed their faithers, so on and sic like. A lot o' them gaed intil larries fan the larries come on ye ken. Callander in Farfar was a boy that had aa plewmen in his larries at ae time — aa ex-plewmen."

*J. Milne at East Ingliston, Angus, 1928. He is wearing a white 'bicycle sark' ready to go out.*
*Photo: R. Buick.*

*Mr Bruce at Overside of Fergus, Aberdeenshire, 1919. That year he sold a pair of horse and two carts and bought this Fordson for £200. The iron wheels, seen here with the cleats on the rear, and the skid-rings on the front, kept tractors off public roads, unless they were fitted with cumbersome bands to prevent damage. The grass sickness that affected horses following the Great War was particularly common in Buchan, and gave the tractor, mostly the 'Davie Broun' and the Fordson, greater opportunities than they had elsewhere.*

Still, the tractor had its limitations. Rubber tyres, which enabled it to go readily on public roads, did not come in until the late 1930s. It was still only a crudely powerful substitute for the horse. Only when Harry Ferguson invented his three-point hydraulic lift and the Ford and Standard motor companies made and developed it as a cheap system during and after the last war did the tractor become a real alternative to the horse. Yet by the end of the 1950s the tractor had caused a massive clearance of lowland countryside.

Willie Murray and Willie Urquhart:
"They speak of the horse comin' back, but na. Aw, there's a new generation of folk . . . the horse will never come back to work ye see. The present day they couldna put on the harness. Na, you canna blame them, see — like I was brought up with them you see. Na, na, they'll never come back, na, na."

With the horses went the horsemen, and this epitaph of Archie Webster's is from the hand of a dwindling band of men whose skills are now part of Scotland's history.

> He lies a'neath the western clay
> A nameless and forgotten cheil
> Yet in the fullness o' his day
> He bravely stepped ow'er mony a field
> The furrows that his plew has left
> The harrow tines hae left obscure
> And there he lies o' fame bereft
> The lowly plewman, humble, poor.
>
> No e'en a marker fur his heid
> Tae mark the passin o' his time
> Tis such as he whan gaen and deed
> Get little mair than poet's rhyme.
>
> His cleeks are oot, his chains are hung
> Intae the thaets tae bide fur aye
> His lines rowed up his work is duin
> Till yokin' time on Judgement day.

GAVIN SPROTT

*At Ingliston, Angus, 1925. There are five pair and the single orra horse on the left.*

## THE LAST O' THE CLYDESDALES

*Words Archie Webster; Music Archie Fisher.*

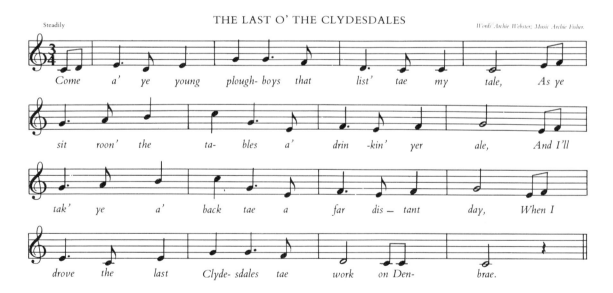

Come a' ye young plough-boys that list' tae my tale, As ye sit roon' the tables a' drinkin' yer ale, And I'll tak' ye a' back tae a far dis — tant day, When I drove the last Clydesdales tae work on Denbrae.

2  There were twa bonnie blacks wi' white faces and feet,
In the hale o' the roond they had never been beat,
An' ye'd lookit gey far twix' the Forth and the Tay,
For tae match they twa Clydesdales, the pride o' Denbrae.

3  They were matchless in power in the cairt or the ploo',
An' my voice and my haund on the reins, they well knew.
There was only ae thocht in their minds but, obey,
In my twa gallant Clydesdales, the pride o' Denbrae.

4  But the time, it wears on, an' the winters grow cauld,
An' horses, like men, can dae nought but grow auld.
But I mind o' them still, as it were yesterday,
For I drove the last Clydesdales tae work on Denbrae.

# ODYSSEY

The Second Collection

# Introduction

'Odyssey has attempted to give history back to the people who made it, allowing them to speak without interruption or editing by an "expert" from outside their culture. It has also given them the central role in broadcasting where they have been ignored for so long. As a generation, these people tholed appalling housing, unemployment, decimation by war and abject poverty to survive with their spirit intact. Through their words, programmes full of honesty, vitality and beauty have emerged, helped by the guiding hand of knowledge and commitment shared by all those who have contributed to this book. I have grown to appreciate even more Scotland's interwoven tapestry of cultures, and have learned from the experience I have had collecting the people's stories. If I have succeeded in reflecting truthfully their enduring human dignity in adversity, then Odyssey has been worthy of them.'

The concluding words of my introduction to the first Odyssey book also serves as a declaration of intent for the present volume and the radio series which inspired it. Yet no matter how strong the material which supports the statement may be, it is interpreted as nostalgia by many an academic historian and media elitist. Having filed it under 'nostalgia', the significance of the material is diminished and dismissed as the fanciful ramblings of old men and women. Giving a talk on Odyssey at one of our newer universities I was confronted with a historian of the old school for whom the document is sacred, and who attacked my case for the use of oral sources in history with the zeal of a defender of the faith. His argument could be paraphrased as follows: old folk's memories are subjective and faulty, when interviewed they tell you what you want to hear and exaggerate to please you more — the resulting transcripts are therefore of no historical value. I conceded that memory could be faulty but facts could be verified against other interviewees or indeed against documentary sources. I argued that oral sources were no more or less subjective than the individuals who brought their own bias to bear on the version of events they wrote down; making the resulting documents approved by the historian as the objectively empirical, in fact little more than ideological constructions. Neither documentary nor oral sources should therefore be held sacrosanct, but regarded rather as complementary yet mutually corrective. On the specific question of exaggeration, I asked him to listen to 'The Clydebank Blitz' which was broadcast that week. There, the enormity of the tragedy had been internalised by the people who experienced it, and for them to exaggerate on any aspect of the subject would have been obscene. Instead, with mutual trust, I recorded harrowing images of a muted intensity which one finds only in the

realm of personal experience, and therefore in oral history. When the only history you have is oral, then the desire is to tell it correctly as affectation would belie the importance of the history and demean the people you represent. In subjects such as 'Gallipoli', where few people remain who can tell the story at first hand, the obligation is not only to record those experiences accurately, but quickly, so that this 'living' version of the event is preserved. For so many incidents crucial to the lives of the masses, there remains no historical record of their participation, except in terms of statistics. That is why the extension of oral history despite its imperfections is essential now, if a democratic perspective on our recent past is to be achieved. Pressure of time on the production of the original radio programmes means that one must be selective in the number of people interviewed, limiting in the time spent with them and aware of contradictory and distorted versions of a story. Yet with careful sifting it is possible to distil the essence of an historical moment from a few people, because the importance the moment held for them will be expressed with honesty and passion. The programmes cannot tell every side of the story, but they do offer starting points on many subjects which would remain underground if Odyssey did not exist.

Within the terms of the Academy, we have here examples of oral tradition, labour, military, craft, minority, industrial and migrant history. But what makes all these subjects come dramatically alive is the extent to which they are personalised through the sharing of a subjective experience. Henri Thierry regarded the people as 'both the victims of history and its ultimate arbiters'. The individual reminiscences collected for Odyssey take on a greater symbolic significance, in that they become a statement for the whole group who experienced an historical incident. Thus the survivors of Gallipoli are the 'arbiters and judges' of those who made their fellows victims of that disastrous campaign. Thus Federico Pontiero's description of what it felt like to be arrested as an alien while his baby is dying, becomes a plea for social justice for all minorities and an end to brutal discrimination. Thus the sense of loss of community and loss of work expressed by the people of Clydebank or Glengarnock becomes a lament for a sense of belonging which the modern urban planners and economists cannot build into a place, a belonging which appears to supply a need deep rooted in the human character.

In Clan Neil of Barra, we witness how one person can express a sense of belonging to a community in a centuries-old tradition. In Nan McKinnon's narrative subjective 'truth' and the collective 'imagination' of her culture merge, yet she relates events which preceded even her great-grandmother's birth by hundreds of years, with a precise surety which reveal the knowledge or *mutho logos* of a predominantly oral culture. The fact that a historian can pinpoint her vivid recreation of the McNeil raids on Shetland to within a decade of the fifteenth century from documentary sources indicates not only the accuracy of oral transmission over such a large space of time, but also the need for all historians to admit to the validity of oral sources. The document gives a factual account, Nan McKinnon paints a word picture which makes the event dramatically alive.

With subjects which deal with rural society, there could be a danger of allowing the beauty of place and subject in e.g. 'The Pearl Fishers' to colour how we examine the relationships within that craft. But while Betsy Whyte's lore of pearling is delightful, it is balanced with her memory of the travellers' running conflict with the figures of authority on the river banks. Yet for the dogmatic Marxist who sees history only in terms of class struggle, there is the salutory and perhaps chastening lesson in that chapter that the travelling folk felt a greater affinity with the landed aristocracy than with those closer to their own social order. Perhaps this is a remnant or folk memory of the older paternalist clan system, in which the travellers played such an important role. Similarly, Annie Finlayson's idyllic picture of the herring lassies sitting knitting on a hillside in the long Shetland gloaming is countered with Eveline Crockett's memory of the long-term effects of young girls lifting heavy barrels. There can be no escapism or romantic yearning for a rose-tinted vision of the past because for the majority of Jock Tamson's Bairns there was more struggle than stability in that past. The trap of romanticising the past is easier avoided by those of the same background as the informants, whose recognition of a directness of utterance dictates the same kind of honesty in those collating the material.

Odyssey attempts to portray a multi-dimensional reality, a democratic range of experience, unconditioned by what I consider to be false divisions. I recall a conversation I had with one respected broadcaster who felt that all the natural poetry in the Odyssey tapes came from those who dwelt in a rural setting, people with a linguistic range and fluency untenable by the urban working class. His is an erroneous belief rooted in middle-class philosophy since the dawn of the Romantic movement — that the peasantry is pure and unspoiled, the harbingers of our traditional culture in a form untainted by either intellectual sophistication or industrial debasement. Herder, the great eighteenth-century German folklorist, summed up the prejudice succinctly in this description of the urban masses: 'The mob in the streets, which never sings or composes but shrieks and mutilates, is not the people.' James Myatt's story of the mongol boy barefoot in the snow in 'Whisky's Awa'?' is told with an eloquent humanity which belies the notion of the urban working class as inarticulate, while the sentiment expressed reveals humanity overcoming conditions that could crush it. The people are the people, town and country.

For socialists it would be easy to idealise the struggle of the urban workers to gain social justice against the power of impersonal coal companies as in 'Mungo Mackay and the Green Table' or against the State as in 'The '26'. But in Mackay's Midlothian we reveal a working class split down the middle in its attitude to a figure of autocratic authority. There are those who find stability in 'knowing their place', their attitudes to the manager mingled with respect and fear. There are those who regarded his reign as tyrannical, a heinous crime against individual liberty. Both sides are the people. The East Fife miners' communities in 'The '26' stress their solidarity and organised physical resistance to the State, clearly defining themselves to separate themselves from the known groups of blacklegs who capitulated. In the making of that programme stories of the '26 were often mingled with those of the 1922 lockout. Such memory lapses could be used as ammunition against oral history, but it does reveal an important psychological attitude of the miners towards the period; that both events are linked as one era of unrelenting struggle. A recent project on the 1972 miners' victory against the Government showed that the old miners saw it as revenge for the defeats of '22 and '26, revealing the inter-relatedness of all historical events shared by a homogeneous group of people.

In a truly democratic history, there can also be no limiting of 'the people' to specific ethnic groups. As Mr Stone in 'Glasgow Jewry' puts it, "Och, the sufferings of the poor Jews wasn't any more than the sufferings of the Glasgow underfed population." Having suffered early on in their history from that very Scottish institution, the Presbyterian Sabbath, both the Jews and Italians have contributed, and still contribute, to the welcome diversity which is Scotland, in their own unique ways. They too are the people. But where, you may ask, are the rest of the people — the landowners, statesmen, officers, socialites, aristocrats and all the other myriad manifestations of humanity? The answer lies in the thousands of books which surround you. They already have their history, written for and by themselves.

We are concerned with building a history from below. With the material supplied in these Odyssey chapters we are gradually collecting the means by which we can understand our society from within. We are not yet at the stage where we can draw all the conclusions about what the recent past has to offer the present. In collecting this evidence, however, we shall be able to provide those with a commitment to the Scottish tradition with the raw material of human experience to help them understand our past. Each subject to emerge from the Odyssey series will eventually reveal the vivid mosaic which is Scottish life this century. Oral history has been called the spectre which haunts the corridors of the Academy; from the evidence in this book, the spectre is now flesh, bone, and blood.

BILLY KAY

# The Clydebank Blitz

On the clear moonlit nights of March 13th and 14th, 1941, over 200 Heinkel 111 and Junker 88 bombers, led by the crack pathfinder unit Kampf Gruppe 100, left bases in France, Holland, North Germany, Denmark and Norway; their destination Clydebank. Clydebank was the first Scottish town to experience the full horror of total war, and forty years on, the physical and mental scars on the place and the people still endure.

Clydebank Town Council had initially been slow to respond to the threat of war. From 1935 to 1937, while other local authorities prepared for civil defence, the Town Council, with the support of the local Labour M.P. David Kirkwood, adhered to the Socialist view that compliance with the right wing National Government Directive was tantamount to condoning its foreign policy and recognising the inevitability of war. The same pacifist stance had been part of the philosophy of the so-called 'Red Clydesiders' during the First World War, and Kirkwood, one of the activists during that period, emphasised his determination to avoid immersing his constituents in the carnage of war. During a pre-election speech in October 1935 he asserted, 'I am all out for peace in the real sense and would not send a Clydebank boy to war upon any consideration. No war for me under any circumstances.' This view was reiterated by Kirkwood's Party leader George Lansbury when he addressed the Labour Party Conference that same month: 'Those who take to the sword shall perish by the sword.'

By January 1937 Clydebank was one of only three recalcitrant local authorities left in Scotland, and it was not until the Government assumed compulsory powers later in the year that the town, potentially one of the prime industrial targets in the U.K., finally carried out Civil Defence preparations.

James Hastings was Depute Town Clerk at the time:
"Once the 1937 Act came into being, we certainly got the go-ahead from the Town Council and we got any support that we needed from them; they not only supported us, they pushed us almost to exhaustion. The net result was that they were in the forefront of the local authorities with their preparations by the time 1939 and 1940 came along."

By the time of the Blitz there were 462 A.R.P. (Air Raid Precaution) wardens in the burgh, of whom fifty were employed on a full-time basis. These wardens co-ordinated the various services which were formed — ambulance teams, rescue squads, decontamination squads, Auxiliary Fire Service, First Aid Posts and A.R.P. Wardens Posts. Houses with gardens were provided with Anderson shelters, huts of various sizes made of curved corrugated steel sheets which were sunk into the ground. The majority of the town's residents, however, were crowded into one- and two-roomed houses in tenements, and these people in the main relied on the ground-floor closes of the buildings for shelter. These entries were reinforced with steel and guarded at either side with baffle walls which prevented splinter from blast entering the closes. Concrete surface shelters were also built, but most folk preferred the cosiness and companionship of the closes. The Clydebank tenements, despite the overcrowding, had developed an intimate communal culture of mutual self-help, something which the Bankies still recall with warmth.

Mrs Richardson:
"Clydebank was a great place, really was. In Clydebank you never walked anywhere but you always got, 'Hello'—always did. Didn't matter what you were, up high or down low, you were always classed the same. Up each tenement close there was nine families—a bedroom and a kitchen, that was all. The toilet was outside on the stair, that's the way everybody lived at that time."

Miss Docherty:
"There was a lot to be said for the old tenement buildings. People cared about each other. John Knox Street was always full of characters, good, down to earth, solid folk."

The 'clarty but cosy' familiarity and bustling energy of the town with its self-contained communities such as 'The Holy City' was like a magnet to people brought

*Kilbowie Road, c. 1937.*

*German bomber over the North Sea.*

up there, so much so that several families evacuated to the safety of the country at the beginning of the war, returned to Clydebank despite the imminent danger of aerial attack.

Patrick Donnelly:
    "At the beginning o' the war, the whole family were evacuated to Tighnabruach, that's across from Rothesay, and we stayed there for a few month. We couldn't stick the country life kinda thing, we stayed in the Marquis o' Bute's house; it was like a big haunted house and we couldn't really stand it. I think most people actually came home. You've got your home and it doesn't really matter how bad things are, you'll just go back to it and just accept it."

During the first year of the 'phoney war' the returnees' decision was vindicated, and people got used to sirens sounding for false alarms or nothing more than the odd German reconnaissance plane. Shortly before the March raids, however, many noticed increased activity above Clydebank.

Father Sheary:
    "A couple of weeks before the Blitz took place, something like lights came down as if German planes were taking photographs of Singers and the Clydebank area in general. We were all out watching the way the sky was all lighted up and we were actually saying to ourselves, they must be

preparing to come to blitz us."

Mr Bain:
    "There was an apprentices' strike on in the Clyde shipyards and the weather couldn't have been better, it was like a summer's day in March and we played a lot of football in the afternoon. Well, I was in the Royal Artillery at the time, on ack-ack, so we were trained for spottin' planes. On the Tuesday afternoon I think it was, there was a plane flying pretty high, and I said, well, it looked like a JU 88—it definitely to me was a reconnaissance plane going over but never thought any more about it. But I've thought plenty of it since, because of what happened on the Thursday night."

The day and evening of the raid were like any other. Many Bankies were at the pictures and dancing when the raid began, presuming the sirens signalled yet another false alarm. For those outside, it was clearly visible that this night would be different.

Mrs Bain:
    "When the raid started my sister and I were over in Blanefield and that's on the other side o' the Old Kilpatrick Hills from here. And we were with two boyfriends and one o' them drove a car. It was the sky, the sky was all lit wi' red, just a red glow in the sky, and comin' over Windy Hill, you could see the whole o' the Clyde Valley. Clydebank seemed to be all on fire."

Miss Docherty:

"The siren went about nine o'clock in the evening and at home my mother was in, my two sisters and myself and we thought, it was just another raid, you know, the sirens had gone before and nothing had ever happened. But before many minutes had passed, things began to fall down from the wall, glass splintering and my mother decided that we'd better really go downstairs into the close."

Despite anti-aircraft fire which kept the planes at a height which normally would have prevented accurate bombing, the perfect visibility and perhaps a measure of luck, resulted in incendiaries setting alight the Yoker distillery at one end of the town, the Admiralty oil storage tanks at the other end, with Singer's wood yard providing the third beacon in the town centre. The bombers ran up and down the line of the blazes, dropping 272 tons of high explosives and 1,650 incendiary containers, the latter described by an eye witness as falling 'like raindrops in a storm or locusts settling upon ripe grain'. To the people in the tenements below it was the beginning of a night of hell.

Miss Docherty:

"Oh dear, the noise was dreadful. I don't remember much until about midnight, it was well past bedtime of course and my mother put me down in a corner to sleep and she said that she was going out to the close for a breath of air and that was the last time I saw her. When I woke up I thought I was still in my bed and tried to, to turn over, but here the clothes seemed very very tight somehow, you know how you pull? My hands were full of stones and they were hot at that. Oh, I knew there was something not right here and I shouted for my mother. Of course there was no answer. Then away down below me I heard my sister calling me and she told me that we had been hit by a landmine and that we were buried away and the building was on fire and she told me to shout as loudly as I could. I seemed to be sinking into unconsciousness, you know, off and on, but my sister made me come awake and we called out and called for help and I couldn't get my leg free, it was caught in one of those big girders and I was told later that every rope they put down burnt in front of their eyes. So I was going into unconsciousness until I heard Father White—one of the curates in the church at the time—and two men speaking, saying, 'Father, we'll break her legs if we pull her like this!' And he said—I remember his answer well—'If she's to come out without her legs she'll have to come because the two of them will burn!' Well, when I heard that I'm telling you I fought like a tigress trying to free myself. Then I remember them pulling, pulling, pulling and with a final tug I came out. And it was an easy matter then for them to go down and pick out my sister because I had been

lying on top of her. So we were taken then to the Rest Centre in Elgin Street and that I'll never forget. The noise and the screams and the cries and in particular I remember my godmother who owned a wee sweetie shop at the corner of Napier Street, and the last I saw of her, her arm was severed from there—and the screams of her . . . and even as a child, I'll, I'll always remember the silence when she died."

Bridget McHard:

"Well I just remember this chap that stayed in the close, John Green was his name, tellin' us to cover wir heads—he saw something through the shutters of the window. Well, I remember putting my hands over my head and puttin' my head down, and that's all I remember until I wakened up and I was buried. It was a funny experience really, I was buried in my mouth and nose, my face down, but I remember wakening up and this terrible dust—in fact I don't like dust from that time. I don't like dust. I seemed to come and go an awful lot. But I know I wasn't taken out until three o'clock on Friday afternoon, and that was from midnight the night before. The only time I saw daylight was when I was gettin' pulled out and I could feel the thing comin' over ma face when I was gettin' pulled out. I'd one brother on one side of me and a sister on the other side of me—they were both killed. But my mother was buried, she was in a cavity sittin' on a chair. The buildin' was on fire and wi' the firemen playin' the hose on the fire and the way my mother was situated, it was like a cavity, and it just filled up with water. My young sister was on her knee and she said that when she felt herself goin' away, or fainting, her hands slipped. She was tryin' to hold onto my sister Eveline and when she was dug out she was sorta pulled up the way and as she looked down she saw Eveline lyin' where she'd fell off her knee and she just told the man that that was her wee girl. So if

*'Clydebank seemed to be all on fire.'*

*What was Tennant's pub. Corner of Radnor Street and Robertson Street.*

Mrs Hyslop:

"A couple came to me—their wee boy . . . they had got out, but he hadn't got out and they came to me, I think it must have been the day after. He was in Graham Avenue, so I said, 'Well, you go back and I'll get the lads to have a look'—they told me where to look. And he had been playing wi' marbles and that's what identified him was his marbles. He had been burned. And it was just bones really that were left. So, they were a Catholic family, terribly worried about him, so we got the wee remains put in a wee box got them buried as they would have liked and when they came back I said 'Yes'—we'd found him. I didn't say how we had found him, and I said, 'Everything was done that you would have done.' There was that wee boy just sittin' playin' wi' his marbles, and that had to happen to him."

The tenement homes became death traps with whole families wiped out in one explosion. The shelters undoubtedly saved many lives during the first night of the Blitz, but only providence could save those near the place of impact of a landmine or bomb. For many, in the microcosm of the Anderson shelters, however, it was possible to remain innocently ignorant of what was going on outside.

Willie Green:

"That first night in the shelter in the Rolls Royce [factory] it was quite remarkable because we found out there was quite a number of talented people, girls, who were singing opera stuff, of that quality —it was unbelievable. And of course whenever a bomb went off there was hysterics, you know, the girls screaming and the men saying 'Everything's alright', and then probably encourage the girls to sing again. We had no sort of inclination what was happening upstairs."

she wasn't killed then she was drowned because the water had come right up to my mother's mouth, she'd tae hold her head up. So that obviously Eveline, if she wasn't killed, she was drowned."

Father Sheary:

"One of the tragic stories is about a family called Semple, and Mrs Semple had quite a large family and they were all young. On that night, she had one in either arm and one on either side of her and she was standing in a close and I think it was an aerial torpedo that struck against Jericho Street, but the blast that came from that took a child out of her right arm and took the child at her left side, leaving her with the child in her left arm and a child on her right side. They two escaped, she escaped and she never saw as much as a rip of hair belonging to the other two children. Frightening; I'll never forget that as long as I live. They disappeared completely —she never saw them again, never, not so much as a rip of hair belonging to them, poor woman."

*Kilbowie Road, looking north.*

Mrs Richardson:

"We used to sit in the shelters and play guessin' games and sing and then 'I Spy'—used to laugh—'I Spy' in the dark! We'd light candles and once we got the 'I Spy', the candle would be put out again and then lit again. And then the sing-songs, it was all the old-fashioned songs, used to love to hear the old folks singing—you know. My mother used to sing 'The Old Rowan Tree', that was her song."

Mary Rodgers:

"There was a church soiree and some of the audience went out and they thought they would be safer in the shelter. And others stayed in the church hall. When the all-clear went, the people were just sittin' like mummies. The door had got blasted off and the blast went in and the people were just sittin' like mummies in their seats there."

Willie Green:

"During a lull in the early morning I went up above ground and I saw Clydebank burnin'—complete panic. People don't talk much about their fears but I can assure you I was scared that night, and more so I think being helpless. You know, if you had a crossbow and just firin' aimlessly, you'd feel you're sorta doing something, but just to sit there. . . ."

The feeling of impotence expressed by Mr Green was shared by a majority of the citizens, who saw little sign of defensive measures being taken, dismissing the guns at Auchentoshan and Dentiglennan as brave but hopelessly inadequate, but praising the 'tram' system of decoys which diverted many bombs to the Old Kilpatrick Hills. The main resistance seems to have come from a Polish destroyer which happened to be in the basin for repair that first night. Clydebank was the first major raid on a Scottish town. It acted as an unfortunate guinea pig, the authorities discovering faults in the system which were only remedied for future attacks.

James Hastings:

"We had, let's say, about 300 or 400 [incidents] —and we only had about ten rescue teams, perhaps

# Rowan Tree

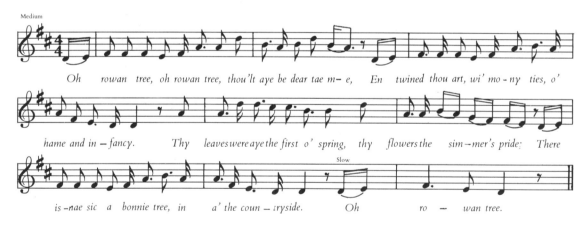

Oh rowan tree, oh rowan tree, thou'lt aye be dear tae m-e, En twined thou art, wi' mo-ny ties, o' hame and in-fancy. Thy leaves were aye the first o' spring, thy flowers the sim-mer's pride; There is-nae sic a bonnie tree, in a' the coun-tryside. Oh ro-wan tree.

How fair wert thou in simmer time, wi' all thy clusters white,
How rich and gay thy autumn dress, wi' berries red and bright.
On thy fair stem were mony names which now nae mair I see,
But there engraven on my heart, forgot they ne'er can be.

We sat aneath the spreading shade, the bairnies round thee ran,
They pu'd thy bonnie berries red and necklaces they strang.
My mither oh I see her still, she smiled our sports to see,
Wi' little Jeanie on her lap, and Jamie at her knee.

Oh there arose my faither's pray'r in holy evening's calm,
How sweet was then my mither's voice in the martyr's psalm.
Now a' are gane! We meet nae mair aneath the rowan tree,
But hallowed thoughts around thee twine, o' hame and infancy.

ten fire appliances, half a dozen or more ambulances—first aid parties, perhaps another ten or so—that we just couldn't cope, and why I say that the thing was chaotic outside was that they had all been sent out and there was nothing more we could do until reinforcements came in from outside. The telephones went—we were dependent on runners. And these were just young lads, they weren't supposed to operate while a raid was in progress; in any event, instead of perhaps twenty or thirty of them reporting, there was only a few reported because, quite naturally, when their houses had been bombed and there was a chance of more aircraft coming over—their parents weren't going to let them out of the shelters to go through a raid to come down and work with us. So communication was just absolutely hopeless. There were fires all over the place, you see, hot ashes from domestic fires got in among the debris from a building, this set it alight. Sometimes the explosion itself had fractured a gas main and set the gas mains alight. My impression was that the whole town was on fire and very little was being done about it. But it transpired that what had happened was the fire engines had run out of petrol—there were only two pumps left in the whole town that weren't damaged. They couldn't get petrol, they'd been hauling the hoses, the wet hoses over debris that included a lot of glass and nails and sharp edges, a lot of their hoses were torn to bits. We found another thing and that was that a lot of the equipment that came in from other areas to help us out, their appliances couldn't be coupled up to our mains because there was no standardisation of mains outlets and fire hydrants in Scotland. So quite a lot of them were standing about doing absolutely nothing. They just could not operate."

Mrs Hyslop:
"Unfortunately the First Aid Post got a hit, so of course the folks all knew me—'Right, we'll go to the Warden's Post'. And about two or three o'clock in the morning, a young woman walked in, she came over to me because I had a white helmet, wanted to know—where was the doctor. So I explained to her this was a warden's post, not a First Aid Post and there was no doctor—and she walked away. I'm sorry to this day that I didn't find out who that young woman was because she went, as I learned later, to the hospital and said 'Look, boys, Clydebank's needing you', and between five and six in the morning, I realised here was men coming in putting on white jackets. They were medical students sitting their exams—and she must have had a job getting her way from our place to the Western Infirmary because there was craters that she would have to dodge with her wee car. I didn't have much time to go out on the streets but I went out periodically just to check how things were. That was Second Avenue there got a direct hit and the place was just obliterated."

Father Sheary:
"The second night of the Blitz was terrifying; as darkness fell, the whole of Singers from Kilbowie Road right up to the boundary of St Stephen's, it was all wood, and it had been hit with the incendiaries the day before. During the daylight we

*Above: A blitzed family with their belongings. Opposite: Dalmuir West tramway terminus.*

*Evacuees queueing for buses in Glasgow Road.*

didn't notice the fire but as darkness came over it, it appeared more like the inferno itself. The red blaze of the burning wood and the darkness of the night."

Willie Green:

"It is a traumatic experience, you know, because you see the town you've lived with disappearing. In Scotland I think this is the only place, except Greenock and Paisley—a whole community you knew and grew up in, things that you'd known all your life, suddenly disappeared."

Mrs Richardson:

"Right from Second Avenue right up to about Radnor Street, all these houses were down, and it really was full of people lying about. Sometimes you seen just trouser legs or legs or arms—and as you went up Kilbowie Road, you know, the bombs had fell there and it was wee tram cars used to run up round there and the tram lines were up, you know, like a jigsaw. And then, right along Crown Avenue, I think there were about three closes left in Crown Avenue standing, the same down Second Avenue, just two closes left. And you think back— 'Did you come through that or did you not?'."

Over 1,200 people lost their lives on Clydeside on these nights, 534 of them belonging to Clydebank itself. Fortunately, thousands of Bankies were evacuated

before the second night's raid, which was even more intensive. Of the burgh's 12,000 houses, only eight remained completely untouched by the bombing. Several people remember standing on the hills surrounding Clydebank, at Gleniffer and Old Kilpatrick, watching their community being devastated. Whether achieved by the authorities or by the people themselves 'trekking' away, the evacuation was efficient and immediately effective, as the population dropped from 50,000 to 2,000 in two days. With unexploded bombs lying around and the threat of another raid ever present, it was a relief for the people to get out of the area.

Mr Bain:

"Clydebank on the following day after the first night of the Blitz, it was like a nightmare. There was buildings still burning, there was masonry, huge sandstone slabs, you know, had fallen down after the fire. The whole place was really in a turmoil. It's just the look on the people's faces, the lost look, you know, really lost."

Mrs Richardson:

"We were leaving on buses, we didn't know what destination we were going to, we just got on the buses and we were going along Great Western Road and I think the Germans thought it was the Clyde—they mistook the Boulevard for the Clyde, and they were droppin' the bombs and the buses were rockin' back and forward but the bus drivers still kept goin' till we got down and it was Bonhill we'd landed in. Well when we landed in the church they supplied us with beds and blankets, beautiful blankets, and we were all lying around the whole church hall, up the centre. The older people, they put all the young ones down, sorted them in their beds, slept there all night, got up in the morning—we were taken down to the barracks, down at Bonhill, and given breakfasts and those that had to go to work were put on buses and that. We travelled like that all the time, up and down, and they couldn't do enough for us."

Willie Green:
"Anyone who stayed unless they were necessary, was really a handicap. And one of the tragedies, you know, there was a certain amount of looting. Yes, I've heard of people who got stuff stolen. Men were re-fixing the houses, you know, wee simple things were stolen, like the wee tumblers out o' Woolworth's, the wee tumbler stands, the wee things that cost sixpence, things like that were all gettin' removed. It's surprisin', people'll take things."

Mary Rodgers:
"There were people that were saying that they had this in their house and the next thing and it got blitzed. They done away with rubbish and they got new stuff. And they'd lost a fur coat in the Blitz and never had a fur coat in their life! It made you laugh at the time."

If human weakness was displayed in the petty looting that went on, it was the overwhelming memory of human dignity and courage that remained in the minds of most folk.

Mary Rodgers:
"After the raid, there was always people passing our house because we lived on the main Kilbowie Road and people were going away out to the hills. This particular day there was this group and this man obviously had a wooden leg, and he had another leg, a spare leg, and he'd a walking stick. He stood and he took the other leg from under his arm and waved it to us and we thought, well, that man had the courage to wave a wooden leg to us and maybe in his simple way of waving to us it would give us courage. You cried and you laughed at the same time. Then another day we seen this group and they passed the window and there's this man carryin' a good-sized picture of the Pope. And although we were Protestants, my mother started crying. She said to me in Gaelic: his faith is so strong in that picture itself that that man feels that he'll be safe."

Alex Nicolson was one of a group of volunteers from the Edinburgh Council of Social Services who came to lend a hand at an emergency station set up after the blitz at the Town Hall.

*Queue at mobile canteen, the morning after.*

Alex Nicolson:

"Different people were allocated different jobs. And they asked me if I would walk up and down the queue, which was increasing ever moment, trying to find out what the people wanted, because in the hall there were tables with assistants sitting taking information, and I could direct them to the [correct] table. If they wanted immediate financial help because all their money had gone, if they wanted to go to stay with relatives, if they needed clothing, food, or information about their own relatives, or to give information of people whom they knew had been killed. If we could get any direct information and just hand it over it saved the people waiting in the queue. I've never seen such dignity, such courage and I didn't hear a grumble that whole day. During all this walking up and down, feeling perfectly useless but at least presumably doing something—I'd been into the hall with information and was standing in the door just coming out again when a man came up to me and gave me a bit of paper and said— 'This is the name of a child who was picked up in a shelter—dead. Would you take it in?' And I said, 'You're quite sure that this is right and the child was dead?', and he said, 'Yes. She was picked up beside my own bairn who was dead too.' And then he stood for a moment and said, 'We're not going to do this to German people's bairns, are we? What good is that going to do?' And I thought, the *courage* of it. There was no resentment, there was no bitterness, it was just a thought, about other people's children."

*Undefeated.*

The morale of the people remained high, aided by the fact that their jobs were secure. Even those evacuated to thirty miles beyond, managed to turn up for the morning shift when industry resumed a few days later. Bombs hit the Royal Ordnance Factory at Dalmuir, the asbestos works and several other targets, but the raid failed to hinder war production to any great extent. Yet for the people who returned to the town there was no escaping the omnipresent images of tragedy. At Dalnottar Cemetery a communal grave was established, where many unidentifiable bodies were buried, with priests and ministers in attendance for days afterwards. People wandered once familiar streets, looking for traces of a life irrevocably lost.

Father Sheary:

"I had married one of the Dorans just shortly before the Blitz and I was talking to him on the morning of the 14th and he went up to try and find his parents and they were blown to atoms. Two or three weeks afterwards I met him, I went back to see what was left of Dalmuir and I didn't know the place, to be honest with you—couldn't find out which was First Terrace, Second Terrace, or Third Terrace. But I saw Denis Doran and he was with his two hands pulling away there, bricks and mortar—and I said, 'What are you doing?' 'I'm looking,' he said, 'for a rip of hair belonging to my family'."

For those remaining alive, a long wait ensued before the authorities found the resources to rebuild the devastated town. A natural resentment developed among those who could compare the aftermath of the Clydebank Blitz with that of other cities which had suffered a similar fate during the war.

Mrs Hyslop:

"Clydebank never got a chance to rebuild. And where Coventry and lots of towns in England which were badly bombed, were given the money to rebuild, Clydebank wasn't."

Miss Docherty:

"Later on in years I went to Italy via Germany and we stopped off at Essen. Really and truly I nearly lost my eyesight. It was built beautifully! The shops were full of goods, and everyone seemed to be so well off, and that stayed in my mind because when I came back to Clydebank after my holiday, there we were, b'God, still sitting in the rubble."

The town was eventually rebuilt, but the communal culture of the tenements with its closely knit family groups could never return. Instead, people were scattered into ill-planned housing schemes where the impersonality of the environment produced in many a sense of isolation. The same could be said of many towns. In Clydebank, however, the possibly nostalgic memory the people have of the pre-war community is

*Funeral of unknown victims at the communal grave, Dalnottar Cemetery.*

overwrought with the terrible personal tragedies most families were touched by. It is a tragedy I felt in Clydebank. Because of the intimate personal nature of the people's reminiscences, I became more emotionally involved with this programme than any other before or since, aware of the tension between telling the true horror of the story while remaining sensitive to the trust the people placed in me. Today, the Blitz is still a potent memory for the Clydebank people, one which will die only when those who lived through it die themselves.

Father Sheary:
"It took me three years to get over the nervous reaction that set in as a result of that. Every time I'd hear a plane, even in peace time, when it came I used to go to pieces for long enough because of the effect that the bombers and the bombs had upon me on that occasion, the 13th and 14th of March."

Bridget McHard:
"I had three sisters, three brothers, there was five of them killed in the Blitz, and my father was killed in the Blitz as well. It was really only my mother and I that survived out the building. My mother and I became very close through it. She still gets upset every March, you know, gets depressed—she's eighty-one now."

Patrick Donnelly:
"I was twelve at the time. Always remember carrying my young sister up to school, Margaret, that was my favourite. We were a pretty close family, you know, up to the Blitz, and that was it. It was terrible. I would say that, for the next three years that I could see myself walking down the streets o' Helensburgh, on my own, and I'd burst out cryin'—it really took me years to get over it. To think I actually had four sisters and a brother, my mother, and that was me completely on my own."

Miss Docherty:
"When I think of the 13th of March, 1941, I often say to myself—that one night changed our whole life. The family, you would say, never ever got together again as a family should be, and when we did we were all changed. I would love to have known my sister and my brother and my mother as a grown-up. In my family, my mother was killed, she was thirty-nine; my eldest sister, she was killed—she was about twenty-two, and my eldest brother was killed, he was just coming up for twenty-one. And I always thought of the old song—'The Flowers o' the Forest are a' Weed Awa'."

BILLY KAY

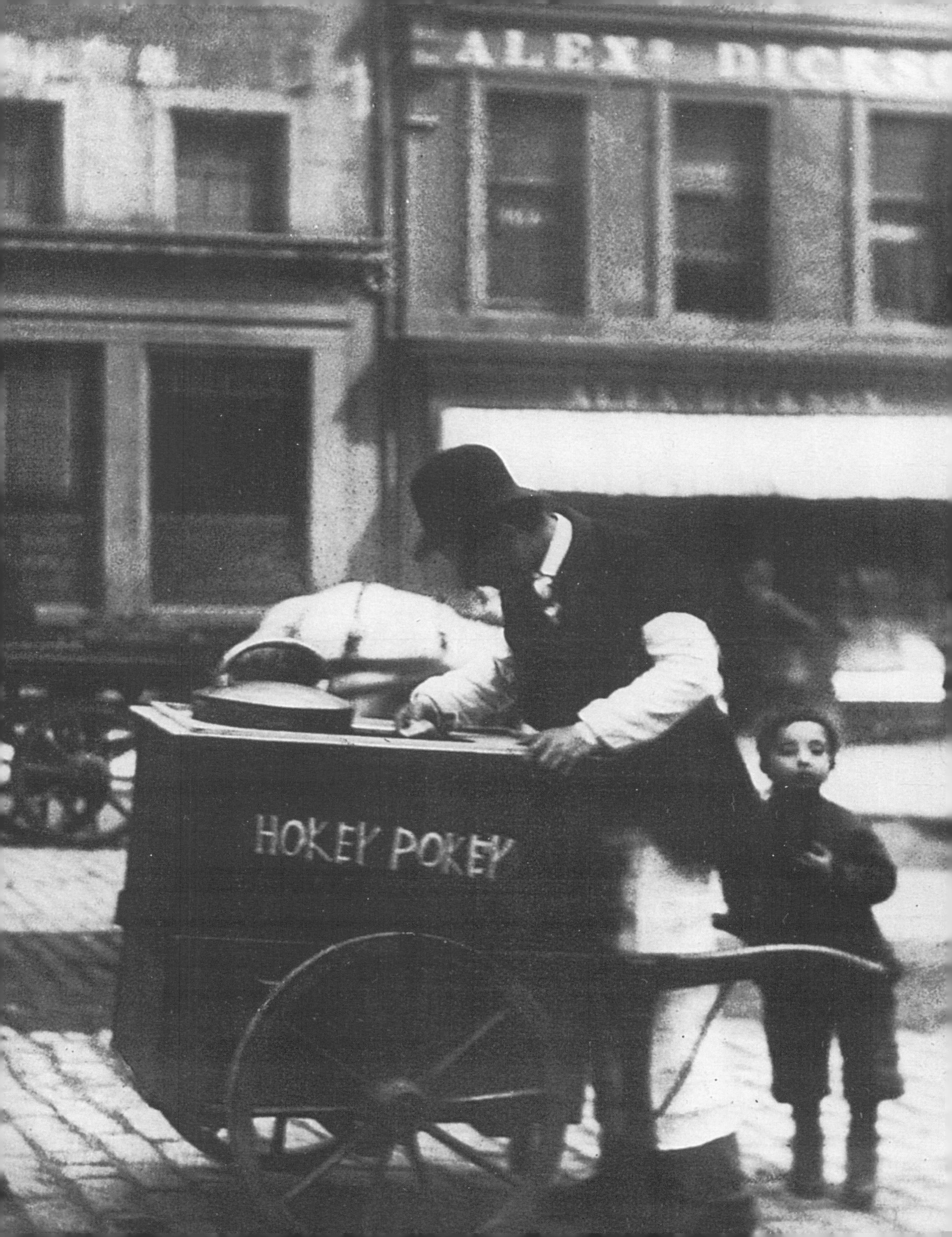
HOKEY POKEY

# Italiani in Scozzia

Italians have a long and varied history in Scotland. They first came to prominence in the wake of the Renaissance in the sixteenth century and it has been established that James IV and VI, both much influenced by Italian culture, employed Italian minstrels to entertain the *literati* who attended the court at Holyroodhouse. Royal favour of a different kind was bestowed upon the ill-fated David Rizzio, ex-Piedmontese musician and counsel to Mary, Queen of Scots. But it was in the eighteenth century, during the so-called 'revolution of manners', that Italian culture achieved its strongest hold. A contemporary writer claimed that 'every girl in Edinburgh who plays the pianoforte learns Italian, and Italian masters are to be found in every street'. The greatest of these was the renowned Italian tenor, Giusto Ferdinando Tenducci, who settled in Edinburgh in 1770. For champions of the native muse, such as the poet Fergusson, the popularity of Italian culture was regarded as a threat. Fergusson satirised the dandies who followed Italian fashion as 'macaronies' and launched a bitter attack on the impact of Italian music in his 'Elegy on the Death of Scots Music':

> Now foreign sonnets bear the gree,
> And crabbed queer variety
> Of sounds fresh sprung frae Italy,
> A bastard breed!
> Unlike that saft-tongu'd melody
> Which now lies dead.

But this influence had been nurtured by a tiny musical élite over the years and it was not until the nineteenth century that the number of Italians increased. The contrast with their well-respected and illustrious predecessors could hardly have been greater. As itinerant street-musicians and entertainers, pedlars of plaster statuettes, organ-grinders and chestnut-sellers, the Italian migrants, dependent as much on their wits as on their trade to earn a living, travelled from town to town on a circuit that covered most of Britain. The sojourn in Scotland was brief and it was only towards the end of the century that Italian migration took on a more permanent form. Thereafter, growth was rapid and between 1890 and 1914 the Italian population in Scotland increased from 750 to over 4,500.

The vast majority of the immigrants to arrive in Scotland after 1880 were peasants from two quite distinct areas of Italy, some 250 miles apart: the province of Lucca in northern Italy and Frosinone in the Abruzzi, south of Rome. The tradition of seasonal or temporary migration was common in these areas but the decision to move further afield, to emigrate overseas, was prompted by the rapid growth in population in the last quarter of the century and the consequent increase in the level of economic hardship. For some, life there was no longer acceptable.

Federico Pontiero:
"My father, he had eight of a family. He was a peasant and of course somebody had to go oot, you

*Opposite: The Hokey Pokey man. 'When they sold this ice-cream, they would say, 'Ecce un poco, Senore'. And the people would interpret that as Hokey Pokey'.–Dominic Crolla. Above: Corn harvest in Picinisco.*

*Ice-cream parlour, Edinburgh, c. 1925.*

know, of the family. So he says, 'You canna make a living here the way I make a living on this small amount of land that I've got. So some of you has got to go somewhere else to make a start in life.' I was glad to come here [Cambuslang], I mean to make some kinda progress in life for my ambition was to live the proper way, no' the rough way. . . ."

Mrs D'Agostino:

"I have only flashes of childhood in Italy. I remember the vast countryside, full of grape-vines, lots of trees and animals and chickens. I used to run wild. I remember running barefooted but there was no such thing as hunger because they grew so much. There was poverty though, it was a terrible struggle. I mean if someone took ill or if someone needed an operation, you had to sell a cow or sell one of your mules and that was a great hardship ·because they would need it. Everyone was more or less the same, glad to escape the hard life they had over in Italy."

The most common route to Scotland at the turn of the century was via London, which was the main centre of Italian settlement in Britain at that time.

Dominic Crolla:

"I had a friend in Edinburgh whose father, when he died, we were all up in his house at night and we were looking for his birth certificate. When we came across it in a drawer we discovered that his father in 1904 or 1905 had been born on the roadside between Dover and London. You see these people had walked from Italy, they'd got lifts on horses and carts and they made their way from the middle of Italy by road and track and boat to London."

Other immigrants came by a more direct route under a system of contract labour organised by recruiting agents in Italy who were in the pay of the *padroni* (employers or patrons) based in London. It seems likely that it was through the *padroni* system that the Italians first came to be associated with the ice-cream trade in Scotland.

Alfonso Barsotti:

"I can remember my dad telling me that a couple of men came into the village an' they were talkin' away, 'We've got these places if you're interested, we can give ye work'. And they started describing the places, that there were theatres and big shops

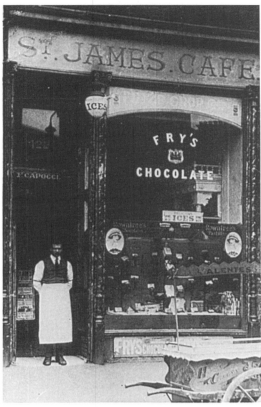

*Ice-cream parlour, Glasgow, c. 1925.*

and so, of course, all the kids in the village were thinking that this was going to be marvellous. The work, it didnae seem much, they thought just stand out there and sell the ice-cream things instead o' us workin' and sawin' logs and drainin' ground and ploughin'—this is money for nothin'! . . . My dad he was about fourteen when he came over. What, of course, they didnae know was that they'd be workin' practically all day and also [that] there was a guy employed just to make sure they only took their wee breaks whenever they should and that they carried out the work. Everywhere he went there was somebody there, you know, just to watch.''

In spite of the difficulties which confronted them some of the pioneer Italians did extremely well. Leopold Guliani from the village of Barga (in Lucca province) is said to have owned over sixty cafés in Scotland and was one of a substantial business group beginning to take shape on Clydeside before 1914. By then the 'Ice-cream Parlour' had become a common feature in most towns and villages in Scotland, for the ice-cream cone, like a drink or a flutter, transcended class differences and was enjoyed by rich and poor alike. There were, however, some sections of the local population who looked upon the growth in the trade of

ice-cream and its Italian associations with considerable misgivings.

The most vociferous complaints came from the United Free Church who condemned the Italians for keeping their shops open on Sundays thereby challenging what was regarded as sacrosanct, namely, Sabbath observance. Furthermore, it was alleged that moral as well as spiritual values were under threat. In evidence to a Parliamentary Committee on Sunday Trading in 1906, it was suggested that ice-cream parlours might be 'morally contaminating' as 'young people of both sexes congregate there after legitimate hours and sometimes misbehave themselves . . . that is the one great attraction of the ice-cream shops and not the ingredient itself'. The police also added their weight to the opposition. Standards of behaviour in ice-cream shops, it was claimed, were low and were 'acceptable only to their alien owners and to people of loose moral habits'.

The ice-cream traders responded by joining forces with the Temperance movement. Although Temperance slogans such as 'lips that touch liquor shall never touch mine' had never had much of an appeal among the majority of the working class, Temperance reformers still continued to encourage alternatives to the temptations of the public house. In 1907 the 'Temperance Refreshment Traders Defence Association' was set up and an appeal, which contained the signatures of over 800 Italian traders in Scotland, was lodged against any change in the legislation. But the pious rhetoric of the sabbatarians were a mere adjunct to a carefully orchestrated and lengthy campaign conducted by the Shop Assistants' Union — a campaign which culminated in the Shops Act 1911 and Sunday closure.

In comparison with the hostility which jaundiced the experience of the Irish and the Lithuanians on their arrival in Scotland the Italians were well received. Anti-alien prejudice appears to have been suspended primarily because the Italians, in the occupations they followed, never represented a serious threat to native labour or wages. Nonetheless minor incidents did take place.

Mrs McGillivray:
"When I used to go to school the kids used tae pull my hair, I had jet black hair, and [tell me] to speak Italian. I spoke Italian, I couldn't speak anythin' else, I couldn't even tell them to stop it.''

Dominic Crolla:
"Many times when the chap would be going round the streets with the barrow they'd get a couple of youths coming up and making a bit of fun because the man couldn't speak English. They'd go up pretending they were going to buy something and when the Italian chap lifted the lid they'd throw bundles of stones or something into the freezer. These boys were only doing it as a prank, you see, but for the Italian man it was a loss of a lot of money because they'd wasted his goods.''

Occasionally the presence of a group of youngsters could be turned to advantage.

Federico Pontiero:
"At the beginning I mean I stood a lot o' abuse, yes, kids especially, because you couldnae speak. Many's the time though you'd get some o' the young boys, they were very good. I gave them 'pokey-hats' and they gave you a hand to shove it [the barrow] up the hill. Some o' the hills you couldnae really shove it yourself because you were trying to shove it up the way and the barrow was pushing down the way. I even pushed the barrow up the Cathkin Braes one morning and you know how much I made? Two pence! Aye, it was heavy, heavy work and it was quite a wee bit hard life tae build up the business. When I did come here the day start seven in the mornin', didna finish till one o'clock, maybe two o'clock in the mornin' and that was for eight solid year. There were one night we went to the pictures, the three o' us and when we went back home, they told us, 'No more pictures!' We hadna a night off nor nothing. I mind o' Mr Rinaldi, I think he was the first Italian settled in Cambuslang, he used to go down the Clyde there and cut the ice. They cut the ice in the Clyde at that time so it must have been an awfu' number of year ago because I never seen a Clyde frozen since! (laughs) It was breakin' ice off for the ice-cream.

*Mrs McGillivray and sister. c. 1910.*

Aye it was a struggle, you know, it wasna money made easy I assure you."

In many cases this hard-earned cash was used to pay off a debt or loan from a benefactor who had provided the finance to start the business. In 1891 a benefit society, *Società di Mutuo Soccorso*, was set up in Glasgow mainly for this purpose. It was much more likely that newcomers would receive assistance from relatives or friends already established in Scotland.

Antonio D'Arpino:
"When I came here to Glasgow in 1922 I didn't know a word and I just had the address in ma' hands, and I was workin' for five, six months and after that a friend o' mine says, 'I'll buy a shop, I'll let you into my trade', and that's how I started."

Mrs McGillivray:
"My father came to Edinburgh in 1902 and in those days you could get a shop and some stock for about £150. After a while, he used to open the shops and sell them to the Italian fellows, you know, as a going concern. First of all he took them on as payin' servants [employees] and then, if they were worthy, he sold them the shop and they paid him so much a week, you see, towards the shop becoming theirs."

A crucial element in this financial transaction, which greatly minimised the risk involved in providing the capital, was a knowledge of the newcomer's background. The information was not difficult to obtain.

Dominic Crolla:
"When they came over all the people from their own village would come over to join them, they would settle where their own villagers were, their own friends. So there's a big crowd from Barga, they've gathered together in Glasgow and the West. Most of them that came here to Edinburgh were from the villages in the Abruzzi and they made for the Grassmarket because it was the most similar place to an Italian piazza. So the Italian colony at that time was more or less centred around St Mary's Street, the Pleasance and the Grassmarket. Everybody knew everybody else."

On entering into a business deal, therefore, the newcomer became enmeshed in a web of social contacts which had their origin in the villages of Lucca or the Abruzzi rather than in Glasgow or Edinburgh. Indeed, it was these links that kept the Italian community together as organisation on a more formal basis was extremely difficult due to the widespread dispersal of the immigrants nationally and the nature of their work. Italian societies were few in number prior to the early 1920s and it was through the family that the traditions and customs of the homeland were preserved.

Mrs D'Agostino:

"Your parents were very Italian, of course, all their thinking was Italian. Every Friday we used to have a whole congregation in our back shop and all the old ladies used to get together and have a good old gossip—I mean they missed the village life. They were very pleasant and polite to their customers but they didn't really mix with them. . . . They were very old fashioned and the girls were kept under a strict rule because they felt that everyone here was much too free and easy."

Mrs Lucchesi:

"My father wanted us to be as much Italian as we possibly could. In the house it was definitely Italian, the food was Italian, we spoke Italian, we had Italian friends and we were brought up that we had to marry Italians. It wasn't only our family for that was a general thing with the Italians. My family consisted of six girls and a boy and we all married Italians. The social life, especially for the girls was very restricted. We got on very very well with the Scots boys who came into the shop and have chats with us but then they stopped asking us out because they knew we wouldn't go out. You could almost say it was forbidden."

Mrs McGillivray:

"I met my husband during the 1914-18 war, he was an engineer sub-lieutenant. When he first came into the shop I thought he was a Rear-Admiral, if you please, with all that gold on his arm! Anyway, I got married to him. You know, the Italian community made me an outcast because I married a Scotsman and because he was a Presbyterian and here I was, a Roman Catholic. Because I was an outcast I used to take him to the Italian dances and I used to hear all the Italian ladies say, 'We don't blame her for marryin' him—isn't he handsome!' And was I happy at that bit, I just turned round and smiled. After that I never went near them because I wasn't gonna allow them to slight me."

Parental control, particularly over the choice of marriage partner, remained strong through the 1920s and 1930s. It enhanced the *italianità* of their children and ensured that the tight social organisation of the community, centred round the tradition of *campanilismo* or village loyalties, was maintained.

In the inter-war years the number of new arrivals from Italy was reduced to a trickle by the restrictive Aliens Act of 1919, consequently the Italian population stabilised at a figure of around 5,500. It was a community, therefore, of older, well-established immigrants who had on the whole achieved a certain degree of security. There was also prosperity. For example, between 1911 and 1931 the number of Italian restaurant-keepers had increased from 278 to nearly 700 and by the 1930s the Italian street-vendor had become something of a rarity. With stability and prosperity also came organisational growth.

*A wedding procession in Picinisco.*

Professional associations such as the *Associazione dei Gelatieri* (Association of Ice-Cream Traders) had branches in Glasgow, Edinburgh and Dundee, and in 1928 the *Sindacato Commercianti Italiani* (Italian Commercial Syndicate) was established. At about the same time the *Collegio dei Parrucchieri Italiani* (College of Italian Hairdressers) was set up in Glasgow. Various cultural associations were also formed, most notably the *Dante Alighieri* society in 1936. On the political front there were other more portentous developments.

In 1923, a year after Mussolini came to power in Italy, a branch of the Italian fascist movement was established in Glasgow comprising mainly members of the war veterans' associations (*Associazione Nazionale Combattenti* and the *Nastro Azzurro*) and some of the wealthier Italian businessmen. According to press accounts of the time fascist meetings held in Glasgow and Edinburgh in the 1920s regularly attracted large audiences. These meetings were social and political gatherings and it was not uncommon, for instance, to find members of the Roman Catholic hierarchy and the Italian Consulate in attendance as well as local dignitaries. In some cases meetings were specifically arranged to coincide with Roman Catholic holidays: for example, the annual reunion of the 'Italian fascisti' was held on August 15th, the Feast of the Day of the Assumption. Most Italians regarded 'the 15th' as the big social event in their year, as described here by a teenager of the time.

*Opening of new hall and sale of work, Italian Fascists. The Italian Consul, Sen. Fronchetti, is right of centre.*

"There always used to be a big picnic to celebrate the fifteenth of August and it was really a good day. Every year the Glasgow Italians, the Dundee Italians, the Edinburgh Italians all got together at some place, some big park, maybe it would be Alva or Stirling or somewhere. We used to have great fun—lots of food and games, tug-of-war and races and things like that. It was really good."

Without doubt Mussolini and his extraordinary brand of fascism enjoyed some support from within the immigrant community. Unlike Mosley's 'black-shirts', the Italian fascists made little impact and there is a conspicuous lack of evidence of antagonism towards the Italians in the 1930s in spite of the growing threat of fascist power on the Continent. The change came with Mussolini's declaration of war on 10th June 1940.

In a night of violence and looting, anti-Italian riots broke out in a number of places including Glasgow, Edinburgh, Falkirk, Greenock, Port Glasgow and Irvine. In one of the most serious disturbances, in Edinburgh, the police had to make several baton charges to disperse a crowd, estimated at over 1,000, which had gathered in Leith Walk. Few areas of Italian settlement were spared.

Marina Barsotti:
"I was in Glasgow when I heard it on the six o'clock news and my mother said, 'You'd better not go to Galston tonight, there might be trouble.' I thought it would be alright because it was just a wee village and nobody bothered us there. Well, this shop here in Wallace Street, a gang of hooligans broke the windows, they came in and over the counter to take the goods away, the likes of chocolate and so on. . . . It was a very frightsome night, certainly was, because you didn't know if you were going to get stoned to death or what was going to happen to you."

The scale and intensity of the violence of 10th June left the immigrant community bewildered and frightened. As Dominic Crolla put it, 'It seemed as if the work of fifty or sixty years had vanished into thin air.' Worse was to follow as the policy of internment of 'enemy aliens' was enforced. Fascists and non-fascists (including some German Jewish refugees) were treated alike.

Federico Pontiero:
"Och, they all started to hate me because I was an Italian. . . . I was up the public park one day

*"Enemy Aliens"? Bothwell Bridge, c. 1920.*

standin' wi' the barra' and this man, he says, 'Get away with that barra,' he says, 'you and Mussolini.' There was a gentleman standin' just beside me and he says [to him], 'Hallo, sir. What's the idea o' you tellin' him "Mussolini"? What has he got to do with Mussolini?' I thought that man had done a great thing and I appreciate that man's spoken for me. You see, I wasna' a political, I wasna' interested in politic at all. . . . That night the war broke out [10th June 1940] my wife, she had a baby dying o' pneumonia. Well the police came up the house, it was about eleven o'clock, and they start to look about and they says, 'You'll need to come with us.' I says, 'I don't know nothing about politic, I've been in Cambuslang most o' my days.' But anyway they took me up the jail and of course I broke doon because my wean was dyin'. The next day the wean died and the priest and the doctor came and they asked the Inspector if they would let me home for five minutes. He said 'No'. So they took us away to Milton Bridge and then from there to the Isle of Man.''

Mrs D'Agostino:
   "They interned most of the men, some went to the Isle of Man, some were sent to Canada, others to Australia. It was just a nightmare really. They took my brothers and one was only eighteen months when he came here. It was very sad because most of them didn't know anything about politics or fascism or anything, even the ones who belonged to the Fascist Club. It was just a social club which, unfortunately, was called the Fascist Club."

Dominic Crolla:
   "Many Italians lost their lives on the *Arandora Star* which was going to Canada with a lot of British troops, German prisoners-of-war and Italians on board. I lost my own father on that ship, yes, the *Arandora Star* torpedoed by a German submarine. I myself was interned in Canada for nearly three years. We were with German prisoners-of-war on the boat and they were singing all the way over, singing that Britain was 'kaputt' and that the war would end very soon. We, on the other hand, about 300 of us who had been in Scotland for years, were all sad with long faces having been separated from our families and not knowing where we were going. . . .''

   Few Italians were interned for the duration of the war unless they were Class 'A' internees, i.e. aliens who represented 'a potential security risk'. Members of this category were deported to Italy after the war. Most of the Scottish Italians had returned home by 1944 and within a few years the community was functioning once again on normal lines. Trade slowly began to improve and in some areas there were unexpected benefits.

Dominic Crolla:
   "It wasn't a very successful business in these days [1930s] because people didn't know anything about spaghetti, wine or olive oil. It only dealt with Italian customers and with Italians who had small shops. . . . But after the war it was a huge success because British soldiers had been in Italy, tasted the

*Mr Dominic Crolla and the staff of Valvona and Crolla Ltd., 1981.*

spaghetti, tasted Italian food, some had been in India and tasted curry, some had been in France and Germany. When they all came back they wanted a change in their kitchen, hence the prosperity, the slow prosperity of Valvona and Crolla Ltd. . . . We were the only ones in Edinburgh at that time from whom they could purchase all these nice goods."

The post-war years witnessed a new wave of immigrants, particularly after 1951 when the Government introduced the Bulk Recruitment Scheme in an attempt to compensate for the acute shortage of native labour in industries such as mining, steel-making and farming. Few Italians remained in these occupations once their contract was completed.

Mrs Lucchesi:
"Italy was very down at that time and the only way that they [Italians] could come over here was to do four years on the farms. After that they were free to take on any work they wanted. The women, they could come over if they were doing domestic work in hospitals or somewhere like that. There was quite a big community here, in fact in Galston they called it 'Little Italy' because right round the farms there was an awful lot of Italians. But after the four years they started getting shops through other Italians telling them there's a shop going to be let and so on. . . ."

Mr Ioannone:
"The farm I went to, it was just like slavery the way ye work there. The Scotchman, the boss, had a two son. All the job they no want to do, I had to do. When I'd overtime to do they just paid me two shillings an hour when everybody else a paid three

shillings or four shillings an hour! After the four years, after that, I start a myself a business, I started with the ice-cream van and after a couple of years wi' the fish and chips and now I have this wee grocery business."

Unlike the pre-war period the migration from Italy in the 1950s and 1960s was on a massive scale: nearly 150,000 immigrants arrived in Britain between 1948 and 1968. As the Census returns show, however, only a tiny proportion of this number settled in Scotland and it is significant that in terms of the origins of the immigrants the composition of the community remains largely unaltered. A recent study of the present-day Italian community (by Ms Terri Colpi) has revealed that 90 per cent of the Italians in Glasgow came from the Garfagnana district of Lucca, while 80 per cent of those living in Edinburgh have connections with Picinisco in Frosinone province. The close-knit nature of the community, however, which was so powerful a feature of the early days, is gradually being weakened by integration and assimilation.

Mrs Lucchesi:
"The younger generation don't want to work late at night and they're just not interested in fish and chips. Although I still have the shop I have to let it out because my family are not interested. . . . Today it's different. My family, we all married Italians, now my children instead, well my son, he's a teacher, he married a Scotch girl, a teacher, and my daughter married a local Scotch boy."

Dominic Crolla:
"Well, it's losing a bit because of the inter-marriage. And it's losing a little because as the

more years pass, the more we're being absorbed into the ways of Scottish life. There's nothing more inevitable than that."

Mrs D'Agostino:
"Well, what I call the new immigrants, they're quite a new breed altogether. They are so entirely different from us that we have very little in common really. This doesn't mean to say that one is better than the other . . . but I think we have acquired a lot of British tastes, British habits. We like our freedom, we don't like to work after a certain hour, we enjoy living a little more gracious life. They're not interested in gracious living, only in acquiring. They're very hard working, I shudder at the work they do because I can remember having done something on the same lines when I was very young and I would hate to go back to that life. To me it's not living, it's just merely existing."

As in the past, most newcomers find employment in the catering trades in the 'pizzarias' and 'spaghetti houses' that have become so popular in the last decade or so. Few settle here permanently and it is partly because of this constant flow of new blood into the community that a strong sense of national identity remains. Other factors are also important, such as the increasing frequency of visits to relatives and friends in Italy and, perhaps equally important, a growing awareness among members of the community that their language and culture ought to be preserved.

Dr Franchi:
"In the last fifteen to twenty years there has been a great movement to keep this link alive. The *Dante Alighieri* society have a number of thriving branches and their forte is simply the spreading of Italian ideals and Italian culture. There are the Saturday morning classes in Edinburgh and Glasgow to teach the young ones exclusively Italian and Italian culture. And every year there is a conference organised, an Italian conference, and this is for the young people to rediscover their origins and to stay together for a few days not only socially but culturally as well."

As in all immigrant groups there will be some who will willingly and quickly adopt the culture and customs of their new 'homeland'. Some will remain indifferent to it and others will try to retain their original identity.

Dominic Crolla:
"Well, I've noticed it in my own family where my oldest girl, she's been to Italy with us on holiday and she loves Italy and came back and wanted to study Italian, whereas my youngest one, she knows nothing about Italy. . . . In the Argentine Games I remember we were all shouting for Italy and my wife was crying when Holland beat Italy 2-1 and my little girl, Carla, she was crying because

*A young Federico Pontiero.*

Scotland had been beaten. I don't want to go through that experience of the World Cup again!"

Clearly, in having a sense of national or cultural identity there is a security, a sense of belonging, an attachment, which meets an important human need. However, the search for an identity has its problems and as Federico Pontiero suggests, in a statement full of eloquence and honesty, perhaps the real search should be for social justice.

Federico Pontiero:
"Who can prove you are a Scots or he's an Italian? Nobody can prove what nationality we have. I mean the Romans, they occupied London for how many years? They occupied Britain for 400 years and how many children's been born in that time? What are they then? To me every people's the same, and I mean every person in this world has the right to live where he wants. This is God's land, it's a God's land for everybody, whether you're black or white or dark or whatever you are."

MURDOCH RODGERS

# Mungo Mackay & the Green Table

Mungo Mackay and his Green Table may not have been unique in the Scottish coal industry during the half century before nationalisation in 1947, but he and his system of industrial and social control earned a notoriety among miners even in coalfields beyond the Lothians. In the Newtongrange area of Midlothian such a lasting impression has been left by Mackay's dominant personality and autocratic paternalism that today, forty years after his death, some older villagers are said still to believe 'Mungo's no' deid yet'.

Mackay, born in 1867, was not a Midlothian but an Ayrshire man. He had begun work as a mining engineer at Auchinleck Colliery before moving to Polton pit, Midlothian, about 1894. Coal mining was by then of course a very old industry in the Lothians. The monks of Newbattle Abbey, evidently the earliest miners in Scotland, were digging coal on the banks of the South Esk river from the thirteenth century until the Reformation. The Marquesses of Lothian, employing colliers as serfs until the Act of Emancipation in 1799, worked the coal around Newbattle and Newtongrange until the later nineteenth century. Then the Lothian Coal Company, formed in 1860 and expanded in 1890, took over production. This company, whose chief director James A. Hood was said to be a millionaire, was only one of half-a-dozen leading coal companies in the Lothians. They included the Arniston Coal Company, Edinburgh Collieries Ltd. and the Niddrie and Benhar Coal Company. With the growth of the export trade in coal and developments in technology, including greater mechanisation, mining in Midlothian began to develop at a much faster pace in the late nineteenth century. The opening of the Lady Victoria pit at Newtongrange in 1890 by the Lothian Coal Company marked the beginning of modern mining in the county. Thus Mungo Mackay's arrival in the district four years later more or less coincided with this 'take-off' of the industry.

Mackay soon became agent and general manager of the Lothian Coal Company and then in 1927 a director. He managed the three pits at or around Newtongrange, where the company's head office was situated—the Lady Victoria, Lingerwood and East-houses. Late in his career, after the death of his fellow-manager Mr Hamilton of Rosewell, Mackay was responsible also for the colliery there, known as Whitehill pit, and for the nearby Polton pit. Mackay died in 1939 and is buried in Newbattle cemetery.

Even in an industry hardly noted in those times for kindly or sympathetic relations between the private coal companies and the miners, Mungo Mackay's paternalism and autocracy were remarkable.

*Opposite: Mungo Mackay in Masonic regalia.*

Authoritarian colliery managers were then one of many occupational hazards that miners had to face daily, but none of his contemporaries appears to have earned quite so much notoriety among Scots miners as did Mackay. In the West Lothian shale mines, for instance, managers like Bryson of Pumpherston and A. C. Thomson of Oakbank attempted to discipline and control their miners both at work and in the more remote villages, but neither succeeded to the extent that Mackay did further east. His techniques of industrial and social control, his ruthlessness in applying them, and his relative success, are rather reminiscent of the old West of Scotland coalmasters recently so well discussed by Alan B. Campbell in his history of the Lanarkshire miners in the century preceding 1874. Mackay could be seen as a survival from an earlier and harder epoch, a kind of early twentieth-century Baird of Gartsherrie.

Tommy Kerr:

"Ah stayed in East Lothian and ah started in the pits in 1926 frae ah wis a lad leavin' the school. Now miners in the Lothians area used to talk about 'Up the braes'—Newtongrange and that area—in whispers. They used to say, 'If there's one place that ah widna like tae work it's up in the area where this man Mackay has the control and the terror struck in the hearts o' the workmen'."

Mackay's reputation spread also in Fife. Some militant miners there, victimised after the 1926 lock-out, sought work in the pits at Newtongrange, no doubt keeping their views well hidden. But on their first pay-day they became merry in the pub and began to sing strike ditties and *The Red Flag*. They were summoned before Mungo Mackay and his Green Table and were back in Fife by nightfall.

The authority that Mackay exercised in Newton-grange, and his personality, are recalled by one of his wages clerks who worked under him for many years in the 1920s and '30s.

James Reid:

"Mungo was a well-built man, about six feet, quite a good lookin' man, moustache. But he had an unfortunate way of speaking to people, always startin' wi' [cough] clearing his throat. Now ah may be biased but he always gave me the impression that I was beneath him. He must have given the miners the verra same, must have. Ah can't tell ye any funny stories about him because ah think he was absolutely devoid o' humour. Ah can't remember ever seein' him smile. But he was the type that demonstrated to the full 'master and man'. There were a class which he belonged to, and there

*Office staff, Lothian Coal Company, c. 1930. James Reid is top right.*

were a class that ah belonged tae. And ah found then although ah was only a young man that if you were a surveyor you were everything, if you were a wages clerk you were a nothing.''

There is no evidence that Mackay ever became a particularly wealthy man. His rise to the position of supreme control that he maintained in and around the villages of Newtongrange, Gorebridge, Birkenside, Arniston, Rosewell, Poltonhall, and Bonnyrigg, seems to have been based very much on his professional skill. Opinion is unanimous that Mungo Mackay was an outstandingly able mining engineer.

Tommy Kerr:

"Ah'm gaun tae pay him a compliment, and it's against the grain. But bein' a miner and aware o' what is essential in minin' is efficiency—both for safety and other reasons—ah would say that Mackay must have been a first-class minin' engineer. If Mackay hadn't played the part that he did in pursuin' a line of road-making in Lady Victoria in all probability Lady Victoria, followin' the War, would hae been shut much earlier than 1981, because when the boom for coal come about the handy coal was taken from the main roadsides and other places and Mackay's roadways stood the test. In fact, it's been often said that he used to have a three-foot stick that he could hold above his

head and if that stick touched any part of the roadway, instructions were immediately given tae get it heightened. So that gives ye an idea o' the man's ability as a minin' engineer.''

Much of Mackay's success in disciplining and controlling the miners of the Lothian Coal Company arose from the fact that the company's pits were run on the contracting system.

Pat Flynn:

"The system o' contractin' wis, there were one man used to go to the bosses in the pit and say, 'Ah'll do this for ye.' And he got a price fur minin' coal. He'd probably say he'd gie ye 5d. or 10d. a ton. And this chap wid hire other people—that's the contractin'. So ma dad, he wis hired.''

Miners, and their unions, were generally hostile to the contracting system and sought its abolition.

James Reid:

"At that time, a man that was on the face, if he worked his five shifts—there were no overtime paid—would be lucky if he had £3 a week. Whereas you, as contractor, was probably takin' home £30. Mungo Mackay believed in this system, which is long gone now, because it was puttin' the workin' man against the workin' man.''

*Newtongrange Main Street and Picture House, 1920s.*

The miners' union in the Lothians—the Mid and East Lothian Miners' Association, which was a purely county union like those in all other Scots coalfields before the 1940s—was not very strong or militant. It was too small, and unemployment among miners, as among other workers, was usually too great for the union to wield much power. It seems to have found no effective answer to the tactics and practices of Mungo Mackay.

Tommy Kerr:

"He tolerated the Trade Union movement but that was all that he did. John Rutherford was a checkweigher appointed by the men. On many occasions Mungo Mackay used the psychology o' imposition, and he would ask him up, the likes o' a trade union official like John, to go to the office and he would keep him waitin' and waitin' and waitin'. This was one o' his methods o' gettin' the first blow in in any negotiations that might have to take place."

As far as the wages clerks of the Lothian Coal Company were concerned, Mackay resolutely opposed any attempt by them to form a union.

James Reid:

"Ah didn't personally try to start a union but we started to talk about it through a wages clerk who went off the rails, started cheatin', and he was found out. Well, he had started two years after me

and of course in the court case his salary came out and he had £1 something more than I had. And we got our heads together. For instance, ah didn't know what Joe Soaps on ma left hand, or John Broon on ma right, had. Ye never knew anybody's wages. There were no scales nor nothing, and of course ah said, 'Look, it's high time we were doin' something.' And ah was told wi' the Chief Wages Clerk: 'You try, or any o' you try, to form a union and you'll be replaced. Period. You'll be replaced.' So that we were actually cowed. Now anybody listenin' to ma story will say, 'Well, why did they stick that?' Well, at that time—we're approachin' it now—there were over three million unemployed. Ah had no degrees, ah'd left the public school at fourteen, ah had nothing. And a job was a job. And that's the sole reason."

Some of the Lothian Coal Company miners, not surprisingly, felt themselves to be in a state of semi-serfdom, little freer than the old Newbattle miners in the times before the Emancipation of 1799. Mackay's power seemed to many to be not merely unchallenged but unchallengeable. He seemed to have complete freedom to practice a policy of divide and rule. Among the office staff the application of this policy took the form of favouritism.

James Reid:

"If ye was on the Staff, ye could get a bag o' sticks, if ye had the right side of his face, a beautiful big bag o' chopped sticks to keep ye goin'. Ah never got sticks. Another difference he made with the Staff was when you were married and ye paid rent and rates. Now at that time it was seven shillings and 1/9d. rates, year after year, there was no jumpin' like what there is nowadays. Well, ye suddenly found out when ye started talkin' seriously about tryin' to all be equal, that one person was payin' seven shillin's, but not the rates. Another person was payin' the full thing. Another favoured person was rent-free. Now seven shillin's and 1/9d. in those days was really something. Then it came to the coal. Some had free coal. Others paid fifteen and ninepence, plus the cartage. In other words, he set the Staff one against another just the same as he did with the miner by his contractin' system."

Of course other private coal companies also operated the contracting system. But this method of dividing and ruling the miners Mackay characteristically extended from their place of work to their place of residence—from the pits to the villages. Some of the contractors and some other miners and villagers acted as spies and informers for Mackay not only in the pits but also in the miners' rows in Newtongrange and the other villages owned or dominated by the Lothian Coal Company.

Tommy Kerr:
"If any organisation was set up he used to query it and find out what its intentions was, and every step was taken to ensure that he was well informed. The contractors of course were the first line o' his defence. They got inflated wages and they acted as spies."

James Reid:
"Ah don't think ah ever once in ma life saw him walkin' through the village. 'Cause he didn't need to, it was like the coal face—he had his informants who told him what was goin' on in the village. The company policeman knew everythin' that went on in the village. The result is he took it up the stair to Mungie Mackay. There were a head timekeeper and another man, who I shall leave nameless, and actually they were just go-betweens. Everythin' that they heard went up the stair to Mungo Mackay. With the result that, as the years went on, he ruled like a king. He really ruled like a king in this village. It's a known fact that a man could have a row on a Saturday night, wi' maybe a pint in him, and got into a wee bit fight, and on Monday he was up in front o' Mungo Mackay because somebody went up and told him. He could actually know that your next door neebour and his wife had a row. It was amazing. You talk aboot Gestapo. It was really good, it was really good."

Tommy Kerr, a militant trade unionist living and working in East Lothian, had no personal contact with Mackay and did not move to Midlothian to work in the pits there until several years after Mackay's death. Nonetheless:

"Ah was aware o' his power over the workers and his representation of the Lothian Coal Company. There's no doubt if ever there were a reputation that could make money for the employers he was the one, at the expense of the employees.
"The powers o' Mackay was so great that if a man didnae attend his work he could phone the local Dean Tavern and instruct the barman: 'This man's not, if he comes in, he's not to receive any drink. He's not to get a pint.' "

Mackay's attempts to recruit informers were not, however, always successful.

Tommy Thomson:
"Well, on Thursday, ah come up and handed in ma tokens, and the rattle, knock on the window, [they] said, 'You're wanted up the stair at four o'clock.' Ah said to maself, 'What have you done already?' When ah went in Mr Mackay's was a long face. 'Tom,' he says, 'ah've a job for you.' Ah says, 'Oh, what's that?' He says, 'I want you to go to Lingerwood pit as an oversman.' Ah said, 'I'll hae tae consider it.' He says, 'Here, where did you get all your experience?' Ah said, 'From ma father and you.' He said, 'Because ah've been hearing good reports about you.' He said, 'Ah've never yet appointed an oversman that's come to me without tellin' the tale. So,' he says, 'ah want to have a check on everything that's in Lingerwood.' 'Well, Mr Mackay,' ah said, 'if that's the case you're no' gettin' me.' He said, 'Come on now, away go home and think it over for a fortnight.' But ah never would take the oversman's job."

Mackay's control over the miners both at work and in the villages, particularly at Newtongrange and Rosewell, was based on the ownership by the Lothian Coal Company of all or most of the houses in which the miners and their families lived. One aspect of his paternalism was his insistence that the miners must keep tidy the gardens of their tied houses.

Alexander Trench:
"If Mr Mackay had been livin' today this village would ha' been a hunder per cent better than what it is, especially the older houses. In these days if you didn't dig your garden there was a man sent down to dig your garden for you and you paid for it. Mr Mackay used to have a walk round himself round the houses to see if the gardens were being looked after. It was a model village all through Mr Mackay. He seen that it was a model village."

Tommy Thomson:
"He used to come down through the village,

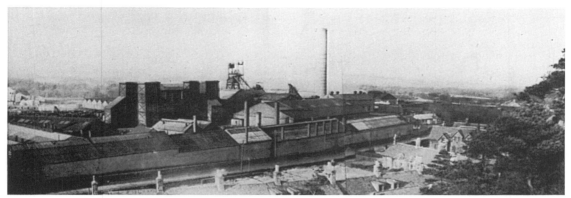

*Lady Victoria pit.*

# The Collier's Song

Now all you jol — ly collier lads, come lis — ten un — to me— You
know how we are sore op — pressed by mast — er's ty — ran — ny; For im
prove —ment o' the mines, n — o leis — ure time is found, Our
child — ren are ne — glec —ted to be work —ing un — der ground.

Our masters are tyrannical and that they must confess,
They overtax their workmen and do them sore oppress;
No other occupation so dangerous can be found,
We cannot call our lives our own while working underground.

The sailor he does plough the main and perils does go through,
But he sees the danger coming which a collier cannot do;
With fallen roofs and fire damp the records can be found,
How hundreds yearly lost their lives by working underground.

Frae Newtongrange and Arniston, frae Polton and Gorebrig,
Frae Birkenside tae Lasswade, Cockpen and Bonnyrigg;
Frae Rosewell tae Newbattle the Lothian men a' say,
We're no the likes o' ither men that works an eight hours day.

*Better quality housing occupied by contractors in Newtongrange.*

walking with his stick, to see how everything was lookin'. And down near the bottom pub there wis a man wi' the name o' Toshie Moffat. Toshie couldna be bothered doin' his garden at any time. So Mr Mackay sent for Toshie to come up to the office one day, and he said to him: 'Toshie, yer gairden's a disgrace tae the raw. What are ye gaun tae dae aboot it?' Toshie looked at Mungie and he said, 'Mr Mackay, ye havenae seen ma gairden right because,' he said, 'there are tatties planted in ma gairden.' 'Oh, no, no, Toshie,' he says, 'they're no' tatties planted in your gairden.' He said, 'The tatties,' he says, 'that you're talkin' about are all long gress.' "

To punish indiscipline by miners down the pits or in the villages Mackay, or his henchmen, sometimes threatened or imposed that traditional weapon of coal-owners—eviction from company housing.

James 'Treacle' Moffat:
    "Mungo Mackay wisna feared tae tell ye if ye done onythin' wrong—'Ah'll put ye out the house.' Ye had tae dae what ye wis telt—or else. His heid man as manager of the Lady was Willie Kerson. An' the under-manager wis Peter Dixon. And they telt ye, 'Ye'll do what ye're told—or else.' An' he says to me one day: 'Ye'll do what ye're told or ah'll put ye out your house.' So ah says, 'Well, ye'll just have to put ez out the house,' ah says, 'ah've a

good home tae go tae.' 'Aye,' he says, 'if ye gang back to yer faither and mither we'll pit them out the house too.' "

Pat Flynn:
    "Now I've heard stories such as Mackay, he'd send for this man, Joe Thomson or whoever, and say, 'Hello, Joe, come in here.' Of course, ye'd go in wi' your hat under your elbow and stand verra much to attention and don't speak until you're spoken to—almost in front of the Crime Squad. And he'd say, 'Ah see you've a son leavin' school on Friday.' And the chap would say, 'Yes, ah hiv, yes, and ah've got a job for him as an apprentice'—ah don't know what it wis, a joiner, plumber, whatever. 'Ah,' he says, 'but ah've got a job here in the pit for him.' And he says, 'But ah'd like ma laddie tae try and dae somethin' better than the pits and ah've got him an apprenticeship.' 'Oh, no, ye'd better bring him up here.' And the chap says, 'Well, ah'd like him to be an apprentice.' And the end of the conversation [Mackay says] 'Either bring him up, start him on Monday, or bring up the keys o' the house.'
    "Well, ye can understand the position o' this man. What's he gonnae do? So thereby another miner, not by choice by any means, ended up in the pits. And that's the way it worked, that's the way his system went on. You can imagine the power that this man had."

*Miners' housing, Newtongrange.*

An elder in the Church of Scotland and first Right Worshipful Master of the Newtongrange Freemasons, Mackay is said to have used both religion and freemasonry in building up his control over the miners.

Tommy Kerr:

"Oh, aye, he was a leadin' figure in the Church. But he was a fly man, he was never sectarian. Ah believe that his association wi' Roman Catholicism was pretty well known in the locality. Ah believe he was friendly wi' the local priests and other people and he conferred wi' them. Many people that ah know in Newtongrange and in the locality got promotion as a consequence o' bein' seen in the church by Mackay."

Pat Flynn:

"Ah wis born in Rosewell. Ma dad was Irish, and he came across to Scotland it must ha' been in the early 'twenties or maybe before that. There seemed to be a hell of a lot of Irish people in Rosewell. A lot o' people referred to it as 'Little Ireland'. Ah often wonder as time goes by why were so many Irish people congregated in the one place? And ah wonder was there so many Protestants congregated in the other half i' the Lothian Coal Company's set-up, namely Newtongrange? An' ah often wonder tae masel, wis this a policy o' Mungie Mackay? Or wis it a policy o' the Lothian Coal Company? As an

individual, ah never heard any concrete evidence to this fashion, but ah wonder, wis he tryin' to divide and conquer? That's what's at the back o' ma head."

Such methods of control, practised by Mackay for about forty years until his retirement in the 1930s, were made possible partly by the deference shown toward him personally and his system by many of the employees of the Lothian Coal Company and their families. This deference may have been to some extent an outcome of many generations of subjection of local miners, stretching back to the centuries when they were the serf-colliers of the Marquesses of Lothian. Whatever the reasons deference certainly oiled the wheels of Mackay's system.

At Rosewell, a few miles west of Newtongrange, Mungo Mackay's writ ran but there it was enforced not so much by himself as by his fellow Lothian Coal Company manager, Mr Hamilton.

Pat Flynn:

"Mr Hamilton was the manager o' Rosewell or Whitehill Colliery. And in the workshops, ye know, the blacksmith's shop, the engineerin' shop, the electric shop, if he happened to be comin', they used tae hae a signal which went: 'SSSSSHH SSSSSH'—which meant, 'Get workin'', or 'Get oot the road', or 'Get lost'. So this went on for years. Every time they heard this noise they used to scatter, ye know, if they were talkin' aboot a game o' football, or dogs, or pigeons, or whatever, they used to scatter. This chap, Mr Hamilton, who was the manager, died. And he lived in a house a few hundred yards up from the colliery. And on the day he was gettin' buried the hearse was passin' by the workshops, so they were peerin' out, lookin', lookin' at this great man passin' in this coffin, and says, 'Oh, look at him, oh.' And all o' a sudden somebody came to the door and went 'SSSSSHH SSSSSH'. And they all scattered. And here's the man goin' by in his coffin—and they were still terrified for him."

Mackay's autocracy even extended to the Newtongrange pipe band.

James Reid:
"He sent for me one day and he said, 'Reid, I want you to be secretary and treasurer of the pipe band.' I said, 'Pipe band?' He said, 'Yes, it's starting this week, and I want them on the right lines. We'll get permission to take a penny off.' So I had to collect the pennies [from the miners' pay packets] and report every month to him. Then he came to the choosing of the tartan, and he went through Maclean, MacDuff, Mackenzie, MacGregor, Mackay. And he stopped at Mackay, naturally. And he says, 'How would that look?' It wis a hellish tartan: it was yellow, and yellow, and more yellow, what ah recollect. Of course it was all the same what I said. 'Aye, we'll have the Mackay tartan for the band.' Well, this actually happened. I had the order made up; it was an Edinburgh firm of kiltmakers. And this morning Mungo Mackay sent for me at half-past nine and he says, 'I've changed my mind. Ye'd better cancel it and get the Royal Stuart.' 'Oh, my God,' I says. I had everything written out: Mackay. The order was already in the post box. Ah had to belt down that road to the post office and I had to plead with the postmaster, 'Look, you've got to open the box and let me get that letter out or I'm shot, I'm as dead as a door nail.' The postmaster knew me and opened up the box and gave me the letter back and I went up and rewrote it for the Royal Stuart tartan."

It was at the Green Table that Mungo Mackay, like some medieval lord of the manor among his serfs, meted out 'justice'. The Green Table was a large table intended for the laying-out of colliery plans.

James Reid:
"Well, he had a fairly large room, and actually all that was in it was some minin' books and this big table, green-covered. And he sat behind and you when you were summoned you were not asked to sit. You stood in front o' the Green Table."

Many miners summoned before the Green Table suffered palpitations.

Alexander Trench:
"Mr Mackay sent for you, to 'go up the stair'. And when you knew you were goin' 'up the stair', it was no joke, you knew what you were goin' tae face. And you had to be clean, a collar and tie on, and go up and see Mr Mackay. And he was very efficient and verra fair, askin' the questions, 'Why did you not do this, why did . . .?' and you had to answer. If you didn't, he fairly rapped you over the fingers for not doin' it properly."

Mackay never presided alone at the Green Table. Always beside him he would place the Lothian Coal Company policeman. This policeman was one of Mackay's chief lieutenants in maintaining his control, industrial and social, over the miners.

Tommy Kerr:
"Ah believe that the policeman were as much subservient to the will o' Mackay as any workmen. The men used the expression in the pits, 'Is you for the Green Table? Some man, eh? Ye're goin' up there to get a bit belabourin'?' The company policeman was only the tool that was used as a psychological threat to the men. Ah never knew o' any violence takin' place any time."

Sometimes Mackay also required the presence of additional henchmen at the Green Table, such as under-managers or pit oversmen. But always he alone did the talking. He alone made all the pronouncements on charges, evidence, and passed sentence on accused miners.

James 'Treacle' Moffat:
"Aye, ma powny run away and when oo went up tae the splint mine the oversman, Jimmy Long, was stan'in wi' the powny. He says, 'What's the powny dae'in up here itsel'?' An' ah says, 'It run away.' It could run harder than me. 'Aw?' he says, 'ye have to see Mr Mackay aboot that.' So ah was sent for. They put a line on your token: 'Gaun up and see Mr Mackay at four o'clock or half-past four.' When ah went up he says, 'What have you been doin'?' And ah says, 'Nothin' that ah ken o'.' So he says, 'You must have been daein somethin'.' Ah says, 'It must be about ma powny runnin' away.' 'Aye,' he says, 'that's right.' So oo had a wee bit blether back and forrit and he says, 'Jist tae learn ye a lesson,' he says, 'oo'll fine ye ten bob but ye'll get it back in three month on your good behaviour.' So ah wis good behaviour for the next three month and ah got back ma ten bob."

Sentences imposed by Mackay at the Green Table included fines—sometimes collective—and of course dismissal from the company's employment, which included loss of a tied house.

Alexander Trench:
"We got fined a pound losing two grease cups.

*Lady Victoria pit bottom, c. 1900.*

Now grease cups were on machinery and they must have got lost some way, with the turning and the moving about as often. And we lost two o' them. So we were fined a pound. But that pound came off the pool. It wasn't one person that lost that pound, it come off the pool where there were about maybe twenty men included in. But that was one of the things, if you lost anything you had to pay for it. You got the choice what hospital you sent the fines to. Most o' them went to Edinburgh Royal Infirmary."

James Reid:
"Now it was genuine, because the next week in your payline you got a receipt from the Edinburgh Royal Infirmary, to thank you for your £1. But the poond at these days happened to be one-third of your total week's wage, which seemed a bit hard to me."

The surviving older generation of Newtongrange and district miners, and their families, who lived under Mungo Mackay's regime until his death in 1939, appear to divide largely into two groups. There are those who respected or even admired him and his system; and those who, with varying degrees of intensity, did not. Only a few take up a middle position.

James 'Treacle' Moffat:
"Well, he was a kind o' bad man an' he was a kind o' guid man at times. If ye went up tae see him, if he sent for ye to gin up, he wid argue wi' ye an' he wid grant ye your side o' the story if he thocht ye wis right."

Mrs Mary McLaren:
"He wis a hard man but right to the core. He got his way, whether you liked it or no'. He was a good man tae this village in every way. If a man was sent to a job it had to be done. And ye never heard o' strikes in thae days wi' Mungie Mackay. He wis a genuine man, a right good man."

John Telfer:
"Well, Mr Mackay was very well liked in the village. He was strict but he was good."

James Reid:
"You'll get people in this village who yearn for the old days, you know: 'Aw, if Mungo Mackay was back; this village is gaun tae hell now.' Maybe so, but ye can put your foot on a man's neck jist a wee bit too hard, you know. That's what ah thought he did."

IAN MacDOUGALL

# The Fisher Lassies

"It was all done for the love o' oor men folk. If we hadn't worked, they couldn't have sold their fish."

This was how Mrs Annie Sellings, now ninety years old, a herring gutter in her early years, summed up the commitment of the women of Scottish fishing communities to the herring industry of the late nineteenth and early twentieth centuries. Fisher girls grew up ready to learn and follow the trade of curing herring for the German and Russian markets. There was a boom in the export of salt herring to these countries from about 1870 to 1914 and these were prosperous times for the fisher people of Nairn and the North East. In their fast and versatile Zulu sail boats, later replaced by steam drifters, they caught huge quantities of herring for the eager and stable curing industry. With their new wealth many built good stone houses, bought fashionable clothes, had grand weddings, and generally enjoyed a high standard of living.

Before this, line fishing, with its endless and repetitive tasks which brought meagre financial reward, was the mainstay of fishing communities and provided only a hand to mouth existence. The lusty appetites of the German and Russian people for salt herring caused a dramatic change in the lives of those who followed the fishing trade, and ushered in a welcome period of hope, happiness and financial security.

From my own town of Nairn, about thirty drifters left in their seasons to fish the herring grounds off Fraserburgh, Wick, Shetland, Stornoway, Yarmouth and Lowestoft. Teenage girls and young unmarried women, mainly relatives of the fishermen, followed soon after, to gut and pack the herring, having previously been engaged by curers for the work. They were provided with accommodation and paid by the barrel. Living conditions were primitive, the pay was miserable and the work exhausting. In spite of all that, however, those who still survive, and most are now very old, in their youth eagerly looked forward to and greatly enjoyed the gutting, especially in Shetland. They loved the independence and comradeship of living away from home in huts with their friends, in charge of their own domestic arrangements, experiencing a temporary period of communal living. It was like a working holiday.

The fishing industry, like farming in the days before mechanisation, required the involvement of the whole family, and women were expected to play their full part. They helped with the line fishing in their home ports by digging up bait, redding and baiting lines, splitting, salting and smoking fish, and finally travelling around the countryside bartering or selling them. When salt herring were being exported on a large scale from the British Isles, it was natural that the women should transfer their energies to supporting this lucrative market. The process of curing was an important related activity which could only be

*Above: The steam drifter 'Glenerne', owned by the author's family. Opposite: Two Nairn gutting crews, Lerwick, c. 1885.*

successfully operated by teams of women workers and
they migrated in hundreds from their homes to large
ports all around the coast, to deal with the continuous
and massive catches of herring being landed by their
menfolk.

William Stewart:
"By the end of the eighteen hundreds there was
something like two hundred boats of all sorts and
sizes pursuing the herring fishing in Lossiemouth. As
the years went by the herring fishery opened in
other areas, but boats started tae get bigger and
then went further afield so that in Lossiemouth the
fishermen started tae go other places—Stornoway,
Lerwick, Ireland, Lowestoft, Yarmouth, Grimsby—
wherever the herring was to be found, the
fishermen followed in their sail boats.
"At the turn of the century came the steam and
in Lossiemouth again, steam gradually took over
from sail. As the steam drifters emerged in large
numbers from all ports, the herring fishing carried
on to unprecedented scale.
"Goin' back to the early days o' herrin' fishin'
there would never hae been the herrin' fishin' if it
hadna been fur the fisher lassies tae gut the herrin'.
And they came from all ports on the Moray Firth—
Cromarty, Avoch, Findhorn, Helmsdale, Burghead,
Hopeman, Lossie, Nairn, was well represented in
the fisher lassies guttin' the herrin'. One wonders at

times just how they survived. The conditions was so
severe that they worked in, especially in the winter
time, in places where snow was deep, the winds
blowin', frost. Nevertheless, it was their bread and
butter and more so, it was their husbands', fathers',
and sons' bread and butter.
"In the nineteen hundreds there was something
like, from Lossie alone, three hundred girls went to
the guttin'. In Nairn there'd probably be half that
number anyway; Burghead and Hopeman equally
much about the same. Buckie, probably five or six
hundred, Buckie and the district, and Fraserburgh
about the same. And all in a', roond aboot these
years, there must have been something like three
thousand girls engaged in the guttin' industry."

A sum of money knows as arles, usually one pound
was paid to the gutting crews as an earnest of their
intention to work for the curer who engaged them.
Before each fishing, representatives of different curers
visited fishing towns to recruit girls for the work. They
arranged themselves in threes, two gutters and a
packer, and worked together, often for many seasons
and in many places, until marriage broke up the
partnership.

Mrs Isabella Stewart:
"The curer called and engaged ye, well asked ye,
and then ye got yer crew, it was three in a crew. It

*Isabella Stewart of Lossie, third from right, with her crew and coopers. Yarmouth, c. 1920.*

wis piece work efter that, ye see, jist whatever much barrels ye could fill. At that time, it was sixpence for a barrel."

Miss Jean Bochel:
"We looked forward to it. I suppose we were like the gypsies, when it came to the time of year, you just sorta, sorted up yer things and away."

The Sumburgh Roost, the confluence of the Atlantic Ocean and the North Sea, creates uncomfortable and hazardous sailing conditions which were particularly dreaded by the fisher girls forced to make the crossing from Aberdeen to Lerwick for the gutting season. Some were sick even at the thought of it, others were dreadfully sick when on board. It gave my mother a distaste for the sea which lasted all her life.

Miss Jean Bochel:
"It was beyond description the boat, you wouldna like tae see it. A lota sickness, a lota girls, just the thought—there was a woman over there, she died just last year, whenever she got the telegram that she was leaving on Monday she would be upstairs lookin' at the sea and she'd be sick before she'd ever go away—just the thought of it made them sick!

"You just lay down where you saw a space, that's all, very much steerage. I don't know how many boats would have left Aberdeen to go to Lerwick because they went by the Aberdeen Steam Navigation Company and they had a lot of extra boats on then and I don't know how many girls but I'm sure there'd be two or three hundred in every boat—exclusively fish workers at that time I'd imagine."

Mrs Eveline Crockett:
"The cattle that was taken aboard that ship was far more taken care of than what we were. We were on the deck and the crew was very sorry fur us, they used tae put tarpaulins ower the top of us."

Miss Jean Bochel:
"Everybody went down, they were very quiet, everybody expected to be sick, but I was quite a good sailor. You had to take your own food, we didn't have any meals or anything there, we didn't have very much money at the time, very poor. I wouldn't have much in ma bag tae take fur eating. And I was a good eater, I still am, and they'd all start bein' sick—sick, I'd go all round their bags and I'd be eatin' all their stuff! So one time coming from Lerwick tae Aberdeen, you know how the Captain comes to the top o' the gangway and sees you all going ashore and he says, 'You over there, you,' points his finger to me to come—and I, face like a beetroot, didn't know what on earth I was going to get a tellin' off for, I wasn't in the way o' gettin' tellin' offs—and he says 'The next time you come, take a nose bag, it would be far handier for

*Dressing up for the photographer was one of the first things the girls did after settling in for the season. Fraserburgh, c. 1895.*

you!' He was seein' me go all round the people and looking to see what was for to eat.

"The Roost was a very bad—I was always saying, 'Where's the Roost, [have] we passed it?' [an old hand said] 'You come and ask me that again,' she says, 'I'll hit ye!' On a calm day it would still be rough."

In Shetland the curers provided the gutting crews with rent-free huts which were unfurnished apart from bunk beds and an open fireplace. In the early days the girls slept three to a bed and lived six to a hut. Their wooden kists, brought from home filled with clothes and domestic utensils, were used as tables and chairs in the huts. Screens were put up at the windows, and a 'glory hole' curtained off for toilet purposes. All this was completed on the first day so that the girls were ready, if needed, to start gutting the next morning.

Mrs Eveline Crockett:
"We had to walk two mile oot tae Gremista and when we arrived at Gremista, the huts that we were gaun intae wes full o' barrels. Fit we had tae dae was empty the barrels oot o' the huts. Then we'd tae take a pail o' water and scrub oot the huts and make them liveable. The curers wasna carin'—they wouldna care less. So therefore, we

*Interior of a herring gutters' hut, in Shetland, with brick fireplace, wooden bunks and wallpapered walls.*

went ben to wir hoosie and—it was a sorta home because we wis nine weeks there. Mind you it wasna like hame, but we made it [like home] and we had bunk beds and there was a hole there they ca'ed the glory hole—the glory hole could tell mony a tale ah'm tellin' ye! (laughs) Well it held mair than pots and pans many a time, but never mind! (laughs) But never mind!"

Mrs Margaret Duthie:
"Ye'd tae take in water in pails from an outside tap ye know and put on pans of water ontae a coal fire, it was always a coal fire. And washing facilities—we'd a barrel o' water, rain water at the door, ye know, and of course, it was just the basin, we'd nuthin' else."

Mrs Isabella Stewart:
"You took your own dishes and mats and everything with ye, ye see, it was jist an empty hut."

Miss Jean Bochel:
"We'd have to paper or paint the place and then take an old chest, kists we called them, and that did for seats and that was our furniture. We used to take pictures with us and we'd leave them, and a mirror and we'd have vases and all sorts—and we'd to provide our own lamp—it was oil lighting we had."

Mrs Annie Finlayson:
"We took our own beds wi' us, chaff, a' oor own beds, our own cookin' utensils. No electric ovens

then nor gas cookers nor nothin', just the open fire. And we made just as good scones and pancakes then as you can do now."

Some girls left home at the age of fourteen to become gutters, usually in the company of older sisters or cousins. So close were neighbourly and family ties at the time that any young girl from the fishing community was warmly and affectionately regarded by the whole group and her welfare and progress became the concern of all. She was expected to 'learn by doing', getting some guidance and encouragement from experienced friends. Already used to many household tasks, mending nets, knitting, sewing, cooking and baiting lines, her fingers adapted in a very short time to the use of the sharp gutting knife and, quickly extracting the guts, she threw them into cougs, and the herring into tubs at the rate of one a second.

Miss Jean Bochel:
"Usually the foreman came and knocked at every door at five o'clock—'Get up, get up, get up.' One girl took a day on, and if it was your day on ye had tae get up and light the fire and boil the kettle, make a cuppa tea and bread and butter—no toast. And then we started work at six prompt and it was prompt—because one was vying with the other, ye see, ye couldna *be* late."

Mrs Margaret Duthie:
"I was a gutter and had all my fingers tied up, you know, and workin' the knife, pretty fast—ye had to. Oh, ye were self-taught. Ye were just thrown in the deep end, just had tae pick up a knife

*Dressing injured hands at the Mission in Yarmouth.*

and start away. But the men were there, the coopers, they were overseein' the work and they would tell ye ye went wrong, ye know. We were all green at the beginning and ye had tae buck up and make a name for yerself sort of thing, and I remember—bein' the youngest, some of them got married and I was left tae get in wi' the older ones, ye know, so I had tae work hard tae keep up with them because we were all number one, two and three crew, ye know, just went by yer barrels, how many barrels ye did in a day, whether you were number one crew or two, like that. And of course I didn't want tae let the side down, I had tae work hard.

"The good crews got goin' tae Ireland ye see. I just went to Fraserburgh one year. But it was always Lerwick, and then, over tae Ireland. We went from there one year to North Shields and then from there down to Yarmouth."

To protect their fingers from the knife working at high speed, the girls tied cotton cloths round their fingers. These were washed daily and the string skilfully secured by hands and teeth.

Miss Jean Bochel:
"We had oilskin skirts and we had kerchiefs on our heads and we tied our fingers with cotton cloths."

Mrs Annie Finlayson:
"Oh your fingers, you had to watch yer fingers, had to be tied up and we got cotton, linen cloths ye know, ye know the flour bags, that the bakers had. Used tae buy them for about fourpence or threepence each, two o' them or three o' them kept us goin', and washed them and bleached them and tore it up in strips for yer fingers, that's how you'd keep your fingers. We'd tae keep them on all day, ye couldna take them off at lunchtime, you just washed your hands thoroughly in hot water. If it was festered, you put a bread poultice on it and sugar in the poultice. Bread poultice and sugar and put it to your finger if you had a festered hand and that cured it. There were no lance—you couldna get it lanced or any o' that sort o' thing, that cured it, nurse it and cured it and it just went away just then. And then you put on a thin cloth to keep it from the salt, and then ye were okay.

"Sometimes ye'd get a mackerel, you know, maybe if ye didna notice maybe grab your hands, and your finger could be pretty sore. But then there were what they called the Red Cross Hut there, what you call a Mission that ye went til if there was anything the matter, and got yer hands dressed which was very good. There was a nurse there, for dressing yer hands. But that was the only thing that was, watching yer hands, ye know. But ye see you were so quick, ye had tae be quick! Unless ye wanta work for no money at all ye had tae be quick ye see."

The hectic process of gutting and packing was interrupted throughout the day while crews carried their full tubs two at a time for rousing. Herring were partially salted in the farlins, but this more thorough salting called rousing was given after gutting, each grade being treated separately in a large tub before packing began. In addition, a handful of salt went in with each layer of herring in the barrel. It was back-breaking work, especially for the packers, constantly leaning over deep barrels stretching to the bottom to arrange the first important tier and working up until they had fitted in about eight hundred herrings.

Mrs Annie Finlayson:
"I think you could do about sixty to seventy in a minute. It all depends on the size of the fish, the size of the herring."

Miss Jean Bochel:
"We gutted and packed three barrels in an hour, three whole barrels in an hour. About seven or eight hundreds—when we gutted them first, but by the time they were filled up there were about a thousand herring in the barrel then. You started with one herring and then ye had one at each side of that and one in the middle. And you did it in three, three along the rest of the barrel, till it came to the middle. It was right across ye see and then ye started to go in then—it was really a work of art—but the bottom tier and the top tier, they were done very carefully, they had to be inspected."

A high standard of packing was demanded, and achieved, as everything had to be perfect for the buyers who tore herring from the tail upwards to taste them. The Russians opened barrels and tipped them up to see if the herring were all the same size. Barrels were chosen at random by the coopers for inspection. The test of a well-packed barrel was that the layers of herring remained in place even when the whole barrel was removed.

Miss Jean Bochel:
"I got away without being inspected because when I started we had a very hard foreman at the time, and oh I've been in tears many a time with him, because if it wasn't done right he would empty it out and he would say, 'You can do anything quicker doing it properly than doing it half shot.' I sure was taught the hard way but in my later years I blessed that man many a time because he saved me pounds. And in anything that you're doing it's easier and quicker to do it the right way than the wrong way.
"It had to be inspected so there was great competition among the girls. In the dinner hour we wouldn't take the hour, ye see, we'd be back quickly to our work tae get some o' this bottom tiers in before the hour to start would come—I would put in the bottom tiers ye see, whenever the hour would start the two gutters would help us to

*Gutting at the farlin, c. 1920.*

*Nairn lassies, Lerwick, c. 1920. Note the tied fingers.*

# Herring Shoals

Ian Sinclair

I'm a fish gutting las-sie gutting her ring's my trade, But I'll ne-ver be weal--thy no for-tunes are made. For ten-pence a bar-rel is all we are paid, Life is hard with the her—ring shoals.

CHORUS

Oh! we'll gut and we'll clean and we'll salt them aw—ay, Fill up the bar—rels and earn a day's pay. And when the job's ov—er we'll be on our way, We'll foll—ow the her—ring shoals.

The work is gey hard and the weather is cold,
But we'll sing while we wait for that catch of pure gold.
Then the drifters sail in, what a sight to behold,
Hurrah for the herring shoals.

We gut and we salt in the sun wind and rain,
Backs almost breaking, hands stiff with pain,
But when next season comes we'll be back here again,
Along with the herring shoals.

The season is over our work is now done,
The men, with their boats and the herring have gone.
Now we've packed up our kists and we're heading for home,
Goodbye to the herring shoals.

FINAL CHORUS
For we've gutted and cleaned and we've salted away,
Filled up the barrels and earned our day's pay,
And now the job's over we'll be on our way,
We followed the herring shoals.

pack up. They would start right away while the other girls, they'd be waiting on the cooper tae come and inspect them and that held them up. So there was a row one time, this girl was mad at us for gettin' started, so the foreman took her, he says 'Come here then,' and he took her over to my barrel, he says, 'When you can do a tier like that you'll maybe be allowed to start right away too,' so that was the end of the story."

Mrs Chrissie Campbell:
   "The coopers was roch and ready, ken what ah mean, they gave an oath noo and again, but ye jist took that in yer stride, ye ken, they were a' good, maist o' them was a' fine chiels ye ken."

'Filling up' was done the day following the first packing, but Mondays were often used for this work because the boats had not yet brought in fresh supplies of fish for gutting. As the salt drew moisture out of them, the herring sank down and fish from other barrels were used for filling up. The barrels, with lids on, were then laid on their sides and had bung holes drilled in them. Pickle was poured in and the barrels left for eight to ten days. After this they were turned on end and the pickle drained off, the lid removed and a second 'filling up' done if necessary. The top layer was then carefully arranged and the barrel sealed at the top. Pickle was poured in until the barrel was filled to capacity. Bungs were replaced and the barrels arranged three tiers high on their sides to await shipment. Two girls and two coopers lifted them up with the help of cleeks attached to the rims. To get the third tier into place they stood on upturned barrels. As well as helping with this heavy work, the girls were called out to bring supplies ashore when the stock boats arrived at Lerwick with salt and empty barrels.

Mrs Eveline Crockett:
   "We hid tae lift barrels and dinna tell me that it didna tell on us in later life, especially if we wis haein the bairns. I mind I had my first baby, the doctor said tae me, 'You fisher quines, I dinnae like tae ging til because yer bodies are finished before ye begin.' We blamed liftin' the barrels o' herrin' on the top, a' tier abune tier. Now that wasna richt—we couldna do it."

   There were no prescribed hours for gutting. When herring came in the girls worked until they were all cleared, however long this took. They were prepared for anything from the lull between catches when there was nothing to do but knit—to the big rush caused by a glut, when the work might last from 6 a.m. till 10 p.m. The obsession with earning a wage for themselves and their families did not prevent the girls from seeing the industry in a wider perspective and realising the importance of their own role within it. This is revealed in the following story of a strike in Yarmouth in the 1920s by the Scots fisher lassies who saw the Scots fleet suffering a disadvantage in relation to the English fleet because of the Scots fishermen's Sabbatarian religious principles.

Mrs Eveline Crockett:
   "The English fishermen went oot on a Sunday and they gathered their harvest and delivered them on Monday which filled up oor farlins. Noo the Scotchmen didna go oot till Monday—they rested on Sunday and of course therefore oor farlins were filled and we couldna manage tae gut the twa. Nae that I have ony what ye would ca' animosity towards the English, no—but I saw it wasn't justice tae gut the Englishman's herrin' and let our Scotchman's herrin' lie tae get an affa puir

*Above: A cooper inspecting the second 'filling up'. Yarmouth, c. 1924. Opposite: Eveline Reid (Crockett) dressed for camera, c. 1921.*

price—gut the lot fur fish meal! So something had to be done about it and I don't like strikes by any means, but the only thing that I could see was that we had tae stop guttin' the Englishmen's fish. So twa skippers came tae me and said tae me, the only thing that ye can dae is stop guttin' them. Well, it wis nae use o' *oor* farlins being stopped, we had tae get the whole lot oot. So I went from yard tae yard and explained tae the girls that it wisnae oor money that kept up oor home, it was oor fishermen's money. Therefore they wasnae gettin' it, owing to this, coming in on Monday and delivering on Tuesday. Now, I took out eight hundred of us, I think. But that couldn't last because the herrin' had to be cured, it had tae be salted or they would have lost the Russian market. Therefore, there was a meeting that night, and it wis decided that half the English fleet would gang oot on a Sunday and the next half would go out the next Sunday which made matters much much better and wir fishermen did get their price and we did gut their herrin'. So the strike was only a two-day strike and it was very successful."

The English fleet were not the only ones to be conquered by Mrs Crockett's ebullient determination.

Mrs Eveline Crockett:
  "I didn't mention that I had twa hours in the jail. That was a'richt, but ne'er mind, I coorted the bobby and I got tae the pictures at nicht wi' him so that was a'richt. That—ah'm nae mentioning—ah canna mention aboot that! (laughter)."

Humour also played its part in keeping the girls' spirits up during the long hours of work.

Mrs Annie Finlayson:
  "There was one incident when we were workin' in Yarmouth at the farlin. There was two ladies that came along watchin' us, stood lookin' at us and we wis all guttin' very quickly. This girl, she was a character, she'd jist make anybody laugh ye know, and one o' this ladies had a soft hat wi' a great big wing, a feather at the top stickin' in it and she says, 'Eh, quines, look at her! Some gull's minus his wing the day!' This is the feather—a seagull she meant ye see. She had the whole place jist laughin'—of course they didn't know what we were laughin' at, for a good job. And you'd hear them sayin', 'Aren't they quick, aren't they quick!'."

The lasting memory of the actual physical work is one of hardship and exploitation. The girls worked as hard as they possibly could in harsh conditions to keep their earnings up, but they considered £17 to £20 a good income for a season, just about the maximum obtainable. In 1911 threepence an hour was paid for filling up. Ten years later it was fourpence, by 1929 sixpence and in 1936 Miss Jean Bochel was getting tenpence. In 1911 for gutting and packing, the three

crew members shared eightpence a barrel. In the 1920s Miss Jean Bochel and her crew were still getting only tenpence a barrel. In 1929, Jean's crew filled 1,100 barrels, earning them something like £15 each plus their filling up money, and this was considered to be a very successful season.

Miss Jean Bochel:
  "No money. Tenpence, which is about four pence in today's money, between three of us for gutting and packing—well say four pence an hour. When we were filling up we got four pence an hour in Lerwick because it was warm. In Yarmouth where it was cold and frosty we got sixpence an hour. Six in the morning till half-past-eight [at night]."

Mrs Eveline Crockett:
  "I wouldna go back tae guttin' again, oh no, and I wouldna put nane o' mine tae the guttin'. No. It wis a primitive wey o' workin'. I hated it, I just hated it! In fact to tell you the truth, I wouldna hae gaen tull't, if it wisna fur helpin' the fishin' industry."

The memories, however, of the companionship among the girls and their brief social hours together are recalled equally vividly.

Mrs Annie Finlayson:
  "Oh, it was lovely, Gremista. Lovely place, away out tae Scotland Point. And then ye had the hills at the back and when ye wasna workin' ye went up there, sat up there wi' yer knittin' and the world was yer own. Ye hadna got a care in the world. Busy knittin' away and ye'd be singin' away, ye know and speakin' away and seein' the boats goin' out and comin' in. Mostly at the end ye know, it was bonny, it was lovely weather ye know."

Mrs Margaret Duthie:
  "The boats used to go out and they played— every one would have a musical instrument and at night, when the sun would be goin' down, you know, there wasn't a finer sight tae see than all the boats sailing about and all the music going—it was just lovely!"

Miss Jean Bochel:
  "We were never idle. Going along the road we would be knitting, going along the road. And of course we went to church every Sunday and the Church of Scotland had a Mission; two ladies—well usually two or three ladies used to be there, they'd have first aid and they were nurses. We got up concerts and ceilidhs of our own and some nights we'd have a dance. But one lady, she didn't think we should be dancing, it wasn't right. We says, 'What's wrong with dancing?' She says, 'There's nothing wrong with dancing, but,' she says, 'you've to go home after the dance.' (laughs) We'd a

*Girls knitting outside the huts at Gremista, Shetland, c. 1910.*

quarrel now and again with one another and then that would be the end of it. There was no time for moods and carrying on. Most of the courting was done during the fishing season, because when we were away from home, well the boyfriends would come up and that was when it was done. Not that it helped me any, I'm not married yet! (laughter)"

The weekend reunion with their menfolk, who amongst hundreds of others had brought in the fish which the girls so deftly handled during the past days, was the highlight of the week. There was plenty to talk about, news from home, reports on catches, prices, wedding plans. The week's hard toil was forgotten as interesting and happy talk took over, soon leading to fun and laughter from the teasing of the men. Home-made scones and pancakes, shop-bought cakes, cheese and ham were some of the delicacies provided by the girls for supper. As the evening wore on, thoughts turned to God in thankfulness for happy family relationships and the love of friends and neighbours. Speaking gave way to singing, laughter to praise, as the well-tuned voices joined together in harmonic renderings of favourite Sankey's hymns, metrical psalms, and paraphrases. For the tie which bound them together most of all, and to which they gave expression every day in honest toil and selfless devotion to each other, was their shared and constant Christian faith. When they sang, 'Will your anchor hold in the storms of life?' they never doubted that it would. Their still

point was God, their 'one for the road' a psalm of praise or a hymn of hope.

Mrs Annie Finlayson:

"Oh yes, we'd oor happy times, oh yes, and if we were finished early on a Saturday then on Sunday of course we always went to church on Sunday, walked two miles into Lerwick, and then of course if the boats were in there's maybe some o' oor own friends, oor own folk, oor own men folk visited us and we'd quite a social life. And then of course we visited one hut tae the other ye know, got all the news o' home. The day the letters came ye went from one place tae see what was doin' ye know— see was there anything new at home.

"Ye all joined in [the singing]. 'Will Your Anchor Hold?', it's a great one, and 'What a Friend we have in Jesus', and another one—it was a great one that was a hymn o' mine that I liked very much too:

> 'The sands of time are sinking;
> The dawn of heaven breaks;
> The summer morn I've sighed for,
> The fair, sweet morn, awakes.
> Dark, dark hath been the midnight,
> But dayspring is at hand,
> And glory, glory dwelleth
> In Immanuel's land.'

I think we had an awful lot o' faith."

MARGARET BOCHEL

# Gallipoli

"Through the narrows of the Dardanelles and across the ridges of the Gallipoli peninsula lie some of the shortest paths to a triumphant peace."
—Churchill

By the spring of 1915, the Allied armies that had marched against the Hun with such gaiety the previous August were bogged down in the trenches of France and Flanders. As casualties on the Western Front mounted, Winston Churchill conceived the scheme of using Britain's mastery of the seas to outflank Germany. When Turkey entered the war on the German side at the end of October 1914, the difficulty of maintaining contact with the Russian Empire had become greater than ever; Churchill's plan was to use sea-power to force a passage through the Turkish kyle of the Dardanelles, take Gallipoli and capture Constantinople.

Gallipoli was the long finger of land thrusting into the Aegean from the Turks' foothold in Europe. To the south stretched the heartland of the Ottoman Empire, on whose coast, just a matter of miles from the site of the coming battles, lay the plain of Troy, where Agamemnon brought his thousand ships to rescue Helen, and from whose shores Ulysses launched his epic Odyssey. The area surrounding the great sea-bridge of the Dardanelles, connecting the Mediterranean and the Black Seas, was rich in the history and legend of war.

Herodotus, Book 7, records:
"And now, as he looked and saw the whole Hellespont covered with vessels of his fleet and all the shore and every plain about Abydos as full as possible of men, Xerxes congratulated himself upon his good fortune; but after a little while he wept."

In strategic terms, the concept of the Gallipoli expedition had much to recommend it. When the straits were taken, an arms supply route would be opened to the Czar. It would also safeguard the Suez Canal, permit armed support for the Serbs, and rally other Balkan nations to the Allied cause—or at least intimidate them from joining the German. High hopes were entertained on all sides of a successful campaign, a hope reflected in the tone of King George's message to the Highland Mounted Brigade as they left England, under the command of Lord Lovat.

George V:
"I send you and your Brigade my best wishes on your departure to active service. I feel sure that the great and traditional fighting reputation of Scotsmen will be more than safe with you and that your Brigade will spare no effort in the interests of the Empire's cause to bring this war to a victorious conclusion."

Lovat's Highlanders were not the first of their people, nor the last, to fight in the Empire's cause, and most of them were Gaelic-speaking crofters, game-keepers, or estate employees on the Fraser of Lovat lands. Few knew the meaning of the word mobilisation when they were called up on the outbreak of the war, and most expected it to be a short affair culminating in the usual imperial victory.

Murdo MacLennan:
"The men that were in those days in the Scouts were outstanding. Strong men, tremendous men. I joined the Lovat Scouts in 1911, and we did drills at the Drill Hall and then we got mounted exercises on the machair. And at that time you had to provide your own horse. When the war broke out I joined the Scouts at a place called Huntingdon and then we rode from Grimsby on horseback to a place called Hunstanton in Norfolk—it took us three days, going round the Wash, through Sandringham estate, and we landed at Hunstanton, where we were until we went away to the war. The war was to be over in six months. That was the sort of conception. Everybody was anxious to get to the war—back in six months. But it was a long six months!"

In the first three months of the war alone, the Allies had lost one million casualties, and First Lord of the Admiralty Churchill's plan to open a second front at Gallipoli was widely seen as the way out of the French impasse. The plan was to land 75,000 men in April 1915 in an assault at the south on Cape Helles and at Anzac Cove, as it would soon be known, a few miles to the north. (In the event, there was to be another major invasion the following August, and the casualty rate was such that reinforcements were constantly being drafted onto the peninsula right up till the final evacuation.) The colonial troops would then seize the Mel Tepe hill, from which, so long ago, Xerxes had viewed his fleet in the Dardanelles, and command the upstream narrows across which he had built his bridge of boats for the invasion of Europe; the narrows across which Leander swam for Hero, and Lord Byron for a bet.

The plan was not, however, to survive the stunning mismanagement that would plague the expedition. For months the Turks had known that the invasion was on its way and had massively strengthened their defences. With days to go, there were no proper maps; there was no real knowledge concerning enemy positions, or water supplies, or landing facilities; even the depth of

*Troops landing from the historic 'River Clyde'. Cape Helles, April 1915.*

the water on the beaches which the army would soon storm was unknown. For the men sailing towards Gallipoli there was an early portent of what was to come.

Murdo MacLennan:

"We went into Alexandria in Egypt and were told to start unloading the saddlery and all the cavalry equipment and put it ashore. Well, we did this and then we loaded back webbing equipment and some of that webbing equipment must have been picked up off the battlefield because some of it was stained with blood."

Eventually, on the Greek island of Lemnos, the invasion force assembled.

Johnny Macrae:

"We stopped the ship and loaded onto small boats to get ashore. When we lowered them into the water they were all leaking, the whole blooming lot of them were all leaking—you were bailing water out the whole time. We arrived on the island and had a walk all round it. There was nothing on it but blooming sand, sand and rocks. The only tree I saw was on it, it was a fig tree, a little wee bitty fig tree, it was not much higher than a stone itself. I'd never seen one before— there was a wee dried fig on it, one dried fig on it, and I ate it."

Within days, the invaders were to meet the Turks. Unseasoned troops stormed ashore under the muzzles of the enemy guns and on one beach alone, five Victoria Crosses were to be won within a few hours of landing. With 2,000 men aboard, the *River Clyde* rammed the shore and attempted to disembark her cargo, in broad daylight. From a matter of yards the Turks shot them to pieces, many dying in the assault launches shoulder to shoulder, unable even to lift a rifle. Soon the ship's special assault-gangways were clogged with the dead and dying. Barely 200 of the 2,000 got ashore alive. An R.F.C. pilot flew over at the time and reported that in bright sunshine the sea was 'absolutely red with blood' from the beach to fifty yards offshore, whipped into a foam by the fantastic rifle, machine-gun and shrapnel fire from the enemy. But despite frightful casualties, the 30,000-strong force managed to hold by the end of that day a bridgehead at Helles and in the north at Anzac.

John Brown:

"We hung out till daylight, outside W Beach. Well, we all went up the beach, got up the top of the rise, spread out in extended order and then we got our first touch of shell fire. We were a bit scared at first, but you couldn't do anything but duck. At that time they weren't high explosive shells, they were all shrapnel and they burst thirty feet up in the air. It was a tongue of land with a mountain across it, right across the peninsula. That

*An illustration of the same landing.*

was the problem, you see, getting past that. It was very heavily fortified, you see."

Murdo MacLennan:

"We came under fire almost immediately after we left the liner. We went in very close and then we started crowding into these coal barges and they took us in to the beach. We came under fire almost at once—rifle fire and machine-gun fire. Of course the barges grounded when they were quite a bit out from the beach and it was a case of jumping over the side. We lost quite a lot of men one way and another—in some places there was barbed wire in the sea and some of the guys were getting mixed up in it. But anyway, we got ashore. That was near Chocolate Hill—the name was given to the place because it was all churned up with shells and trenches, and it looked like the colour of chocolate. It had been cultivated in some sort of way before we landed there and there were water melons and tomatoes growing about the place, but they didn't last long. Some of the guys lost their lives going out after water melons between the two lines."

Within a fortnight it was clear that the invasion had lost any impetus it might once have had. There were already 25,000 casualties, all the reserves and most of the shells had gone, and the two landings still held just five square miles of the peninsula. The guns of the artillery were rationed to two shells a day, and the King's 'poor bloody infantry' settled in on their beachheads, eye to eye with 'Johnny Turk'.

John Brown:

"They were anything from 25 to 200 yards away. You see, between a front-line and a support trench, you have a communication trench. So when we took one of their front-line trenches, you worked your way along the communication trench and built a barricade, and threw bombs over it at them. They were home-made bombs at the time, pound jam tins filled with bits of shrapnel, gelignite and a fuse— that gave you five seconds. Sometimes they would throw one over and we would pick it up and throw it back again before it got time to explode—we were just taking a chance. There was shells coming in all the time. You were a wee bit better in the firing line than the supports. In the firing line, see, you didn't get the shells so bad, we were so close to their own men they were afraid they would hit them instead of us.

"There was one fellow, they called him Bun Craig, jolly type o' fellow, he came round the corner o' the traverse—he'd a hole in his cheek, right through. He must have had his mouth open but a bullet had gone right through one cheek, out the other. And he says, 'Here, Jock, look what the so 'n' so's have done tae ma face!' And he was splutter, spluttering blood all over the place, ye see. Well, anyway, we'd tae tie him up, and he wanted

*A shell from the Turkish gun 'Asiatic Annie' bursts in the sea near Cape Helles. The men shelter under the cliff.*

# Banks of the Bosphorus

March

Pipe Major J. Robertson

*John Brown, a survivor. c. 1916.*

a smoke. Here he found that he couldn't smoke—
kept blowin' the smoke out through the hole in his
cheek! You heard him swearing—we had tae hold
his cheek tae let him get a smoke!''

Johnny Macrae:
"Oh, they were just ordinary trenches, you
know, with a firing step. You had to watch yourself
there, you know, there was sniping all the time,
you know, day and night.''

Murdo MacLennan:
"I was a sniper for a while myself and it's
not a very nice job. There was a big tree in front
of us, and we fixed steel plates in it. You
went out there before daylight and you were
there till night, overlooking the Turkish trenches.
Once they started to shell this tree with high
explosives and they nearly blew it out of the
ground. But they never hit the fellow that
was in it, no—but he was chittering with fright

for about a week after he got out of it that
night. A fleet of destroyers used to come in
during the day and fire away at the Turks.
When the *Queen Elizabeth* used to fire her
sixteen-inch guns, while the flames lasted
from the muzzle of the gun, you could actually
see the shadow of the shell leaving it.
    "There was a lot of poor work with our
own guns—some of their shells falling among
us, you know. Before you went in you were
frightened. But after you got mucked in, the
fear sort of left you. Sometimes conditions
were so bad you didn't care whether you were
shot or not. When the whistle blew, you just
went over the top and ran like steam, through
the wire and into the other fellow's trench
and went at it, hand to hand. Rifle and bayonet,
yes. You fired from the hip, you know, you
were right in among them.''

By June, the plague of flies that infested the place
were growing fat and bloated on blood. Conditions
became worse than ever, and men broke teeth trying to
eat the army ration biscuits upon which they largely
existed.

Murdo MacLennan:
    "Bully beef and hard biscuits—that was it.
Sometimes you had to pound them up with an
entrenching tool before you could even look at
them.''

*Making bombs from empty jam tins.*

*Anzac Cove, troopships landing.*

Johnny Macrae:

"The food that was on the peninsula was just a lot of bully beef and biscuits, hard biscuits, and tea. But sugar was scarce, and so was milk. And water was scarce as well."

Poor food and grossly insanitary conditions led to massive losses through disease and sickness.

Murdo MacLennan:

"One of the worst features of the peninsula was disease—dysentry, malaria, trench fever. Trench fever was where men were overloaded with lice, and sores got to be all over them. Dysentry was deadly. In five days you would see a stalwart man reduced to a wretch, they just laid down and didn't even bother going to the rear. It was terrible, and I think the dysentry was due to the fact that the dead weren't properly buried. The ground was hard and they weren't buried deep enough and when heavy rain came you could see a man lying in his grave, you could see his face and his hands. We got our water out of wells that were dug in the cemetery and I think that had a lot to do with it. We lost a tremendous lot of men with the dysentry."

John Brown:

"And then my hands were all one mass of septic sores. They're still shiny to this day. You got septic sores with your hands rubbing against the side of the trenches. We used to carry a bag of bandages and a wee bottle of carbolic acid, you put a drop or two in some water and bathed the sores. And all the time a lot of us were rotten with dysentry. I managed to dodge it. But I took jaundice, yellow jaundice. But it didn't make any difference, they were so short of men you just had to fight on."

Murdo MacLennan:

"Ships were being sunk on the way out and we were short of everything and there wasn't much coming ashore in the way of medical supplies. The men were sometimes tearing their underclothes to wrap round their wounds."

By August the Allies were ready to attempt another offensive, centred on Anzac and Suvla Bay to the north of it. At Suvla, 25,000 men were to storm ashore and across the bed of the dried-up Salt Lake. Almost 40,000 fresh reinforcements were to break out from the Anzac bridgehead, and put an end to the Turks. Given proper leadership, they would have, but the chain of command broke down completely. At Suvla, the attackers spent

*Soldiers crossing the Salt Lake at Suvla, August 1915.*

the whole day wandering on the plain, held back by just 1,500 Turks without a machine-gun among them. Not till dusk did they advance and take Chocolate Hill, after a 24-hour delay in which the Turks were rushing reinforcements to the front. At Anzac the charge took place in broad daylight across a front just 200 yards wide—in the first few days alone, 4,000 men died, and seven Victoria Crosses were awarded. At Sari Bair, the commanders considered sending in the Australian Light Horse in a cavalry charge—but they were finally dismounted and charged Battleship Hill. Half of their 1,200 men were dead in minutes. Not till the end of August did the battle come to an end and 45,000 Allied soldiers were casualties in those weeks alone.

John Brown:
"Now we went over the top after three or four hours bombardment in the morning. We were told to take three lines of trenches. We cleared the first and we cleared the second and we went into the third and the third was a dummy, it was only a foot deep. We got an awful cutting up there, we lost about 400 men in that stunt. You had to chase them out with the bayonet, you see, you had to go over and chase them out. It was just hell, I don't like to describe it, you just dived in hoping that he would clear off! After a trench was taken it was just dead

all over the place, full up of dead, and we had to live among them, until we could dig another trench alongside and fill them in, you know, in the old trench. Sometimes the trench had so many dead in it, you didn't know where to put them. We sometimes had to bury our own dead in the sides of the communication trench—you just dug a hole down from the top, put it in, and one or two sandbags on top. But them that were killed in between the lines, they lay there all the time. And after a stunt the place was living with maggots, crawling with maggots, you see. It was absolutely one desperate stench, but if it was a while since the action, if it was quiet for a bit, the smell died down and wasn't so bad, if the wind wasn't in the wrong direction."

Many of the soldiers in the Gallipoli invasion forces were not native-born Englishmen. Scottish regiments like the Highland Light Infantry and the King's Own Scottish Borderers saw action on the peninsula, as did Welsh and Irish soldiers, Sikhs from India, and the incomparable Anzacs, insubordinate and brave in equally heroic proportions.

Murdo MacLennan:
"They were very fine chaps. Reckless to a

*Australians freezing by their dugouts, November 1915.*

degree, you know, they were mostly the Light
Horse. I came across a lot of them and they were
quite the finest set of men I have ever seen. Oh yes,
great physique and good appearance. Aye,
wonderful men.''

Angus MacVarish:
   ''They were great friends of the Scottish soldiers,
but they didn't like the English so much at all.''

Murdo MacLennan:
   ''The man in the next bay to me was a Gurkha
and I got very pally with him. I gave him a wrist
watch that wasn't going but he didn't mind that.
He said, 'You are my blood brother', and this is the
mark he put on my hand with his kukri [Gurkha
knife]—it'll never go away. It's been there sixty-six
years now. Whatever he put in it, I don't know. He
used to give me chapatties and that sort of thing,
and, oh, they liked their rum ration, the Gurkhas.
They were very fond of the rum. When the ration
would come round, they would say, rum tonight,
charge tomorrow! You often got an issue of rum,
you know, before you went in for an attack,
whether it was to boost your morale or not I don't
know.''

   Not all of the incidents on the peninsula were tragic,
and the soldiers thought up ingenious ways to keep
their spirits up.

John Brown:
   ''Once we made a fiddle, a Japanese fiddle, just a
box with a handle, very crude, but we managed to
get a tune out of it. We put a field telephone wire
on it for a string and hair from a mule's tail. We
just used to boil the hair to get the grease out of it
and we managed to get it to play, just the usual
Scottish tunes, you know.''

Murdo MacLennan:
   ''On one occasion on the front-line, Gallipoli, the
officers thought, well, we'll get our pipe band
together and we'll play a selection (laughing)—we
were only about 75 yards away from the Turks at
the time. So they got a hold of Pipe Major Donald
Macmillan and got that band gathered together and
they set up their pipes. Well, boy! did we pay for
it! There was grass, long white grass in front of the
trenches and they set the grass on fire with shell
fire and oh it was terrific, terrific! The Colonel
said, 'Well, this is a good idea for making the Turks
waste a lot of ammunition!' (laughter).''

   It was becoming increasingly clear to the General
Staff that the campaign was a failure, and as autumn set
in with the prospect of severe weather in the near
future, even the once-high morale of the army began to
drain away. Hugh Cameron had been priest in
Castlebay, Barra, and at the age of forty had
volunteered as chaplain to the Catholic soldiers with

*Father Hugh Cameron, Chaplain to the Lovat Scouts at Suvla.*

the Highland Mounted Brigade at Gallipoli. The entries in his private diary reflect the falling spirits of the soldiers, and the endless round of life on the peninsula—shelling, sniping, stand-to's, listening posts in no-man's-land, scouting, disease, burial parties, and growing hopelessness.

Father Cameron:

"Mass this morning at six-thirty. What a figure I must have cut—muddy slacks, tunic covered with dirt, unshaven. Luckily the guns were quiet, but a few bullets were coming over the parapet and whistling over my head. The strain on my back and through stooping was awful. All the men were at Holy Communion. One of the Mallaig boys was shot while on sentry—lucky boy, just a scalp wound. Yesterday we were heavily shelled. Major Grant was badly wounded last night while spying. One of the Moidart boys was killed, a bullet through the head while standing on the firing bank. Terrible shelling this morning."

By November the weather was worse than ever, but the generals and politicians still argued about evacuation. The British guns were down to a ration of two shells a day each, and winter clothing had still not arrived. Many units were at half-strength, and Staff estimates of an evacuation-casualty rate were around 40 per cent or 40,000 men. As the weather worsened day by day, the prospect grew of the whole army being cut to ribbons on storm-lashed evacuation beaches. On the 27th of November, the worst weather in forty years hit the Gallipoli peninsula.

Willie Fraser:

"That night there was thunder and lightning and the Turks—I think they thought they were going to wallop us off Suvla Bay—they let a dam go way up in the hills, down through Chocolate Hill, and the rivers got flooded. All our trenches were flooded to the top. We couldn't get a rifle to fire in the muck—and then the frost set in and in the morning an awful lot had frostbite."

Murdo MacLennan:

"Things were so bad we had to get everything we could lay our hands on to light a fire. It gives you an idea of how bad things were when we weren't even firing at each other. For two nights we could see each other quite plain round the fires."

The rain lasted for a full twenty-four hours, and then the wind veered to the north, increased to hurricane force, and brought snow—the first snow the Anzacs had ever seen. Sentries froze to death at their posts and when the storm subsided, the army had lost a tenth of its strength. Two hundred men were drowned, 5,000 disabled with frostbite, and another 5,000 also hospitalised. Evacuation fever gripped the increasingly bitter army.

Father Cameron:

"Rumours of evacuation. The sooner the better. None of us will be sorry to leave this damned hole of a graveyard where so many brave men have fallen in vain. We are all having visions of Egypt, where they will send us next. This is for my own use and I can put down my own thoughts for they are the thoughts of all of us. From start to finish Gallipoli has been a most abominably managed business. Had the fine material available been properly handled we should long ago have been in Stamboul instead of holding three miles of flat dominated on three sides by the Turks. We were up on those heights more than once and bad leadership in high places lost them to us. That is what makes the temper of the army so bitter. Our Brigade are to fight our way out. I shall send this diary by one of those who go before me in the hope that it may eventually reach home if I do not. Oh Lord, give me the grace to do my duty like a man."

The rumours were correct—the army was to be evacuated, whatever the casualty rate. The retreat in fact was the only success of the whole campaign. With incredible luck, the army got off Gallipoli with scarcely a casualty—its secret phased withdrawal worked to perfection. The weather held just long enough for the army to get away.

# Farewell to Cape Helles

Retreat                                                                                Pipe Major William Ferguson

John Brown:

"I volunteered to stay in the front-line till the end but we didn't know everyone had gone till the afternoon, when one of our fellows nipped back to the support to get some water and when he came back he says, 'Here, fellows, there's not a bugger in the support!' So we had the wind up then, good and proper, in case Johnny Turk put in an attack. If he had, I don't know what we'd have done. There was just twenty of us, instead of two or three thousand. When it got dark it was just absolutely awful, you know. Time, och it was like years, like

*Lord Kitchener at Gallipoli. Kitchener decided that evacuation was inevitable.*

waiting for years, you see. I never put in such a time in my life, waiting, waiting, absolutely sick with anxiety.

"Well, we were withdrawing from all points, and as we went down there was more and more of us till there was quite a wee battalion of us. When we got down onto the beach one of the brasshats met us, and he was nearly crying with relief to see us arriving there. He didn't expect to see us make it, you see. But we got to the beach at last, and onto a barge and out to a destroyer. We were so beat, so fatigued, we could hardly climb up, but we were hauled up and we just threw ourselves down and I remember one of the sailors looking at us, and he says—'Oh, poor buggers'."

Willie Fraser:

"So we got to the beach in the dark and we got through the wire and then we knew we were safe because the barges were waiting. And all of a sudden, as we were going off, we heard a jangling on the barbed wire. There was this mule that had been left behind, and he came charging down, you know, and into the wire, and that's the last I remember seeing of Suvla Bay—a mule dangling on the barbed wire about thirty yards from the beach."

In the nine months of the Gallipoli campaign, the Allies deployed half a million soldiers, and half of them became casualties. Turkish losses probably were higher. The assessment of those who remember the peninsula sixty-six years after leaving it is still tinged with some bitterness about a campaign to whose fighting soldiers no special medal was ever awarded.

*John Brown, 1981, fashioning a fiddle. He made his first instrument on Gallipoli.*

Murdo MacLennan:

"Well, there was a shortage of everything—medicine, bandages, ammunition for guns and rifles, food, water. For a while we just got a pint of water a day for everything."

John Brown:

"The officers, we hadn't any feeling against the officers, they were in it the same as us. But the high-ups, we didn't think so much of them, we didn't think we were getting a very fair do from them. I never felt I would get off Gallipoli, never thought it was possible. If we didn't get killed, we would die of starvation or disease, you understand. That's what we feel about Churchill. He was detested, the man was always detested for that—by those who knew the place. It's a place you hardly hear mentioned, though you hear plenty about the rest of the war. I believe it was squashed, the whole thing was squashed. I had a year in France but it wasn't anything like the horrors of Gallipoli."

Murdo MacLennan:

"Oh, the country was bled white, bled white. Where I come from, there were seven young men killed, out of a total population of a hundred. It was the same all over the Highlands. There was a lot of mismanagement. You were put in to attack in broad daylight, what they called stunts. 'We'll try a stunt,' they'd say, and they'd put in a battalion or thereabouts and they would be massacred."

Due to the numbers involved, the tragedy of Gallipoli has passed into the folklore of Scotland's working people. But bitterness is not the prerogative of the ordinary soldiers who saw service there. Lord Lovat, invalided out of the peninsula with dysentery, wrote from hospital to his wife about the campaign, with a damning indictment of the whole Gallipoli adventure.

Lord Lovat:

"It is more than clear that Winston alone was the inspiration of this tragedy. The Gallipoli expedition properly carried out would have been brilliant; great strategic possibilities and with combined action (Army and Navy) very little risk; carried out piecemeal, sailors first, driblets of soldiers second, more driblets of soldiers third, starvation of guns fourth, failure to observe Balkan trouble fifth, plus final debacle on arrival of guns and supplies through Serbia, it was disaster. It will be up to date and probably to all eternity as sordid and miserable a chapter of amateur enterprise as ever was written in our history."

IAIN FRASER GRIGOR

# The Pearl Fishers

## THE PEARL FISHER

*Where the Tay, the Earn and the Isla flow*
*Threadin wi siller the plaid o' the strath*
*Kneedeep in river shallows gaes the pearl fisher,*
*Wi sunbaked, wind-hardened face bent on the water.*
*Keen-eyed, he peers intae the shingle bed,*
*For the fabled shell, the yin he dreams o'*
*The secret, hidden, unexpectit yin tae make his fortune.*

*For that he tholes the cauld and bous his back*
*For oors and days, aften wi nae reward.*
*He never heeds the warld aroon*
*Wha's sichts and soonds a' melt awa.*

*His lassie's een an breists, his bairnies' lachter,*
*Firelicht, gowd o hairst,*
*Birdsang wi the day dawning,*
*The fiddlers' rant wi the feet dirlin;*
*His faither deid, his hame brunt doon,*
*His siller tane or his dochter hured,*
*It a' means nowt tae him, noo deif an blin*
*As if by warlock cantrip tane,*
*Tae a' but the socht for prize:*
*The ae perfect and priceless pearl.*

—Sheila Douglas

'The ae perfect and priceless pearl' has been 'socht for' in the rivers of Scotland from before Roman times. It is said that pearls were one of the prizes sought by the Phoenicians when they landed in Britain. At that time most of Britain's rivers were the habitat of the river mussel which produced the pearls but today Scotland is one of the few places left in Europe with some of its rivers unpolluted. Over the last 300 years there are records of the great quality and quantity of Scottish pearls and we are fortunate today that the river mussel can still survive in so many rivers of the Highlands and the north-east free from the pollution of industry.

The most common pearls are found in oysters in Oriental seas and these pure white, round, precious jewels are most people's image of what a pearl looks like. The river pearls can vary enormously in quality but they also vary in colour and lustre which can make them more interesting than the Oriental variety.

The traditional belief, the world over, was that the pearl was formed from a grain of sand which irritated the oyster or the mussel. This belief is not far from the truth but it is now more certain that the pearls are formed by a parasite which enters the shell. An irritation sets in which the mussel isolates and gradually covers with layer upon layer of mother of pearl. This process can take many years and it is now

*Opposite: A pearl fisher, Bill Abernethy.*

evident that many of the mussels can be up to 150 years old. The river mussel can only survive in clean, fresh water and this is why so many of the fast flowing rivers of the Scottish Highlands are so perfect a habitat.

In the *Book of the Pearl*, published in 1908, there is a record from as early as 1560 when 'large, handsome pearls' were sent from Scotland to Antwerp. In 1620 a great pearl was found in the Kellie burn in Aberdeenshire; this was carried to King James by the provost of Aberdeen, who was rewarded with 'twelve to fourteen chalder of victuals about Dunfermline and the Customs of Merchants goods in Aberdeen during his life'. There are also accounts of how between 1761 and 1764 £10,000 worth of pearls were sent to London and sold from ten shillings to one pound six shillings per ounce. In 1861 a German merchant travelled through the districts of the Tay, Doon and Don and interested the local people in gathering pearl mussels. 1862 was a particularly good year, owing to the dryness of the season and in the low water unusually large quantities of pearls were found. The *Book of the Pearl* brings its history up to the turn of the present century with accounts of pearls bought by Empress Eugenie and Queen Victoria herself.

Until recent years this long tradition of pearl fishing was continued almost exclusively by members of the travelling people who, in between seasonal farm work in the summer, camped by the rivers and searched for pearls.

Peter McMillan:

"It was fifty years ago that I started with my father, we all pearlfished then, my uncles and brothers and cousins. I think the whole family used to go up to the Spey to pearl fish, all the season, from April to September, and we got a lot of good pearls then, big ones, you know, and some small stuff and that. I've seen dozens of us fishing together, not only my family but other families too in the travelling family class, we always fished. We used to meet up there every year and we all fished in the Spey, and the Tay, the river Morrison, the Conan, we fished all these rivers in our younger days.

"But it was a hard life then for us youngsters, it was very hard. Travelling from one place to another, up and down the river, way over to Blairgowrie, down the Tay and away up to Glen Lyon—horse and cart then, or a caravan. We all went under canvas then and we camped there all summer, you know, pearl fishing all the time, as long as the river was fishable, like."

The river mussel is usually found in the bed of the river and very often almost completely hidden from view.

*Pearling from a boat.*

Bill Abernethy:

"The equipment is simple, all you need is a forked stick and a glass-bottomed bucket to cut off the ripple of the water. You can wade to quite deep water, maybe five or six feet, but if it's any deeper than that, you need a boat. You see the bottom of the river with your glass and you pick up the shells, it's just as simple as that. But there's other little wrinkles that you've got to know—where the pearls are and things like that. There's certain weeds that grow and certain types of gravel and all that comes into consideration, the flow of the water and things like that. There's quite a few things that you've got to know to be successful at it."

Betsy Whyte:

"My father and most travellers made their own boats for pearl fishing. They used to get wood from a sawmill or something, wide planks. They weren't deep these boats and they were shaped a bit like, you've seen a snow plough at the front, well, they used to bend their wood over like that at the front, and the back was straight. It was completely flat on the bottom and maybe just about twenty inches deep, just shallow boats. They put planks along the straight back and these planks would act as a seat if you were sitting in the boat and when you were pearl fishing you lay on your belly on top of these planks with your head over the side of the boat. I used to watch them sitting making them, getting the wood and getting it fixed together and then you've got tar, I'm sure it was tar you put on them to make them waterproof. And a lot of the travellers did the same. They were very light, you could carry them on your shoulders when you were shifting about, if the water was too shallow, you could just put it up on your head and walk with it,

it was that light. And yet they were strong, 'cause sometimes if the water was deep enough you were moving down the river, he'd get us all into the boat and it was great, we used to scream, laugh and carry on and he says, 'If the baillies haven't seen me, they're sure to have heard me.' Because they chased us about that much up the river, you ken. And all the travellers' boats were built like that. Just simple things but they worked.

"From a very early age, we got to recognise the pearl shells, a lot of folk call them mussels but I never connected them with a mussel. They're a bit like a mussel but much longer and flatter. You can get them about ten, twelve inches long, very big and sometimes they get a bit damaged. Did you ever see an auld burned boot? Well, you get shells much the shape of that and almost as big and these were the ones we loved to get, they were almost sure of a pearl but sometimes they were disappointing too because the pearl might turn out to be brown or blae coloured and these were valueless. Very rarely you got tiny seeds of black pearls but in all those years of fishing my father never got a decent sized black pearl. They're very rare but they are there, but he never happened to get one. There were lots of different shapes and sizes of pearls and you often got things just like a pearl but it was just a big cluster sticking to the shell and this was very disappointing. These were valueless although they were nice to look at. Then you would often get two or more pearls in a shell or sometimes a cluster of tiny seed pearls and you could get something for them, for setting in rings and brooches. Then there were brown pearls and they were valueless. But sometimes you could get a lovely clear pearl and a fine size, maybe the size of a round pea, and take it home and by the time you

*Travellers' camp.*

got home with it, it had turned blae. Pearls did this with some people and with other people they would keep their purity. I've seen my father saying to a man that had got this big blae pearl, 'What are you doing with it?' 'Aw,' he would say, 'I'm just going to throw it away, it's no use.' He says, 'Give it to me.' So he got it, a good size of pearl, about pea size. He took it home and says, 'Maggie, put that pearl in your bosom for two or three days,' and its purity came back. You know pearls will do that. There are certain people that they will not keep their true colours with. They change. My mother was one of these people that they would keep their true colour with. My father didn't keep the money to himself, he wouldn't do that. He maybe felt like it but the travelling folk believe that if they do anything like that, they'll get paid back double for it so he shared the money with the man that had found the pearl and he says, 'Don't tell me you got that for thon pearl.' He says, 'I did.' He wouldn't believe him, he says, 'I cannae believe you.' 'Well,' my father says, 'that pearl was as pure as anything when Maggie had it for a few days.' So he would hardly go pearl fishing without my mother being there. She was just one of these kind of folk that was lucky at opening shells and that pearls kept their colour with."

The pearl fishers lived and worked by the rivers, their popularity varying according to the attitudes of the local landowners and their estate workers.

Betsy Whyte:

"We used to get chased a lot off the river but it wasn't because of taking pearls, it was always because they thought you were maybe poaching for salmon. Well travellers, they wouldn't care less about salmon because they would prefer trout, you

ken. And anyway they had a sort of thing with the landowners, the gentry, as we called them, because the gentry would often stand and speak to traveller folk and ask them questions about what they were doing and they understood us much better than anybody else and they tolerated us on their grounds. They would give you a piece of ground and you could live there and they knew that they could trust us not to touch the salmon and they would ask for a pearl but they always paid for the pearls.

Sometimes my father would go and give the lady of the house a pearl, he says, 'I'll give you this pearl if you'll give me a permit to fish this part of the river,' the part that they owned and they rarely refused. But that didn't keep the water bailiffs from chasing you off and breaking the boat. My father used to take great pains to hide his boat when he was going home at night because although they were very light, you didn't fancy carrying them home every night along the banks of a river, so he used to hide them in . . . grass or undergrowth—a certain way to try and hide them from the water baillies or they would chase you. I've seen it come into fights between travellers and water baillies but only if the traveller had a permit. If he didn't have a permit, he would just go quietly off the water and that was it. But if he'd got a permit from the landowner he'd just keep fishing away and ignore the bailiffs, you ken, and hae them screaming and cursing across the river, and he'd just fish away and never let on and then after they'd brought the police, they would take out their permit and say 'I've a permit to fish here from Lady So an' So', you ken, whoever it was. There's quite a lot of big estates in Perthshire, landowners, and most of them were very familiar with the travellers. If a traveller was in difficulty or trouble with the police or with fishing in the rivers, these folk, they understood right away what the travellers would do and what they wouldn't do. And what they could trust them with and what they couldn't trust them with, that sort of way. So they had what they called 'their own travellers' come here every year and I've often seen ladies in Perthshire, when an old traveller passed away, paying for the burial and everything. If there was an old woman or an old man left on their own, they would never say to them 'You'd be better going into a home or something', they understood them better than that."

For most people in the past pearlfishing was a seasonal job and for many it still is. But Bill Abernethy has made pearlfishing a full-time occupation and fishes practically all the year round, travelling all over Scotland.

Bill Abernethy:
"I just like it because it's a good job, you can go where you want and travel the country and you meet a lot of people at the rivers. There's no any hustle at the job, you've no set times from nine o'clock here or six o'clock there and all this sort of thing. You can please yourself, there's no any pressures put on you, like say you were an office worker or some job like that where you had responsibility, but at the pearl fishing there was never any push.
"My father and his brothers were at the pearl fishing at the beginning of this century and back as far as 1890. My father and his uncle started pearling here in Scotland, but at that time there were more pearl fishers than now, for a various number of reasons. At that time there wasn't the same pollution in the rivers, they were more or less free, and there were no cultured or artificial pearls or anything. All the pearls that were on the market were natural pearls, they were either freshwater

pearls or pearls from the sea, and the prices were quite high according to the value of money for other jobs. A good pearl, say maybe in 1910, you would get £60 for it. Now that's near a year's wages for an ordinary man working."

The largest pearl that we know of today found in a Scottish river was found by Bill Abernethy in 1967. Today it is on show at Cairncross' jewellery shop in Perth.

Alistair Cairncross:
"The Abernethy pearl is so perfect that when we saw it first of all we immediately thought of creating the most marvellous pendant with it and the lilac tint in the pearl demanded a very special colour of diamonds to go with it. However, when we thought about it afterwards we decided that it was so lovely that it would be a crime to drill it to create a mount for it. We therefore decided just to put it on show so that the rest of the world can have a look at it whenever they feel so inclined and we have a special case in the shop in which the Abernethy pearl sits in majesty."

Bill Abernethy, who found the pearl, describes how he found it.

"Sometimes the flood covers beds of them [mussels] with leaves. It was like that on the Tay, you know, where I got the Abernethy pearl, the pearl, the big pearl. I'd fished it the year before and there hadn't been any shell but in a big back wash there had been a lot of leaves in the winter floods that had been washed down. The next year when I went, another flood had shifted them and here was a bed of shells looking up from the sand. I started digging them and then I dug this shell, it was just about that size [demonstrates] but it was about that

*Travellers camp by the river.*

breadth when I put the stick in you know, it would
hardly go in, it was that wide and I knew when I dug it,
I said, this is a good shell, because the shell with the
good pearls, there's usually a bit of a twist on it.
When I dug it I put it in a corner of the boat and
when I came to cut the shells I had this one at one
side and I knew there was a good pearl in it but
what I didn't know was that it was twice the size
of what it was supposed to be, you see, it was a
freak of nature. It was just like a duck's egg sitting
in it. You know, when I opened the shell it was just
a huge bump covered in the meat and the only
thing that I was worried about was, I knew it was
round, I thought there might have been some mark
or something on it. The pearls are encased in the
meat, they're not attached to the shell, they're
encased in the meat and when I squeezed it out of
the meat there wasn't a mark on it. I carry a bottle,
you know, for putting the pearls in, it was that big
that I couldn't get it in the neck of the bottle and
so I wrapped it in a docken leaf and put it in my
pocket. That's how it came to light."

There are many stories about the largest, most
perfect pearls that people have found.

Betsy Whyte:
"I remember one pearl that my father got and it
was very big, much bigger than the average pearl,
almost marble sized, a small marble. By seven or
eight o'clock, they all went home together and this
uncle of mine, when he was coming past, my
mother said, 'Look.' 'Any luck,' he says, 'I never
got a thing,' and she says 'Look' and he says 'Ach, a
blowed bead,' and he just hit her hand underneath,
you ken, and sent it right over among a heap of
stones at the riverside, ken they wee chuckie stones
at the side of the river. My father jumped after it,
you ken, he'd been packing up his things and hiding
his boat and when my uncle saw them desperately
looking he says, 'It must have been a pearl right
enough.' So in the end they hunted for hours before
they found it, but they did get it. And my uncle
says, 'Well, I just couldn't believe a pearl that size,'
and my father got a good price for it in Perth."

The pearls found in Scottish rivers have a great
variety of colour and shape and this is now an
important part of their appeal.

Neil McCormick:
"You get some beautiful pearls, different colours,
different shapes, different sizes. You can get them
barrel shaped, pear shaped, button, like flat on the
bottom and round on the top, that's button; round
ones are the hardest to find, it's usually buttons or
peardrops or all different, you can even get them
like a corkscrew, you know. They're unique,
there's no two the same, hardly any two look the
same."

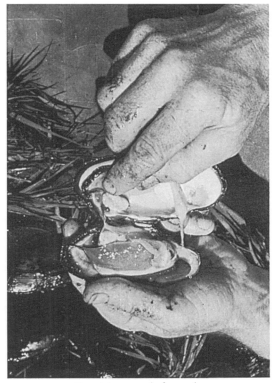
*Examining mussels for pearls.*

Bill Abernethy:
"You get them all colours, you can get them
pink, mauve, purple, white, creamy coloured,
salmon pink, all the different colours of the
rainbow. The sea pearls, you know, they're more or
less all one colour. One pearl's the same as the
next, but a Scotch pearl, you can get a brooch
made up or a necklace and every pearl's different,
they're individual, and that seems to appeal to
people as well, it makes them look more, what
should I say, natural because they blend in with,
more or less, the colours of the country."

Today there is only one jeweller in Scotland who
buys river pearls. Alistair Cairncross in Perth creates
settings and designs for the pearls found in this country.
His is a family business which has dealt with pearls
since 1869.

Alistair Cairncross:
"The pearls we feel are completely individual,
the beauty of the pearl, the Scottish pearl in
comparison with an oriental, or cultured pearl for
that matter, is that they have a very very subtle
quiet lustre, they're not as brilliant as an oriental,
but their colouring is very much more subtle and
there's a hint of the misty hills in the background in
them. They, being different, require, we think, a
different form of presentation and over the years

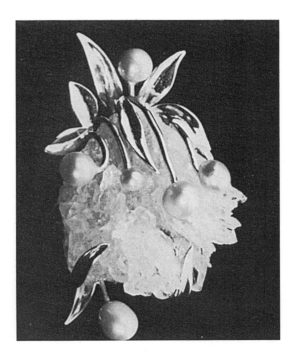

*Pearls and rose quartz.*

we have developed a series of designs which not only show off the pearls in their own individual way but are indicative of the atmosphere of the background in which the pearl was found. For instance, rhododendrons and rowans, a lot of the berries—blaeberries, crowberries, cranberries; this allows us to create a slightly different character to each mount.

"The supply of the pearls is rather restricted with the result that we have to try to use every pearl which has any beauty or lustre at all. Having asymmetrical designs, we're not restricted to trying to match sizes of pearls and they don't have to be round so that we can make the most use of the pearls that are available. The other type of pearl which gives us a certain amount of pleasure in using is the slightly Baroque looking pearl which might have what we term a bad end, in other words, the nacre of the pearl hasn't covered the whole pearl and it's a nice little puzzle how to use this to the best advantage so that the bad end is hidden in the mount and yet the pearl itself is happily proportioned in the design so that the whole thing looks perfectly natural and as though nature had meant it to be that way."

Bill Abernethy:
"Way back in my father's time there were jewellers all over Scotland bought pearls. There was a large number of pearl fishers and a large amount of pearls available. Tourists could buy a pearl say even in Coupar Angus here or Blairgowrie or small

village jewellers. All the jewellers had a few Scotch pearls for sale. At that time there was umpteen nomadic pearl fishers going about, if they hadn't the time or the inclination maybe to go to Edinburgh or up to Aberdeen or Perth, that's where they got a bigger price for them, they would just sell them to the local jeweller. In fact there was one of the travelling crowd that goes about, he got a big pearl in the Earn, just below Crieff it was, and he went into this baker's shop and he tried to sell the pearl to the baker and the baker says 'I'll take the pearl, and anytime that you want bread,' he says, 'you can come in here and you'll get it free, if you'll gie me the pearl.' And the deal was made there and then and he had more or less a lifetime's supply of bread for this pearl. That's how the baker worked him, but I think the baker got quite a good price for that pearl because it was really a fine stone, you know; but that's how he done the deal!

"There was one particular pearl that was got in the South Esk, I think it was about 1906 by a nomadic pearl fisher by the name of 'Cove Pitcaithlie' and he travelled about all over Scotland. There was, like, several hundred pearl fishers at that time going all over the country and they just called him Cove. He got this pearl and it was a pink ball that he got, up in the South Esk just above

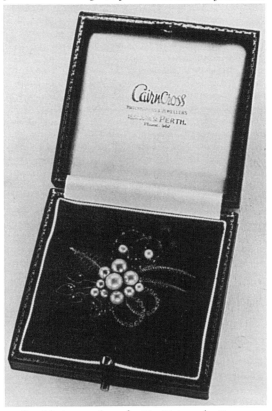

*Scottish river pearls set for Her Majesty the Queen.*

Brechin, and it was thirty-seven-and-a-quarter grains. It was a lovely pearl and he went into the local jeweller up in Brechin and the local jeweller offered him £20 for it. But the Cove Pitcaithlie knew that it was worth more than that and the jeweller wouldn't give him any more. Anyway it seems to have transpired that the jeweller made out that the Cove had come by the pearl other than fishing it and as he was coming out of Brechin to go down to Edinburgh to sell the pearl there were two policemen coming, legging after him and they shouted to him. But the Cove, he surmised that there was something up and he put the pearl in the cup of his clay pipe, you see, and covered it up with the tobacco and they came up to him and they asked him about this pearl and he said he didn't know anything about a pearl. But they arrested him. They said, 'You've been in a jeweller with a pearl and he's offered you £20 for it.' But they had to let him go because they couldn't find the pearl on him but he had the pearl in his clay pipe and he left Brechin then when they let him go and he had to walk to Edinburgh because he hadn't any money. He got £100 for that pearl and it was worth more even than that, but he took the £100—a hundred gold sovereigns he got for it. That pearl was sold to an Austrian count but where it went after that, they didn't know. But that one came off the South Esk, it was thirty-seven-and-a-quarter grains because my father asked the jeweller that bought it in Edinburgh because Cove Pitcaithlie, he stayed with my grandmother here in Coupar Angus and he was on about this great pearl he had. He had all thir gold sovereigns, and when they went through to Edinburgh they asked the jeweller, 'Oh aye,' he says, 'we bought that pearl, it was thirty-seven-and-a-quarter grains right enough.' They thought that the Cove was exaggerating a bit because he tended to exaggerate, but this was genuine, you know, a genuine find."

Although pure white pearls are sought after, the great prize was to find a black pearl.

Betsy Whyte:
"For years they were all hunting for a black pearl; they said they'd get a fabulous price if they could get a black pearl but I've never heard of anyone getting one except seeds, tiny seeds which weren't much good.

"You know, if you burn a pearl it'll turn black but as soon as it's handled a bit it just crumbles away. But there was this lady and she was dying for a black pearl and I think the temptation must have been too much so this woman burned these pearls and sold them to the lady. Two, they were black and shiny when she sold them. Later some of them went back to the lady's house and she said, 'You know, I don't know what's happened to these pearls, I put them away safely in the drawer but I could never find them. I questioned everybody in

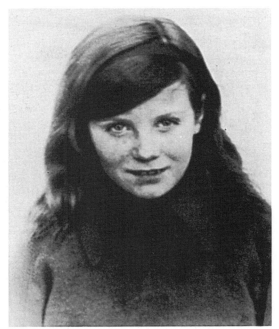

*Betsy Whyte.*

the house and they were never found.' But, of course, they'd crumbled away, you see they do that when they're burned."

Black pearls are so rare that many legends and perhaps some wishful thinking has surrounded stories about them.

Bill Abernethy:
"Mary, Queen of Scots, had several necklaces and brooches in Scotch pearls and I think it was Lord Darnley that stole her jewellery and sold it. But she also had a necklace of black pearls which is very rare, black pearls are very few and far between you know. But you do get black pearls and at that time, as you know, the rivers were full of pearls here and it wasn't any great difficulty to get a few necklaces together but to get a black necklace was a different story. The black ones had probably been saved up for Mary, Queen of Scots, and it was made into a necklace. When she was taken to England and her jewellery was either stolen or confiscated and whether it was broken up and sold or not. . . . But the story goes that the black necklace of pearls was bought in a junk shop in Aberdeen away back at the beginning of this century for two shillings and sixpence. That was the story that went about. The boy that bought them for two shillings and sixpence knew the value, he was a pearl fisher from Stirling, that's all I can tell you about it. Where they went to after that, I don't know but that's the story, whether it's true or no, you've just got to take it at its face value."

ISHBEL MACLEAN

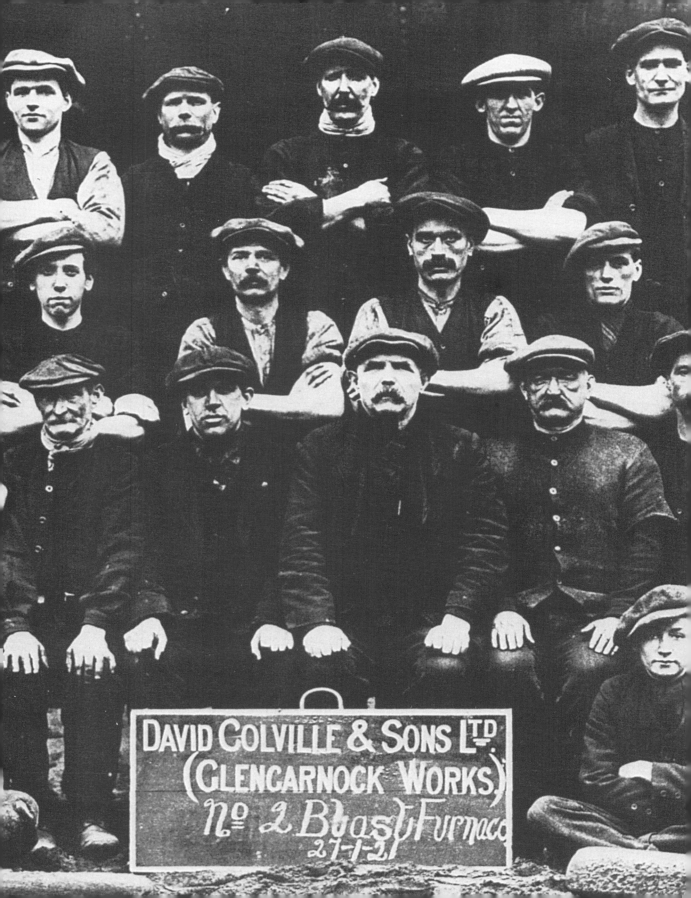

DAVID COLVILLE & SONS L™
(GLENGARNOCK WORKS)
N° 2 Blast Furnace
27-1-21

# Glengarnock Steel

On 21st December 1978, steel was made in Glengarnock, north Ayrshire, for the last time: its owners, the British Steel Corporation, had deemed the open hearth furnaces there to be obsolescent, a decision ratified by the Government.

On that day, just prior to the final charging of the last furnace in operation — the 'H' — four of its team scrawled their names alongside one of its five doors. Time has already partially erased their signatures but the informed onlooker, stopping to ponder over the reasoning behind such an action, does not take long to come to a conclusion: these men wanted it to be known that they had witnessed the demise of the open hearth process in Britain. They were the last link in what had become, over the past eighty-six years at Glengarnock, a traditional industry. But before steel had been produced in Glengarnock there had been iron. The laying of the Glasgow/Ayr railway in 1840 dispelled any doubts that local industrialists James Merry, Alexander Allison and Alexander Cunninghame may have had as to the viability of an ironworks on the shores of Kilbirnie Loch. If supplies of coal, iron and limestone in the area were to run out then these raw materials could thereafter be easily imported. More importantly, the pig iron produced could be quickly dispatched.

Thus by 1843 eight blast furnaces were producing iron which found its way to Europe and America. As these markets began to make their own iron and the supply of local ironstone became exhausted, the company, now owned by John Charles Cunninghame, son of the original founder, and his cousin John Cunninghame, decided that the time had come to make steel. Four eight-ton Bessemer converters were installed (1885-1920) and seven years later, in 1892, the first of the open hearth furnaces was built followed closely by a rolling mill and a structural department.

Over the years a variety of products were to be dispatched from the works: pig iron, shells (during the First World War), rails, sleepers, fish plates, joists, angles, tees, channels, bars, blooms, slabs and flats.

The establishment of an iron and, eventually, steel works at Glengarnock attracted men from far and near. For not only was there the chance of male employment: the thread and net works and woollen mills of the neighbouring town of Kilbirnie and Dalry

*Blast furnace workers–date unknown (probably late 1920s).*

*Above: Furnace workers, c. 1921. Opposite: Lithuanian women and children in Glengarnock.*

proffered work for their womenfolk. Not surprisingly, families from Ireland, England, Spain (from where much of the ore for Glengarnock's iron furnaces was eventually imported), Italy, Poland and Lithuania were attracted to this industrial pocket of essentially rural Ayrshire.

Robert Whitelaw:
"Mother came from Workington—a sort of steel working community, too. I presume the works was slack there and they came up here when the steelwork was being enlarged and more people came into it. They came from Workington in the 1890s—her mother and five of the family came up here for the work."

Joe McAuley (second generation Lithuanian):
"When they came to a certain age they had to go into the Russian Army. And father had a brother in the army; and when he was home he says, 'Brother, if there's anything you can do to avoid the army, do anything at all. Because really, the conditions is really not too pleasant.' So the result wis father made up his mind: he came over here to Scotland.
"Well, it was just farming [in Lithuania]. Ah'll tell ye the way they lived then: they had a small holding an' whitever grun they cultivated there it was for their own use, for the winter. And then if they had a pig, a sheep and a horse—if they had a surplus— they ta'en it tae the market. And they worked sorta on a barter system: they exchanged jist for something that they really required.
"There was no schooling there. None o' them got

any schooling. Mother—if she was takin' note o' anything—used to sit and draw strokes tae she came tae ten. And then she put a top on ten and she went along until she had another ten."

Laura Buchanan:
"I can remember them [Lithuanians, known locally as 'Poles'] coming off the train because it was a local man in the steelwork who met them aw—he was a foreman there or a manager. They couldn't say a word of English that I remember. And they all had tickets on their backs [saying Glengarnock, Ayrshire] when they came off the train. They seemed all to come just in one batch. The men came first. Ah don't remember when their wives came. But they did come. And they had big families after they came here, quite a lot o' them."

Many Ayrshire men, too, sought a start in the steel works, regarding it as an attractive alternative to life down the local pits.

John Ramsay:
"Instead of going to the pit that first morning, ah went to the steelwork; and sat and waited till the manager passed me. Ah chased up the manager and asked him for a job. He took me tae a foreman that already said he didn't require anybody, told him to start me. After Ah'd worked a short time, till about nine o'clock, the foreman came to me and says, 'You didn't tell me that you worked in the pit.' Ah says, 'It's quite obvious if you look at me.' Ah never worked any place else—at that time still

having on my yorks or knee strings. 'So why did you leave the pit and come here?' So ah says, 'Wait.' And ah pulled up ma shirt at the back. He says, 'You're supposed to go back to the pit, ah'll have tae send you back.' But when he looked at ma back he says, 'You're going back to no pit.'

"Ah was skinned from the hips up to the back of the neck. The company that owned the pits also owned the steelwork and they were very economic with their rails down the pit. And time and again the hutch would jump the road and you had to lift these hutches on. And the only method of doing it was turning your back on the hutch, putting in a spragg to hold it in position. Then you put your back against it and heaved it on to the road. Your back got skinned from the neck right down to the buttocks. Ah never saw a drawer with anything else but a skinned back. And, well, that's the reason that the engineer foreman decided ah wasn't going back to the pits."

With such an influx of people (in 1841 Kilbirnie's population totalled 2,631, in 1851 it was 5,484 and by 1901 it was 7,207) the hamlet of Glengarnock which hitherto contained very little more than an inn and Kilbirnie's station, mushroomed. Families settled not only along its Main Street but within the steelworks site itself in rows upon rows of single-storey houses, serviced by the company store and its celebrated liquor annexe, the 'Billy Ruffin' (the local interpretation of 'Bellorophone', after the famous British warship that

took Napoleon to exile in St. Helena).

Although working conditions regarding safety improved with time, older hands still referred to the works as the 'Slaughterhouse'. The following account concerns the Bessemer plant where air was blown through holes in the bottom of the cupolas into molten iron, initially causing slag and molten metal to be thrown out rather violently.

Joe Smith:

"Ma faither wis brought home. He was burnt—claes were burnt aff him. See, when you're drawing in these bogeys from the vessel—ken, a cupola—slag keeps bubbling and this yin must have been right full up. Ken, the wye it bubbles oot and it caught alight and they took him hame. Ah think they took him hame in a cab, a horse-drawn cab, aye. An' he come in—oh, he wis an awfae state. And would you believe the treatment he got efter that—ah remember—leeches pit on his back—leeches! And whenever they were full they were pit intae salt so they would vomit up their thingmae so they'd be used again and then pit intae a jar. This wis a doctor's idea. Aye, they did that wi' leeches, ken—burns—bad burns. Ah seen it—ah seen as much as three leeches on his back— his bare back. He was quite a bit aff before he was right again fur workin'. But he wouldnae need tae be right better. It was as quick as he could get out tae work because there were nae money. Ah don't know whether we wur gettin' any compensation.

*Blast furnaces and pig beds (taken from a supplement to 'The Metal Industry', 3rd June 1927).*

Ah think aw he got was a lift fae the
workmates—ken, subscribin'."

The attitude of the private owners of Glengarnock
Steelworks as to sanitary conditions was not portrayed
in an enthusiastic manner by their former employees.
Until the erection of amenity blocks at the Mill and
Melting Shops in the 'fifties and 'sixties respectively,
washing-up facilities were very basic and the men had
to take their meal breaks alongside their work.

John Williamson:
"They had wee cabins built in the Melting Shop
and that's where everybody had to eat. And to
make tea, you had to put a steel plate in the
furnace, heat it, and boil your can. That's how you
made your tea. And you just sat beside your job and
ate. And if there was a lot of dust, well, you just
absorbed the dust along wi' your meal. It helped to
fill a hole. . . . The modern worker would lay an
egg if he saw the way we worked in these days.
You got a two-and-a-half gallon zinc-coated pail
and you filled that with water and that hung on a
hook outside the cabin, open to the atmosphere and
open to all the coke and alloy dust that fell around
it. And that was the water that you drank—that
was the water you made your tea with."

Andrew Dick:
"Well, ye got bits o' scrap—flat—ones that ye
could lift. Ye'd tae throw them intae the door o'
the furnace—into the bay, an' pull them out when
they wis hot and put them up on a couple of bricks
and used that. Ye toasted in below that. And ye'd
get your [tea] drum, an old syrup tin, an' boiled it
that way."

George Barclay:
"As far as washing-up when yir day was finished
as many as possible got around about the one
washhand basin, an old sink and a cold tap goin'
intae it.
"There were no hot water facilities. If you got
hot water, you were fortunate. Because it meant
you were working outside the shop someplace. You
were at the Mill and you got a bloom end and ye
got an ordinary bucket and you put it on the top o'
it till the water was warm. And that was you—you
had warm water tae wash your hands at the end o'
yir shift."

James Vann:
"The sanitaries were open, were dry closets.
That's what they were, aye. Like a lot of canaries
in a tin box, aye!"

The tremendous heat and heavy nature of the work
required special clothes.

George Blair:
"Well, they [melters at the open hearth furnaces]
wore the blue flannel pants and shirts—that was to
take the sweat, and the wee cap. Fireman's caps,
they called them—they were just a thin black
material. Well, you'd mibbae jist go in wi' a new
one an' go in some place where there was heat
and—psssst—it was burnt!
"Ah used tae go down tae the store and get the
hand leathers. They were good. They must've been
about six inches b'eight: they jist cut a nice slit and
jist slipped their hand through. So that was
protection [for the palm of the hand].
"The melters wore a white scarf—that was a
sweat rag. You had always that tae wipe—you
know, you wis gettin' blinded whiles wi' sweat.
Because if you wis working, it was running off
your broo.
"We wore a canvas apron: you had it down
below yir knees an' it protected against any burns
or splashes."

William Dubordieu (second man at one of
Glengarnock's iron blast furnaces):
"You'd tae take two shirts wi' ye when you were
workin'. When you were bye wi' the one, you ta'en
it off and pit oan a dry one, blue flannel shirts, they
ate up the sweat, y'see. Then we had a thing we
pulled over wur boots to save wur boots fae gettin'
burnt, we were in hot sand [pig beds were moulded
in sand]. They were jist made of the beltin' offa the
different machinery and wooden soles and you
nailed it roon aboot; and then you laced it roon
your boot. And that done tae ye wur bye wi' the
cast. But you werenae long in takin' them oaf after
you were bye wi' them. You couldnae walk aboot
wi' them, you know—you could have tripped."

Wanda Mackaveetch (daughter of a pig lifter at the
blast furnaces):
"They had t'get moleskin trousers. They were
thick, thick, thick. . . . They needed something to
keep the heat out of their legs. Because when they
went to their work they wore long johns—drawers
we called them. They never wore socks, they got
white linen, usually, and they rolled it round their
feet and all round their legs and they pulled their
drawers down to there [ankle]. That's the way they
went to their work—no socks, wi' the moleskin
trousers.
"They were expensive then, too. You coulda
got an ordinary pair of trousers cheaper, but the
men had t' get those."

Work, however, was not always available in the
area: the slumps and booms of heavy industry were felt
keenly in Glengarnock, a village that lived by and for
steel. When jobs were scarce, families would move on
to hopefully more secure climes.

Matt Yuill:
"At the end of the nineteenth century, many
families, when work was slack, went off to the

U.S.A. to work in the pits there. If trade got better in Scotland, many returned. My mother recalled—as a little girl sailing back to Scotland up the Clyde—the families sat in the hatches, tidying up before they reached the tail of the bank. I last saw my Grandma going off to America—her seventh crossing of the 'Herring Pond', the Atlantic Ocean. This seems to convey to me the idea that, ach, it wasn't very big: it was just a pond. You know, you just went across."

John Ramsay:
"Dalry men were generally known as Chinks. That's supposed to have originated from somebody that had emigrated to Waterbury, a favourite place for Dalry people before the development o' the motor industry in America. And there'd been a queue at this employment gate in Waterbury where they made watches and there was a Chinaman in it, also a Dalry man. When they got up to the employment office—there had been quite a few refusals—the official asked this man, 'Where do you come from?' 'Ah come from Dalry.' 'Oh, come in.' Started right away. So they asked the Chinaman next. He says, 'Me Dalry man, too!' So he got started as well! And that's how Dalry men are supposed to have got the nickname, Chinamen."

Ironically, it was war—the Great War—that was to bring expansion and prosperity to Glengarnock Works. David Colville and Sons of Motherwell, backed by Ministry of Munitions money, refurbished the ailing furnaces and built a new open hearth melting shop and a rolling mill. By 1919, 3,000 were employed, the highest labour force ever recorded.

The village of Glengarnock grew in confidence during such a thriving time: the friendly rivalry that always existed between its inhabitants and those of Kilbirnie, on the other side of the Garnock River, became more evident.

Ellen McConachie and Helen Kennedy:
"Ye put the links [chain by which a pot, etc. hangs over a fire from the 'crook' or iron hook] on as you needed: drew them forrit as you needed—an' whatever size you needed.
"They used tae say that wis why the kettle never biled in Kilbirnie. For they had it on the top link!"

While Glengarnock was dominated by steel, its inhabitants were, in the main, only first generation industrial workers: most still had an affinity for the country and rural skills could be relied upon when money was scarce.

John Ramsay:
"Ma father was what was known as a good pot filler. He could turn his hand to get a rabbit or wild duck or 'cushies' or wood pigeons, they're better known as. One night he said to me, 'Come on, Ah know where there's a hare feedin'.' And he

*Jock Ramsay outside his home in Kilbirnie.*

lifted a net, and we went away up this road to a gate. He put the net on a gate and he says to me, 'Now, when the hare comes into that net, get it, break its neck.' Well, Ah looked at him. Ah says, 'Listen, don't tell me that a hare's gonnae run intae a net on a gate when there's only an occasional bush round that field along wi' a wire fence.' He says to me, 'Just you lie there and when it comes in the net, get it, ah'm telling ye.'
"And away he went down to the bottom of the field and ah could hear him rattling two stones together he'd picked up. Sure as he said it the hare come running up and stopped aboot ten or fifteen yards from the gate, looked round, then it dived through the bars of the gate into the net and it let out a squeal. Well, ah was a bit soft-hearted and ah put ma hand in and got the hare b' the ears and threw it out behind me and away it went quite happy, ah suppose.
"And he came up. 'Where is it?' he says.
"Ah says, 'Where's whit?'
"'Where's the hare?'
"'Ah never seen any hare.'
"'You're a damned liar,' he says, 'the hare went intae that net.'
"Ah says, 'Naw it didnae. Ah never seen any hare.'
"'Listen,' he says, 'this is your education: when a hare gets disturbed in a field where it's feeding at night, it'll go through nothing else but a place where there's a gate. And that hare went intae that net, ah don't care whit ye say.'
"Well, he was right!
"Another time, ah saw him sitting stringing horse hair through ears of corn. Ah never asked him any questions, ah just watched him. And when he had quite a bundle o' these horse hairs strung corn, he says, 'Come on.' And he took me up tae this field

where there was cushies feedin'. There was a plantin' run alongside it. Well, naturally, the cushies got up when we went up and we went along the edge o' this plantin' and scattered this corn and then hid. Well, in a short time the cushies went back down to feed and ah saw a few of them begin tae flutter their wings and give a jump and when there was half a dozen like this, he says, 'That'll do.'

"And we went along and picked up the cushies. They couldn't fly because the horse hair had entangled their wings—the corn was over their gullet but there wur plenty of horse hair trailing behind tae entangle their wings and they couldn't fly. That was another way of getting cushies!"

Such escapades must have provided welcome relief—as well as welcome food during hard times—for those forced to live literally on the job. The Long Row, the Front Row, the Square, the Pond Row (next to the reservoirs containing water for the works' steam engines), the Coal Lye, the Store Row and the Railway Cottages were sandwiched between furnaces, slag heaps and railway lines.

Sanitary arrangements within the 'Raws' (Rows) were primitive: drinking water was got from pillar wells, outside toilets were shared one per three households and, unlike the later works' houses—the 'Hill' and the inaptly named Cornpark—there were no wash houses. Slop water was thrown into sheughs, open channels which ran alongside the houses' front doors to a common sewer; and household rubbish was deposited in 'mickeys', or ashpits, nearby.

Joe McAuley:
"Well, when we wis goin' to bed, if wur feet wis dirty and that, we sat on this sheugh and washed wur feet and got prepared there for bed."

Helen Kennedy:
"In yir entry wis where ye kept yer pail o' clean water and yer basin to wash in. There was a lovely, big barrel on a stand outside. And we collected the rain water in it: and you washed your face wi' the rain water. In winter there were ice floatin' roon aboot an' it hit the side o' yir basin an' tinkled all roon aboot." [shivers]

Large families crowded into rooms and kitchens in the labyrinth of homes situated within the works or in the village of Glengarnock itself where conditions were only marginally better. Thus there was room for only the bare essentials of furniture: belongings, as well as coal, had to be stored under set-in beds in many cases.

Joe Smith:
"We had three in-set beds. Ma father and mother slept in the kitchen—the big wan in the kitchen —and we slept whit they cawed the 'jail'! Part a it would be shown tae the kitchen, like, and the rest

o' it would be in between the room and the kitchen. The other bed was jist the full length, ken; it was curtained tae.

"Aw, ye had tae have curtains. There was nae privacy, ye had tae have yur claes on a chair near the bed. . . .

"You used to have neighbours in. Sometimes you couldnae come oot a bed till they went away! Ken, they wid blether away there! But if you were in the room it was a different thing. Well, the girls were in the room—three girls were in the room."

Joe McAuley:
"There was no mattresses in thae days. They made a big, big tick; and we went over to the farm and we got straw and they filled this tick wi' straw and they put it on the bed. And that's what you lay on. That was ma mattress. But the cushions was good aw the same because they was always feathers. Mother, every Christmas, she would buy either a goose or a duck or a drake or something like that and she would pook the feathers off it and she would save these feathers and then put them intae cushions. But wur covering was good. It was a big tick and it was filled wi' feathers—just like a continental quilt. Well, this is what we covered wursheves wi'. And it was warm."

Helen Kennedy:
"We hud a meal and a flooer [flour] girnal [meal chest]. Ma mother goat it as a weddin' present: she worked as a farm servant at a farm at the Longbar [next to the steelworks, now a housing estate]— that's a long time ago. And the one side held a bag o' meal and the other a bag o' flour. And in below held things for bakin'."

But there was no doubt at all that in such cramped surroundings a housewife's pride and joy was her dresser.

Ellen McConachie:
"Like a sideboard, but it had two doors. And then abin that were wir three drawers wi' glass handles on them. And then there wir a big rack and this rack hid like wee shelves wi' bars across an' we hud plates in it: a big plate and two wee'er yins like would haud a turkey nooadays—kinna Willow pattern. An then at this place where the wee drawers were there wir mibbae two or three ither plates—if ye wir lucky enough t' hiv what matched. And if they didnae match, well, that was alright— you made them fancy!

"And we hud mibbae a hauf a set o' cheeny: an' if ye wur lucky enough ye hud twa hauf sets. And sittin' on the flat bit, we hud a pair o' wally dugs an' whit they would cry noo a fruit thing. It wis kinna crystally—cut gless, likely it would be. An' a photae o' yur lawd or yir swank!

"Ye've seen a jug and ewer? Well, we hud two o' that—jist sittin' up beside this gless thing; and sittin' beside that wis the two wally dugs."

Glengarnock's good fortune after the 1914-18 war was to be short lived. The miners' strikes of the 'twenties and the emerging worldwide economic recession spelled hardship for its steelwork families. The works' owners had to introduce a programme of rationalisation: in 1930 the emerging company of Colvilles Ltd., under the direction of Sir John Craig, designated Glengarnock as a producer of structural steel. The works' structural department, producing in the main girders (hence the local name still used, the 'Girder Shop') took on a more sophisticated image: five years later it pioneered electric arc welding. Such a development was introduced, however, at the cost of Glengarnock's blast iron furnaces: these were closed down in 1930 as iron production was now to be concentrated within Clyde Iron Works. As a result, families began to move away from the area in the vain hope that work could be had elsewhere for by now Britain was in the grip of the Depression. In 1933 only one furnace was in operation in Glengarnock and some families lived on 'broo money' for nigh on five years (1930-35).

The food a family eats is a good indication of the financial circumstances it is experiencing. In Glengarnock, like everywhere else, good fare was enjoyed when business was booming—a pig lifter would enjoy a breakfast of half a pound of bacon and half a dozen eggs or eat two pounds of steak in one sitting. But the lasting memories of food, like those that follow, are held by people who know what it is like to go wanting.

James Jennings:
"It used to be an occasion when all the men in the area would walk over the Fairlie Moor from Dalry. Ye knew when they came back, that you were gonnae get fish for your dinner because this was them goin' over to Fairlie, to the boats, to try and scrounge some fish fae the fishermen who were comin' in. We used to say, 'That's ma Daddy away to Fairlie. We'll get fish. . . .'

"And you could rest assured, on the way back, they'd be into a potato field or a turnip field. And this was how they lived. They would go out in the middle of the night and scrounge things. Those days made, no' necessarily criminals, but offenders, out of people who otherwise wouldn't have resorted to that type of thing. Because they had families to feed. . . ."

Ellen McConachie:
"Tatties and dab at the still [stool]. . . . Well, on a winter night or a winter day yer mother had a big poat o' tatties bilin' ready, sittin' up oan the hob. Aye, it was a big stane poat—no' enamel, ken—it wis too cauld.

"So oot come the stool—nae cover [tablecloth] on it—jist oot come the stool an' a saucer o' salt. An' ye got yer potato—lifted a potato and peeled the skin oaf it and ye dabbed it in the salt an' ye ate it. If ye liked, ye cud get a wee bit butter tae it.

*Opposite: Railway cottages on site at Glengarnock works.*

"Mibbae it wis yer tea, mibbae it wis yer dinner—jist as it suited."

The harsh dictates of the Means Test caused many people to perjure themselves in order to get a reasonable income for their families:

John Dempsey:
"Well, we come onto the Means Test and this is where ma father and ma mother got the hard en' o' it. Because whenever we got a job in the Guide Mill, ma father didn't get anything. He was unemployed and we were supposed t' keep ma father. If ah worked for three month, then he got nothing—which forced us t' say, 'We've left the house.' Ma eldest brother was married so we'd all say, 'We're living with ma brother.' That was to get something from the Labour Exchange when we weren't working; and something for ma father to get because he couldn't say that we were in the house keepin' him."

The ramifications of the Means Test were to have violent repercussions in Kilbirnie: on a February night in 1931, the Riot Act was read. Local Communist leaders, backed by Glasgow members of the National Unemployed Workers' Movement and contingents of supporters from nearby Beith and Dalry, as well as Glengarnock, had marched to the town's Walker Hall where local councillors were holding a meeting.

Dick Sneddon:
"Well, the street was black from the Masonic Hall to the Walker Hall; and black on the ither side, right to the bridge. Oh, the crowd in front o' the Walker Hall was massive. . . . It was night, ah would say aroon aboot half-past seven we'd actually land there. Now the demonstration, ah suppose, would be advertised aforehand. Well, the councillors must have asked the policemen t' be there that night. There must've been oh, hundreds o' policemen between the Commercial Hotel and the Walker Hall—*in* the building.

"The deputation came out and said that the answer wisnae satisfactory. . . . Now the Riot Act, it seems, wis read inside the building. It seems that someb'dy hud come out—the policeman concerned—and the Riot Act was then read. . . . But ah've always mind o' the strap [of helmet] comin' down—the inspector—and that must've been the sign for them tae draw their batons. . . . Well, ah don't know whit made me bury ma head in among the crowd—you know the way it all broke up—but ah've always mind o' gettin' this blow on the shoulder and then taps. . . . Ah wus frightened, aye, very frightened! Ah think everybody wis frightened. Ah mean, the people o' Kilbirnie had never seen anythin' like that in their life before! There wurnae one person armed in that demonstration because there were wimmen in it—an' children—wi' wee prams."

*Main Street, Glengarnock–looking eastwards towards Glengarnock Railway Station.*

George Henderson:

"Communists are not born: they're bred. And to this day in Kilbirnie you have Communists who were converted at that time."

It was to take another World War—the 1939-45—to remedy the situation: steel is a crucial commodity during such a time and Glengarnock steel was to be used in shipbuilding. The men began to go back to work. . . .

Helen Kennedy:

"Ma husband was goin' oot t' his work this Thursday night—two tae ten—he hid goat three shifts—goat three days broo an' three shifts an' this wis marvellous. Well, when you goat the three shifts, the week before that you only goat three days broo which was twelve and six. Well, that had t' do ye t' the next again Friday. 'Ah've fill't a [football] coupon in the paper,' he says. 'It'll only cost fourpence haepenny t' send it away. Will ye post it fur me?' Ah sayed, 'Oh, alright, ah'll see.'

"So away he went tae his work an' ah says, 'Oh, my, that coupon t' post. Ah've fourpence haepenny. Fourpence haepenny would get me three eggs in the mornin'. Ah don't know whit t' dae!' An' ah didnae know whit tae dae. An' ah waited an' ah waited an' wunnert what ah wid dae. Ah says, 'Och, him an' his coupons. Ah'll jist buy three eggs!'

"So on the Saturday he wis checkin' his coupon. His coupon come up. It wis mibbae a hundred and forty [pounds], ah cunnae hae mind. Bit it wis quite a loat a money. Oh, me! He nivir spoke t' me for three weeks efter it. Oh, ah wis cut, ah wis upset!

An' he says, 'Ah asked ye t' post that coupon!' Ah says, 'Ah know you asked me t' post the coupon but you'd a hud no breakfast nor neither wid the weans hiv had a breakfast if ah hud posted that coupon.' Well, he come roon an' he says, 'Oh, right enough, it mibbae wid a went doon'."

After 1945, hand-to-mouth existence was no longer paramount and the steelwork families began to find more time for leisure. More money meant more sophisticated activities were enjoyed but some, like the two that follow, gained momentum and still survive today.

Anna Williamson:

"I can remember it was an all-night sitting before the [Kilbirnie] Flower Show. And my cousin and I used to get the Friday afternoon off school to go and gather rushes. We would gather armfuls of rushes and they were all put into these vases and whipped off! The rushes were used for floral art, as you might say—to hold the flowers in position. But in the morning, when everything was ready, they had the Co-op coal cart—horse and cart—and it was the joy of our life if we were the one that was picked to sit and hold something steady on the cart. But more often I seemed to be the one that had to walk up carrying something—which wasn't quite so nice, you know. My father tried all sorts of gadgets. His whole life was flowers. But the garden wasn't a thing of beauty. The garden was full of wee boxes covering the flowers to keep them clean! If we got an east wind from the steelwork—sometimes at the weekend—I don't know what they did but there was a great deal of pollution came. And I've seen him heartbroken if he had something not covered and it got dirty.''

Joe Smith:

"We were wans fur fitba—day and night. Ah've seen us goan' fur wur tea and comin' back. . . . The gemm was on. You just got in a gemm. You hud tae get a partner fur the opposite side. It would start wi' abit mibbae, say five or six at the start on each side and then b' the end a it they'd be very near twenty-two on each side! But they had always tae get another wan tae go on the opposite side: and the gemm would go on tae night and we were wans fur bed.''

By the 'fifties, however, two major local authority housing estates were built in Kilbirnie and the drift of Glengarnock families to more modern homes outside the village began. Their going spelled the beginning of the end for the community. Of the five Co-op departments, three public houses, eleven shops, a licensed grocer and two banks, only a hairdresser, the licensed grocer, a sub-post office/newsagent, a public house and a social club remain today. Not that the loyalty of some of Glengarnock's inhabitants was easily dissuaded.

Jackie Clark:

"Ah still think that this village of Glengarnock is due a better destiny than what it's getting. There's nothing to me to beat a village life and some people come into ma shop that I haven't seen for a long, long and weary and the first thing they say, 'Well, poor Glengarnock! But if there was a house built in Glengarnock, ah would come back to it tomorrow.'

"Let us restore places where we used to be and fill the gap sites. Ah organised a petition and a thousand signed to try and do something about the village of Glengarnock. And the authorities stated that the people who signed this didn't belong to Glengarnock. The petition was left to people who came into my shop and, after all, it's only a wee village shop. Ah had people who came from all over, visiting the steelworks, travellers, people who belong to Glengarnock, people who had emigrated abroad who'd come back to Glengarnock who said,

'In the name of heavens, what's happened to this place?'

"We've had to look at dilapidation for so many years that we really had to do something. I erected a cross—a ten-foot cross—and on that cross was, 'GLENGARNOCK, DIED OF NEGLECT'.''

Although the village of Glengarnock had begun to run down, the works continued to be the major employer in the Garnock Valley (Glengarnock, Kilbirnie, Dalry, Beith and Lochwinnoch). In 1968, following extensive alterations to its rolling mill, it was taken over by the British Steel Corporation. But, basically, the open hearth furnaces remained as they had been after the First World War. Newer, quicker, more efficient processes, coupled with marked foreign competition and a fall in the demand for steel, contributed to the demise of the Glengarnock Melting Shop in 1978. A reduced rolling mill operation, employing just over 200 people, has continued, its survival due to the establishment of the 'Glengarnock Agreement' which promotes job flexibility—something which would never have been tolerated a few years before.

However, recent figures show increased productivity there and hopes are high that more hands may be taken on in 1982. This cannot be soon enough for the 31 per cent at present unemployed in the Valley.

Government authorities are valiantly trying to introduce new industries to the area but those firms which have been attracted by specially built premises and financial incentives are still in embryo, employing relatively few local people. The future is bleak.

Helen Kennedy:

"It's jist history repeatin' itself. It is. Because wir lifeblood was the steelwork an' the [iron] furnaces. An' when the furnaces closed down, there was a loat went away. And there the steelworks is the same an' they're goin' away because the steelworks is closed doon. It's jist a tragedy. An' an older body, seein' it happenin', it's jist heartbreakin'. Because you were intendin' t' bring up yer grandchildren in the area. They'll need to go away fae here t' look for work—if they can get it ither places. Where in Scotland are they goin' t' get it?"

LORNA LEWIS

*Derelict melting shop in winter 1979/80.*

# Clan Neil of Barra

"The McNeills originally came from Ireland and they used to say in Gaelic 'Clann Neill nam piob's nam breacan sibh a thug a chreach a Eirinn'—Clan Neil of the pipes and tartan that came from Ireland to raid and stayed."
—Nan McKinnon

Lying as it does at the southernmost end of the Outer Hebrides, Barra has never been the most easily accessible of islands. The advent of air travel has helped to alter this, but for most, the journey from Oban to Castlebay by sea, is still one of some five hours—when a direct route is taken by MacBraynes ferries and when the weather is favourable. The island of Barra and its adjacent islands of Vatersay and Mingulay have successfully retained Gaelic culture and identity where other islands have been swamped by the tide of outside influences. This is probably due to a number of factors. Firstly, the island's relative isolation in geographical terms. Secondly, and related to this, the close-knit nature of the community. Thirdly, Barra's adherence to the Catholic faith, which, along with the islands of South Uist and Eriskay, gave it a sense of separate identity from the other islands of the Hebrides. It also spared the island the cultural ravages of over-zealous Presbyterianism which destroyed Gaelic oral and musical tradition in other areas of Scotland. Therefore, while the historical experience of Barra, and the history of Clan Neil, shares much in common with that of other Highland areas and clans, the survival of a lively, comparatively unbroken oral tradition has given the island something of a closer affinity with the past. Through this we are fortunate in being able to glean some idea of the clan days, not from the history book, but from the passing of oral tradition from generation to generation through the centuries.

The McNeills of Barra are undoubtedly of very ancient lineage. Martin Martin writing in 1695 tells us that according to the genealogists of his day, the chief of the McNeills was the thirty-fourth of his name who had possessed Barra in unbroken descent. The Old Statistical Account states that the McNeills originally came from Ireland, related to the O'Neills of Ulster, and that they were in possession of Barra before the 'Danes'. It is at least certain that they were there during the Norse occupation of the Hebrides. Niall of the Nine Hostages who ruled at Tara in Ireland from 308 to 405 is commonly regarded as the progenitor of the clan. It is believed that his ancestor 'Niall of the Castle' came to Barra around 1030 as vassal to the King of Norway and married one of his daughters, his progeny remaining in feudal homage to the Norwegian Crown until 1266.

Other Clan historians, however, have held that the progenitor was a norseman named 'Njal'—McNeill being the same as Nilsson—perhaps Njal of the race of Ketil Flatneb who ruled the Hebrides during the tenth century. What is important, however, is that they held identity from a common progenitor and that as an established clan in Scotland we can go back no further than the eleventh century. The construction of the original Keep of Castle Kisimul probably began around the same period. In Scotland the McNeills of Barra have always been regarded as chiefs of the clan, above the cadet branches found in Gigha and Knapdale. The traditional clan lands were the islands of Barra, Vatersay, Mingulay and all the islands south to Barra Head, but as late as the seventeenth century the McNeills were in possession of part of South Uist, before being driven out by the McDonalds of Clanranald at the battle of North Boisdale in 1601. During the clan period they feature as allies of the McLeans of Duart and links between the clans were close.

Under the clan system the relationship between the chief and his clan, in Barra as elsewhere, was a well-defined one, what has been described as a 'mixture of autocracy and communism'.

Roderick McNeill:
"They were like one family. The chief had to

*Above: Kisimul Castle. Opposite: Barra from Vatersay.*

allocate the land and the fishing banks as well. He also had to arrange marriages and generally to order the lives of all his people. Where one of his men was in rather dire straits, for example if twins were born in a family, one of the pair was taken into the castle and brought up there as one of McNeill's own family."

McNeill's responsibilities also extended to replacement of cattle lost by tenants and admission to the castle of those with no family who had grown too old to look after themselves. The arranging of marriages was an important duty of the chief as Martin Martin discovered in Barra in 1695:

"When a tenant's wife in this or adjacent islands dies, he then addresses himself to McNeill of Barra representing his loss and at the same time desires

*Sixteenth-century graveslab showing Hebridean birlinn.*

that he would be pleased to recommend a wife to him. Upon this representation McNeill finds out a suitable match for him and the woman's name being told him immediately he goes to her carrying with him a bottle of strong waters for their entertainment at marriage, which is then consummated."

The paternalism of the chiefs extended to a responsibility for discipline.

Archie McDonald:
"The McNeill had a day every year for judging what happened through the whole year. If there was any crime of any description they [the clanspeople] would have to come forward and he was giving judgement—what would be if there was any punishment or anything like that, and it was always on horseback. He was always sitting in his saddle over at a place on the west side of Barra called 'Judgement Seat'. The site is still there. If there was anything wrong it was always put straight, on a straight tack and the rules were laid down to them."

Rent to the McNeills was paid in kind, in military service and in produce such as corn or livestock.

Roderick McNeill:
"The islands to the south of Vatersay—they were all inhabited at that time, paid their rent in kind—wool and birds' feathers and no doubt oil and the actual flesh of the birds. There was one bird that was regarded as a particular delicacy, the *fachaich*. The *fachaich* is the young of the puffin. They were paid as part of the rent. Now the place where this rent was delivered called Port an taigh mhal can still be seen at a place called Nask."

The people of Mingulay and the other islands where the fachaich was harvested do not seem to have used ropes as they did on St Kilda, but clambered among the rocks like goats.

The esteem with which the McNeill was held, in Barra at least, was humorously referred to by James Wilson in his *Voyage Round the Coasts of Scotland*, published in 1842. There Wilson relates that in ancient times the custom was for the herald to sound a horn from the battlements of Castle Kisimul and proclaim 'Hear ye people and nations listen, the great McNeill of Barra having finished his meal, the princes and kings of the earth may dine'—a good story which the historical sceptic should not judge too harshly.

Tales of the clan days are told by the older people on the island with familiarity, as if a centuries-old event had occurred but a few years previously. Not surprisingly, the Barra men have been noted for their seamanship from earliest times, and the fortunes of the Barra people have always been inextricably bound up with the sea. The sight of McNeill's Galleys or 'Birlinns' as they were called, setting off on a raid, was a familiar one in the olden days.

*Cattle on the beach at Vatersay.*

Archie McDonald:

"Oh, they were great pirates, they could manage that. There were no use of them trying to get a hold of them on the high seas."

Ruaraidh the Tartar, chief of the McNeills from 1598 to 1622, seems to have been particularly notorious in this respect, and was none too scrupulous in means of adding to his revenue. He was comparatively safe as long as he confined his attentions to French or Dutch vessels but he extended his piracy to the coasts of Ireland where he looted an English vessel and spread such terror that his exploits came to the attention of Queen Elizabeth who complained strongly to King James VI of Scots.

Roderick McNeill:

"King James summoned Ruaraidh but he did not obey. He was kidnapped by McKenzie of Kintail who brought him to Edinburgh. His defence to the King for his action then, was that he was merely avenging the King's own mother who had been beheaded at the orders of Queen Elizabeth. James thought it politic to let him go!"

Raids by the Hebrideans on Shetland, and Orkney in particular, were frequent, the largest invasion of Orkney taking place in 1460. It is told in contemporary accounts how the Hebrideans burned, plundered and ravaged the country, massacred the inhabitants without regard to sex or age, and carried off whatever cattle or other property they could lay their hands on.

Nan McKinnon tells of one raid by the Barra men on Shetland and of 'Gille Dubh Thangasdail'.

Nan McKinnon:

"McNeill wanted to go to Shetland for a raid—they used to raid one another and take all the cattle and sheep and everything. Anyway, McNeill took Gille Dubh Thangasdail with him. Gille Dubh was a strong young man, the only son of a widow that lived down at Tangasdail. He was the strongest man in Barra and McNeill was afraid of Gille Dubh. The chief of the Shetlanders at that time was a man named the 'Bauch Sealltainneach'. He was called the 'Bauch' because of the style of his whiskers—the bauch is the male goat. 'Now,' says McNeill, 'if the Bauch Sealltainneach is getting the better of me, you take my side, but if I'm getting

# Fliuch An Oidhche

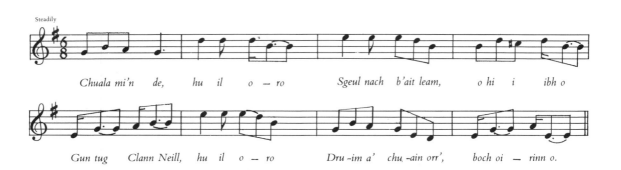

Chuala mi'n de,    hu il o — ro    Sgeul nach b'ait leam,    o hi i    ibh o

Gun tug    Clann Neill,    hu il o — ro    Dru -im a' chu -ain orr',    boch oi — rinn o.

Gun tug Clann Neill, hu il oro
Druim a' chuain orr', o hi i ibh o
Luchd nan seol ard, hu hil oro
'S na long luatha, boch oirinn o.

Luchd nan seol ard, hu il oro,
'S na long luatha, o hi i ibh o
Nam brataichean, hu il oro
Dearg is uaine, boch oirinn o.

'S nam brataichean, hu il oro
Dearg is uaine, o hi i ibh o
'S iomadh bairneach, hu il oro
Glas a ghluais iad, boch oirinn o.

'S iomadh bairneach, hu il oro
Glas a ghluais iad, o hi i ibh o
Agus duileasg, hu il oro
Donn a bhuain iad, boch oirinn o

Fliuch an oidhche, hu il oro
Is gum b'fhuair i, o hi i ibh o
Ach thug Clann Neill, hu il oro
Druim a' chuain orr', boch oirinn o.

WET AND BITTER THE NIGHT

I heard a tale, which sore disturbed me
That Clan Neil have taken again
to the seas.

Though wet and bitter the night
Clan Neil have put to sea
Many's the black rocky shore
they've raided.

They of the high sails
and of the fleet ships.
Men of the green and scarlet banners.

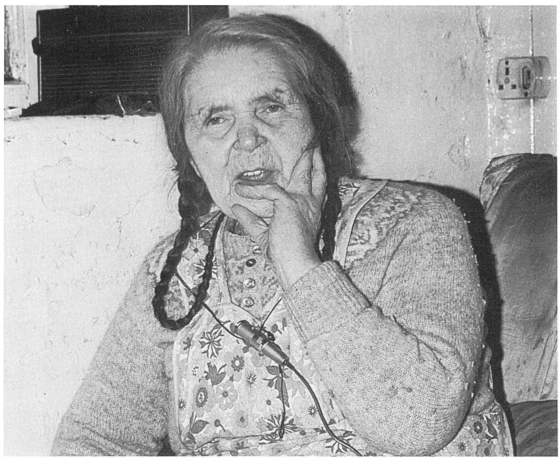

*Nan McKinnon at home in Vatersay, 1981.*

the better of him just let me carry on.' Anyway, they started fighting and the Bauch was getting the better of McNeill, so Gille Dubh went to his aid to help him and he killed the Bauch Sealltainneach. When McNeill saw that the Bauch was dead, he ordered all the cattle and sheep in Shetland to be raided and taken with them. But Gille Dubh Thangasdail turned on McNeill. 'No,' he says, 'it was I that did this and not you. It was I that killed the Bauch Sealltainneach and I've more right than you to the plunder and if you don't go to your birlin [boat] as fast as your legs can carry you, I'll do the very same to you.' So McNeill had to leave everything to Gille Dubh. The cattle and sheep were returned to their places in Shetland and Gille Dubh got the Bauch Sealltainneach's daughter and married her. He built a castle in Scalloway in Shetland and it still stands—well, the remains of it—and it's the very same shape as Castle Kisimul."

Another of the most notable characters to survive in the oral tradition is 'Marion of the Heads', a fifteenth-century wife of one of the McNeills of Barra. She

herself was from Coll but she gained notoriety in Barra as Marion of the Heads after the death of the chief when she ruled during the minority of their son. She had the habit of decapitating those she took a dislike to, including her two stepsons who might have had a better claim to the chiefship than her son. She had a servant behead these boys and then she took the heads herself down to the cemetery, washed them in the well and gave them Christian burial there. Nan McKinnon relates the strange story of how one of her victim's sons wrought uncanny revenge on Marion's servant, who was responsible for carrying out her series of executions.

Nan McKinnon:
"The father went to where the heads of his sons were, so as to bury them at Borve. He carried them in a cradle and when he was coming along and taking a short-cut across a place called Cliff, one of the heads spoke and said 'Father, you'll go to the island of Fuday and there's a young woman there that I ought to have married and she's bearing my child. Go and bring her home with you and look

# A Bhradag Dubh

Very Free

A' Bhradag Dubh    O hi o    hu    A bhrist na glas-an    A ho    ri

ho ho a o oh hi uu ri ho    Fal u    a ho    Ho hi ho    u.

| | | | |
|---|---|---|---|
| Ge de bh'agaibh riamh | Barraidh bheag | C'aite na dh'fhag thu | Is Gilleoghnan |
| O hi o hu | O hi o hu | O hi o hu | O hi o hu |
| Ach Barraidh bheag, | Chrian dhubh chlachach | Niall a' Chaisteil | Mor an gaisgeach |
| A ho ri ho . . . | A ho ri ho . . . | A ho ri ho . . . | A ho ri ho . . . |

| | | |
|---|---|---|
| Bheireadh a fion | Air ghaol uisge | 'Sa chuireadh cruidhean |
| O hi o hu | O hi o hu | O hi o hu |
| Dha chuid eachaibh | Loin a sheachnadh | Oir fo'n casan |
| A ho ri ho . . . | A ho ri ho . . . | A ho ri ho . . . |

## THE BLACK BESOM

(Uist Woman)    *You Black Besom*
*What have you McNeills ever had*
*but your little Barra–wee,*
*bare, black, stony Barra.*

(Barra Woman)    *What we have had, the*
*likes of you could never*
*aspire to*
*Neil of the Castle*
*Neil Frasach*
*the warrior, great Gillionan*
*who shod his steeds with gold*
*and gave them such wine to drink*
*that they disdained to touch water.*

after her well and she'll bear a son and he'll seek my revenge.'

"So the poor father went for the girl and took her home, looked after her and it came to pass that she had the son as was foretold. He grew up and when he was twelve years of age it happened on a hot day in summer that they were shearing sheep in Borve and this young boy was walking round they that were shearing sheep. One of the men asked him, 'Now, my boy, just you take that cuman [a water bucket] and bring me a drink from the well.' The boy took the cuman, filled it with water and when he was coming back he let it fall on a rock and broke it to bits. He went back to the man that asked for the drink and he says, 'Oh, I'm so sorry, I've broken the cuman.' 'Oh,' the man said, 'my boy, don't cry, I'll drink from the well.' And he went and the boy followed him and when he bent down, bent his head down to get his drink, the boy took a sword from the sleeve of his coat, hit him at the back of the head and left his head in the well. 'Now,' he says, 'that's what you've done to my father.' Whether it was instinctive or whether the boy was told about it remains a mystery, but it did happen."

Marion herself met her fate in 1540 when the Barra people apparently revolted against her. She had one last request, that she be buried not in Barra but in Coll. On the day, however, that the party set out with her body to Coll, a northerly gale blew up and she was buried off Vatersay at Capal Mor Nan Ceann, the chapel of the heads, outside the chapel, and standing upright facing Coll.

Despite the fact that almost the entire population of Barra were of Clan Neil, some families of different clans were to be found, for example McKinnons, who came from Elgol in Skye in the sixteenth century as grazing constables to McNeill of Barra. Perhaps the most interesting story, however, is that of how the first McPhees came to Barra, and ultimately the island of Mingulay.

Nan McKinnon:
"The McPhees of Colonsay, the first one that arrived in Barra was a Kenneth McPhee and that was at the time when all the people of Eigg were burned to death in St Francis cave by McLeod of Dunvegan. Kenneth McPhee who was married to McDonald of Eigg's daughter was the only one to escape. They had a baby son three or four months old and McPhee went to his own home after he escaped from the cave, wrapped the baby in a blanket and took it to his own boat. He didn't care where he went to, as long as he'd get away from the horrors of Eigg. He landed in Barra, built a sort of house for himself and married again.

"Now one day years later, McNeill of Barra was wondering why he wasn't seeing anyone coming from the island of Mingulay [with his rent]. He sent a boat with a crew over to the island and one of

the young men that was in the crew was the baby that was brought from Eigg by his father. He was seventeen years of age by this time and when they landed over at Mingulay one of the older men said, 'Just go up and see what's doing.' They didn't see anyone, there was no sign of life, and he went up to all the houses and found they were all dead. Some of them had pots on the fire, some of them were lyin' on the floor, some of them were in their beds. And och, he rushed down and when he was gettin' near the beach he called at the pitch of his voice, 'Oh, God,' he cried, 'they're all dead!'

"The men in the boat said, 'Well, is there anything the matter with them? If it's any disease or a plague or anything, you've got your stomach full of it and you'd better stay along with them,' and they pushed their boat away and left the poor boy cryin' there on the rocks. So he stayed there till nightfall and it got dark. He went right round the island, right round to the south of Mingulay and built a shelter for himself. Fortunately he had a pocket knife and he used to kill the sheep, and it's said that he lived mostly on the fat of the sheep. He was there for six weeks alone and he used to climb to the top of the hill—it's called McPhee's hill to this day—to see if any boat was coming. No, he wasn't seeing any and he was there for six whole weeks, but then his father was wondering what had happened. He went down to McNeill and said, 'I was wondering what happened to my son, he was one of the crew.' McNeill never answered him and Kenneth McPhee knew that there was something he didn't want to tell. 'Now,' he says, 'if you don't tell me what happened to my son the lowest stone of your house will be the highest of it. You'll suffer for it.' So McNeill said, 'Well, Kenneth, your son was left over in Mingulay the day they were over to see what was wrong with the Mingulay people. Seeing it's happened just you pick your own men,' he says, 'and go to Mingulay and it'll be yours as long as any of your family lives.'

"And McPhee picked his own men, went to Mingulay, and they had it free of rent till such time as Colonel Gordon bought Barra in the nineteenth century and made them pay rent."

As a clan, the McNeills of Barra did not participate in the disastrous rebellion of 1745. Prudence determined the action of most of the Highland chiefs on that occasion. The repercussions, however, were to be great for Gaeldom as a whole, and not just the small minority of clans who had participated in the Rebellion. The real significance of Culloden was that it was the prelude to a massive government assault on the political, social and economic structure of the Highlands. The whole weight of government was employed to dissolve every tie between chief and clan and to abolish all distinction between Highland and Lowland Scot. Government legislation alone, however, could never have achieved this, and what was to be ultimately responsible for the end of the clan

*Eoligary House, built c. 1790. Residence of Colonel Roderick McNeill, the 40th Chief.*

system was summed up by A. J. Youngson as 'contact with and acceptance of the economic usages and ambitions of commercial and industrial capitalism of the Lowlands'.

For the majority of clan chiefs long accustomed to moving in the cultural spheres of both Gaeldom and Lowland society, the transition from a patriarchal figure to a capitalist landlord was a fairly easy one. In this respect the '45 Rebellion merely acted as a catalyst to accelerate modernising tendencies already at work in the Highlands. The overriding priority in estate management became commercial profit as against the number of able-bodied men on the clan lands. This transformation took place in Barra as elsewhere and ended the role of the McNeill towards his clan as it had been known. The first group to feel the winds of change were the tacksmen or middle class of the old clan system. There was little place for them in the new order and rather than succumb to transforming to business like farmers, most chose voluntary emigration. This was to prove one of the great catastrophies of Gaeldom in that it deprived the Highlands of its natural middle class and the ordinary people of their natural leadership. There was much 'voluntary' emigration in Barra between 1760 and 1790. Colonel Roderick McNeill wrote in 1790 'deploring the loss of so many decent people', but he was to be the last proprietor of Barra to express regret at the emigration of his tenants. Perhaps due to its relative isolation and the close-knit nature of the community, Barra was later in manifesting the deterioration in relationship between chief and

clansmen, but in 1822 the last chief of the McNeills in the direct line, General Roderick McNeill, succeeded his father.

Nan McKinnon:

"It was prophesied centuries before that it would be Ruaraidh, the seventh Ruaraidh, that would lose Barra, and it came to pass that it was the seventh Ruaraidh who had to sell Barra. He started glassworks down at North Bay, went bankrupt and had to sell Barra to pay his debts."

*Eoligary House with demolition squad, 1975.*

*Thatched houses, Barra, c. 1900.*

As in all the seaboard areas in the Highlands, the kelp industry became very important in Barra in the late eighteenth century, early nineteenth century. Kelp was an extremely lucrative activity for the clan chiefs given that in 1794, tenants received on average £2.5/– a ton, while the chiefs sold it at anything from £10 to £22 a ton. Rents were also raised during this period and thus the chiefs scored a double bonus. By 1814, however, the price for kelp began to fall and General Roderick McNeill came into kelp on a falling market. The alkali works he built at North Bay between 1830 and 1833 were a financial disaster. Hard pressed financially to raise cash, McNeill divided every croft in Barra in two, charged the same rent and thus doubled the apparent value of his property. General McNeill's memory has probably benefitted from comparison with his successor as proprietor, Colonel Gordon of Cluny. The following letter, however, written in London in July 1825 to the Rev. Angus McDonald, at a time when McNeill was frantically trying to organise his commercial enterprises in Barra, is a sad testimony to the last chief of McNeills in the direct line.

"I think it but fair candidly to tell you that the conduct and tone of the good people of Barra, whom every day's experience teaches me cannot be depended upon from their fickleness, idleness and stiff necked prejudice, has produced in my mind a decided revolution. Every man, my good sir, has a right to do the best he can for himself in his own affairs — if one set of servants won't do, the master must try others. I cannot afford the slow operation of waiting till John or Thomas or Hamish are pleased to be convinced that McNeill after all was right and could not have meant to cheat and ruin them. No, Mr Angus, I see my way sufficiently clear before me, but if I am to ensure myself an ample harvest, I must have fishers and kelpers who will cheerfully do my bidding. In the name of common sense abandon all idea of condescensions on my part to your spoilt children. Pray do not ask me as my resolve is not to be shaken. So if you mean to keep your flock together, look to it. I can easily fill up the vacancies. Say to the fishermen that if they do not within 8 and 40 hours after this proclamation bend their energies to the daily prosecution of their calling as fishermen, I shall turn every man of them off the island were they steeped to the ears in debt. Say to those who are about to emigrate I sincerely wish them well through it and assure those who have signed and repented that their repentance comes too late. So help me God they shall go at all events from my property, every man, woman and child."

McNeill, however, went bankrupt and Barra's vastly increased population of some 2,300 were unemployed and quite unable to pay the inflated rents McNeill had imposed during the kelp boom. Barra was put in the hands of creditors and was bought for £42,000 in 1839 by a speculator called Menzies. In 1840 Menzies put it up for sale at Paxton's Coffee House in Inverness where it was purchased for only £38,000 by Gordon of Cluny. Thus, after forty generations of McNeills of Barra it had been sold twice in one year. Colonel Gordon was to be responsible for some of the most barbaric evictions in the Highlands during the last century.

Nan McKinnon:
"They just lived on the rocks in Barra and there's an old man lived beside us, he was our neighbour where I was brought up and he used to tell us that his father, who was born down in Uig there at the jetty, had to flee at such short notice that they took the roof off the house in the morning and slept under the same roof that night in another place.

"Gordon evicted the crofters from the whole island of Vatersay, and from the adjacent islands, and from Tangeval—they were evicted from all those places."

The onset of the potato famine in 1845–46 blasted the Barra people's last hopes of retaining life upon their small unproductive patches. By 1847 the critical proportions of the famine in Barra came to the attention of the authorities. Colonel Gordon had provided some employment on roadworks but in August 1846 these projects had been abandoned and the workers dismissed. Informed by his factor that at least 8,000 bolls of meal would be required to prevent widespread destitution, Gordon, who lived in Aberdeenshire, made arrangements to 'send 900 Bolls'.

By January 1843 none of these had arrived in Barra and the island was quoted as the most wretched of all Highland estates. Colonel Gordon hit upon a somewhat novel solution to the problem and solicited Government through the Home Secretary to purchase Barra for a penal colony. Fortunately he was told 'it would not suit'.

In the three years between 1848 and 1851 Gordon was responsible for the transportation to Canada of some 2,715 people from his estates in Barra and South Uist.

The coming of the Crofters Commission in 1883 marked the turn of the tide in the fortunes of the Barra people, as elsewhere in the Highlands. Slowly but surely the economic conditions of the island began to improve but there still remained an acute shortage of land due to the letting of large tracts of land to outside farmers. On the 8th of September 1900, the farm of Northbay, one of the largest on the island, was illegally occupied and others quickly followed the same fate. The most daring series of raids was carried out by men from the island of Mingulay who successfully established their community on Vatersay between 1900 and 1908.

By the turn of the century then, the lot of the Barra people, as elsewhere, had improved greatly; most importantly the crofter now had security of tenure.

Archie McDonald:
"Barra was thriving very well in the early part of the century, fishing was great, there was a lot of

*The Herring Boom, Castlebay, c. 1910.*

*Peat carriers and Barra ponies, c. 1915.*

herring, with whitefishing in the winter, and the seafaring boys were away at sea and doing well till that mass defeat of the '14 war came and struck. Families were scattered all over. In Barra most joined the Royal Navy and a lot was in the Merchant Service too, that never came back. After all that the First World War boys were going to come home, they told them they would come back to a land flowing with milk and honey, aye, that was the show till the Depression of the early 'twenties struck. All the beautiful herring boats were drawn up, there was no market for herring and no market for fish. The same thing happened with cattle and sheep and everything went down, and the Merchant Navy also went down at that time. That's what happened really till the next boost came and the next war hit us again. The last war saw a big difference in Barra, in all the islands I think, but I think it was noticed more in the smaller islands. A lot of old people was left and the younger people moved away. It was sad. It was depopulation in a way but in the last few years there's been a halt—maybe things are changing."

Today the population of Barra appears to have stabilised, and the drain of young people away from the island halted to some degree. The traditional means of livelihood—crofting, fishing, the sea, are still the backbone of the community. Recent co-operative ventures have been fairly successful as has the establishment of a fish processing plant, but for the young people, employment in oil-related industries has probably been of greatest importance in job terms.

One thousand years after the arrival of Niall of the Castle in Barra, McNeill is still the predominant name in the island and the majority of the local population are still Gaelic speaking. Clan McNeill, however, have scattered to all corners of the globe, well illustrated by the fact that the present chief is an American. Wherever the McNeills were to go, identity was never surrendered easily.

D. J. McLean:
"When the clearances was on they left. Some of them landed in Cape Breton and they put up their own places there and called it Barra Glen and there was 400 McNeills in it."

During the later eighteenth and nineteenth centuries the Highland clan was to become popular amongst romantics and the notion of the 'braw John Heilan' man' decked in his clan tartan, tramping the glen, was born. It was an image exploited by the military establishment who would successfully channel the energies of the clan regiments against 'Britannia's' enemies. The romantic image of the Highland clan has been an enduring one, perpetuated by advertising, the media and the popularity of 'tartan and heather' societies. It is indeed fortunate that people like Nan McKinnon can still remind us of the depth of Gaelic oral tradition, and provide us with something approaching a truer impression of the clan period.

BILLY ROSS

# SCOTLAND
## SOBER AND FREE
### The Temperance Movement 1829 ~ 1979

People's Palace Museum
Glasgow Green
3 October 1979 ~ 31 January 1980
10 am ~ 5 pm daily, 2 pm ~ 5 pm Sundays
Admission free

# Whisky's Awa'?

In Scotland an estimated 75,000-112,000 people over the age of fifteen have what is termed 'a drink problem'. Alcohol abuse, according to bodies such as the Scottish Council on Alcoholism, is the cause of many health and social problems, and the contemporary advertising campaign of the Scottish Health Education Unit, which is designed to either shame or scare Scots into drinking less, is widely known.

Similar but voluntary efforts of past generations to cope with excessive drinking in 'whisky-injured Scotland' have been all but forgotten. Temperance and teetotalist principles are now out of favour, badly understood and often confused with Gradgrind Calvinism and Scottish sabbatarianism. Few people realise the social impact which the temperance movement had in Scotland, or the cultural enrichment which it brought to people living in squalor, misery and hopelessness. Indeed, the essence and humour of the movement can be best heard from oral sources, which bring to life the dry and often passionless reports of the various temperance societies.

Temperance was introduced into Scotland in 1829 by John Dunlop (1789-1868), a philanthropic lawyer from Greenock. The cause was taken up and the message spread by William Collins, the Glasgow printer, who not only gave it considerable personal and financial backing, but put his press into its service. Their ideas were considered at best absurd, and at worst insidious, by a nation which prided itself on its conviviality. When Chartists and radicals in the early 1830s embraced teetotal principles wholeheartedly, many industrialists and established church ministers felt threatened. Workmen who compared their enslavement to drink with the enslavement imposed by their employers were considered a menace, and those who took to preaching against drink were effectively usurping the authority of the church. Radicalism and temperance were closely associated for over a century, Conservative interests resting naturally with those of the brewers and distillers.

Although the temperance movement cannot be described as a homogeneous or unified movement, neither can it be seen in terms of a minority or sectarian interest. From small beginnings, it grew to touch upon almost every facet of life in Scotland. By the turn of the century, the sum total of temperance effort had resulted in a radical change in attitude towards excessive drinking. The 'convivial topers' of an earlier age were now looked upon as irresponsible drunkards, and had the Scottish M.P.s been left to their own devices, temperance legislation in Scotland would have

*The brothers who founded the Independent Order of Good Templars in Scotland, 1869 (wearing the coveted regalia).*

been much more extensive than the ineffectual Temperance (Scotland) Act of 1913.

Temperance was a driving force in both local and national politics. Local politicians fought the loose licensing laws of the time, while at a national level, M.P.s pressed for legislation. It was the candidate of the Scottish Prohibition Party, Edwin Scrymgeour (1866-1947) who unseated Churchill in Dundee in 1922, and the Scottish Independent Labour Party members who accompanied him to Parliament in that year were likewise supporters of either temperance or prohibition. Those involved in left-wing politics who 'took a drink' were frowned upon, and a co-operative society which did not practise temperance principles could not become a member of the great Scottish Co-operative Wholesale Society.

Temperance principles came to be accepted by all churches. Every Presbyterian church had its Band of Hope, while the Catholic churches had their own temperance societies, established first by Father Mathew in the 1840s.

Ultimately, the various temperance organisations such as the Good Templars, Rechabites and Sons of Temperance and the bodies of the left—the I.L.P., Clarion Scouters and Co-operative societies—had managed to provide for their members an alternative, drink-free society. There were public houses and other places of entertainment without alcohol fed by a flourishing soft drinks industry; concerts of temperance songs sung by temperance choirs in temperance halls; coffee houses and tea rooms; temperance hotels; teetotal pleasure steamers; financial benefits in the form of lower insurance premiums. Indeed, one could go from the cradle to the grave, without stepping outside the movement.

Mrs Kerr:
"There were five generations of us in Good Templary. I was carried in to the Order, and I came right up through the Order. My mother was a singer, and my aunts were singers, and in the Good Templars they were known as the Gibson Sisters. It was just natural for me to carry on there."

Robert McKechnie:
"We had at that time a Cradle Roll. So more or less your name was added almost as soon as you were born. But I took a very active part in the Juvenile Lodge, from say five years old onwards and at that time, all the children around our area were members of the Juvenile Lodge. When we reached the age of roughly fourteen, we were transferred into what we looked upon as the 'big' lodge."

The problem of child drunkenness should not be underestimated. Until 1913, children could collect drink from the pubs for their parents in jugs and mugs.

James Myatt:
"At that time, when we went up for a pint of beer and it was filled up, they used to let you suck the froth. If a boy was going for beer for his father, you said 'Gaun up for beer, Wullie? Aye right, I'll come with ye'—so we went up and had a suck at the froth of the beer."

The Bands of Hope therefore made tremendous efforts to educate children against alcohol. Besides this, they were a source of free entertainment and great enjoyment.

Jan Goudie:
"It was really quite something. I don't remember what age I was but in your young days your entertainment and places to go to were more or less organised by churches, and one of them was called Paddy Black's Mission. And you used to go in there, and you got handed a big enamel mug. And if there was a crowd, you all got packed tight in. And they gave you a bag of buns going in. There would be someone would give you a talk you know—a religious talk, and about the slides you were going to see.
"You were always in a bit of a quandary as to what to do. In the one hand you had a bag of buns, and then they'd come round with scalding hot tea. And you'd this mug of tea, and if you laid it down, it got kicked over. If you put your buns down, they disappeared. So you held on to your tea, kept your buns in your lap, started eating your buns, and you got drier and drier. People were joggling you, it was a free-for-all, and the noise! I can still remember it—it was unbelievable!
"Quite often you couldn't finish your buns, or you were going to keep one to take home. If you thought the slides were lousy, you started throwing the buns.
"But the reason why most of the kids went to the Band of Hope was that unless you went to the Band of Hope or the Sunday School, you couldn't get to Paddy Black's Trip. And that was something. The carters round about, like Robb in Commerce Street, Lurdies, all these people, used to decorate their carts, either put forms on them or layers of straw, and all the kids could sit on them. The horses were beautifully groomed, with all their fancy decorations and plumes, and what have you. And all the local bands—the pipe band, the B.B. Bugle Band, all the bands interspersed in this very very long procession—there must have been about sixty or seventy carts. And you either went to Bellahouston Park or Pollok Estate—one of these places. The whole of Glasgow used to turn out to watch this trip going away."

Mrs Kerr:
"Outings and trips, and they celebrated different nights—Halloween nights, and my mother had always a big dumpling on for Halloween nights and there was the guisers, all dressed up. Prizes went for the best-dressed guiser. Every occasion, Christmas and all those occasions."

# The Drunkard's Raggit Wean.

MUSIC BY THE KIND PERMISSION OF MESSRS D. SWAN & CO.,
70 Buchanan Street,
Of whom Copies of the Tune, with Piano-Forte accompaniment, may be had.

WORDS BY PAUL ROOKFORD.

With Feeling.

A wee bit rag-git lad-die gangs wan'-ren thro' the street, Wad-in' mang the snaw wi' his wee hack-it feet, Shiv'-rin' i' the cauld blast, greet-in' wi' the pain, Wha's the puir wee cal-lan'? he's a drunkard's rag-git wean. He stans at il-ka door, and he keeks wi' wist-fu' e'e, To see the crowd around the fire, a' laugh-in' loud wi' glee; But he daur-na ven-ture ben, tho' his heart be e'er sae fain, For he man-na play wi' i-ther bairns, the drunk-ard's rag-git wean.

Oh see the wee bit bairnie, his heart is unco fou,
The sleet is blawin' cauld, and he's dreepit through and through;
He's speerin' for his mither, an' he wun'ers whar she's gane;
But oh! his mither she forgets her puir wee raggit wean.
He ken's na faither's luve, an' he kens na mither's care,
To soothe his wee bit sorrows, or kame his tautit hair,
To kiss him when he waukens, or smooth his bed at e'en,
An' oh! he fears his father's face, the drunkard's raggit wean.

Oh pity the wee laddie, sae guileless an' sae young,
The oath that lea's the father's lip 'ill settle on his tongue;
An' sinfu' words his mither speaks his infant lips 'ill stain,
For oh there's nane to guide the bairn, the drunkard's raggit wean!
Then surely we micht try an' turn that sinfu' mither's heart,
An' try to get his father to act a father's part,
An' mak them lea' the drunkard's cup, an' never taste again,
An' cherish wi' a parent's care their puir wee raggit wean.

*Temperance song. Inset illustration by George Cruickshank, from a Scottish Society for Suppressing Drunkenness publication, 1852.*

Temperance organisations often brought some colour and excitement into the lives of children, and the right to wear regalia, which accompanied membership of the Good Templars, Rechabites and Sons of Scotland was an added bonus.

Martin Robertson:

"One thing I will always remember was the fact that when I was initiated into the juvenile branch of Good Templary, officers had to wear their regalia round their neck. I envied them that right from the start and I wasn't satisfied until after about a year in the Order I was promoted to holding an office. The regalia which the officers of the Lodge wore was a purple collar, with the words 'IOGT' on one side and our motto, 'Faith, Hope and Charity', on the other. Now as youngsters we were all keen to wear one of those regalias."

The magic lantern show, which was the staple entertainment of the Band of Hope, often excited the imagination.

J. B. Owens:

"I was a regular attender at the Gairbraid Church Band of Hope in Burnhouse Street, Maryhill. I have never failed to remember some of the scenes, particularly of sea-coasts or lighthouses, and when I have been, in the course of my business life, to places like Peterhead and Fraserburgh, and also into Banff and Buckie, where some of the glorious scenes of setting suns are to be observed, I've always remembered that the first time I had witnessed such glorious scenes was at the Band of Hope, through some of the slides that those good people tried to show us. Because they lifted us completely from what was a working-class life—none of us had ever seen the sea."

Jan Goudie:

"Two slides I can distinctly remember. One of the head of Christ with the crown of thorns, all in lurid, vivid colours. And another slide was a photograph of a pub door with all the adverts for spirits and beers, and three wee waifs, different sizes, standing outside the door. There was a talk about that, on the evils of alcohol, and what it did to the poor mother and the children, and the next slide had a song on it—something like 'Father dear father come home'—inferring that the kids were starving and all the rest of it."

Mr Kerr:

"When I was very young, I joined the Band of Hope in our church in Hamilton. They had marvellous meetings. I always remember one in particular, a Mr Gibb gave a lecture and he had alcohol with him. He was giving examples of the uses of alcohol. He says, 'You know, away up in Alaska, they don't have fires as such. They don't have fires with coal or wood, or anything like that

*Pledge card of J. B. Owens.*

because there is no wood or coal.' So he says, 'They use alcohol,' and he says, 'I'll let you see how it's done.' And he poured the alcohol into a receptacle, and put a match to it, and it went in flames. He says, 'This is the use of alcohol. It's the only good use of alcohol—to get a wee bit heat.' So this was the lecture we had in the Band of Hope."

William Brown:

"It was a year or two before the First War, and this American lawyer—his name was Tennyson Smith—he seemed to be carrying on campaigns on temperance in different places. He came to Motherwell, and was there a fortnight, with a meeting every night, and it climaxed in what he called 'A Trial of Alcohol'. Now on the Town Hall platform they had set up a sort of mock court with a dock, and a judge's place and so on, and there was a judge, jury, two counsel—and a bottle of whisky in the dock. The whole thing was overseen for legal purposes by the Town Clerk of Motherwell at that time, a Mr Burns. Now when the trial started of course, it was just a case of saying a few words from each counsel, and then they brought in their witnesses. Tennyson Smith's witnesses were, of course, very vehement against drink. The other chap, the defender, had only a few witnesses, but one of them was a local doctor who testified as to the medicinal value of spirits. But after the two counsels had made their closing speeches, the result was inevitable—guilty—and the judge pronounced sentence of death on the bottle of alcohol.

Somebody brought in a basin or a pail with a hammer, and they smashed the bottle into this pail. And that was the whole thing finished. It was quite a thrilling night for Motherwell because at that time we didn't have the cinemas as much as we have now, and of course there was no TV and no radio."

Band of Hope leaders made up poems to try to impress upon children the addictive qualities of drink. The following is from Mrs Sykes' vast repertoire.

Bessie Sykes:

*A little grey mouse one fine summer's day,*
*Said to his mother, "I'm going away.*
*I'm tired of this place, it is not very gay,*
*And I've made up my mind not to stay here alway."*
*His mother was sad, and heaved a great sigh,*
*And said "My dear son, very sorry am I.*
*But if you must go, one thing I must say,*
*If you're once in a mousetrap, you'll ne'er get away!"*
*"All right," said the mouse, so plump and so grey,*
*As in the bright sunshine he trotted away;*
*And smiled, as he thought of his mother's advice,*
*Though she was the oldest and wisest of mice.*
*As he went on his journey such strange things he met,*
*But he said to himself, "I've not seen a trap yet,*
*And I'll not be afraid, though mother did say,*
*'If you're once in a mousetrap, you'll ne'er get away'."*
*Soon mousey grew hungry and longed for some food,*
*"Oh," he cried, "I can smell something good;*
*'Tis cheese! Toasted cheese–I know very well!"*
*And he ran to the spot from whence came the sweet smell.*
*"A dear little house! Oh can it be real?*
*Just the place for a mouse to have a good meal.*

*The door is just open–I don't mean to stay."*
*But the door held him fast–he could not get away.*
*To remember his mother's advice was too late,*
*And bitterly now did he moan his sad fate.*
*His mother and home he saw never more,*
*Just because he once entered that fatal trap door.*
*My tale has a moral, though simple 'tis true,*
*The drink is the mousetrap, the grey mouse is you;*
*The drink is the bait, a delusion and snare,*
*And you will be caught, if you do not take care.*

Mr Kerr:

"Our minister took the Band of Hope you know. He used to come in, and the first thing he'd say 'How many letters is the Pledge?' Of course he only wanted the Pledge—P-L-E-D-G-E—six letters. And this was always the wee things that started things away. And then every week you said the Pledge. Every week.

*I promise here by Grace Divine,*
*To take no spirits, ale or wine;*
*Nor will I buy nor sell nor give,*
*Strong drink to others while I live.*
*For my own good this pledge I take,*
*And also for my neighbour's sake;*
*And this my strong resolve will be,*
*No drink, no drink, no drink for me."*

Adults often found that signing the pledge was of great help in their attempts to break free of drink addiction, and many of the Gospel Missions tried to help them.

James Myatt worked in the Tolbooth Mission at Glasgow Cross in the early 1920s:

*Women queueing to enter the Tent Hall, c. 1890.*

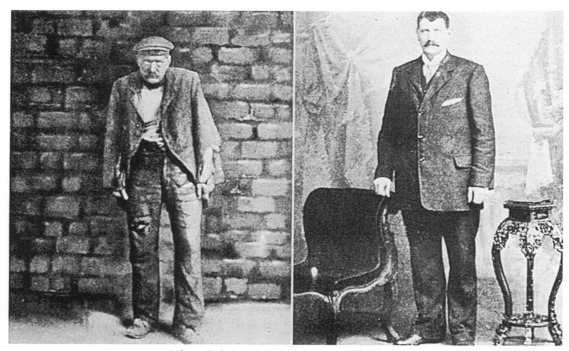

*Jimmy Byars, before and after (1910 and 1912)–a Trophy of Grace of the Tent Hall.*

"They would take a notion and go to the Tolbooth and sign the pledge at the Tolbooth. 'I promise to abstain from liquor, alcohol in any shape or form', and the funny bit was, when they signed that, they kep it! They'd keep it maybe for a month, two month, three month, longer, just by signing that pledge. And that was an excuse—you could hear a man say 'C'mon, have a pint, Wullie.' 'Naw—I've signed the pledge, I've signed the pledge.' That was all right—nobody pressed them when they said they'd signed the pledge. They were tryin', they were doin' their best, to get better conditions, to make better conditions for themselves.

"The Tolbooth Mission held gospel tea meetings and, periodically, Muffler Meetings. You had to be in a better class—even although I was unemployed I had to wear a collar and tie because I was a member o' the mission. For the Muffler Meetings the chairman and everybody put on a muffler, to invite the people, to encourage the people, wearin' mufflers to come into the meetin'. And they had a tea meetin' and maybe gave them a pie, cakes or something like that. And the whole idea was to preach to them, try and get them to sober up and become members of the Tolbooth—all the missions did that."

Such mission halls were popular throughout Scotland, and played an important part in the religious education of working-class people, succeeding where the established churches had failed dismally. In Glasgow, mission work was co-ordinated by the Glasgow United Evangelical Association, established in 1874 in the wake of the triumphant visit of Moody and Sankey. The G.U.E.A.'s best-known work was done in the Tent Hall in Steel Street, off Saltmarket. The mission had its origins in a gospel tent on Glasgow Green, where open-air meetings reached thousands who had never been inside a church, and from 1875 to 1979 it specialised in the care and reclamation of drunkards.

Mrs Sykes:
"Jimmy Byars was one who got converted at the Tent Hall, and many were in the same boat at that. And I've a feeling it was Jimmy Byars who said he believed in miracles—that the Lord could do wonderful things. Jesus turned water into wine—well, the Lord turned beer into furniture for him. And there were people who used to be all right, and their downfall was drink and they started again by getting converted in the Free Breakfast and took up life again and became real trophies.

"There used to be a lady—her name was Mrs Dunbar—in the Tent Hall who looked after that section of the work—women and girls who were outcasts from society. Maybe drink was their downfall, or some other thing. And they would come in, and she would look after them. She would clothe them if they needed clothing, feed them if they needed feeding, all in connection with the Tent Hall work. And she would try and get them a new start in life and help them on the way."

# Whisky's Awa'

Not too fast

Ay weel may ye wond – er, sae lang keep it un – der, Wi' our

face to the grund – stane, our back to the wa', But our

warst fears are en – ded, our for – tune has mend – ed, We're

fed and well fend – ed since whisk – y's a – wa.

I mind our wee big – gin wi' scarce – ly a stick in't, Our

bed was the floor on a wee pick – le straw, Sae

seld – om we cook – it, sae hung – ry it look – it, That the

starved mice for – sook it, but whis – ky's aw – a'.

See noo, whit a change–we've a weel-stockit girnel–
Abundance o' bannocks, wi' hams ane or twa;
Our fire it is cheery–sae dull ance and eerie–
Can shelter the weary–since whisky's awa.

Ye thoughtless, who rin on the rough road to ruin,
Come, join total abstinence!–join ane and a'!
For naething can mend ye, nae kind friend will fend ye–
Nae guid will attend ye, till whisky's awa!

Bessie and Seth Sykes were a Springburn couple who became known throughout Britain for their evangelical and temperance teachings. Their mission began on the streets of Glasgow during the General Strike.

Bessie Sykes:

"There was a lot of children and people couldn't get on holiday in the summer of 1926 for they had no money to do anything like that, and we got the idea to start these meetings, to gather the children together up at Alford Street, and the parents became just as interested. And we started in the summer of 1926 and went on for three years—every summer for three years. And at first, we wondered how they would go—we had a kind of handful at first, but it grew and grew all the time, until night after night we had quite a good following. It was amazing the people that gathered round, and where they came from.

"From Monday to Friday without fail we had the meetings. We carried this little organ, the organ was getting kind of done that we had. I used to say that it had asthma, bronchitis, it was developing consumption, and we were badly needing another organ. But, it was going to be difficult to get one—a portable organ. But here, before we knew anything about it, the children and the friends of the meeting, they gathered between them and got us another organ to take the place of the one that was on its last legs, and it was presented to us to carry on the work in those meetings. They all put

*Mrs Bessie Sykes at her new organ, c. 1928. The organ is now in the People's Palace.*

together and they put a wee plate on it saying it had been presented to us by the children and friends who attended the meetings."

Peter Donnelly:

"In those days, hundreds of children congregated round about the streets and played out in the open, because most of the houses were single ends, and room and kitchens, and there was nothing else for them to do but go out and play in the streets. And word would come round that Seth Sykes was coming. And he appeared in Gourlay Street—he used to walk up the centre of the street, and he wheeled a trolley with the organ on it, and all the kids following him from the further ends of Springburn.

"He used to hand out bills, and it said 'Mr and Mrs Seth Sykes, assisted by the Tiny Tots Trio' (that was the three kids—they sang gospel hymns, and Mrs Sykes played the organ).

"He never took any collections at his meeting—he was a tramway driver or conductor. The only time I ever knew him to take a collection was when he got the Salvation Army band to come up and add a bit more entertainment to it one night, and there was a big turnout for that. And as he mentioned himself, he never took collections, but he was taking one that night for 'the best band in Springburn'. Then he would have other nights that were kind of gala nights, when he would ask all the kids to wear paper hats."

Open-air meetings were a common feature of temperance work, and the speakers were sometimes subjected to harassment.

James Myatt:

"There were six Open Airs at Bridgeton Cross at that time, back in the 1920s. There was the Bethany Hall, the Christian Volunteers, the Salvation Army and the Cairter's Mission, the Mill Street Mission. And there was one in Muslin Street. They could all get crowds at that time. I was the Staff Sergeant of the Christian Volunteers, in charge of the Open Air, and there used to be crowds at each meeting. And what happened, the publican of Hillcoats' Pub, the man in charge, complained about the crowds obstructing his door. So he sent for the police and the police cleared the pavement a bit, but they couldn't put us too far out. Of course in those days there were no motor cars or anything, and we could spread out a bit into the street. So he complained, the police came—but it was the rule that you couldn't disturb a gospel meeting—that was the rule. But you could be asked to move on. So he asked them to move on and I was singing a song, later on, after he had spoken to us, and we asked the crowd to come out. And after he had spoken to us I was singing this hymn, 'Courage Go On'. And the last verse is 'When burdens oppress ye and trials cast down, Remember, remember there

*Scrymgeour holding an open-air meeting, Albert Square, c. 1913.*

waits you a crown'. And as I was singing, I looked up, and on the lintel of the door was 'J. Burdons, Licenced to sell wine and spirits and tobacco'. And it was such a coincidence—'Burdens oppress ye'—you know, that was what I was talking about—such a coincidence me singing 'Burdens oppress ye'—and he was trying to oppress us, telling us to keep out of the way!''

A Dundee Good Templar remembers the open-air meetings held by Edwin Scrymgeour, founder of the Scottish Prohibition Party.

Martin Robertson:
"About 1913, Ned started a series of open-air meetings in the Albert Square which was known as the Speakers' Corner in Dundee, where advocates not only of religion but all the different political parties and sometimes even hawkers, addressed big meetings on Sunday evenings. Now I can easily remember one occasion when I happened to be there, though I was quite a young man at the time, when a questioner in the audience threw up the question at Neddy—'Ned, you're fond of a smoke. If I promise to give up drinking, will you give up smoking?' Ned took him at his word, he says 'I'll

stop smokin' now.' And he took his pipe out of the top pocket of his jacket, turned round and threw the pipe away into the grounds of the Albert Institute. He says, 'That's me finished with smoking.' He says, 'I hope you'll come back next week,' he says, 'and let me know if you have stuck by your side of the bargain and stopped drinking.' ''

The temperance movement was always an international movement, and there was a frequent exchange of ideas and personnel between Scotland, other European countries, the U.S.A., Canada, Australia and New Zealand. In 1908, for example, Scrymgeour's Scottish Prohibition Party sponsored a Scottish tour for Carrie Nation, the 'Bar Room Smasher' and a veteran of the Kansas Whisky Wars.

Carrie and her followers believed in direct action, and had smashed up saloons when public prayer failed to work. Describing herself as a 'hatcheteer', she always appeared on public platforms with a Bible in one hand and a hatchet in the other, and some of the small hatchet-shaped brooches distributed on her 1908 tour have survived.

Carrie Nation was a feminist; the pursuit of women's rights and the cause of temperance were often synonymous.

*Carrie Nation poster.*

Robert McKechnie:

"That's another thing as far as the Good Templar Order is concerned. It was the first organisation (1869) that allowed women to take part in its meetings. The women were entitled to the same rights and privileges as the men. And there were very few organisations at that time where women were permitted to take part. And a number of women of outstanding merit were in the Order in the early days. Here in Largs for instance, the first woman to be Provost of Largs was a Good Templar—Mrs Morris. She was superintendent of the juvenile work in Scotland for over twenty years. Another instance of training in the Good Templar movement which fitted people for social work/public work, and she became the first woman to be Provost here in Largs."

Both women and children suffered terribly because of male drinking habits, and the spectre of 'The Drunkard's Raggit Wean' was unfortunately all too real.

James Myatt:

"In the winter of 1916, she couldn't afford to buy me boots. And I was workin' deliverin' milk, for the dairy at the corner of Tylefield Street, in my bare feet, with snow. And I met this wee mongol boy—on coming home after delivering my milk this wee chap was sitting in the public house door, crying his heart out. And I says, 'Whit's wrong?' 'Ah canny walk am cauld, ah canny walk am cauld.' And I lifted him and put him on my back, put his two bare feet in my pockets of the jacket I had, and took him down to the house that way. And I had my bare feet.

"Up by the Templeton's Carpet Factory in Fordneuk Street there must have been a boiler or something underneath the pavement, for there was a square stone that was always dry in the snow, and it was always warm. We used to stand on that—I wasna the only boy y'know—we used to stand on that and heat wur feet."

Poor people drank to forget their pain and misery.

James Myatt:

"I was black leadin' the grate one day when this woman came to the door and oh, she was all excited. She says, 'Oh, will ye come, Jimmy?' she says, 'there's a man being buried opposite us and there's nobody there to say a prayer nor nothin'.' So I went along to this street off Dalmarnock Road; the van was outside or rather the cab—the paupers' cab, and this man was at the door, outside the close, and he said, 'Is it you that's doing this job?' I said, 'Yes.' He said, 'Well hurry up—I want away.' So I went up to this house—nothing, absolutely nothing. The only thing that was in the house was this coffin and two tripods, you know, and a big tall man with a military moustache, and a woman at each end. Both of them were drunk and they were sitting crying. I looked in the fireplace and it was only a fire made up wi' bricks. Well what could you do? I said a prayer, read a scripture, and then the man came up. He said, 'Give us a hand here, Mac.' So I gave him a hand to shift the coffin into the paupers' van. The paupers' cab was a cab with a square box hanging fixed at the bottom. You put the coffin in there and anybody that wanted to go to the cemetery could go into the cab but he shoved the man into this long box and away he went.

"People drank sometimes to get them out of their misery. If they got a few coppers in their hand they were up to the nearest pub and had a bit of conversation with people and that, and it passed their time and helped them to forget for a while.

And the Labour Party at that time were very worried about it too and that's a thing that amazes me today, the Labour Party were advocating teetotalism and all that for the worker. They said that the drink was a tool of the master to keep the people sodden wi' drink and they wouldn't think of their conditions and fight for better conditions. And the Labour Party was strongly against strong drink at that particular time."

Robert McKechnie:
"The founder of the Labour Party, Keir Hardie, was District Chief Templar of Ayr District Lodge, and it was there he made his first speech, in a Good Templar Lodge. Out of the west of Scotland particularly at that time, practically all your leading political Labour workers were Good Templars, or had been Good Templars, and were still total abstainers."

Harry McShane:
"You take the most of them that were councillors in those days. They were all teetotal. There was P. G. Stewart, the first Labour Lord Provost, and his brother. Teetotal PG. And Maxton was teetotal. All the Clydeside M.P.s till George Buchanan in his latter days was seen with a bottle of beer in his pocket. That was in his latter days. For most of his life he was teetotal."

Robert McKechnie:
"If you go back, you find that the trade union movement was very much indebted to the Good Templars for the presiding officers. They got their training in the Good Templar Order and then they went to trade union meetings and were able to get up and express themselves.
"Of course the Co-op in those days was a total abstinence movement. They didn't have any

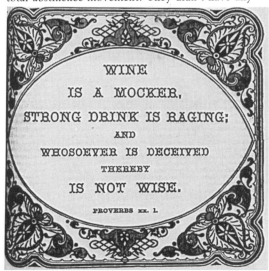

*Text from Scottish Temperance League publication.*

licences—liquor licences or anything of that nature. That's practically a modern trend as far as the Co-op is concerned."

In spite of the work done by the temperance movement, the drinking problem in Scotland is as bad, if not worse, than it was at the turn of the century.

James Myatt:
"Alcohol in those days seemed to have a different effect. Now they want to stab, they want to fight, they want to rape. In those days they wanted to *sing*. You always saw a drunk man singing. . . . It sort of cheered them up, the alcohol in those days. But not now—it seems to turn them into animals."

Temperance work lost all the ground it had gained for a variety of complex reasons—two World Wars, which introduced many to drinking, the unpopularity of prohibition in America, the poor quality of Scottish temperance legislation, the advent of other attractions for young people.

Martin Robertson:
"Unfortunately, two World Wars created a decline in the movement, mainly because the men who were called up in the Forces enjoyed or were persuaded by the NAAFI to start beer drinking. This led to them sticking to that in their everyday life, making the work of our Order doubly hard. Over the years, temperance, instead of being a byword in the country is now something of a backward step. Despite all other endeavours to attract new members, several things have come in the way. To mention but one thing, we had strong juvenile lodges until the advent, strange to relate, of rock and roll. Now it may seem strange to mention rock and roll, but believe me, we in our lodges knew what it meant. Our youngsters failed to attend our meetings because they were out practising their rock and roll.
"In this modern age, they think they're more sophisticated and if you mention temperance to many of them, they'll ask ye 'What is temperance?' There's also the fact that the membership of churches has deteriorated rapidly not only in Dundee but all over the country, with the result that ministers do not have the opportunity of advocating temperance. In fact I know in my own church, we were reduced to one temperance service per quarter. This I believe has now resulted in one temperance night in the year. The Church of Scotland which used to spend maybe a matter of one or two days on the question of temperance [during the General Assembly], now devote, I believe, only one afternoon in the whole week's session to advocating temperance, and again, it's attended mainly by women. Notable absentees being the ministers."

ELSPETH KING

# The '26

If anything else of historical importance happened in 1926 we could be forgiven for overlooking it, so much was that year dominated by the General Strike and miners' lock-out. Both events directly affected masses of ordinary working people, and both provided for many people the most intense, exhilarating, or depressing experiences of their lives.

This was the case, as elsewhere, in the East Fife coalfield. The coalfield extended eastward from Kirkcaldy along the Firth of Forth to Leven, and included mining towns or villages such as Wemyss —East Wemyss, West Wemyss, Coaltown of Wemyss—Buckhaven, Methil, Coaltown of Balgonie, and pits such as the Michael, the Wellesley, Muiredge, Lochhead, the Rosie, and Wellsgreen. The pits were owned by either of two private companies, the Fife Coal Company and the Wemyss Coal Company. The miners' county union in Fife had split in 1923, mainly over issues of internal democracy and leadership; and when the big events of 1926 unfolded there were still two rival unions in the county—the 'Old' Union, whose general secretary was the right-wing Labour M.P., William Adamson, and the more militant

Reform Union, whose secretary, Philip Hodge, had been expelled from the Independent Labour Party for opposing Adamson in the General Election of 1924. The Reform Union, as a breakaway, had not been allowed to affiliate to the national miners' union, the Miners' Federation of Great Britain, and therefore did not receive relief funds distributed through the Federation during the 1926 struggle. During the General Strike and the miners' lock-out, Reform Union members were much more active than those of the 'Old' Union.

A big industrial struggle had almost broken out in the summer of 1925, when the miners had been threatened by the coalowners with severe reductions in their wages. But the struggle appeared to have been avoided by an eleventh-hour retreat by the Conservative government headed by Stanley Baldwin, which agreed to pay a subsidy to the coal industry to maintain miners' wages at their existing level. The subsidy was to be paid for nine months, until the end of April 1926. In the meantime, in semi-secrecy, the government began to prepare for any major industrial struggle that might come with the ending of the

*Above and opposite: A mass meeting in Fife during the lock-out, addressed by A. J. Cook, General Secretary of the Miners' Federation of Great Britain.*

*Buckhaven Committee, Fife Miners' Reform Union, 1924. John McArthur is third from right, front row.*

subsidy in the spring of 1926. It was determined never again to be caught unprepared, as it had been in 1925.

The Trades Union Congress and the unions, with some exceptions, such as the Miners' Federation, did nothing, claiming that any preparations on their part for a struggle might prejudice the chance of an agreed settlement of the crisis in the coal industry. Such a settlement, union leaders hoped, would come out of the recommendations of the Samuel Royal Commission, which had been appointed by the government soon after the crisis in 1925. To the more militant trade unionists — and of these there were strong groups among the miners of East Fife — the Samuel Commission was merely a smokescreen behind which the government was preparing for a confrontation with the miners and other unions.

At the end of April, all attempts at agreement between the miners and the coalowners having broken down, the miners were locked out until they agreed to accept severe reductions in their wages, amounting in the case of Fife and other Scots coalfields, to about 22 per cent.

Peter Fitzpatrick:

"Well, at the beginnin' o' the lock-out we got the option, whether tae work on a reduction o' wages or be locked out—that was the only alternative—fight fur our wages. So that was us locked out; and from then on it got worse."

A few days later, on 4th May, contrary to the expectations and even the wishes of the leaders of the T.U.C., the General Strike began. It was intended to demonstrate the moral and practical support by the unions as a whole for the miners in defending their wages and conditions against the coalowners' attack.

John McArthur:

"The General Strike was an event of staggering importance to all of us who had been active in the workers' movement. We had dreamt of the day when all workers would stand solid one with the other. I can remember in trying to work out what 1926 would mean—that we felt we would have to have a series of meetings in order to get our message across. I don't think many people because of bitter disappointments in the past actually felt that the General Strike would take place. The main area for holding meetings of an area character was Denbeath Bridge, and a number of us decided to hold a meeting on the Sunday prior to the General Strike. We had to cancel it for lack of attendance. But the General Strike when it took place we had a meeting the next Sunday and one could hardly see the back of the crowd."

Coal and railways were leading industries in East Fife and both were well unionised. It was therefore not surprising that, as in other industrial areas of Britain, the response to the call for a General Strike was very solid in East Fife, and that the railwaymen, road transport workers, Methil dockers, and other groups came out on strike. (Some miners also refer to their struggle in 1926 as a strike but really it was a lock-out.)

Though the miners, whose union was the largest and most militant in Britain, could draw on the relatively recent experience of their national three months' lock-out in 1921, as well as much similar experience of industrial struggle, the local organisation of the locked-out men and of the General Strikers had to be set up swiftly. This spontaneous and generally effective formation of lock-out or Strike committees, and their handling of the manifold questions that arose out of the crisis, demonstrated the resourcefulness and organising power of ordinary working people.

John McArthur:
"The period of the General Strike was a very enlightening and, looking back on it, very educative period. As the Strike developed and all loose edges were being tucked in, the Strike consolidated and a feeling of elation, of strength, of new-found strength, this solidarity of the workers, created an extraordinary atmosphere among working men, their wives and families.

"In our own area we had probably as good working-class organisation as any that had been set up. We had worked this out prior to the General Strike so that when the General Strike took place an immediate meeting of the Trades Council was called and the plan for action was laid down. The

Methil Co-operative Hall, with its ante-rooms, was taken as the Strike headquarters. It was got from the Co-op and was continuously in use, even during the night. . . .

"The Council of Action or General Strike Committee was formed by means of having a central strike committee under a convener, and each convener had a department to look after. There was a subcommittee that was in charge of permits, in charge of transport. . . . There was also the question of defence and organisation of pickets. There was built up a communications group and the East Fife Motor Club approached us and offered their services as couriers and despatch riders. This augmented the push bikes and one or two cars that were made available to us. There was the committee set up to deal with entertainment, so that there would be adequate means of keeping people entertained, preventing any question of boredom, and so on. And here we tried to get built up concert parties and groups that would do concerts and entertainment in halls or even when the weather was suitable outside entertainment as well."

William Wilson:
"I can remember the concerts very vividly—in

*Kidd's Jazz Band, Leven, 1926. William 'Mosie' Murray at the piano.*

fact our own Jimmy Shand, who was born and brought up just a mile down the road from Coaltown of Wemyss and here at East Wemyss, playing to concerts and also to dances."

Peter Fitzpatrick:
"Aye, aye, they'd have dances, concerts. Up at Buckhaven we used tae hae them. There's a boy cried Patrick Burns, he played the fiddle. And Brannan—he played the dulcimer. Tam Brand, he played a fiddle. And the same boys used tae gang aboot through the week, travellin' tae Dundee and Edinburgh and different places, playin' on the streets, collect money fur the soup kitchens."

As the funds of both Fife miners' unions were low, collecting money to keep the struggle going became an essential part of activity in East Fife as elsewhere.

George Simpson:
"I was in Buckhaven Town Silver Band. And we went up tae Arbroath, then on tae Dundee and then stayed in Dundee for the rest o' the week, doing the streets there. And we gathered oor collections which was totalled up every day for tae come back to East Wemyss. We went frae there, a' the villages right up the coast. At Dundee I think we finished up with £175 for the week in collections. We was in Stonehaven in the Square there for two hours playin', and we followed that wi' goin' up in Aberdeen and sleepin' in the Labour Halls off Union Street and we lay on the floor there and there were old ladies comin' in to see that we wis gettin' fed and some o' them were bringing a pitcher o' soup and we got free lunches in the Arcade and Union Street. The band broke up intae pieces, three pieces, and they went into the halls for the dancin'. We got money that way."

The best—most economical and fairest—way for the Strikers and locked-out men to organise their food supplies was by setting up communal kitchens or soup kitchens.

William Wilson:
"The village got together and we had what was known as the soup kitchen in these days and luckily for me, I was able to have two soups. I got a soup at the school and came home and my soup had been collected for me by my mother. So in fact I didn't do so badly, did I?"

The menu and amount of food available from the soup kitchens varied from one village to another, depending on the ingenuity of the organisers, the generosity of donors, or the flat refusals by some local farmers, the success of poachers, and other factors.

Alex Warrender:
"The folk was gettin' less tae eat. You were

relying on the Co-operative Society at that time to dae what I thought was a great thing—they allowed you to take credit on condition that you signed your name, that you'd pay back this amount o' credit that you had got. After the strike it was duly paid back."

Ebenezer Campbell:
"Oh, well, the soup kitchens was a godsend. Well, you was lucky if you got a plate o' soup and maybe a mashed potato or a bit o' corned beef or something like that. That's a' that could be afforded. It was a' on a sheet, ye ken, you couldna come the day and say there were fower in the family and come back in the morn and say there was just yoursel'. There was nae cheatin'."

William 'Mosie' Murray:
"Ma specific job at that particular time was to organise the soup kitchens and also provide finance. This was done successfully for a period of over seven months. And I would like to state on behalf of the traders in Leven, they were pretty good, and also the outlying farmers who supplied us with potatoes, turnips, and various other ingredients that was necessary for to make soup. The people at lunchtime came with their pitchers or their jugs and received a jugful of soup and as much bread as would do them until the following day at lunchtime. At tea time we also tried to give them a mug of tea and margarine to put on the bread which they already had. That was the staple diet of the people at that particular time. The farmers were good, but at times we couldn't receive the stuff from the farmers, so, being desperate of course, we used to go to the outlying farms and take it. That perhaps wasn't etiquette but necessity as far as I'm concerned knows no law. The main proposition was that the people had to be fed and we were determined that they would be fed."

Alex Warrender:
"Well, we were a bit luckier living near the beach because we were able to gather whelks, limpets, and mussels and bile them in cans on the beach and that gi'ed us something tae eat. For people livin' further inland couldna get that."

James Sinclair:
"They used tae get into the tattie pits and help theirsels through the night—firewood, anything that was possible to get. In fact I remember getting stopped one night wi' the policeman, carrying a five-foot pit prop down, and as you know, in the pit when ye was boring holes you used these pit props as a lance, and the policeman [says] 'Whaur are you goin' wi' that?' he says. [I] says, 'Surely get to take oor own pit prop home, that's oor born right, that's oor born right!' (laughs) I think the police were pretty sympathetic, they turned a blind

*Leven miners soup kitchen staff. William 'Mosie' Murray is third left, front row.*

eye to a lot. But we used to go at night and poach rabbits."

Peter Fitzpatrick:
"I've seen me comin' in wi' maybe aboot eight or ten rabbits—gie some o' them away because I knew I'd be goin' out the next day fur mair. I used tae go and do a bit o' fishin' tae. And when I came in wi' the fish I used tae gie them away. People a' helped one anither, it was the only way tae survive. Some of the farmers you couldna make them understand that you werena' on strike at a', that ye were locked out, they couldna understand that. They thought that ye were out for more money and we werena, we were just out fur tae keep what we had. But they werena wantin' you mixed up along wi' their workers in case it would cause trouble among them. I never met ony farmer yet that wis what you could say co-operative. In fact, I was along by Largo and thae places and ony farmer ye went to fur tae get stuff, they wouldna gie ye it."

Footwear became another problem, as boots and shoes wore out and it was difficult to afford repairs.

Peter Fitzpatrick:
"As far as the boots was concerned, I used tae go along the beach tae the rubbish bings. I'd gather old boots, dismantle them and take off them what would be serviceable fur us and I used tae repair other people's boots—girls from the school, boys

from the school, men fur walkin' about. Some o' the men had maybe had a bit copper or two aboot them yist tae club thegither and gie me maybe threepence a piece or sixpence a piece or anything like that tae comin' on two or three bob. I used tae go along tae Kirkcaldy and buy a piece o' leather in a shop there and that was good leather fur maybe repairin' their good boots—kept us goin' in feetwear that way."

The lack of money meant lack of very basic amenities, including necessities such as razor blades.

James Sinclair:
"Black Jock was an old miner—thick black

*East Wemyss miners' gala, 1926.*

beard—this is how he got Black Jock. And he used to sit on his easy chair on his hunkers—you know how miners do, sit at a corner. The insurance man come in one day and Mrs Cunningham, she was away looking for the insurance book, and the insurance man, he's eyeing Jock up who hadna had a shave for a week. When Mrs Cunningham came back he says, 'Excuse me, Mrs Cunningham, but does your monkey bite?' When we told that story Jock used to go raving mad you know!'' (laughs)

On 12th May, nine days after it had begun, the General Strike was suddenly and unexpectedly called off by the General Council of the T.U.C. Strikers at local level, such as East Fife, thought they were winning the struggle; they certainly did not think they were losing it. But the T.U.C. leaders, forced against their wishes to call the Strike in the first place, included a few, such as J. H. Thomas, the Railwaymen's leader, who wanted to end it as soon as possible. So great was their haste to do so that they did not even trouble to ensure that the men called out on strike in support of the miners returned to work on the same terms as before. Consequently, there were widespread attempts by employers to worsen working conditions and victimise activists—attempts which were in the main unsuccessful because even more workers came out on strike in protest, and also because the Prime Minister, Baldwin, used his influence with employers to persuade them to mitigate their attacks. The Miners' Federation refused to endorse the T.U.C.'s decision to call off the Strike, and in East Fife, as in all the other coalfields of Britain, the miners remained locked out. Though rank-and-file activists in other unions did all they could to continue practical and moral support for the miners, there was a widespread feeling that, as in 1921, the miners had been betrayed by the leaders of the other unions. For six months, from mid-May until almost the end of November, the miners struggled on courageously—but alone. Conditions became increasingly difficult. Rents went unpaid, meagre savings ran out, clothes were wearing out. In most mining villages in East Fife, the soup kitchens continued to cope efficiently; but in a few, such as Coaltown of Balgonie, where organisation was less effective or rations more meagre or there was greater isolation, the outlook became very bleak. Here and there a few miners, unable any longer to endure the privations suffered by their families, began from October onward to drift back to work. Religious belief actuated others to do so—belief which did not recognise any need for industrial struggle or even for trade unionism. But despite all difficulties the great majority of the miners in East Fife held out until their union, at national level, eventually called off the struggle toward the end of November.

Alex Warrender:
"Well, as the Strike wore on and there were no sign o' the miners gonna get the benefit of it, some people wanted to go back to work. A few of them

*A Fife miner of the period.*

belonging to this district got up in the mornin' and awa' to the pit. Efter a day or twa it was noticed that some folk was goin' oot ower early, so they decided to put pickets on. And I believe some of them got a bit o' a doin' afore the police was brought in to escort the blacklegs to their work. But, as far as I can mind, a lot of them was blacklisted for years after it. They maybe had a job but they never had nae freends during that time.''

Harassment of the blacklegs varied in intensity from violence to humorous ridicule.

James Sinclair:
"He [the blackleg] had this pony, and the men went up one mornin', painted it aa white like a zebra, the straw hat, its ears through, slippers on its feet and tied it to the bottom o' his stair. And Ned came down in the mornin' and here's the pony

tethered to the stair and he looks at it. (laughs) John Macdonald, he made up a poem about it: 'Old Ned looks at the pony'. I can always remember the last lines, it was, 'Aince I thocht ye a gallant wee steed, But noo ye're neither a horse nor a cuddy'.

"[Another blackleg]—we called him Geordie John Jesus for a by-name, you know. We were up at Buckhaven, two or three of us one night, when Mr Bence, who kept goats—one had broken loose and it was followin' us doon the road in the dark. So we got the idea o' takin' it down and tying it on Geordie's door. And went away across the other side o' the street and lay down. When George opened the door—he's pullin' one way and the goat the other and we were lying screamin' wir heads off, watchin' the carry on! (laughs) Oh the tricks we used to play!"

George Simpson:
"I mind one old man and he had a son. His son had went oot and into the pit, and then the next mornin' he couldna get up. Somebody asked where he wis, ye ken, he kent he wisna at his work and here he was lying in his bed and his faither had hit him wi' his pit belt, ye ken, and had opened his head and he wasna able tae get up."

Peter Fitzpatrick:
"There were a terrible lot [of blacklegs]. They were comin' from Methil and they were comin' over by the beach and into the colliery. That's how they come in, direct up and through the office. And there were some o' them getting food taken down to them and kept there. They come up fur me,

well, they sent a message up fur me frae the house to see if I'd come up and cut some coal fur them. I said, 'I wouldna cut a bit o' bread fur ye, never mind coal for youse.' So even after the Strike was finished, wi' me refusin' tae oblige them, they kept me idle for aboot another six or seven months for reprisals. But blacklegs, oh, you couldna count how many blacklegs they were."

Mrs Agnes Henderson:
"The next door neebour was a blackleg at Muiredge Pit, and of course he got polis protection and ah wish ye'd seen the crowds that came ahent him at that time, bringing him hame. I wouldna hae the name o' it for love nor money. It's true. Ah wouldna hae the name o' it. I'll tell ye everybody was down on him. I mind one day I was pitting out ma washing, ma bairns' nappies, and I was that roozed at him being a blackleg I went doon and I flung a stane at him one day. I was that roozed— you can imagine—well, you had nothing and he was getting a pay! And I had my claes oot and ye ken what he did? He came and he cut ma rope doon and landed all ma claes on the ground. I took ma stretcher and I battered it ower his head, so I'm tellin' you he didna half catch it for that. You can imagine thae days you had to stand up for yoursel' or if you didna you was doon the chute, you wis, you was doon the chute. Well, he maybe was a blackleg but he had to pay for it later on, for if he went oot he was like as if he was hunted; and passin' the Bank Corner a' the young men just sneered at him for a long time. But it faded away as a' thing fades away."

*'Pit Bing Girls'. Miners' gala in the 1920s.*

During the nine days of the General Strike and the six months of the miners' lock-out, there was sometimes conflict between the miners and the police, especially over picketing.

William 'Mosie' Murray:

"We had trouble, on one occasion we had mass pickets at the Leven station for to try and stop an incoming train that was passing through but we were met by a big contingent o' police under the auspices o' their Inspector. They immediately drew their batons and set about the pickets without getting any provocation at all."

Alex Warrender:

"Well, a beer lorry came frae, I think it was Younger's o' Alloa, making for St Andrews or some o' thae places. But it come this road. And when it got the length o' Muiredge, it turned to come doon the Wellesley road. It was stopped and was telled to turn back and he refused. So they couped the lorry. Of course barrels o' beer was burst open, and it was runnin' on the pavements and somebody went for the police and there were about twenty or thirty police come up in nae time. Several people was arrested and wheeched awa' in a van, and the rest when they saw the policeman comin, maybe

me included, we run oot the road. Well, twa or three different place it happened, no' just this area."

The conflict with the police at Muiredge led the Strike committee to create a Workers' Defence Corps to protect pickets. This Corps eventually numbered 750 men, under the command of former wartime sergeant-majors and N.C.O.'s. It was the biggest force of its kind to be formed anywhere in Britain during the General Strike.

James Sinclair:

"They upset a beer lorry at Muiredge and the crowds were a' there, a' the men and spectators watching us. I can see the beer runnin' down the drain yet! Anyway, Inspector Clark he drew up his constables all on the one side, in front of the Co-operative, but across the road there was about four or five hundred tons of road metal and he chased the men on to the top o' this and ordered them to disperse. However, when he charged, he made the biggest mistake ever he made in his life. You could hardly see daylight for chunks o' road metal! Must have been unfortunate for him: he got hit right in the face wi' a bit. He wasna very well organised, that charge. I don't suppose there were a police

*Protest march by East Fife miners to Thornton poorhouse, June 1926.*

*John Bird, Bowhill (West Fife) militant miners' leader, dressed for a stunt as a 'Special Constable' in 1926.*

inspector round about that was hated as much as what he was, you know."

As in every other mining area, there were a considerable number of arrests during the lock-out.

William 'Mosie' Murray:
"I was addressing a meeting at the Shorehead at Leven when I was ruthlessly hauled off the box, taken up to the local court and given thirty days' imprisonment in Saughton Jail for sedition. In the hall I was in in Saughton Jail, 'B' Hall, the whole of the Bowhill Strike Committee was incarcerated. There was John Bird and the Chairman, the Secretary, and the whole o' the committee of the Bowhill miners' union. And I may tell you, they put us through the mill. They had us out in the fields, pulling sugar beet and we never got our back up. Our food was deplorable. I'll give you the menu: in the morning they gave us a stone jar full of porridge, or lumps of porridge, no milk, that was your breakfast; at dinner time we had some watery soup, and at tea time one slice of bread an' margarine and tea without sugar or milk. That was our diet on which we had to pull sugar beet. Every week they had a concert for the inmates o' Saughton Jail but we were not allowed to attend. We were not allowed any library books or any comforts of any description. They were making sure that once you were in there you would never come back."

John McArthur:
"A foreigner—I think he was Austrian—named Kitchen, had made a foolish speech during the Strike. He was impulsive, was carried away, his English was not too good and he was arrested. The lads who were in control of the defence organisation were concerned about what was going

*John McArthur, c. 1926.*

*Miners at work underground, Wellesley Colliery, Methil, 1926.*

to happen to him, because he was not a recognised leader of the strike or the trade union movement. Although he was married locally and had a family he was not naturalised, and the question was to avoid deportation. Those lads in charge in Kirkcaldy arranged with the fiscal that he should get a nominal fine and there should be no deportation but they went back on this. He was fined and ordered to be deported. This was one of the tragedies in this area, in Kirkcaldy area especially, because this lad was deported, wandered around Europe, and finally committed suicide."

Almost seven months after it had begun, the lock-out ended in the later part of November with the defeat of the miners. No other group of workers suffered as severely as they. Their wages were reduced and their working hours lengthened from seven to eight per day. Along with the General Strike the lock-out had been the biggest labour struggle in Britain between the wars. After the calling off of the General Strike moderate trade union leaders began to declare their belief that the whole concept of a General Strike had proven a failure, though in fact it had been in many ways a remarkable demonstration of working-class support for the miners. The year 1926 proved to be a watershed for the trade unions and the broad working-class movement. From that time onward there was a

movement away from confrontation and toward greater co-operation, even collaboration, with employers and government—a movement that on the whole lasted until recent times. In the coal industry, the year 1926 left much bitterness among the miners. It made them more than ever determined to seek the nationalisation of their industry—a step taken eventually by the post-war Labour government in

*Wellesley Collier, 1926.*

1947. But a more immediate result of the prolonged lock-out in '26 was the victimisation by the coalowners of many of the more militant miners.

William 'Mosie' Murray:

"Now as far as myself was concerned, after the General Strike I was unable to get work of any description, any description at all. I went round the pits. I was victimised. I went to the various builders and the various other employers in Leven, but whenever my name was known as Murray, that was me out. And I was actually on the Labour Exchange for approximately six to seven year. Fortunately after that I was employed by Leven Town Council for thirty-two years."

Some of the more militant miners who were victimised were forced to find work as best they could. Some became local insurance agents; others as 'shilling-a-week men', or door-to-door salesmen. Quite a few of those victimised were forced to leave the East Fife coalfield altogether in search of work. Some of them emigrated to Canada, Australia or the United States; others moved to pits in other coalfields in Scotland or England. Most of those who were victimised but remained in East Fife remained active in the miners' union and in one or other of the three main political parties that enjoyed the support of the miners:

the Labour Party, Communist Party or Independent Labour Party. Some in due course became burgh or Fife county councillors, leading figures in the local Co-operative Societies, respected the more for the suffering they had undergone and the leadership they had given in '26. But whether they remained or moved away, East Fife miners, like tens of thousands elsewhere who had struggled through the lock-out, looked back on 1926 as the most memorable year of their lives. A good deal of the reputation for industrial militancy which today still attaches to miners was earned for them by their long drawn out struggle in 1926. Often closely knit communities living at some distance from more urbanised workers, miners had over many decades of hard working and living conditions developed strong loyalties and powers of endurance that made it difficult for some other people to understand what they saw as mere stubbornness and almost mindless militancy.

Peter Fitzpatrick:

"Ah think they were a pretty reasonable, honest set o' people, the miners. In fact, I've never met a class o' people as reasonable and understandin' as what the minin' class wis. People away frae the pits that never wis near them thinks that the miners had horns on their head but it's no true."

IAN MacDOUGALL

*David Proudfoot, a leading militant miner, speaking in front of banner during the 1926 struggle.*

# Glasgow Jewry

Jews have lived in Glasgow at least from the beginning of the nineteenth century. It is thought that the earliest Jewish inhabitant was Isaac Cohen who purchased his Burgess Certificate to trade as a hatter in 1812. He was joined by Jews who were engaged in a wide variety of occupations in the city: merchants, agents and auctioneers, optical and mathematical instrument makers, furriers, jewellers, manufacturers of 'French Fancy Goods' and makers of artificial flowers. James Cleland, writing in 1831, made the following observations on the newly established community:

"A Jews' Synagogue was opened in this city in September 1823, Mr Moses Lisenheim is their Priest, Hebrew Teacher and Killer [*shochet*—a Jewish butcher authorised to kill animals according to the Laws of Shechita]. The Feast of Tabernacles, which used to be celebrated by the Glasgow Jews in Edinburgh, is now observed in this City. A Burial Ground is about to be opened in Hutchesontown for the interment of the Seed of Abraham. Edward Davies, son of Mr Edward Davies, Optician, was the first that was circumcised in Glasgow; the rite was performed by Mr Michael on 18th July 1824. . . . The Jews are 47 in number, viz. Males, 28 — Females, 19; above 20 years of age, 28 — below do., 19. Born in the following countries, viz.:— in Prussian Poland, 11 — in various parts of Germany, 12 — in Holland, 3 — in London, 5 — in Sheerness, 10 — and in Glasgow, 6."

Growth was slow and in 1860 it was estimated that there were still only twenty-six Jewish families resident in Glasgow. The community, though small, was conspicuous by its success and according to one contemporary, non-Jewish writer, displayed all the virtues of mid-Victorian respectability: "The Jews in Glasgow . . . are moral, industrious, educated and some of them wealthy. . . ." The majority of the Jews lived north of the Clyde and it was not until the mid-1870s and 1880s, with the arrival of immigrants from Eastern Europe, that expansion into the south side of the city, and into the Gorbals area in particular, took place. By the end of the 1880s the centre of the Jewish population had shifted away from the Garnethill area, where a substantial new synagogue had been built in 1879, towards the densely populated Gorbals district where accommodation was cheaper and life undoubtedly rougher. It was more than the waters of the Clyde that separated the wealthy, well-educated, anglicized Jews of Garnethill from the 'greeners' of the south side.

*Opposite: A Jewish cap-making factory, Oxford Street, Gorbals, c. 1915.*

Most of the newcomers were Yiddish-speaking Jews of Russian and Polish extraction seeking refuge from the religious and economic persecution that was the lot of the Jews under Tsarist rule.

Mrs Braverman:
"I come frae Dubna *guberniya* in Russia and I was born, I think, in 1891. I remember I was always running around, going to the market. It was in a big square and the old ladies used to sit with their shawls round them, freezing cold, and they'd sit by a fired top and warm their hands. The potatoes used to be roast on there and some people would bring a pot and take maybe six potatoes home. . . . Everybody was poor. The pogroms were gettin' so bad that I was told they used to go into a house and they'd pull a baby's tongue out! I was told that and I felt terrible and I thought I'd like to go down to the barracks to see what these people looked like but they were just ordinary soldiers. Anyway, people were nervous in case things got worse and that's the reason they left because things weren't so good."

Mr Stone:
"My folks were married in Suwalki, that's in Lithuania. They were penniless. Round about 1880 it was enacted that all Jews were liable for military service. Well, there was the difficulty with the dietary laws bein' infringed and they wanted time for worshippin', so they decided to get out. The problem was how to get over the border. My mother related that the young girls would chat to the border guards while the rest of the Jews skipped over. Once you had a foot over the border that was you safe, you were in Prussia. They hitchhiked tae Hamburg and the main thing tae notice, they'd practically no food. Water, herring, and black bread, that sustained them. It was pure chance whether the ship arrived in Leith, Cardiff or Liverpool."

Some may have used Glasgow merely as a staging point for their ultimate destination, America, *die goldene medine*, the golden land. Others had settled elsewhere in Britain and had come to the Gorbals via London, Manchester, Leeds, Newcastle and also Dundee and Edinburgh. It was estimated that in 1903, of a total Jewish population of 6,000, about 4,000 lived in the Gorbals district alone. Visible evidence of their presence was not difficult to find. There were synagogues in Oxford Street and South Portland Street, the latter built at a cost of £9,000, a *Talmud Torah* school (a religious education school) with a roll of about 400 in Buchan Street. In Oxford Street there was

*Three Jewish upholsterers, the Gorbals, c. 1915.*

a 'Zionist Free Reading Room and Library' and in Portugal Street, the Glasgow Hebrew Benevolent Loan Society had premises which opened shortly after its foundation in 1888. In addition, there were more than sixty Jewish stores and workshops in the vicinity.

Mrs Aitken:

"It was nearly all Jewish shops and Jewish firms in the Gorbals. There was the Fogels, the corner of Hospital Street and Cleland Street, there was the Jewish bakery at the corner of Dunmore Street. Gleicken, the gown people were there and the Ashers as well. The Gerbers, the Woolfsons, them that had all the jewellers, the shops in the Trongate, they came from there. There were small cabinet-making businesses and upholstery work right up to Cumberland Street. . . . Some o' them kept stock in one o' their rooms for customers to come up and see what they wanted and they could get them everything. They all opened little shops, just doing alterations and repairs to suits and everything. There was no provident checks or anything like that, everybody had a wee connection of giving credit and goin' to collect it. It was a great place the Gorbals."

Mr Grossman:

"Gorbals Cross on a Sunday mornin'. That was a wonderful thing! If you wanted to meet anybody you just went along to Gorbals Cross. Well, there were different groups—tailors, cabinet-makers, travellers, and so on—and they'd all be discussing different things, their trades, politics, football. There would be crowds all over, every Sunday mornin'."

A considerable proportion of the occupied male population were self-employed and many of the small-scale businesses that were set up in this period were financed through loans supplied by the Glasgow Hebrew Benevolent Loan Society. In 1901, for example, the Society granted 175 loans.

Mr Glasser:

"These loans were granted free of interest mainly to pedlars and travellers and that gave them the basis for making a living from the stock that they

could buy and sell. They used to go to the outside of Glasgow, to Uddingston, Baillieston and into the mining communities like Hamilton, Coatbridge and Airdrie to sell their wares. They were selling various things, braces, mouth-organs, games, small things that needed small money for stock. When they became a little wealthier they paid the money back. Two people out of the community, who were more affluent, would sign as guarantors so that the fund would never be depleted by loss."

On occasion, capital could also be obtained from some of the wealthier and more established members of the community. Initially, profit margins were low.

Mr Tobias:

"They had a hard, hard life at the beginning. Ma father told us that he used to get up at maybe three or four o'clock in the morning and rush down to the Gorbals to see if he'd missed the time to go to his work. They'd no clock, nothing! The poverty was absolutely diabolical. He had a trade, he was a blacksmith and he worked for twelve years for this company and the boss was a real slave-driver! . . . Well, he went to a firm in Glasgow, a Jewish company of merchants called Shaunfield & Co., Hope Street and they supplied him with an anvil and bellows and equipment to start up on his own. They supplied him with steel to do the work and some of the merchants gave him a little credit. He

*Mr Tobias and some of the work force.*

*A Jewish bakery in Main Street, Gorbals, c. 1910.*

started his own business in 1900 in MacFarlane Street in the Gallowgate and many a week he'd come home with hardly a penny in his pocket after he'd paid one or two bills. It wasn't easy going.''

Mrs Taylor:

"My husband was a traveller in the credit drapery line. He owed half o' Glasgow I think (laughs). Later he started to go out and canvas for gold, old gold bullion and he did quite well. Then he was selling watches, clocks, jewellery, he'd buy up stock in shops that were giving up and he'd clean and polish it up and take it to the 'Barras' to sell. Oh, if I had £2 in a week I was lucky. We always kept a few pounds back for his stock but I was always diggin' into it! Yes, you could get help from the Board of Guardians or the Parish but we would never think of going to these places. No. We just took what we could get and just struggled away."

There were some among the immigrant community, however, who required this kind of basic assistance. In 1901, for instance, the two main relief organisations in Glasgow, the Jewish Board of Guardians and the Hebrew Ladies' Benevolent Society, between them dealt with over 500 needy cases. It was a measure of the degree of poverty that existed among the foreign Jews that a number of additional relief organisations were set up in the 1890s and early 1900s. These included the Boot and Clothing Guild, the Sick Visiting Association, the *Hachnosas Orchin* (society for welcoming strangers) and the *Hachnosas Kalla* (society for providing the bride with a dowry). Collectively, the objective was the same, namely, 'to promote self-respect and independence among the recipients of help'.

These organisations were remarkably successful in

that few immigrant Jews found their way onto the parish relief books. The allegation, frequently made during the chauvinistic campaign which led to the Aliens Act of 1905, that the Jewish immigrants were adding to the local rates burden was thus refuted in Glasgow. Nonetheless, the sudden appearance of, what was thought to be, a large Jewish immigrant population, quite different in status and background from their respected co-religionists, created unease. There was opposition to the group as Jews and as immigrants.

As early as 1893, J. A. Hammerton in his *Sketches from Glasgow* was depicting the quintessential Jewish stereotype:

"He has a rather sallow complexion, and his face is fringed with straggling black whiskers. He wears a frock coat that was black in the long ago. He is earnestly conversing with a fair companion, rather gaudily attired, but good looking for her nationality. . . . A glance at him is sufficient to proclaim him a son of Israel. He is a money-lender in the city — like not a few of his tribe — and his conversation has reference, no doubt, to some advantageous bond he has received."

As the *Jewish Chronicle* was later to remark: 'Take away the stilted style and the writing of this passage hardly shows a very agreeable spirit.' One area where this manifested itself was in house-letting.

Mr Stone:

"Before the First World War it was very, very hard for a Jew to get a house. One landlord after another: 'No Jews!'. If your name was Finkleberg then he'd say, 'No'. So you just changed it to Faulkner or something and if you didn't have a semitic nose then you might get it."

Occasionally, the Jews came under attack because of their religion. In a period when the Churches were heavily involved in 'mission-work' at home and abroad it did not pass unnoticed that an 'Eastern quarter' had appeared in the midst of the city. To counter any 'threat' a Glasgow Jewish Evangelical Mission was established in 1907 and there were also visits paid to the city by members of the Society for the Propagation of the Gospel to the Jews. One of the major criticisms concerned the Jewish violation of the Sabbath, a theme also taken up by the trade unions in the campaign to prohibit Sunday trading.

Sabbatarianism provided a useful front for what was essentially an economic grievance — excessively long working hours. In a submission to the Trades Council in June 1908 the Glasgow and District Furniture Trades' Federation concluded:

". . . we think we ought to have secure protection that our valued Sunday shall not be broken down and trampled underfoot by the unthinking foreigner in his greedy pursuit of financial gain."

It was the exploitation of cheap immigrant labour and the threat which this posed to working hours ('our valued Sunday') and to wages that was the main concern of the unions. The need for protection was not lost to the immigrants themselves. For example, in 1905 an Independent Jewish Cabinetmakers' Association was set up only to collapse the following year when its meagre funds were exhausted after a three-weeks long dispute with a group of Jewish employers over Sunday working. More successful was the International Tailors', Machinists' and Pressers' Union established in 1894 in Crown Street, Gorbals, and with a membership of over 220 by 1902. In a dispute in the same year the union succeeded in winning a 15 per cent increase in piece-rates and in the following year supported the Tailors' Society in their nine-month long strike. This type of behaviour made an important contribution to the gradual process of integration.

Most of the Jews who were involved in trade unions were also active politically. Zionism, which was still only in its infancy in the early 1900s, attracted a great deal of support in Glasgow and, indeed, in later years it was said that Zionism had 'all the force of a religious creed' among the Glasgow community. It was through the Workers' Circle (*Arbeiter Ring*) that much of the political activity was channelled.

Mr Glasser:
"There was a branch in Main Street, Gorbals [c. 1915]. Downstairs there was the communal baths and the 'steamy', where you washed your clothes, and the top flat was rented by the Workers' Circle. The activities were two-fold. One was associated with *Poale Zion*, that's the Zionist workers and this organisation was linked to the Labour Party and a number were members of that. There were others, quite separate, who were essentially interested in

their social welfare. They would negotiate better conditions, shorter hours, time off for *Shabbos* [Sabbath] and so on. There were quite a number integrated into the socialist parties. There were members of the I.L.P., the Independent Labour Party, the B.S.P., the British Socialist Party, and the S.L.P., the Socialist Labour Party—these were different grades of socialism."

Mr Stone:
"The Workers' Circle, aye, they were very active workers. They turned out some worthy people, men like Manny Shinwell, you know. He, along with what they later called the 'Red Clydesiders'—Kirkwood, Geordie Buchanan, Jimmy Maxton—these fellas had no hesitation in comin' and givin' us a wee talk. Jimmy Maxton, I remember him tellin' us that when he went to school he saw the utter futility of teaching a class o' children that had no boots and were obviously without any breakfast. Och, the sufferings of the poor Jews wasn't any more than the sufferings of the Glasgow underfed population."

It was possibly because they shared in the poverty that surrounded them that there was, by all accounts, little active opposition to the Jews at street or tenement close level. Communal relations appear to have been little different to those experienced by other 'foreigners', whether from Ireland, Italy, Lithuania or Edinburgh. The immigrant Jews in fact lived a fairly self-contained and independent existence, well organised but poor, tolerated but not accepted.

In the early days some of the customs imported from the *shtettl* in Eastern Europe were maintained in a community characterised by its orthodoxy.

Mr Grossman:
"There were marriage-brokers, *shadchans*, they brought boy and girl together. It was more common then than it is now, you never hear of it now. The weddin's all took place in the synagogues. Oh, they were lovely weddin's, class, real class. A Jewish wedding in those days was catered by the local Jewish butcher, there was an odd one that was catered outside but no' many. It would be under the supervision of a *shomer*, a man who looks after these things. They were really good. The best hall in those days was the Trades House in Glassford Street, that was supposed to be a nice class wedding."

Mrs Aitken:
"Our parents, they were very strict with us. There's only one in our family out of ten children that married out. In those days it was a terrible thing to do. We never got going out on a Friday night until after ma parents were gone. My father would be readin' his *Talmud* [the main Rabbinical text] and we would be in the room just havin' a talk with some other friends. The neighbours would come in for a little while and that'd be it. On

*Oxford Star F.C., 1910. Top left: Mr Grossman.*

Saturday we were so modern that we went out. We did our bit o' shoppin', and brought the messages in and quietly put them away *then* we went in and spoke to ma parents! (laughs)"

Strict observance was also displayed in other areas of community life.

Mr Grossman:

"I was president then [1910] of the 'Oxford Star' football team. You couldnae meet a nicer set o' boys, they were all Jewish boys who lived around Oxford Street in the Gorbals. I don't think we played on the Sabbath. Well, we never played near the Gorbals, if we did play we played away in another district. I may tell you the candid truth we'd hundreds o' people used to come and watch us. That was a regular occasion."

Mr Glasser:

"They went on holiday to places like Dunoon, Innellan and Rothesay, these were the places in the early part of the century. If you were orthodox and observed all the ritual dietary laws then you had to carry all the various utensils in a hamper: pots, pans, crockery and linen as well for the beds. You couldn't go down without having a *minyan*, that is, ten people to make up a prayer meeting. As most of the families weren't very affluent, the father would return to Glasgow and do his work for the week and come back on the Friday before the Sabbath. He'd bring some food, among which was the black bread, the salt herring, and the *chala* [a twisted loaf of white bread], small pieces that were suitable for the Sabbath along with the wheaten loaf. The loaf

was used for making the *Kaddish*, the prayer for bringing in the Sabbath and the prayer of the blessing of the bread. It was observed strictly and with due diligence and care just as if you were at home."

Much depended on the attitude and influence of the parents for the new generation were being exposed daily to a culture which at points challenged their *Yiddishkeit* (Jewishness). A major problem was the absence of a Jewish day school.

Mr Grossman:

"I went to Rose Street School. They were nearly all Jewish children and we used to come in half-an-hour later than the rest o' them because they said their prayers at that time. In those days we didn't say any prayers to my knowledge—I might be wrong, mind ye, maybe I was too late in gettin' into school! We had teachers to teach us the various things and we went to little *chedarim* [small, traditional, religious schools] and they maybe had some pupils. Other times you might have a teacher come to the house to teach you, you were lucky if it was a twenty-minute lesson and then he dashed away to another house. That was quite common in my day and I was born in Glasgow in 1885."

The establishment of the *Talmud Torah* school in 1895 improved the provision for instruction in Hebrew and religious education but, although the number on the roll remained consistently high, it is difficult to determine the level and regularity of attendance at classes held three times a week after school hours. Few children in the Gorbals district, Jew or Gentile, would

have relished the prospect of extra schooling.
Some Jewish children experienced other problems of
an equally 'serious' nature.

Mrs Woolfson:
"When I was at school I was challenged by one
of my friends and I was asked whether I was a
Protestant or a Catholic and I said, 'No, I'm a Jew.'
So I was then asked whether I was a Protestant Jew
or a Catholic Jew. Well, I went to a Protestant
school so I said, 'I'm a Protestant Jew!' (laughs)"

Mr Latter:
"I was playing for the Southern Y.M.C.A. at the
time and we were in the amateur cup, doing quite
well and thinking that possibly we might win it.
We'd won our previous round and then some guy
produced a protest against me. He dug up this old
rule that if you played for the Y.M.C.A. ye had to
have two consecutive attendances in the Bible
Class! Well, I was desperate because I really
thought we'd a chance o' winning this cup. I
thought about it and decided to go. Surely it canna
be all that bad, I'll no' open ma mouth, no' sing any
hymns or anything like that. So when I went I sat
at the back, kept my mouth shut the whole time,
expecting a bolt from heaven to come down and
strike me (laughing). I made my two appearances
and that meant I could carry on playin' for the
Southern Y.M.C.A. Anyway, this guy must have got
the needle and thought that he'd have tae try
something different. So he sent an anonymous letter
to my aunt and this was eventually passed on to my
Dad. In the letter it said, 'If you want to find your
son on a Saturday afternoon you'll find him in
Glasgow Green playin' for the Southern Y.M.C.A.
and if ye wonder where he gets to on a Sunday
night, he's at the Bible Class!' Ye can imagine, it
caused ructions in the family. It would be a fairy-
tale end to say that we won the cup but we were
knocked out in the next round (laughing)."

By the 1920s and 1930s aspects of the old way of life
had changed and in some cases disappeared altogether
as increasingly the younger generation adopted the
habits and culture of the host society. Yiddish, for
example, which had been spoken in most houses, was
doomed to extinction. One Yiddish newspaper after
another folded—the daily, *Evening Times*, the bi-lingual
monthly, *Jewish Life* — until finally in 1928 the weekly
*Jewish Voice* succumbed to become the *Jewish Echo*, the
Glasgow community's English language newspaper.
Only the middle aged and elderly took advantage of the
large collection of Yiddish and Hebrew books
(estimated at over 1,000 in 1934) in the new Gorbals
library. There was a much greater laxity in Sabbath
observance, for those in business adopted a more
pragmatic approach and many of them kept their shops
open on Saturdays. It was not unusual to find Jewish
supporters on the terraces at Ibrox, Parkhead or
Cathkin Park, home of the now defunct Third Lanark.

Mr Latter:
"There was quite a good support for the Thirds,
whether some of it was due to me being Jewish and
playin' for them I don't know. The fact that I was
playin' on a Saturday was no different to somebody
having to keep their shop open on a Saturday to
earn a living and, of course, I was gettin' good
money. Even though I was playin' on the Sabbath I
was a sort of wee tin god because I was playin'
professional football and possibly enhancing the
Jewish image as it were."

The theatre, the cinema and the dance-hall all drew
large Jewish crowds. These were venues that in
previous years would have been out of bounds and
regarded as inappropriate and potentially harmful to
the orthodox Jew. Yet, Jews not only owned some of
them but performed in them as well.

Mr Tobias:
"There were two comedians, Peel and Curtis,
they were on for a long time. They were quite
famous and were heard all over the English circuit
as well. Peel and Curtis, Blass and Spilg, these were
their original Jewish names. Then there was a
young man called Ike Freedman, his real name was
Solomons, and he came from the East End of
Glasgow and he was very popular amongst the
Glasgow people. He used to perform in the Palace
Theatre, the Metropole and went round most of the
circuits. . . . Oh, there were plenty of jokes about
the Jewish people in Glasgow but they were all
taken in good part. It was give and take on most
occasions."

Humour was, of course, one way of coping with
injustice and prejudice which the Jews encountered.
For although the immigrant community had travelled
far along the road towards acceptance there remained
a suspicion, an antipathy towards the group.

Mr Stone:
"I got the sack for being a Jew! The war was on,
this was 1916, and the boss come in and says 'I don't
want a German Jew' and told me to get out. I was
*born* in this country. . . . Well eventually I found
myself in the army and I remember when I got to
the barracks there was a Jewish lad on duty serving
out the breakfasts. He was dishin' it out with a big
ladle. You just had to take what you got, bacon and
all. And there was this big hefty lad sitting opposite
me and he shouted, 'You bloody Jews make sure
you get the best.' So this fella just put down his big
tray and he belted, really clobbered this chap. The
fella next to me turned round and asks, 'You know
who that is?', and I says, 'No'. He says, 'That's
Myer Stringer, the Scottish boxing champion'. . . .
Because of the provocation Myer was exonerated
and they realised they might as well make use of
him so they made him a gym instructor!"

Prejudice was not as easily handled in peace-time. The Churches, for example, still continued to display evidence of intolerance in their treatment of Jews. To cite but one example, in March 1938, at a time when the newspapers were full of accounts of the suffering of the Jewish population in Germany and Austria, the Moderator-Designate of the General Assembly of the Church of Scotland, in a speech entitled *The Enigma of the Jew*, commented:

"... there are only two ways to treat the Jews, and they are to fight them or to convert them, and Britain's desire is not to fight them but to see them converted to accepting the pure and unsophisticated principles of the Christian religion as their faith."

This unwillingness to accept the Jews in their own right occurred elsewhere. There were bowling clubs, for example, in Glasgow, which refused to accept Jewish members, and it was because of discrimination that Jewish golfers founded their own club, Bonnyton Golf Club, in 1928. In housing there was the case which George Buchanan, I.L.P. M.P. for the Gorbals, brought before the House of Commons on 12th February 1935. It concerned the refusal by one of Glasgow's leading builders to allocate a house in the new King's Park estate on the grounds that the person 'belonged to the Jewish race'. The company policy was changed almost immediately but the ignorance that lay behind it was deep-rooted and was to persist.

It would be misleading to exaggerate the importance of anti-semitic feeling in the inter-war years but foolish to ignore it. It may well have contributed to the rapid growth in the number of Jewish organisations in this period, particularly Zionist groups. Its effect on the community must, however, have been tempered by the knowledge that on the continent the plight of the Jews was much worse. News of the persecution of the German Jews led in August 1933 to a boycott of German goods in the city and almost overnight a whole series of relief organisations sprang up. Support came from a number of quarters, from Willie Gallagher, the Communist Party member to Lord Marley and Mrs Anthony de Rothschild, all of whom appeared at protest and fund-raising meetings in Glasgow. From 1933 onwards refugees began to arrive.

Mr Glasser:
"We had an organisation in Glasgow known as the Central British Fund for the Relief of German Jews, there was also an organisation set up by the members of the Federation of Women Zionists, it was known as the Glasgow W.I.Z.O. The refugees who came over here were sponsored by Jewish families and became members of the family until they managed to get resettled. The children were dispersed in two's and three's throughout the community. There were quite a number of professional people among the refugees, doctors and dentists and so forth. For example, in 1934, Dr Karl

Abenheimer arrived in Glasgow. He had an extensive knowledge of psychotherapy and psycho-analysis and was quite outstanding. He was so proficient that he taught the doctors here because psychoanalysis was practically unknown until he came here. . . . Bringing the children over, well, it affected every individual because you realised what was happening."

Most of the refugees were from Germany and Austria. There were some who came from further afield, for example, from Singapore, but they were sponsored in the same way.

Mrs Simon:
"When we arrived in Glasgow the billeting officer said, 'Have you got any relatives here?' I said, 'I have one person and that is God' (laughs). We were taken to the Beresford Hotel and then to the Y.W.C.A. It was our Passover and I told my daughters that they're not to eat bread. I didn't know you could get *matzos* here. So the matron phoned Mr Glasser and sent us to Geneen's Kosher Hotel in Abbotsford Place and they were wonderful to us. The whole Passover week was paid by Geneen's."

*Geneen's Kosher Hotel, c. 1928, regarded as the centre of the Jewish community.*

*Calderwood Lodge Primary children: the Festival of Succot.*

The sponsorship scheme worked efficiently and well and the newcomers who decided to settle here adapted to life in Glasgow with apparently little difficulty. The Jewish community, by this time, was quite widely dispersed for the drift away from the Gorbals had started almost as soon as family finances would permit. The movement was always to the south of the city: first to Govanhill, then to Battlefield and Shawlands and later to Newton Mearns, Netherlee, Clarkston and Giffnock. The poorest Jews remained in the Gorbals as did the Jewish shops, workshops and warehouses.

Mrs Taggart:

"I came from Palestine as they called it then in 1944 because I had married a Glasgow fella, he was a soldier. I went first to his parents' house in Parkhead and then we went to the Gorbals to Thistle Street. There were quite a few Jewish families but I couldnae speak to them—they couldnae speak Hebrew and I couldnae speak Yiddish! I was there about eleven years in that house, it was only a single-end, a sub-let really, but I really liked the Gorbals there, really friendly people. I used to get fruit really cheap. There was this man with a fruit barrow and 'cos I come from Palestine he used to give me oranges and all kinds of fruit cheap. One day he saw me walking along the street and he stopped me and told me that there's a horse running by the name of 'Palestine' and that I should back it. I did and he won, he won the Derby! . . . It was the shopping I really liked. If

I wanted any Jewish food, I went to the Jewish shops, especially the Jewish bakeries, they were really beautiful. On a Sunday morning standing in a queue to buy the cakes and muffins from the Jewish shop. We used to look forward to Sunday mornings!"

With the massive redevelopment of the Gorbals in the 1960s the last vestiges of a Jewish presence in the area disappeared. In 1965, the Board of Guardians set up a special house-purchase scheme to help needy families and those who were living in substandard houses in the Gorbals area were moved elsewhere, to be replaced by Punjabi and Kashmiri immigrants from the Indian subcontinent. Today, in an area which was once a leading centre of Zionism, there is now a large mosque under construction, evidence of yet another phase of immigration.

The Glasgow Jewish community, estimated to be 11,000 to 12,000 strong, is centred now in Giffnock, a district occupied almost entirely by members of the professional and business classes. The social and economic division of a hundred years ago no longer exists, or at least not to the same extent, and in terms of associations and societies, the community has never been better organised. There remains, however, the thorny problem of assimilation.

Dr Jesner:

"There are many groups in the community and the umbrella organisation is the Glasgow Jewish Representative Council which represents all the organisations in the West of Scotland. There are welfare organisations: the Jewish Welfare Board, the Jewish Old Age Home, the Association for the Mentally Handicapped, the Blind Society. There are religious organisations, the synagogues, the Ritual Council which looks after the ritual slaughtering of the meat, and the *Beth Din* [Jewish Ecclesiastical Court]. There are many other organisations such as the Friends of the Hebrew University, the Jewish Graduates Group, the Association of Jewish Ex-Servicemen, the *Yeshiva* [a Jewish learning centre], the Zionists, the Jewish Choral Society and so on. . . . Yet I don't think the community is as religious as it was a generation ago. There has been some inter-marriage and I think there's little doubt that inter-marriage has been increasing. Most of the Jewish community are displeased by this because they feel that it is undermining the strength of the community and weakening the threads of the history of the community."

Mr Tobias:

"There's only one progressive synagogue in Glasgow that takes in the people who have mixed marriages—it's an easy outlet for them. I've never been in a progressive synagogue because I'm completely orthodox and I'd like ma family to follow me. Ma daughter is very orthodox but ma son's not so hot! He won't do any harm so long as

I'm here, I know he won't do anything to upset me. Well, he's forty-seven now and I'm now seventy-seven (laughs)."

Mr Stone:

"You've got assimilation now. I'm not sayin' anything for it or against it but that is the position. Then there's Sabbath observance, well that's no' in the same class as before. I'm sure if you went down to Bonnyton Golf Club you'd find quite a congregation there on the Sabbath. Where you will see it is during the festivals then you'll see the synagogues crowded but for the rest, no."

An important development in the struggle to maintain the Jewish faith and Jewish culture was the establishment of the first Jewish day school in Glasgow in 1962.

Mrs Woolfson:

"I think there were about nineteen in the first class, today we've got about 220 in the school. We have eight classes plus a nursery and teach the full range of primary subjects. In addition, we have all the Jewish subjects, the Hebrew language, spoken and written. Bible study, our traditions and festivals. We actually participate in the festivals as they come through the year so the children are actually living their Judaism as well as learning it from books."

Education of this kind undoubtedly creates a greater awareness among the children of being Jewish and it will be further enhanced by the plethora of Jewish youth groups and societies set up for that purpose. For their parents and grandparents, apart from their own religious beliefs, external events have produced the same effect. The Balfour Declaration of 1919, the tragedy of the Holocaust, which, as Dr Jesner has said, 'coloured our whole way of life', the creation of the State of Israel in 1948 have contributed to raising the level of Jewish consciousness. It has not, however, prevented the Glasgow Jews from making a major contribution to the life of the city in, for example, politics, business and medicine. Nor has it created any conflict of loyalty.

Mrs Woolfson:

"I think that Jews very much identify themselves with the place of their birth. I feel very Scottish and I'm very happy to be in Scotland and have a little foothold in Israel as well for my daughter was married there recently. Funnily enough, there's quite a large community of Scots in Israel, and it really came to the fore last year when they held a Burns Supper and the people clamoured to take part!"

Mr Glasser:

"Let me put it to you this way. There are five million Scots living in Scotland and there are about twenty million Scots living outside the country. In all these places, Canada, America, New Zealand, there are Scots societies called 'Sons of Scotia', Burns clubs and so on. St Andrew's Day is celebrated and the people identify with Scotland. They talk of the 'motherland' but they are loyal to the country that they're living in. The Jews in this country are likewise."

The transition from being a Jew in Scotland to being a Scottish Jew may not, at times, have been easy, but it seems by now to be completed.

Mr Stone:

"I mind when I had that experience here of being turfed out o' my job for bein' a Jew. I said to myself maybe I'd be better gettin' out of this country. Well, I haven't left yet 'cos I don't know a better one (laughs). I'll tell ye something interestin' now. In that wonderful Mitchell Library we've got here in Glasgow—it's a veritable paradise—you can go in there and find not only English but Scottish poetry translated into Hebrew. I came across this Burns collection translated by a Tel Aviv fellow. And it really gave me a great thrill to see 'Auld Lang Syne' printed in Hebrew. I'm no' much of a singer but it goes like this:

עָבְרוּ יָמִים מִכְּבָר (Auld Lang Syne)

יַחְדָּו עַל פֶּלֶג שָׁטְנוּ אָז
כָּל עוֹד הַיּוֹם זָהָר;
הֵרִימוּ רַחֲבֵי-יַמִּים —
עָבְרוּ יָמִים מִכְּבָר.

הַפִּזְמוֹן:
לְזֵכֶר הַיָּמִים עָבְרוּ... וכו'

יָדִי לְךָ; הַב לִי יָדְךָ,
רֵעִי גֶאֱמָן-יָקָר!
לְךָ, נִשָּׂא כּוֹס שֶׁל בְּרָכָה
לְזֵכֶר יְמֵי-כְּבָר!

הַפִּזְמוֹן:
לְזֵכֶר הַיָּמִים עָבְרוּ... וכו'

כּוֹס רְוָיָה לְךָ וְלִי,
נַטִּיב הַלֵּב, נִשְׂכָּר!
כּוֹס-חֶסֶד בּוֹא נָרִים יַחְדָּו
לְזֵכֶר יְמֵי-כְּבָר!

עָבְרוּ יָמִים מִכְּבָר

הֲיִשָּׁכַח יָדִיד קָדוּם
וְלֹא יְהִי נִזְכָּר?
הֲיִשָּׁכַח יָדִיד קָדוּם
מִן הַיָּמִים מִכְּבָר?

הַפִּזְמוֹן:
לְזֵכֶר הַיָּמִים עָבְרוּ,
לְזֵכֶר הַיָּמִים,
כּוֹס-חֶסֶד עוֹד נָרִים יַחְדָּו
לְזֵכֶר הַיָּמִים...

אָהַבְנוּ רוּץ בֵּינוֹת הָרִים,
אָרוֹת פְּרָחִים בַּכָּר,
אַךְ רָגֶל זֶה בְּצַקָּה, צָעָה —
עָבְרוּ יָמִים מִכְּבָר.

הַפִּזְמוֹן:
לְזֵכֶר הַיָּמִים עָבְרוּ... וכו'

רוֹבֶּרְט בָּרְנְס [ROBERT BURNS]

MURDOCH RODGERS

# Up the Valley

The men and women who work in the lace factories of Ayrshire's Irvine Valley are heir to a long tradition of skilled weaving. The Galston Kirk records of the 1570s mention both walkers and wabsters living in the parish, weaving wool spun locally and brought to them by the customer. Local tradition has it that Protestant Flemish and French Huguenot refugees settled in the Valley in the later sixteenth and early seventeenth centuries, introducing the advanced draw loom and the skills of pattern weaving. Typical Valley surnames such as Scade, Frame, Gebbie, Howie and Fleming probably arrived with these immigrant groups, and 400 years later the same names will be found among the lace, madras, terylene and silk weavers of Newmilns and Darvel.

Woollen goods continued to be woven in Galston well into this century, but for the Valley as a whole, wool was eclipsed by linen manufacture arising from Government aid after 1727. The wealth generated by the linen industry was such that Newmilns built a fine Town House in 1739, and farmers' sons were attracted into the older burghs in such numbers that the 'new town' of Darvel was established in 1751 to house the increase in population. The linen boom was also aided by the improvement in roads following the Turnpike Act of 1766, which facilitated the supply of outside flax to the Valley lint mills, and the transport of the finished article to the merchants of Glasgow and Paisley. Increased contact with these larger manufacturing districts also led to the introduction and eventual specialisation in finer fancy goods. The first silk loom was set up in Galston in 1781. By 1791 forty out of fifty-five of the town's looms were engaged in producing this luxury article. The availability of cheap cotton from India and the improvement in the thread spun on Crompton's mule led also to a specialisation in fine muslin weaving in the 1790s. Many Ayrshire women augmented the family income by engaging in tambour work, sewing beautifully intricate lace insertions into the muslin gauze woven by the man of the house and eventually fashioned into the flowing gossamer gowns which adorned the ladies in the Age of Sensibility.

This was the Golden Age of the master weaver with his indentured apprentices, high wages for his craft and spare time to indulge in self-education and religious and political disputation. The weavers formed the vanguard of the radical Reform and Home Rule movements which flourished in Scotland in the decade following the French Revolution. The United Scotsmen and Friends of the People revolt in 1797 and the Radical Rising in 1820 both required Government spies and force to suppress them. During his Scottish tour in 1819 the radical writer William Cobbett

*Above: Detail from a tamboured muslin sampler, Ayrshire, c. 1800. Opposite: William Allan at Jacquard handloom, c. 1885.*

answered the weavers' petition to come to the Valley to address them. So fired was he by the commitment of his audience, he wrote, "I would go a thousand miles to see the looks of these Scotchies—especially at Newmilns."

The days of the independent master weaver were numbered, however, as adaptation to the new fabrics led to increased dependence on outsiders for the supply of materials. A class of middlemen, or sma' corks as they were known locally, developed; agents who transported the webs of up to 400 weavers to the Glasgow manufacturers who in turn supplied the agent with the warp yarn and payment to bring back to the artisan weavers. Some weavers actually walked across the muirland path to deal with the Glasgow manufacturers directly but the majority answered the carriers' cry of 'Ocht or nocht fur Glesga' when his cart set off for the city. The corks of course were local men who 'graduated' from weaving work.

John F. Morton:
"My great, great grandfather had a warehouse, what ye called a wareroom in the old days, and he collected all the handloom cloth and he hauled it on his back or in a barra or whatever into Glasgow. I think he went twice a week and eventually I think he got a horse and cart

and took it to Glasgow. But originally he went over the moor. He walked over the moor to Glasgow with the actual bundles o' hand made muslin."

This system was to last throughout the rest of the hand loom period. Despite the decline of hand loom weaving elsewhere, the weavers at work in Newmilns increased from 550 in 1842 to 952 in 1872, while the numbers in Darvel similarly doubled. This was partly due to the successful introduction and adaptation of the Jacquard machine onto the hand looms in 1838 by a local mechanical genius, Joseph Hood. The Jacquard enabled weavers to produce intricate patterns on curtains, table covers and bed covers, products whose very diversity helped the industry to survive. The finesse of the Valley product was able to resist growing competition from machine-made articles throughout the nineteenth century, enabling the weavers to continue in their now quasi-independent state until almost the dawn of the present century. The weavers, however, could not resist market forces and the nineteenth century saw more troughs than booms for the artisan weaver. The mood of the period is expressed in the following examples of local poetry. The first, semi-humorous in vein, refers to the necessity to employ the weavers' children as soon as they are able to walk.

*Main Street, Darvel, c. 1880. Handloom weavers outside their cottages.*

*A weaver said unto his son*
*The nicht that he was born*
*My blessings on your curly pow*
*Ye'll rin for pirns the morn.*

The next sums up the frustration of the weaver, thirled to the corks and manufacturers:

*Trade it was slack an' wages sma'*
*An waur than that tae bear.*
*Agents an' corks in ruthless thraw,*
*Sought oot each scob and tear.*

*Doon gaed their glesses on his claith*
*Whene'er a shot seemed missing.*
*Wi' stoppages, they werenae laith*
*His sma' returns tae lessen.*

It took the American Civil War and the total embargo on raw cotton which came as a result of it in the 1860s to ring the final knell on the days of the handloom weaver. In the resulting distress many families left the Valley while some turned to the new pits outside Galston for work. The old textile tradition might have died completely if it had not been for the enterprise and vision of one Alexander Morton. The period of transition between the machine lace period and the handloom days was just within living memory in 1981.

John Woodburn:
"Ma grandfather had what they ca'd a two loomed shop and he wis a Galston man, Roxburgh they called him. It wis the staple industry. I mean it wis in my day that, hearin' the handlooms goin' even at night. I remember what they were like right enough jist like a big lace loom on a very small scale—they had shuttles and cards and then they worked them wi' their feet of course—treddles. The women worked the same time as the man, oh aye, that wis a well known fact. At that time there werena the same discipline, they could come off it fur half a day and go up tae the curlin' pond or something like that."

Alexander Morton was himself a weaver of fine madras or 'leno' curtains, who on the death of his brother continued the latter's business as a sma' cork. Up until then curtains were sold to the merchants unbleached and unfinished. By finishing the curtains himself and selling them directly to stores from Glasgow to London, Morton built up a profitable business. It was on one of his selling trips to London that he saw the Nottingham lace machine at work at an industrial exhibition. Despite his failure to convince a majority of the conservative Darvel weavers and agents to help him finance the scheme and bring alternative industry for the declining handlooms, and despite the opposition and reluctance of the Nottingham industry to sell him their looms,

Morton succeeded in bringing the first lace machine to Darvel in 1875. Within ten years there were over 100 in the Valley and shortly afterwards Darvel, Newmilns and Galston replaced Nottingham as the world centre of the lace furnishing trade. The confidence of the new class of manufacturers in their market for the product is revealed in the fact that by the early 1900s individual Valley firms had opened factories in Barcelona, Oslo, Gothenburg and Columbia, Pennsylvania.

In the Valley a new social order emerged with master and worker on different sides of a widening divide. The alienation of the workers was exacerbated in 1897, when after a long and violent wage strike and lock out, the manufacturers won a hollow victory over the recently organised Newmilns Textile Workers Union. The collective memory of professional strike breakers and imported 'foreign' English blacklegs left the workers with no illusions as to the break-up of the old homogeneous community, and the bitterness remained well after the union was recognised in 1914. The thrawn individuality of the handloom weaver, however, continued on both sides—the manufacturers rarely uniting in association with one another, but determined to dominate the workers, the workers resentful of their loss of liberty and the obvious wealth of the nouveau riche.

Carmichael James:
"They used tae blow the hooters, there's a hooter went at half past six in the mornin' and then it went at nine o'clock for the breakfast; went at twenty-past nine for shift men tae come back in; went at ten o'clock again for them that was away for their breakfast; went at one o'clock, went at two o'clock. Then it went at six o'clock and twenty-past six for the backshift men tae go back in. An uncle in Dervel, he's dead noo, Rab Hamilton, he was a weaver and a tenter tae, I worked beside him. Rab used to tae say about Dervel, when they were arguing aboot the slaves and that, 'See the darkies, the darkies are wicer than us,' says he. 'They have to leather the darkies tae their work wi' whips. See here in Dervel, they just blaw a horn and everybody's runnin' tae it.'

David Drummond:
"They were the meanest lot ever ah seen, ah think, the manufacturers aboot here. They've a' big hooses. One, Alexander Morton, built a big castle there, Gowanbank. This was years ago, before ma time—they asked the men to come oot tae work a Saturday fur him and he would see them alright. He gave them a poke o' readin' sweeties! Ye know, thon sweeties wi' 'I love you' on them—they got a poke o' sweeties each fur their Saturday mornin's work. And then he built a castle! That's true! Tae tell ye the truth we never got naethin' aff them that we didna work fur."

The 'readin' sweeties' story has perhaps gained in

*Interior of lace mill, Newmilns, c. 1900.*

momentum through the generations but it does reveal the 'them and us' attitude which quickly established itself.

Robert Black:
   "It was Alexander Morton that brought, you could say, prosperity here, oh there's no question about that. But he was a hard man too, you know—we'll leave it at that! (laughing)."

John Woodburn
   "He wis of the kind that had tae rule the roost or he wouldna hae naethin' to do wi't. He wisnae an overgenerous man, he was a hard man tae work fur. In 1882 he built Gowanbank and that gave the show away. He showed how much [profit] was in the trade."

   Many of the new firms manufactured madras and chenille curtains, in addition to satisfying the insatiable Victorian and Edwardian demand for lace bedspreads, wall hangings, tablecloths and beautifully styled curtains. The Nottingham lace machine was not dissimilar to the Jacquard handloom so the inherent knowledge and skills of the Valley weavers were easily adapted to machine

production, while the piece rate system gave the weaver the opportunity and incentive to earn higher wages than anyone else in the factory, thereby helping restore the weaver's pride in his craft in the new environment. The reaction of the worker paid a set wage to the weaver's obsession with output was a mixture of envy and humour.

James Hunter:
   "They hated some o' the patterns. They had tae be up and doun the ladders behind their machine, up onto the Jacquards to change cards, reverse them and what have you. One o' the stories when ah started wis one o' the weavers had decided tae take a short cut comin' back down and jumped over the front o' the machine and had went over on his ankle. A couple o' men ran over to help him and he says, 'Don't bother with me,' he says, 'get the machine on!' The first week ah started I remember running past this machine and the weaver comin' chargin' after me, cursin' and swearin'—the draught o' me runnin' past him would knock his machine off and interfere wi' his wages! And ah couldna believe this but it turned oot, if there were a door left open, the weavers that were makin' their own pay always came

chargin' over and kicked the door and cursed at whoever had dared leave this open tae interfere wi' the machine.

"I remember when I was only fifteen I used tae love tae annoy the old weavers. I would hide behind the machine and you could always watch the rhythm o' the machine and start whistling as if the machine wis squeaking. So the weaver would rush for his oil can and he would oil where he thought the squeak was comin' from. So I just stopped for a minute or two, moved along and started again and it wis guaranteed that he would rush for this oil can, there was no way this machine would get put off for the lack of oil—they always seemed to have an oil can in their hand, the weavers."

Robert Black:
"I was thirteen years of age [c. 1914] . . . you started as a boy at what we called the ravelin' aff—strippin' the bobbins. From that ye went tae the shuttlin', fillin' the shuttles. And then it was the spoollin', [when] a spool is emptied you took it off an' tied a full one on, ye see. You went onto shifts then, ye were what they called a shiftboy. Ye had juist tae learn the loom as ye could. A weaver would say, 'Let me oot for a smoke, Bob', and you would watch the loom till he came back in and you gradually picked it up tae the best o' yer ability, ye see.

'At that time, a weaver nearly had tae die before ye got a chance o' a loom! (laughs) But gradually ye got ontae a machine, an' that was that. Lace weavin' was a job ye were learnin' all the time, you could be years and years in the lace workin' a machine and suddenly you would meet something that you hadn't met with before—there were so many different weaves, single action, double action, Swiss, Madras and comby. If you were on a good machine, it was in good order, you did a good job. In the early days, if the loom wasnae gaun, yer pey wasnae gaun—you only got paid on what ye made. Now a weaver has a guaranteed wage. They can still make extra if the machine's really goin' well, but there is a guaranteed wage. Conditions are better now."

Carmichael James:
"I can go back three generations in ma connections wi' the lace. Ma grandfather came up here frae Nottingham an' he worked wi' Mortons . . . I think it would be when the first power looms came. James was his name, Jack James—in fact that was his by-name—English Jack! Ma father was in the lace a' his days. When ma faither wes a schuilboy, he used tae rise early in the mornin' an' gae out wi' ma granfaither an' help him tae shuttle. He came back an' got his breakfast an' went tae the schuil. He cam back fae the schuil an' went back in tae about six o'clock at nicht tae help ma

granfaither tae shuttle again. Well, ma faither got nuthin' for that—it went on ma granfaither's pey.

"I was the Dux boy o' the schuil . . . but I'd tae go in tae the mull. Ye had tae hae money tae go on [to higher education], so ma faither hadnae the money. Ye juist had tae go tae the mull or the pits. That's how things went on about here.

"There used tae be a train come in here at twenty-past six in the mornin', an' it was like Hampden Park, about five or six hundred came off it, to work in Darvel. They'd never hae got workers for a' the factories in Darvel. An' I'll tell ye wan thing when I was a boy, the lace weaver would be one o' the best paid workers in Britain. The folk wi' the biggest complaint in the mills was the women. Oh the manufacturers took a rise oot o' them for years—low wages."

Wages in the mills have varied a great deal over the years reflecting usually the market for the product. The fact that there have been few major strikes this century, however, reveals a measured acceptance of wages in the trade. The same acceptance may also be due to the fact that wages were always compounded by families in which perhaps mother, father, daughter and son all contributed to the weekly household income. In such a unit a small individual pay rise could mean a large increase in income while a prolonged strike could bring immediate economic disaster.

The sense of continuity in weaving from previous centuries to the present day is strengthened by the fact that not a few of the manufacturing class are descended from the original Flemish and Huguenot weavers and that people engaged in the modern industry can speak of direct connections with the hey-day of the handloom period. Such a man is John Hood whose firm still repairs the Valley machines today and whose great-grandfather, Joseph Hood, introduced the Jacquard machine there in the 1830s. Working as he has with the lace machines all his life, Mr Hood has a special admiration for the class of tenters who lie between weaver and manufacturer in the factory hierarchy.

John Hood:
"The tenter was the main man. They were the people that had to put the cloth on the machine and they had to know what the machine could do. You can mention Willie Gold, Davy Lawson, Tommy Rankin, Tommy Morton, Borland, at Stirling and Aulds, Jim Craig, Jim Craig's father . . . they're too numerous tae mention."

James Craig:
"I was what they ca' a tenter. A tenter, when things break doon he's the fellow tae sort it. The job itsel wes interestin' big variety, an' ye'd tae have a guid knowledge o' the trade fae beginnin' tae end o' the product. Weavers, oh there were guid weavers, there were some weavers that werenae just sae hot, and there were ithers that just

## Derval Dam

Medium

It happened on a Lammas Nicht As I gaed oot for a stroll I

had nae gone sae ve — ry faur Tae I daunered doon by the Toll. I

daunered on an' daunered on Tae Derval Dam I did pass And

wha dae ye think was staun- in' there But a bonnie wee servant lass.

CHORUS

Whaur a'e gaun, gie me yer haun' How dae ye do, says I, Haud

up yer heid ma bonnie wee lass, And din — nae luk sae shy.

Whaur dae ye bide? Whaur dae ye stey? Come tell tae me yer name. Will yer

faither no be ang —ry noo If I wis tae see ye hame?

We stood a while an' crackit
   About a thing or twa
We werenae thinking o' the time
   Tae the staurs gaed a' awa'.
She drew her shawl aboot her heid
   And solemnly did exclaim,
Says she, 'Young man, ye'll keep yer word,
   Ye promised tae see me hame.'

And noo that we are merrit,
   And happy as can be,
Wi' twa wee bairnies by oor side
   And anither yin on oor knee,
We'll sit aroon our ain fireside,
   And talk o' days gaun past,
But I'll ne'er forget that nicht I met
   Ma bonnie wee servant lass.

*Mills and bleachworks on the Irvine from the southern slope of the Valley, c. 1890.*

didnae seem tae cotton on tae it. The guid weaver wes worth his weight in gold tae ye."

The lace looms were manned twenty-four hours a day by three shifts of workers. The weaver's insistence on keeping his machine going even precluded the usual lunch break.

Alec Black:
"I used tae carry a can an' a piece tae my faither. He sat the en' of the loom an' et his piece. Nou, tae keep the tea warm we used tae go an' put it on top o' the safety valve in the boilerhouse an' when he wanted his tea he sent me down tae the engine man tae get it."

Carmichael James:
"Somebody came up wi' yer hot piece and yer can o' tea an' ye just sat by your loom an' ate it—tane in the black lead an' everythin'. An awfu' durty job, the lace, awfu' durty."

Robert Black:
"When ye left the factory, ye wis as black as the ace o' spades. That lead that they use for the combs, ye see they can't use where the shuttle runs . . . it's black lead, like graphite [they use]. Ye was polished like a black man."

Fortunately the factory workers could balance their hours in the hubbub of the factories with time spent in the peaceful beauty of the surrounding countryside.

Carmichael James:
"I've seen us in shifts, in the guid weather in the summer, five or six o' us, we used tae feenish at twa an' hurry an' get away up the watter tae swim. And in the backshift, ye wes droppin' [finishing the shift] at eleven. Instead o' gaein' hame an' washin' yersel . . . ye went hame, lifted a towel an' a bit soap an' went doun tae the Irvine—a guid summer's night . . . did that . . . oh it used tae be great! Did a lot o' things in the countryside. Walking was a great thing. Then in the spring ye went fur peeser's [peewit's eggs], in the autumn ye went fur rasps. There wes a place up there ye'd fill a basket ony time. We used tae rake the countryside—roun' the ferms an' lift the eggs for the fermer . . . but he didnae haund them intae him. (laughs)"

By the 1920s and '30s the factories had established their own work rituals and practices, the humour of which was often directed against young apprentices. The latter had to suffer horseplay and indignity in order to be accepted into mill society.

Carmichael James:
"It was a custom when a boy stertit in the mull, the women got a haud o' ye, ken . . . yer private parts—used tae rin, but they got ye—that wis you in the lace then! Then when ye were boys ye got sent a' the daft messages if ye wis stupit enough tae go. Ye were sent for left-haunded screwdrivers, or

a pail o' steam, or . . . 'Awa' ben there an' tell the warper tae gie ye a long staun [stand]!'

"If ye wes a guid riser, ye got the keys an' opened the mull in the mornin'—maybe got hauf-a-crown for it. Well ye maybe opened a swing door, an' afore ye even got the light on, the first thing that met ye wis a big pot or a big ba' o' black lead—hit ye richt in the face gaun in in the mornin'. Did it no' mak a mess o' ye! The backshift left it fae the nicht afore.

"There wis ae fella used tae get the gaffer's watter ready tae wash his haunds at droppin' time. So this nicht the gaffer gaes ower an, 'Oh ya,' he says, 'ye've aboot burnt the haunds aff us. Whit the hell . . . did ye no' pit only cauld watter in it?' 'Aye,' says the fella, 'the cauld watter's at the bottom.' (laughs) He wis some man that."

Alec Black:
"This weaver made a mistake, he had made an awfu' long darn. He wis sent for to the Gray Room [where they check the lace for faults] an' he said tae the Gray Room foreman, 'It's no' possible for me tae hae a long darn . . . I never hiv long darns!' The foreman says, 'Well, ye've just walked through ane, we hung it over the door!'"

The Greige (or Gray) Room staff are mainly women whose job it is to repair and finish the piece.

Mrs James:
"I startit when I wis fourteen. I went tae whit ye ca'ed the measurin' o' the cloth. Efter, ye got a step up, an' ye went tae the drawin' tae look for the faults. Ye wis there for aboot a year then ye went tae the dernin'. Well, ye got six weeks tae learn the hand dernin'. Ye could either be a machine derner or a haun derner. But when they got a machine, there's nane o' them wad leave so ye just had tae gae tae the haun dernin'.

"It was an auld Mrs Glen that learned me. Ye got dernin' everythin'—spools, shuttles, holes, great big derns wi' maybe six row oot o' them. Well, ye had tae learn tae pit a' that in the pattern. See the like o' that flower there [indicating a lace table cover], well if there were a bit missin' in that flower ye had tae sit an' dern it so's that it would be the full flower. Ye were never coontit skilled."

One of the reasons for Alexander Morton's original success with his leno curtains was the importance he placed on good design. The survival of the lace trade is partly due to the beauty of those Victorian designs and the continuation of a line of designers such as John F. Morton, who could adapt the tradition to suit modern taste. The sudden death of Mr Morton in 1981 weakened one of the pillars of the Valley trade.

John F. Morton:
"My faither an' mither were both designers—ma faither was wi' ma grandfather in Holland in 1912—he was a tenter and they were building a new factory. My wife's grandfather, he set up a factory in Sweden. But this is the only place now that makes lace to any extent.

"We do the designing which is drawing freehand and then it goes to this squared paper. The colours are a code for the [Jacquard] card cutting people, and they cut the cards according to what we put on the paper. We are commissioned to do these designs by local factories, by factories in Nottingham, Spain, Austria and India. Every country has a different idea of design—characters; swans, angels, floral, old-fashioned, Victoriana, modern.

"There's one manufacturer, he 'phoned me here an' told me tae come up to one of the local bars. I went away up wi' the umbrella over the head and it was really comin' down, bucketin' down an' he was standin' outside in all the rain, quite inebriated. Now they had just newly whitewashed the wall [of the pub] and the rain was trickling down over the wee parapet at the bottom o' the wall. Says he, 'Right, that's what I want ye tae draw!' We had that as a design an' this is whit ye had tae draw, rivulets running over the parapet o' the wall! A character!"

The effect of the industry was not confined to the factories. The Valley towns were always recognised by outsiders for the beauty of their window decorations, due to the range of local curtains available to them. During the 1930s and the 1950s a day was set aside during Darvel Fair holidays for the crowning of a Lace Queen, a day on which to show off the beauty of the staple industry.

Robert Black:
"You come intae Darvel at the bottom end there and honestly you could hardly see a building for lace . . . lace curtains draped in practically every house in the village—fantastic!"

Morag Ritchie:
"At the time I was Lace Queen I worked in a sample department . . . I still work in an office in a lace factory. Each lace factory was asked to nominate two employees who had to be resident in Darvel and unmarried. The firm I worked in had some new designs and I was allowed to choose a design and the dresses were made locally. I'll never forget the thrill . . . and I'll never forget a sea of faces . . . to me it looked like ten thousand people. A lot of people, mostly I think with Valley connections would come back. It was a day that families got together. I think the town has lost a lot by this bein' dropped.

As the Lace Queen festival died so the very existence of lace came under threat in the slumps which followed the boom years experienced by all textile manufacturers during and in the year immediately following the Second World War. In the 1960s I.C.I.'s synthetic terylene fabric, with its lightness and drip-dry properties, appealed to the housewife more than the more expensive and less convenient lace product. Many factories changed over to terylene production. It was a change received with ambivalent feelings by the work force.

Jim Hunter:
"The lace weavers reckoned there was no skill [in it] . . . just a wee boy's job watchin' the terylene machines. They used tae laugh, called them toys, 'Are ye watchin' the wee toys?'"

Carmichael James:
"You went this wey tae yer work, clean as anythin'. It was an' awfu' easy job. Ye see ye'd only a warper, a weaver an' changers. There were nae darnin' wi't, nae mendin', nae shuttlin', nane o' that. Ye maybe watched fower [machines] . . . maybe twa or three o' these wadnae stop a' shift."

Most of the factories which did not buy terylene weaving machines went out of business. The shrewdest manufacturers who maintained diversity in their production were rewarded with the demand for dress lace which was fashionable in the 'swinging '60s'.

J. F. Morton:
"Durin' the boom o' the 'sixties we did a table cover for a local firm. The next time we saw the cover it had a Mary Quant label on it! It was for a poncho she had cut out a hole in the middle and put a zip on it . . . two holes for the arms and that was it. I don't know what it would be sold at but it would be more expensive than what it would be sold as a lace table cover, that's for sure!"

Jim Hunter:
"They were workin' night and day for months and months, twenty-four hours a day, just tae get this dress material oot. They were sellin' no' jist yards . . . miles tae America. It was in a' the big magazines . . . models wi' it in *Vogue*. It was supposed to be the world beater but like all other things it jist came to an end."

The liquidation of numerous lace firms in the decade following 1955 resulted in many lace machines being sold abroad, thus opening up future competition for the Valley product. Those firms which survive in Newmilns and Darvel today make mainly terylene and lace nappery. Whereas the trend was towards cheaper synthetic goods in the '60s, today it is the firms exploiting the specialist luxury end of the market who have more reason to be confident about the future.

Mitchell Allan:
"There are eleven firms in the Valley making

lace. We see the lace going on and on provided we keep our old machines in good condition and provided we keep tabs with the market. We've concentrated our markets in Europe using the old traditional skills and designs that this industry had and this firm kept since 1881."

Ironically, it is a return to an older fabric in the Valley's textile history, silk, which is helping Mr Allan's firm, Haddow, Aird and Crerar, retain its work force. The chance survival of Madras looms in Morton, Young & Borland of Newmilns not only provides that firm with a good American market but gives the industry a direct link with the muslin curtain handloom weavers of the nineteenth century.

Morton Dewar:
"During the late 1950s and early '60s the cotton weaving industry was in severe decline and many of the companies took advantage of the Government's scheme which enable them to scrap looms and receive payment for doing this. We nearly closed our Madras department but just at the time that closure seemed inevitable, orders started to come through from America . . . and these have continued to this time."
The last major slump in the staple industry of the Valley fortunately coincided with the rise of employment opportunities in the engineering factories of Kilmarnock. In the 1980s we witnessed the collapse of that town's prosperity with the withdrawal of Massey Ferguson and the resultant increase in the ranks of the unemployed along the banks of the Irvine. Many Valley mills are on short time with several facing possible closure. Now more than ever it is to be hoped that imagination in marketing can be allied to the skills of the weavers to guarantee a future for this unique traditional industry and its beautiful products.
Hope for the future is based on examination of the past, which has given this experienced tenter faith in the manufacturers' ability to endure.

James Craig:
"They've gone through a' their bad times, they survived. They started away wi' the old lace curtain, they got on tae coloured cord an' silk, and when that began tae go, they startit anither thing—the terylene. And they're still in it, they're still survivin'. It's the history o' the lace trade—they're survivors."

BILLY KAY

# Acknowledgements

The editor would like to acknowledge a special debt of gratitude to all those interviewed for the Odyssey series: without their contribution this book could not have been written.

I would like to thank the author of the preface and of the individual chapters, whose enthusiasm and commitment to the material has made my job as an editor an agreeable and stimulating task.

I am grateful to BBC Scotland (Radio Management) for promoting the Odyssey series and allowing access to their resources in the compilation of this book. I wish to thank in particular Stewart Conn (Head of Drama, Radio) whose initial enthusiasm for the idea of Odyssey did much to ensure its success at a later date and Christopher Irwin for allowing access to BBC resources in the compilation of this book.

Thanks also to Gavin Sprott and the staff of the Country Life Section, National Museum, Edinburgh, for their help in acquiring and processing photographs from a wide variety of sources which give a stunning visual element to the book.

Introduction     Valda Grieve and Martin Brian and O'Keefe Ltd., for permission to use 'Scotland Small?' from *The Collected Poems of Hugh MacDiarmid*.

### From the Gorbals to Gweedore

*Photographs*     *Radio Times* Hulton Picture Library. St Andrews University Library. North of Scotland Hydro-Electric Board. Country Life Archive, National Museum. *The Scottish Catholic Observer*. Private collection: Mrs Coll.

*Songs:*     The singing of Kevin Mitchell.

### Fishermen Of Kintyre

*Photographs:*     Angus Martin, Ian Y. Macintyre, Mrs Elizabeth Morrison, Mrs Annie McMillan, the late John Martin, William Blair, Mrs Annie McMillan, Ms Mary MacArthur, the late Mrs Marion (McIntyre) Lyon, Mrs C. (Gilchrist) Munro, A. Mathieson, Robert Miller. Poem: George Campbell Hay.

### The Lanarkshire Lithuanians

*Photographs:*     Private collections; the author, Mr Frank Gilligan; Miss Anne Russell

### St. Kilda

*Photographs:*     C.L.A. National Museum. Private collection; Janet Chalmers.

Song:     'Cumbra H-Irteach' reproduced from the Gesto Collection by permission of the Trustees, National Library of Scotland. English version by Paul MacInnes.

### They Fairly Mak Ye Work

*Photographs:*     Dundee Public Libraries; St Andrews University Library; D.C. Thomson & Co. Ltd.; Baxter Brothers; N.B. Traction Group, 31 Forfar Road, Dundee; Private collection; Tony Patterson, author of *Churchill—A Seat for Life*.

Song:     Mary Brooksbank; the singing of Jim Reid.

### Da Merry Boys

*Photographs:*     Shetland Islands Council Library; Dundee Museum and Libraries; Private collection; Bobby Peterson; individuals whose photographs are in the care of Shetland Islands Council Library.

*Music:*     Tom Anderson; Bobby Peterson.

School of Scottish Studies for use of tapes SA 1975/163, B5 164A and SA 1970/249 B10. The families of the late Magnus Fraser and James Gordon. Alan Bruford, editor *Tocher*, for permission to use extract from *Tocher* 22.

### The Seven Men of Knoydart

*Photographs:*     The *Glasgow Herald* and *Evening Times*; *Radio Times* Hulton Picture Library.

*Song:*     Hamish Henderson.

### Poets and Pioneers

*Photographs:*     Private collections.

Thanks to those who advised on translations. *Tocher* 32 for permission to make use of 'Manitoba' sequence (SA 1971/98 B11). The School of Scottish Studies for use of following tapes: SA 1974/253–259–260–266, SA 1975/5–6. SA 1978/51–52–96–100, SA 1979/60–62–69–71–72–73.

### Mountain Men

*Photographs:*     *Radio Times* Hulton Picture Library; Scottish Tourist Board: Private collections; Tom Weir, Bob Grieve, John B. Nimlin, Alex Small.

### Will Ye Gang Wi' Me, Lassie

*Photographs:*     C.L.A. National Museum; National Galleries of Scotland. *Dundee Courier and Advertiser*; Angus Folk Museum; John McLaren Cowper.

*Newspaper extract: Stornoway Gazette.*

The School of Scottish Studies. Tape SA 1968/248 A1 first printed *Tocher* 30, 1979.

A Weel Plou'd Rig

*Photographs:*   C.L.A. National Museum; Kinross-shire Antiquarian Society: Private collections; Mrs MacLeish, R. Buick, Mrs Simpson, Allan Baron, Mrs A. Westwood, R. Buick, R. Ewan, Harry Davidson. Mr MacLeod, Bruce Walker, James Brown.

*Music:*   Archie Webster, author of *Denbrae*; Archie Fisher, who composed the music and contributed sterling work to the series.

The Clydebank Blitz

*Photographs:*   Clydebank District Libraries (thanks to Pat Malcolm). Thanks to Gerard Boyle for contacts.

Italiani in Scozzia

*Photographs:*   *The Glasgow Herald.* Yerbury Galleries, Mrs M. McGillivray, Mrs E. Di Ciacca, Mr F. Pontiero.

Mungo Mackay & the Green Table

*Photographs:*   Scottish Record Office. Lodge St Mary's, Newbattle. James Reid, Mr Yuill, David Spence.

The Fisher Lassies

*Photographs:*   Margaret Bochel. Country Life Archive, National Museum of Antiquities. Thanks to Ron Grant for contacts.

*Song:*   'The Herrin Shoals' was written and performed for the radio programme by Ian Sinclair of Mirk and Caledonia.

Gallipoli

*Photographs:*   Imperial War Museum. B.B.C. Hulton Picture Library. Ian Boughton, John Brown, Mary Kate McKinnon.

The Pearl Fishers

*Photographs:*   Country Life Archive, National Museum of Antiquities. *Scotland's Magazine.* A. & G. Cairncross Ltd. Betsy White, William Moodie, William Elder.

*Poem:*   Sheila Douglas.

Glengarnock Steel

*Photographs:*   Mrs A Munro, Mr Joe Smith, Stephen Ruxton, Mr John Dempsey, Miss Maggie Bell, John Lewis.

The original material for 'Glengarnock Steel' came from a Manpower Services Commission Project, sponsored by Cunningham District Council, British Steel Corporation and the S.D.A.

Clan Neil of Barra

*Photographs:*   Mary Kate McKinnon, Nan McKinnon, Barbara MacDermott.

*Songs:*   The singing of Flora McNeil.

Thanks to Paul MacInnes, Morag MacLeod and Anne Cullen for assistance with the Gaelic.

The '26

*Photographs:*   National Library. John McArthur, William Murray, A. Wilson, Mrs Thomson, the Misses Proudfoot.

Glasgow Jewry

*Photographs:*   City Archives, Glasgow. B.B.C. Hulton Picture Library. Dr J. Miller, Mrs Woolfson, Mr M. Tobias, Mr P. Brooks and Ms J. Brooks. Mrs Nyren (née Geneen). Mr James Gillies (People's Palace).

*Song:*   The Mitchell Library, from *The Hebrew Anthology of English Verse*, Ed. Ruben Avinoam (Tel Aviv, 1956).

Whisky's Awa'?

*Poster and Photographs: People's Palace Museum, Glasgow. B. Aspinwell, University of Glasgow.*

Up the Valley

*Photographs:*   James Mair, Victor Albrow, Norman Chalmers, Joseph Hood & Co., Newmilns; Haddow, Aird & Crerar, Newmilns; Morton, Young & Borland, Newmilns; National Museum of Antiquities; Jean Paton, Robert Black, and Fleming & Co.

My thanks to Jim Hunter for contacts and James Mair of Newmilns for his excellent thesis on the lace industry.

I would like to extend personal thanks to Norman Chalmers for his unstinting support; Murdoch Rodgers for his guidance concerning the oral material, and proof reading; my secretary Joan Raffan for her professionalism in organising and transcribing the Odyssey tapes; to Beth Nairn and Margaret Scott for transcription. Finally, I must thank my wife, João, for her tremendous support and patience throughout the making of this book.